032061

612 MAC

HUMAN LIFE

Don Mackean

John Murray

D0543094

612. MAC

AYLESBURY COLLEGE
LIBRARY

032061

© D. G. Mackean 1988

First published 1988 by John Murray (Publishers) Ltd,
50 Albemarle Street, London W1X 4BD
Reprinted (with revisions) 1993, 1994, 1995

All rights reserved.

Unauthorized duplication contravenes applicable laws.

The drawings (except those listed on page iv) are by the
author, whose copyright they are unless otherwise stated,
and whose permission should be sought before they are
reproduced or adapted in other publications.

The copyright holders of photographs are listed on
page iv.

Typeset in Linotron 202 Melior

Printed and bound in Hong Kong by
Wing King Tong Co. Ltd

British Library Cataloguing in Publication Data

Mackean, D. G. (Donald Gordon)

    Human Life
    1. Man. Physiology – For Schools
    I. Title
    612

ISBN 0-7195-4500-5

To the Student

This is a textbook to help you in studying human biology for the GCSE. You will be following the GCSE syllabus of only one Examination Group, but this book contains the material needed by all the Groups. For this reason, among others, you will not need to study or learn everything in the book.

Furthermore, the emphasis in GCSE is on the ability to understand and use biological information rather than on committing it all to memory. However, you will still need to use a book of this sort to find the facts and explanations before you can demonstrate your understanding or apply the biological principles.

Text The text is written at two levels. *Core text* is in ordinary print and contains subject matter which occurs in nearly all the syllabuses. *Extension text* appears on a coloured background. It covers topics that are beyond the basic syllabus requirements or that are included in only one syllabus. The extension topics are printed in colour in the list of topic headings at the beginning of each chapter.

It is therefore quite possible to concentrate only on the core material. If, however, you have a particular interest in biology or if parts of the extension material are included in your syllabus, you should read the extension material, either when you come to it or later when you are sure you understand the core material.

Questions The questions within a chapter are intended to test your understanding of the text you have just read. If you cannot answer the questions straightaway, read that section of text again with the question in mind.

Most of the questions at the end of the sections and those grouped at the end of the book are taken from the specimen examination papers published by the GCSE Examining Groups. Many are designed to test your ability to apply your biological knowledge. The question may provide certain facts and ask you to make interpretations or suggest explanations. In such cases, the factual information may not be covered in the text.

Looking up information The index, the contents pages and the headings at the beginning of each chapter are there to help you find the information you need. If the word you want does not appear in the index, try a related word. For example, information about 'sight' might be listed under 'vision', 'eyes' or 'senses'.

Cross-references You will find frequent cross-references in the text to other parts of the book e.g. (page 123) or (see page 45). This is simply to tell you that the word or the topic is more fully explained, or described from a different aspect, in another part of the book. However, you need not interrupt your reading to look up the pages referred to unless you find you must do so in order to understand the passage you are studying.

Updating information In any textbook, information about pollution, recycling, conservation and international agreements or legislation on these issues rapidly becomes out-dated. You should check the date of this impression before relying too heavily on specific figures and other data related to these topics. When studying these topics, make sure you are referring to the most up-to-date figures and other data that you can find.

Practical work Given standard laboratory equipment, you should be able to do any of the practical work described in the book. You will probably not have time to do it all, however. This is why the book gives the expected results of the experiments. You can then understand the design and purpose of an experiment even if you have not been able to do it yourself.

Acknowledgements

The author and publishers are very grateful to all the individuals and organisations who have provided photographs or given permission for photographs to be reproduced:

Cover
The Image Bank (photographer M. Tcherevkoff)

Chapter 1
Fig 3 Farmers Weekly Picture Library; Figs 4, 5 Heather Angel; Fig 6 Biophoto Associates; Fig 7 Tony Langham; Fig 8 Picturepoint; Fig 9 Hertfordshire School Library Service, Marlborough School; Fig 10 (a) Barnaby's Picture Library; Fig 10 (b) The Hutchison Library

Chapter 2
Figs 2, 4, 6 Biophoto Associates; Fig 7 Gene Cox; Fig 10 Philip Harris Biological Ltd

Chapter 7
Fig 3 Eric & David Hosking; Fig 5 Colin Green; Fig 9 Heather Angel; Fig 13 Biophoto Associates

Chapter 8
Fig 1 (P Morris), 17 (J Swedberg) Ardea; Fig 2 Eric & David Hosking; Figs 3, 9 Heather Angel; Figs 4, 5, 6, 12 Biophoto Associates; Fig 7 ICI Agrochemicals; Fig 11 Nature Photographers Ltd; Fig 13 NHPA; Fig 15 ADAS Aerial Photography Unit, MAFF, Crown Copyright; Figs 18, 21, 22 Bruce Coleman; Fig 19 The Hutchison Library; Fig 20 Photo Library International

Chapter 9
Fig 2 Ford UK; Fig 3 Pete Addis; Figs 5, 7, 9 Thames Water Authority; Fig 8 A Pasking/Water Research Laboratory; Figs 10, 17 Picturepoint; Fig 11 Warren Spring Laboratory; Fig 13 Charles Brady/Audio-Visual Productions; Fig 14 Cleanaway Limited; Fig 15 British Nuclear Fuels plc; Figs 16, 24, 25 Bruce Coleman; Fig 18 (E Mickleburgh), 22 (J Mason) Ardea; Fig 19 Biophoto Associates; Figs 20, 21 Nature Photographers Ltd; Fig 23 Mid-Glamorgan Land Reclamation Unit

Chapter 10
Figs 3, 4, 5, 10 The Hutchison Library; Fig 11 Save the Children Fund/Mike Wells; Fig 13 Mark Edwards

Chapter 11
Fig 3 Tony Langham

Chapter 12
Fig 8 Philip Harris Biological Ltd; Fig 11 K E Carr & P G Toner

Chapter 13
Figs 2, 12, 20, 25 (b) Biophoto Associates; Fig 23 Barnaby's Picture Library; Fig 24 Science Photo Library; Fig 25 (a) Philip Harris Biological Ltd

Chapter 14
Figs 3, 11 Biophoto Associates; Fig 9 Philip Harris Biological Ltd; Fig 13 Swiss League Against Cancer

Chapter 15
Figs 4, 8 Biophoto Associates

Chapter 16
Figs 2, 3 Biophoto Associates; Fig 7 Leo Mason

Chapter 17
Figs 7, 9, 20 Biophoto Associates; Fig 11 Steven Green; Fig 15 Professor W J Hamilton; Figs 16, 21, 25 Vision International; Fig 19 Birth Atlas, New York; Figs 17, 18 Sally & Richard Greenhill

Chapter 18
Fig 5 (a) & (c) Rank Organisation; Fig 10 Leo Mason

Chapter 19
Fig 4 British Dental Health Foundation; Fig 5 Biophoto Associates

Chapter 20
Fig 2 Biophoto Associates; Fig 17 Tony Langham, reproduced from Ishihara's Tests for Colour Blindness, published by Kanehara & Co Ltd, Tokyo; Fig 19 Sally & Richard Greenhill

Chapter 21
Fig 1 Sporting Pictures (UK) Ltd; Figs 10, 12, 15 Biophoto Associates

Chapter 22
Fig 2 Biophoto Associates

Chapter 23
Fig 10 Tony Langham

Chapter 24
Fig 1 Barnaby's Picture Library; Fig 4 Vision International; Fig 5 Biophoto Associates; Fig 9 Marc Henrie; Fig 22 Sir Ralph Riley

Chapter 25
Figs 2, 13, 20, 21 Biophoto Associates; Fig 5 J v den Brock (Biozentrum der Universität Basel); Fig 12 Heather Angel; Fig 16 A Shell Photograph; Fig 17 ICI; Fig 18 St Mary's Hospital Medical School

Chapter 26
Figs 1, 3 Science Photo Library, Fig 5 Thames Water Authority; Figs 6, 10, 11 Tony Langham; Figs 7, 8 J. Sainsbury plc; Fig 9 Vision International

Chapter 27
Fig 1 Tony Langham; Fig 2 Sally & Richard Greenhill

Page 1 Biophoto Associates; *page 49* Nature Photographers Ltd; *page 97* Sporting Pictures (UK) Ltd; *page 221* Vision International; *page 247* The Hutchison Library

The following photographs are by the author: Chapter 3, Fig 8; Chapter 7, Fig 17; Chapter 11, Figs 6, 9.

The full-colour illustrations on pages 4 and 5 are by Pamela Knight; Fig 24 on page 174, Figs 13, 15 and 16 on pages 186–8, Fig 4 on page 250 and Figs 1 and 2 on pages 277-8 are by Charles Bannerman. All other artwork is by the author.

The cover design is by Peter Theodosiou.

The following Examining Groups are acknowledged for their permission to reproduce examination questions from their specimen GCSE papers:

London and East Anglian Group for GCSE (L)
Midland Examining Group (M)
Northern Examining Association (N)
Southern Examining Group (S)
Welsh Joint Education Committee (W)

The letters and numbers which follow each question indicate the name of the Examining Group and the number of the paper from which the question is taken. For example (N2P) indicates that the question is from Section P of Paper 2 of the Northern Examining Association.

Contents

SECTION 1
Some Principles of Biology

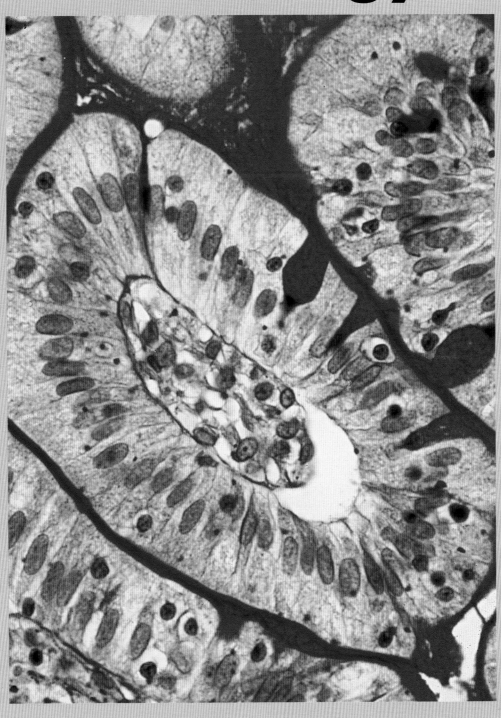

Humans as Living Organisms

Characteristics of Living Organisms

Classification

Differences between Plants and Animals

Characteristics of Mammals

Humans as Mammals

Special Human Features

Humans are living organisms in a world which contains a great many kinds of living organism. Living organisms may be very different from each other in their structures – think of trees, insects, elephants, mosses. But they all have certain things in common. They all grow, feed, breathe and reproduce, for example.

Characteristics of Living Organisms

Whether they are plants or animals, large or small, warm- or cold-blooded, all living things have the following characteristics:

Breathing Most living organisms take in oxygen from the surrounding air or water and give out carbon dioxide. Animals may have special structures such as lungs or gills which help to make this exchange of gases. With large animals you can see the breathing movements that exchange the air or water. With plants and most animals you would have to test the air or water round the organism to show that oxygen was being taken up and carbon dioxide was being given out.

Feeding It is fairly easy to see animals taking in food. Green plants make their own food from air and water by a chemical process in their leaves (photosynthesis, page 41). This feeding is not obvious but it can be shown by experiments. Fungi and bacteria feed by dissolving plant and animal tissues (usually dead tissues) and absorbing the liquids produced. In all living organisms the food is used for growth and energy production.

Energy production (respiration) For organisms to live, they must produce energy. This energy drives the chemical processes in their bodies that keep them alive. When you see animals moving about, they are obviously using energy. If a creature can keep warmer than its surroundings, it is evidence that energy is being released. It is not obvious that bacteria, plants and fungi are producing energy but there is plenty of experimental evidence to show that they do.

In all living things, the energy is released by a process called **respiration** (not to be confused with 'breathing'). During respiration, food is broken down to carbon dioxide, and energy from the food is set free for use in the body. Many organisms need oxygen to break the food down. Respiration is the reason for oxygen and carbon dioxide being exchanged by breathing.

Excretion Some of the products of the chemical processes in living organisms are poisonous and have to be got rid of. Carbon dioxide produced during respiration is removed by breathing. Animals produce urea and other nitrogen-containing substances which have to be removed from their bodies. The removal of these waste products, together with excess salts taken in with the food, is called excretion.

Growth Food is used for growth, as well as for respiration. Most living organisms start as tiny eggs or seeds and grow in size and weight. They also change their shape as they grow and become more complicated.

Reproduction If an organism is alive, sooner or later it is likely to reproduce itself. Bacteria and single-celled creatures simply keep on dividing into two. More complicated organisms have reproductive organs and produce eggs which grow and develop into new organisms.

Responding to stimuli (sensitivity) Living organisms are sensitive to changes in temperature, light, chemicals and pressure in their surroundings. We call these changes stimuli. A light touch or a shadow falling on a non-living substance, such as a stone, will have no effect on it. A living organism, such as a cockroach, will respond to a touch or a shadow by running away. The touch is a **stimulus** and the running away is a **response**. Plants respond to light, to gravity and sometimes to touch. But they respond slowly compared with animals.

QUESTIONS

1 If acid is dropped on a piece of chalk or marble, it gives off carbon dioxide. Does this mean that the chalk is living? What other evidence would you need to convince you?
2 Make a list of the processes in your own body that need energy to make them work.
3 If a crystal of copper sulphate is placed in a strong solution of copper sulphate it will get larger. Why is this not 'growth' in the same sense that plants and animals grow?
4 Choose any animal you know well and describe briefly the ways in which it exhibits the seven characteristics of living organisms listed above.

Classification

Living organisms can be grouped into five 'kingdoms'. Not all biologists agree that this is the best way to group or 'classify' them, however, and sometimes other ways are used.

1 Bacteria and blue-green algae These are single-celled organisms which do not have a proper nucleus (page 12) in their cells. Most of them live in water or soil and play an important part in decay and recycling. Some bacteria cause disease in humans.

2 Protista are single-celled organisms which do have a nucleus. Most live freely in fresh water or sea water. Some of them cause human diseases such as malaria.

3 Fungi This group includes toadstools and moulds as well as the fungi that cause diseases in crop plants.

4 Green plants In their leaves, green plants can absorb sunlight and use its energy to build up the food they need for survival.

5 Animals These organisms cannot make their own food. They have to take in food by eating plants or other animals, or the dead remains of either. Humans are classified as animals.

Each of the five kingdoms is divided up into smaller groups. The plant kingdom contains mosses, ferns and flowering plants, for example.

The animal kingdom can be divided into **vertebrates** (animals with 'backbones') and **invertebrates** (animals without 'backbones'). The invertebrates are not really a proper biological group because they include organisms that differ greatly from each other, such as worms, insects and snails (Figure 1). However, it is convenient to call these animals 'invertebrates' to distinguish them from the vertebrates.

The vertebrates are divided into five classes:

(a) fish (strictly speaking there are three classes of fish),
(b) amphibia (frogs and toads),
(c) reptiles (snakes, lizards, tortoises),
(d) birds,
(e) mammals (Figure 2).

All vertebrates have a central nervous system consisting of a brain and spinal cord. The brain is enclosed in the skull and the spinal cord is protected by the vertebral column (spinal column or 'backbone').

Apart from the fish, all vertebrates breathe by means of lungs. They all have jaws (except for some primitive fish). In most vertebrates (though not in birds) the jaws carry teeth.

The fish, amphibia and reptiles are all 'cold-blooded'. That is, they cannot regulate their body temperature in the same way that mammals do. Fish have the same temperature as their surroundings. Amphibia and reptiles may warm up or cool down when their surrounding temperature changes. Birds and mammals keep their body temperatures at a steady level, however. They are usually warmer than their surroundings.

Fish, amphibia, reptiles and birds all reproduce by laying eggs. These are fertilized externally in most fish and amphibia, and internally in reptiles and birds.

Differences between Plants and Animals

Plants and animals differ in the way they feed, in their cell structure, in their sensitivity and in their ability to move about.

1 Feeding Plants can make their food from substances with small molecules: carbon dioxide, water and salts. From these small molecules plants build up larger molecules by a process called photosynthesis (page 41).

Animals cannot make their own food. They have to get it by eating plants or other animals. Their digestive systems break down large food molecules

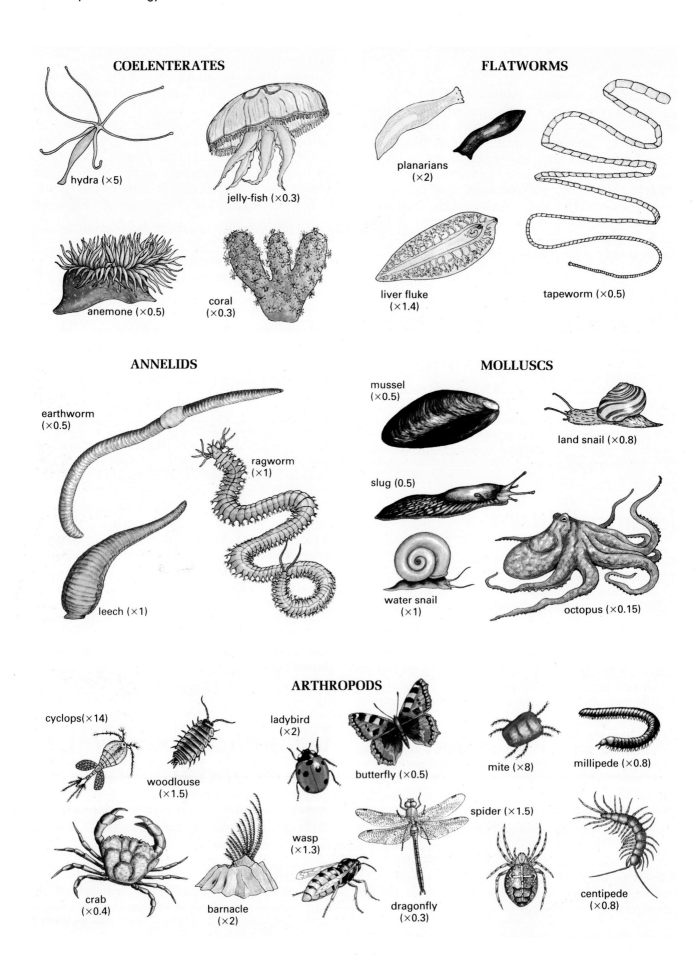

Figure 1   Invertebrates (only five groups are shown)

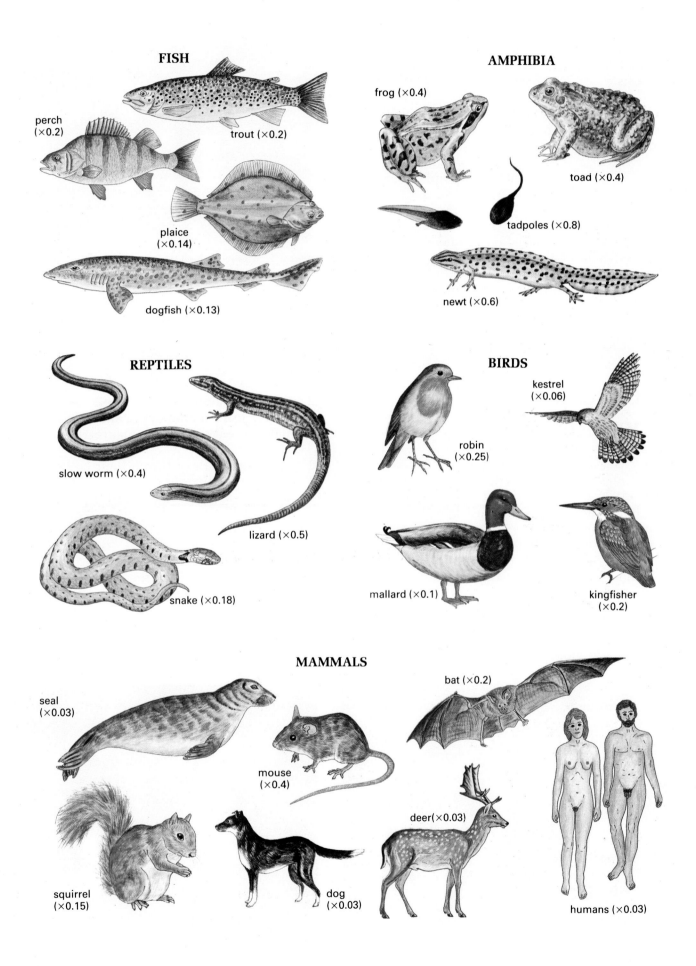

Figure 2   Vertebrates

into smaller molecules which their bodies can absorb.

Thus in animals feeding involves a breaking-down process while in plants it is a building-up process, or synthesis.

2 Cell structure   Plant cells have cell walls made of cellulose. Cells in plant leaves and stems contain chloroplasts, small green structures which assist in photosynthesis. (Cells are described in Chapter 2.)

Animal cells never contain chloroplasts and they do not have cell walls.

3 Movement and sensitivity   Most plants are rooted in the soil and do not move about. Most animals can move about freely.

When animals receive a stimulus, they often respond rapidly and the whole animal moves. Most plants respond slowly to stimuli and only parts of the plant move, such as the stem, the leaves or the petals.

Characteristics of Mammals

Mammals have all the vertebrate characteristics: brain, spinal cord, skull, vertebral column and lungs. They are 'warm-blooded', so they can keep their body temperature steady, even when the surrounding temperature changes.

The following are characteristics of mammals:

1   Mammals, except for the Australian platypus and spiny anteater, do not lay eggs. Their eggs are fertilized internally and are kept in the female's body for weeks or months while they develop into embryos. They are born, that is they come into the outside world more or less fully formed (Figure 3).

Figure 3   Most mammals produce their young fully formed. The cow is giving birth to a calf, with a little help from the farmer. The calf is still partly enclosed in the amniotic sac (page 168).

Figure 4   Mammals feed their young on milk. Five of the piglets are suckling from the sow.

Except for animals such as the Australian kangaroo (marsupials) the embryos are nourished by an organ called the **placenta** while they are developing inside the mother (see page 168).

2   Female mammals feed their young on milk produced from **mammary glands**, until the young animals can eat solid food (Figure 4).

3   They have hair or fur on their bodies (Figure 5). This may be an obvious dense covering as in cats and dogs, sparsely distributed bristles as in pigs, or a simple tuft like the one at the end of an elephant's tail.

4   In all mammals, the internal body space is divided into two regions: the **thorax**, which contains the heart and lungs, and the **abdomen** which contains digestive organs, liver, kidneys and reproductive organs. The two cavities are separated by a sheet of tissue called the **diaphragm** (page 114). Other vertebrates do not have a diaphragm.

Figure 5   Mammalian characteristics. The gerbils are covered with fur; they also have ear pinnae and vibrissae (sensory whiskers).

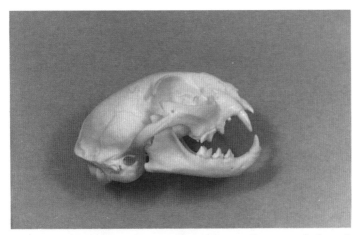

Figure 6 Skull of cat, showing the different shapes and sizes of teeth for holding prey, cutting flesh and crushing bones.

5 In most but not all mammals the first set of teeth, the 'milk' teeth, is shed early in life and replaced with a set of permanent teeth.

6 In most mammals, but not, for example, in dolphins, the teeth are of different shapes and sizes (Figure 6) and are adapted for special functions. For example, incisors are adapted for gripping or cutting, and molars for crushing or grinding.

In a reptile or a fish, the teeth are usually all the same shape, forming rows of simple sharp spikes or pegs which grip the prey.

7 Sweat glands occur only in mammals, but not all mammals have them. Cats have sweat glands only in the feet. Whales do not have sweat glands at all.

8 Although birds, reptiles and amphibians have ears (hearing organs), only mammals have the structures called ear **pinnae**. These are the flaps which project from the head and direct sound vibrations into the ear (Figure 5). Whales, seals and most other mammals that live in the sea have no ear pinnae.

9 Mammals differ from all other vertebrates in the much greater development of their brains. Part of the front region of the brain has developed into two large **cerebral hemispheres** (see page 213). Biologists think that this region is responsible for learning and intelligence as well as many other activities which make mammals a successful group.

Primates The mammals include about 18 subgroups (orders). Examples are the carnivores (such as lions and wolves), rodents (such as rats and mice) and insectivores (such as shrews and hedgehogs). One of these orders is the primates. The primates include lemurs, monkeys, apes and humans. These mammals are mostly adapted for life in trees. They have quite large brains, well-developed eyes set in the front (rather than the sides) of their heads, and five fingers and toes which can grasp and grip. Their teeth are not specialized for a particular diet in the way that those of carnivores or herbivores are.

Humans as Mammals

1 Birth Human eggs are fertilized internally and the young develop in about 38 weeks inside the mother, obtaining their food and oxygen through the placenta (page 168). The young are born fully formed but helpless. They depend on their parents for food and shelter for many years.

2 Suckling The mammary glands of the females form the breasts. These contain fatty tissue and milk-producing glands. The young suck the milk from the breasts. Normally it is their only source of food for several months.

3 Hair Apart from the palms of the hands and soles of the feet, human skin is covered with hair. This grows longer and more densely on the head, the face and chest (in males), and in the armpits and the pubic regions.

4 Diaphragm Humans have a diaphragm which separates the abdomen and thorax. The diaphragm plays an important part in breathing (page 142).

5 Milk teeth Children have 20 milk teeth which they lose between the ages of six and twelve. The milk teeth are replaced by 32 permanent teeth.

6 Teeth shape Human teeth are not so varied in shape as, for example, those of a dog. There are differences, however. The incisors have chisel-like crowns which cut off pieces of food, and the molars are broad and knobbly for crushing the food.

7 Sweat glands All parts of human skin contain sweat glands. They play a part in temperature regulation.

8 Ear pinnae Human ears have pinnae which project from the side of the head. Whether they are important in directing sound waves into the ear is not clear, however.

9 Brain The human brain is very large in proportion to the body size, and the cerebral hemispheres are particularly well developed. This probably gives humans a learning ability and intelligence which is greater than that of the other mammals.

Special Human Features

Upright posture By standing upright instead of on all fours, humans leave their hands free to manipulate tools and weapons. This means they can build shelters, defend themselves against predators and develop writing and other technical skills. Some of the apes can also use their hands, but only

Figure 7   Manipulation by human hands. Notice the opposable thumb and forefinger holding the thermometer.

Figure 8   Humans have the power of speech

Figure 9   Stored knowledge. Unlike other mammals, humans can pass on the knowledge resulting from many years of study and research.

(a) The Alaskan Eskimo may experience temperatures down to −30°C. The clothing must provide an effective layer of insulation.

(b) The temperature in Mali may be +35°C or more. Little clothing is needed.

Figure 10   Human adaptation to extremes of temperature

humans can bring the thumb to oppose any one of the fingers so that the pads face each other. This is called an **opposable thumb** (Figure 7).

Speech Other mammals communicate with each other by sounds. But they cannot exchange very much information other than warning sounds, threatening cries and greeting signals. No other mammal has organs that can produce speech, however. Nor has any other mammal a brain that can use speech to pass on detailed information (Figure 8).

Learning and intelligence The combination of speech, writing, memory and ability to learn from experience helps humans to survive all kinds of hazard. Also, by speaking and writing they can pass on information to their children so that they can benefit from all the learning of the past (Figure 9). It may have taken our ancestors thousands of years to change from hunting to agriculture. Now, however, the information is available and can be used at once by anybody. We learn by watching others and by reading and listening. This is all part of human culture, which is not shared by any other mammal.

Adaptability Humans are not specialized mammals. Their forearms are not flippers for swimming, wings for flying or hooves for running. Instead, humans use their simple, five-fingered hand, with the aid of intelligence and memory, to make machines and buildings so that they can reach and survive in almost any part of the world.

By wearing clothes, building houses, storing food and passing on information, humans can adapt themselves to be independent of their surroundings. They can carry on the essential living processes in both very hot and very cold climates. No other single species of mammal can do this (Figure 10).

QUESTIONS

5 What is the main difference between green plants and animals? Suggest some other differences.

6 Make a list of all the mammals you can think of. Choose one of these and say how it differs from humans.

7 Humans are described as unspecialized or adaptable mammals. How does this apply to their choice of food?

CHECK LIST

- All living organisms
  - (a) breathe, exchanging oxygen and carbon dioxide
  - (b) feed
  - (c) produce energy from food
  - (d) excrete the waste products of their chemical processes
  - (e) grow
  - (f) reproduce
  - (g) respond to stimuli.

- Humans are living organisms, classified as mammals in the vertebrate sub-group of the animal kingdom:

Kingdom...............	Animal
Sub-group	Vertebrate
Class	Mammal
Order	Primate

- Like other mammals, humans
  - (a) give birth to young
  - (b) suckle their young on milk
  - (c) have
    - (i) sweat glands and hair on the body
    - (ii) a diaphragm separating thorax and abdomen
    - (iii) ear pinnae
    - (iv) two sets of teeth in the lifetime
    - (v) specialized shapes in the teeth
    - (vi) very large cerebral hemispheres in the brain.

- Humans differ from other mammals in their
  - (a) upright posture
  - (b) speech
  - (c) highly developed brain
  - (d) adaptability.

Cell Structure

How tissues are studied to see cells: the microscope; taking sections. Cell components. Plant cells.

Cell Division and Specialization

Cell division and growth. Specialization of cells for different functions.

Practical Work

Preparing, observing and drawing plant and animal cells.
Tissue culture.

Tissues and Organs

Definitions and examples of tissues, organs and systems.

Cell Structure

If you cut a very thin slice of a plant stem and study it under a microscope (Figure 1), you can see that the stem consists of thousands of tiny, box-like structures. These structures are called **cells**. Figure 2 shows a thin slice taken from the tip of a plant shoot, photographed through a microscope. Photographs like this are called **photomicrographs**. The one in Figure 2 is 60 times larger than life. So if a cell appears to be 2 mm long in the picture, you know it is only 0.03 mm long in life.

Thin slices of this kind are called **sections**. If you cut *along the length* of the structure, you are taking a **longitudinal section**. Figure 2 is a longitudinal

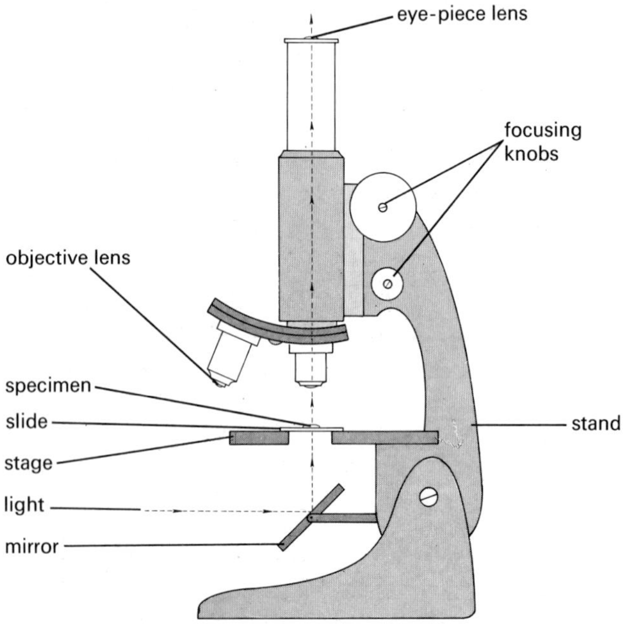

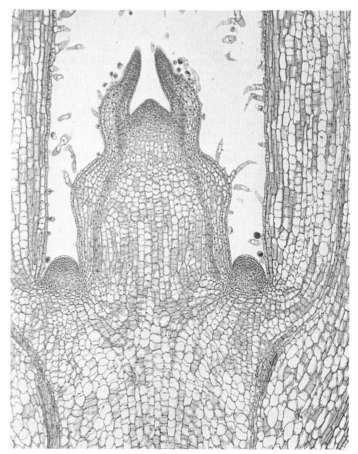

Figure 1   The microscope. Light is reflected by the mirror and directed through the specimen into the lenses of the microscope. These lenses produce a greatly magnified image of the specimen. This can be either studied directly or photographed.

Figure 2   Longitudinal section through the tip of a plant shoot (×60). The slice is only one cell thick. Light can pass through it, allowing the cells to be seen clearly.

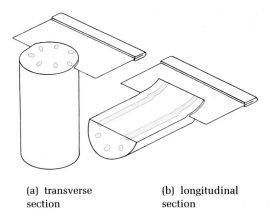

(a) transverse
section

(b) longitudinal
section

Figure 3   Cutting sections of a plant stem

Making sections is not the only way to study cells. Thin strips of plant tissue, only one cell thick, can be pulled off stems or leaves (see Practical Work, page 18). Plant or animal tissue can be squashed or smeared on a microscope slide, or treated with chemicals to separate the cells before studying them.

Figure 5 shows a group of cells scraped from the human cheek lining and smeared on a microscope slide. Figure 6 shows three of these cheek cells magnified 1500 times.

All cells have a **cell membrane**, which is a thin boundary enclosing the **cytoplasm**. Most cells have a **nucleus**.

section which passes through two small developing leaves near the tip of the shoot, and two larger leaves below them. The leaves, buds and stem are all made up of cells. If you cut *across* the structure, you make a **transverse section** (Figure 3).

It is fairly easy to cut sections through plant structures just by using a razor blade. To make a microscopic study of animal structures is more difficult because they are mostly soft and flexible. Pieces of skin, muscle or liver, for example, first have to be soaked in melted wax. When the wax goes solid it is then possible to cut thin sections. The wax is dissolved away after the section has been cut.

If you examine sections of animal structures under the microscope, you can see that they too are made up of cells. Animal cells are much smaller than plant cells, however, and need to be magnified more. The photomicrograph of kidney tissue in Figure 4 has been magnified 700 times to show the cells clearly. Sections are often treated with dyes, called 'stains', so as to make the structures inside the cells easier to see.

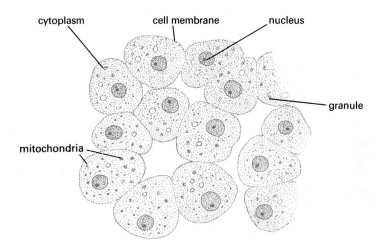

Figure 5   A group of animal cells, for example, cells from the lining of the cheek.

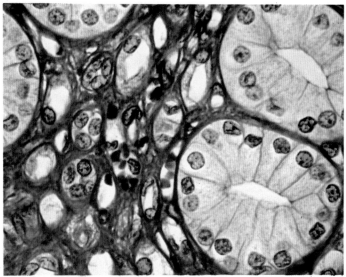

Figure 4   Transverse section through a kidney tubule ($\times 700$). A section through a tube will look like a ring (see Figure 13 (b) on page 16). In this section, there are about ten cells in each 'ring'.

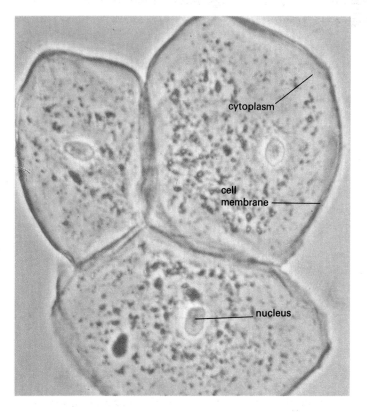

Figure 6   Cells from the epithelium lining the cheek ($\times 1500$).

Cytoplasm   Under the microscope cytoplasm looks like a thick liquid with particles in it. In plant cells you may be able to see it flowing about. The particles may be food reserves such as oil droplets or granules of starch. Other particles are structures which have particular functions in the cytoplasm.

For example, **mitochondria** are tiny structures which supply the cell with energy. Chemical changes in the mitochondria release energy from food substances (page 28). The energy is used to drive other chemical reactions in the cell.

When studied at very high magnifications with the **electron microscope**, the cytoplasm no longer looks like a structureless jelly. It appears to be organized into a complex system of membranes and vacuoles.

In the cytoplasm, a great many chemical reactions are taking place. These keep the cell alive by providing energy and making substances that the cell needs (see pages 19 and 28).

The liquid part of cytoplasm is about 90 per cent water with molecules of salts and sugars dissolved in it. Suspended in this solution there are larger molecules of fats (lipids) and proteins (pages 19-20). Lipids and proteins may be used to build up the cell structures, such as the membranes. Some of the proteins are **enzymes** (page 22). Enzymes are substances that control the rate and type of chemical reactions taking place in the cells. Some enzymes are attached to the membrane systems of the cell. Others float freely in the liquid part of the cytoplasm.

Cell membrane   This is a thin layer of cytoplasm round the outside of the cell. It stops the cell contents from escaping and also controls the substances that enter and leave the cell. It allows oxygen, food and water to enter, and waste products to leave. It also keeps harmful substances out of the cell. In this way the cell membrane maintains the structure and chemical reactions of the cytoplasm.

Nucleus (plural = nuclei)   Most cells contain one nucleus, usually seen as a rounded structure embedded in the cytoplasm. Drawings of cells may show the nucleus darker than the cytoplasm because, in prepared sections, it takes up certain stains more strongly than the cytoplasm does. The nucleus controls the types and quantities of enzymes produced by the cytoplasm. In this way it regulates the chemical changes taking place in the cell. As a result, the nucleus determines what the cell will be – for example, a blood cell, a liver cell, a muscle cell or a nerve cell.

The nucleus also controls cell division. This is shown in Figure 11 on page 14. A cell without a nucleus cannot reproduce. Inside the nucleus are thread-like structures called **chromosomes** which can be seen only when the cell is dividing. (Chromosomes are described more fully on page 222.)

The term **protoplasm** may be used to describe the cytoplasm, nucleus and cell membrane together.

Plant cells

Figures 5 and 6 show a few animal cells. Figure 7 is a photomicrograph of plant cells in a leaf (palisade cells, see page 42). Figure 8 is a simplified drawing of two of the cells.

Plant cells differ from animal cells in several ways;

1 They all have a **cell wall** outside the cell membrane. This is a non-living layer of cellulose, which allows liquids and dissolved substances to pass freely through it. It is not selective like the cell membrane. (Plant cells *do* have a cell membrane but it is not easy to see or draw because it is pressed against the inside of the cell wall. See Figure 9.)

Under the microscope, plant cells are quite distinct and easy to see because of their cell walls. In Figure 2 you can see only the cell walls (and some of the nuclei). Each plant cell has its own cell wall but the boundary between two cells side

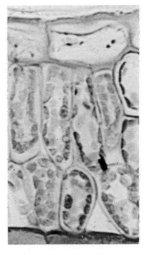

Figure 7   Plant cells. This is a section through a leaf. The tall cells are called palisade cells (×460).

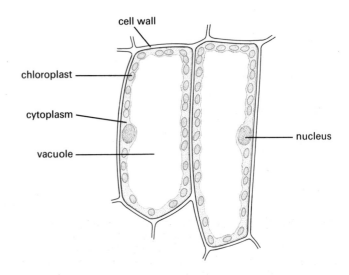

Figure 8   Palisade cells from a leaf

by side does not usually show up clearly. Cells next to each other therefore appear to be sharing the same cell wall.

2 Most mature plant cells have a large, fluid-filled space called a **vacuole**. The vacuole contains **cell sap**, a watery solution of sugars, salts and sometimes pigments. This large, central vacuole pushes the cytoplasm aside so that it forms just a thin lining inside the cell wall. It is the outward pressure of the vacuole on the cytoplasm and cell wall that makes plant cells and their tissues firm. Animal cells may sometimes have small vacuoles in their cytoplasm but they are usually produced to do a particular job and are not permanent.

3 In the cytoplasm of plant cells are many structures called **plastids** which are not present in animal cells. If they contain the green substance **chlorophyll**, the structures are called **chloroplasts** (see page 41). Colourless plastids usually contain starch, which is used as a food store.

The shape of a cell when seen in a transverse section may be quite different from the shape of the same cell seen in a longitudinal section. Figure 9 shows why this is so.

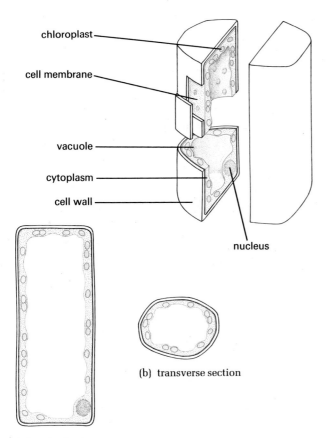

(b) transverse section

(a) longitudinal section

Figure 9   Structure of a palisade cell. Although cells look flat in sections or in thin strips of tissue, they are in fact three-dimensional. So they may seem to have different shapes depending on the direction in which the section is cut. If the cell is cut across it will look like (b). If it is cut longitudinally it will look like (a).

QUESTIONS

1 (a) What structures are usually present in all cells, whether they are from an animal or from a plant?
   (b) What structures are present in plant cells but not in animal cells?
2 What cell structure is largely responsible for controlling the entry and exit of substances into or out of the cell?
3 In what way does the red blood cell shown in Figure 1 on page 125 differ from most other animal cells?
4 How does a cell membrane differ from a cell wall?
5 Why does the cell shown in Figure 9 (b) appear to have no nucleus?

6 In Figure 4, the cell membranes are not always clear. Why is it still possible to decide roughly how many cells there are in each tubule section?
7 (a) In order to see cells clearly in a section of plant tissue, would you have to magnify the tissue (i) ×5, (ii) ×10, (iii) ×100 or (iv) ×1000?
   (b) What is the approximate width (in mm) of one of the largest cells in Figure 4?
8 Make a simple drawing to show what a longitudinal section through Figure 13 (b) would look like.

Cell Division and Cell Specialization

Cell division

When plants and animals grow, their cells increase in numbers by dividing. Each cell divides to produce two daughter cells (Figures 10 and 11). Both daughter cells may divide again, but often one of the cells

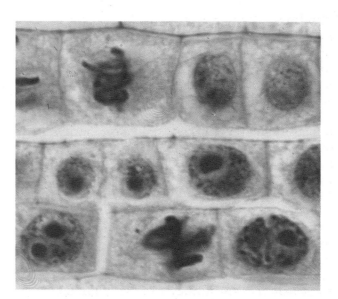

Figure 10   Cell division in an onion root tip (×750). The nuclei are stained pink. Most of the cells have just completed cell division. Chromosomes are visible in some of the cells.

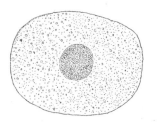 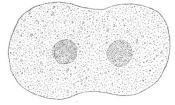 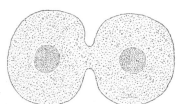 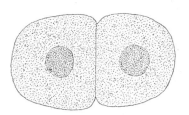

(a) Animal cell about to divide.

(b) The nucleus divides first.

(c) The daughter nuclei separate and the cytoplasm pinches off between the nuclei.

(d) Two cells are formed. One may keep the ability to divide, and the other may become specialized.

Figure 11   Cell division in an animal cell

grows and changes its shape and structure and becomes adapted to do one particular job. We say that it becomes **specialized**. At the same time it loses its ability to divide any more. The other cell is still able to divide and so to continue the growth of the tissue. **Growth** is, therefore, the result of cell division, followed by cell enlargement and, often, cell specialization.

Cell division also replaces the cells which die at the end of their life span. Cell division in the red bone marrow of the skeleton produces millions of new blood cells each day (page 126). Skin cells, which die and flake off all the time, are replaced by the basal layer of the epidermis (page 159).

Specialization of cells

Most cells, when they have finished dividing and growing, become specialized. This means that

1 they do one particular job;
2 they develop a distinct shape;
3 special kinds of chemical change take place in their cytoplasm.

The changes in shape and chemical reactions enable the cell to carry out its special function. Nerve cells and muscle cells are examples of specialized cells.

Nerve cells   A nerve cell is shown in Figure 12 (e).

1 Nerve cells conduct electrical impulses to and from the brain.
2 Some of them are very long and connect distant parts of the body to the spinal cord and brain.
3 Their chemical reactions cause the impulses to travel along the fibre.

Muscle cells   A muscle cell is shown in Figure 12 (c).

1 Muscle cells produce movement.
2 Like nerve cells, they are very long.
3 Their chemical reactions enable them to contract.

We say that specialized cells are **adapted** to their function. This means that their shape and their chemical reactions are particularly well suited to the jobs they have to do.

The specialization of cells to carry out particular functions in an organism is sometimes called '**division of labour**' within the organism. Similarly, we can think of the special functions of mitochondria and other cell structures as 'division of labour' within the cell.

QUESTIONS

9 Look at Figure 4 on page 160. Where do you think cell division might be taking place? What effect might it have?
10 Name the specialized cells in Figure 7 on page 115. Suggest what their function might be.
11 Look at Figure 4 on page 160. When a basal cell of the skin divides, which daughter cell becomes specialized and which one keeps the ability to divide again?

12 Look at Figure 1 on page 42. (a) Whereabouts in a leaf are the food-carrying cells? (b) What other specialized cells are there in the leaf?

Tissues and Organs

Some microscopic organisms consist of one cell only and can carry out all the processes necessary for their survival (see page 256). The cells of the larger plants and animals cannot survive on their own. A muscle cell could not obtain its own food and oxygen. Other specialized cells have to provide the food and oxygen needed for the muscle cell to live. Unless these cells are grouped together in large numbers and made to work together, they cannot exist for long.

Tissue   A tissue such as bone, nerve or muscle is made up of many hundreds of cells. These cells are of just a few types. The cells of each type have similar structures and functions. So we can say that the tissue itself has a particular function. For example, nerves conduct impulses, muscle cells contract. Figure 13 shows how some cells are arranged to form simple tissues.

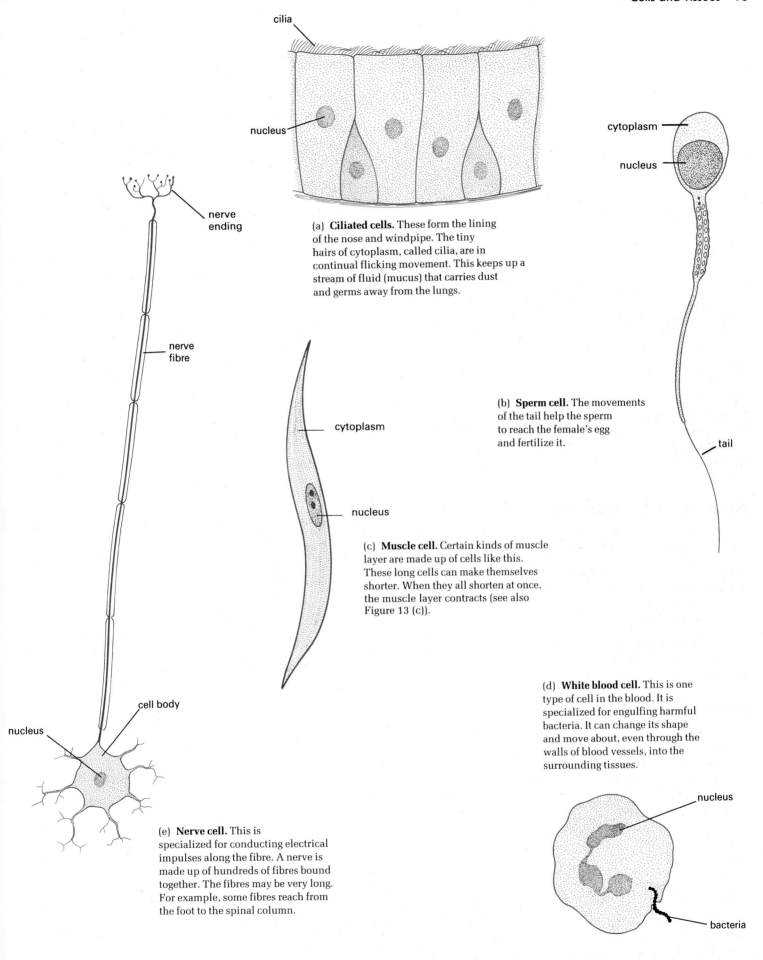

cilia

nucleus

(a) **Ciliated cells.** These form the lining of the nose and windpipe. The tiny hairs of cytoplasm, called cilia, are in continual flicking movement. This keeps up a stream of fluid (mucus) that carries dust and germs away from the lungs.

cytoplasm

nucleus

tail

(b) **Sperm cell.** The movements of the tail help the sperm to reach the female's egg and fertilize it.

nerve ending

nerve fibre

cytoplasm

nucleus

(c) **Muscle cell.** Certain kinds of muscle layer are made up of cells like this. These long cells can make themselves shorter. When they all shorten at once, the muscle layer contracts (see also Figure 13 (c)).

(d) **White blood cell.** This is one type of cell in the blood. It is specialized for engulfing harmful bacteria. It can change its shape and move about, even through the walls of blood vessels, into the surrounding tissues.

cell body

nucleus

(e) **Nerve cell.** This is specialized for conducting electrical impulses along the fibre. A nerve is made up of hundreds of fibres bound together. The fibres may be very long. For example, some fibres reach from the foot to the spinal column.

nucleus

bacteria

Figure 12   Examples of specialized cells (not to scale)

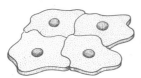

(a) **Cells forming an epithelium.** An epithelium is a thin layer of tissue, such as the lining of the mouth. Different types of epithelium line the windpipe air passages, food canal and so on. They protect these organs from physical or chemical damage.

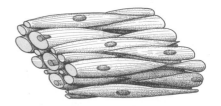

(c) **One kind of muscle cell,** forming a sheet of muscle tissue. Blood vessels, nerve fibres and connective tissues will also be present. Contractions of this kind of muscle help to move food along the food canal. They also make small blood vessels narrower.

(b) **Cells forming a small tube,** such as a kidney tubule (see page 153). Small tubes like this carry liquids from one part of an organ to another.

Figure 13   How cells form tissues

(d) **Cells forming part of a gland.** The cells make chemicals in their cytoplasm. These are released into the central space and are carried away by a tubule like the one in (b). A gland such as the salivary gland is made up of hundreds of cell groups like these.

Organs consist of several tissues grouped together to make a structure with a special function. For example, the stomach is an organ which contains tissues made from epithelial cells, gland cells and muscle cells. These cells are supplied with food and oxygen brought by blood vessels. The stomach also has a nerve supply. The heart, lungs, intestines, brain and eyes are further examples of organs in humans.

A system is the name given to a group of organs whose functions are closely related. For example, the heart and blood vessels make up the **circulatory system**, the brain, spinal cord and nerves make up the **nervous system** (Figure 14).

An organism is formed by the organs and systems working together to produce an independent plant or animal.

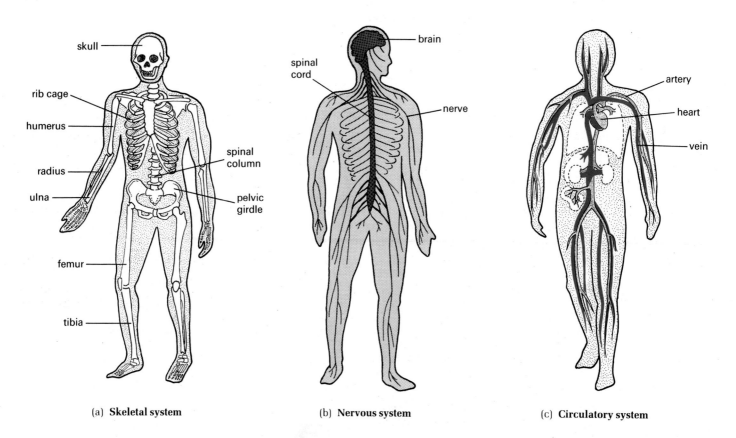

(a) **Skeletal system**

(b) **Nervous system**

(c) **Circulatory system**

Figure 14   Three examples of systems in the human body

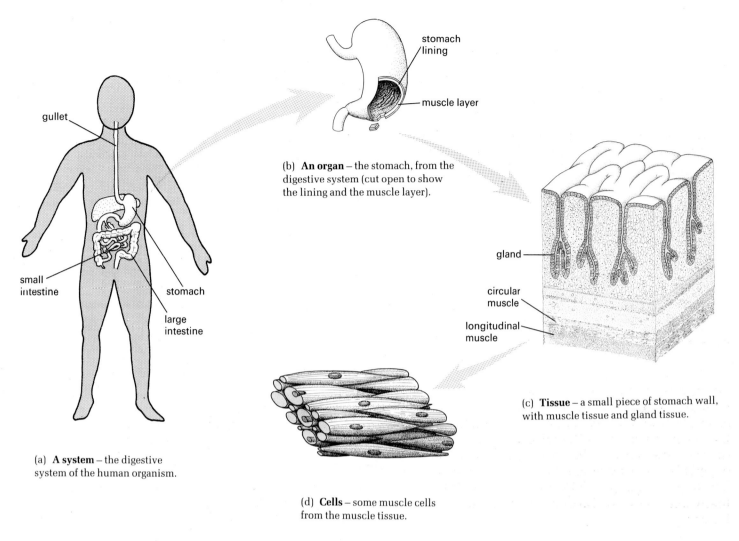

gullet

stomach lining

muscle layer

(b) **An organ** – the stomach, from the digestive system (cut open to show the lining and the muscle layer).

gland

circular muscle

longitudinal muscle

small intestine

stomach

large intestine

(c) **Tissue** – a small piece of stomach wall, with muscle tissue and gland tissue.

(a) **A system** – the digestive system of the human organism.

(d) **Cells** – some muscle cells from the muscle tissue.

Figure 15   An example of how cells, tissues and organs are related

Tissue culture

Biologists can take samples of developing animal tissues and separate the cells by using enzymes. If the cells are placed in shallow dishes containing a solution of food substances, they can grow and divide. This technique is called **tissue culture**. The cells do not become specialized but may move about, touch each other and in time cover the floor of the culture dish with a layer, one cell thick. At this point, they stop dividing unless they are separated and put into fresh culture vessels. Even so, most mammal cells stop dividing after about twenty divisions.

These tissue cultures are used to study cells and cell division and to test out new drugs and vaccines. They are also used to culture viruses and to test whether new chemicals can be harmful. For some tests and experiments, tissue cultures take the place of laboratory animals.

Large-scale tissue cultures are being developed in order to obtain cell chemicals which may be useful in treating disease.

QUESTIONS

13 Say whether you think the following are cells, tissues, organs or organisms: lungs (page 141), skin (page 158), ovary (page 165), blood (page 125), multi-polar neurone (page 208), ovum (page 164), *Amoeba* (page 256).

14 Say what tissues are shown in the following drawings: Figure 11 on page 185; Figure 9 on page 211.

15 Look at Figure 5 on page 114. Which of the structures shown do you think are organs? What system is represented by the drawing?

16 (a) Make a list of the ways in which cells can be studied.

(b) For each method of study, point out one way in which the results may not represent what really happens in living cells.

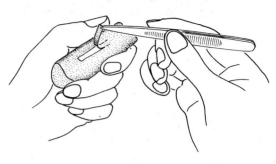

(a) Peel a strip of red epidermis from a piece of rhubarb stalk or . . .

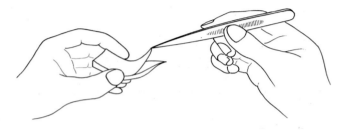

(b) . . . peel the epidermis from the inside of an onion scale.

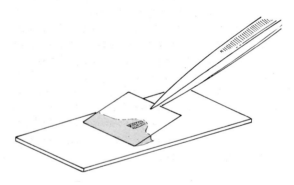

(c) Place the epidermis in a drop of weak iodine solution on a slide and carefully lower a cover-slip over it.

Figure 16   Looking at plant cells

PRACTICAL WORK

1 Plant cells

The outer layer of cells (epidermis) from a stem or an onion scale can be stripped off as shown in Figure 16 (a) and (b). A piece of onion or a rhubarb stalk is particularly suitable for this. Place a small piece of this epidermis in a drop of weak iodine solution on a microscope slide and cover it with a cover-slip (Figure 16 (c)). Then look at it under the microscope. The iodine will stain the cell nuclei pale yellow and the starch grains blue. If you use red epidermis from rhubarb stalk, you will see the red cell sap in the vacuoles.

2 Animal cells

Use a spatula or tooth-pick to scrape some of the lining from a piece of windpipe from a sheep or pig. Smear the material on to a clean slide and mix with a drop of water, followed by a drop of methylene blue (Figure 17). Cover the drop with a cover slip as shown in Figure 16 (c) and examine under the high power of the microscope. You should be able to see cells from the windpipe lining with the nucleus stained blue.

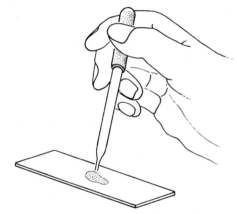

Figure 17   Add a drop of methylene blue

CHECK LIST

- Nearly all plants and animals are made up of thousands or millions of microscopic cells.
- All cells contain cytoplasm enclosed in a cell membrane.
- Most cells have a nucleus.
- Cytoplasm contains food reserves and structures such as mitochondria.
- Many chemical reactions take place in the cytoplasm to keep the cell alive.
- The nucleus directs the chemical reactions in the cell and also controls cell division.
- Plant cells have a cellulose cell wall and a large central vacuole.
- Cells are often specialized in their shapes and activities to carry out particular jobs.
- Large numbers of similar cells packed together form a tissue.
- Different tissues arranged together form organs.
- A group of related organs makes up a system.

3 The Chemicals of Living Cells

Cell Physiology
Description.

Chemical Components of Cells
Water, proteins, lipids, carbohydrates, salts, ions, vitamins; their chemical structure and role in the cell.

Enzymes
Definition. Methods of action. Effects of temperature and pH. Enzyme specificity. Intra- and
extra-cellular enzymes.

Practical Work
Controlled experiments. Catalase. Effect of pH and temperature on enzyme reactions.

Cell physiology

The word 'physiology' is used to mean all the normal functions that take place in a living organism. Digestion of food, circulation of blood and contraction of muscles are all parts of human physiology. The next three chapters deal with physiological events in individual cells.

The physiology of a whole organism is, in some ways, made up of the physiology of its cells. If all cells need a supply of oxygen then the whole organism must take in oxygen. Cells need chemical substances to make new cytoplasm and to produce energy. Therefore the organism must take in food to supply the cells with these substances. Of course, it is not quite as simple as this. Most cells have specialized functions (page 14) and so their needs are different. However, all cells need water, oxygen, salts and food substances. And all cells consist of water, proteins, lipids, carbohydrates, salts and vitamins, or substances derived from them. **Metabolism** is the word used to describe all the chemical changes that take place in our cells and, hence, in our bodies (see page 30).

Chemical Components of Cells

Water

Most cells contain about 75 per cent of water and will die if their water content falls much below this. Water is a good solvent and many substances move about the cell in a watery solution. Water molecules take part in a great many vital chemical reactions. One is photosynthesis, described on page 41.

The physical and chemical properties of water are different from those of most other liquids. And because of these properties, water can support life as no other liquid can. For example, water has a high capacity for heat (we say it has a high thermal capacity). This means that it can absorb a lot of heat without its temperature rising high enough to damage the proteins in the protoplasm (see page 20). However, most cells are damaged if they are cooled below 0 °C, because at this temperature water freezes and ice crystals form in the protoplasm. (Oddly enough, rapid freezing of cells in liquid nitrogen at below -196 °C does not harm them.)

Proteins

Some proteins are part of the structures of the cell, such as the cell membranes, the mitochondria and the chromosomes. These proteins are called **structural proteins**.

There is another group of proteins called **enzymes**. Enzymes are present in the membrane systems, in the mitochondria, in special vacuoles and in the fluid part of the cytoplasm. Enzymes control the chemical reactions that keep the cell alive (page 22).

Although there are many different types of protein, they all contain carbon, hydrogen, oxygen, nitrogen and sulphur. Their molecules are made up of long chains of simpler chemicals called **amino acids**. Amino acids have the general formula

$$\boxed{R}-\underset{\underset{H}{|}}{\overset{\overset{NH_2}{|}}{C}}-COOH$$

where $\boxed{R}$ is an arrangement of carbon and hydrogen atoms forming either a chain or a ring. The —COOH group makes the chemical an acid and the —NH_2 group is called the amino group.

19

There are about twenty different amino acids in animal proteins, including alanine, leucine, valine, glutamine, cysteine and lysine. A small protein molecule might be made up from a chain such as, say, glycine–valine–valine–cysteine–leucine–glutamine– and so on, for a hundred or so amino acids.

Each different protein has the amino acids arranged in its own particular order. The chemical linkage between each amino acid and its neighbour is called a **peptide bond**. Two amino acids joined together form a **dipeptide**. Three form a **tripeptide**. More amino acids than this make a **polypeptide**.

A long polypeptide molecule becomes a protein when the chain of amino acids takes up a particular shape as a result of cross-linkages. Cross-linkages form between amino acids which are not neighbours, as shown in Figure 1. The shape of a protein molecule has a very important effect on its reactions. This is explained in the section on 'Enzymes' on page 22.

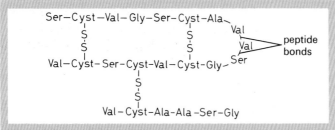

Figure 1   A small imaginary protein, made from only five different kinds of amino acid. The cysteine groups are cross-linked through pairs of sulphur atoms.

Denaturing   When a protein is heated to temperatures over 50 °C, the cross-linkages in its molecule break down. The protein molecule loses its shape and will not usually regain it even when cooled. The protein is said to have been **denatured**. Because the shape of the molecule has been altered, it will have lost its original properties.

Egg-white is a protein. When it is heated, its molecules change shape and the egg-white goes from a clear, runny liquid to a white solid. You cannot get the liquid protein back again. The egg-white protein, albumen, has been denatured by heat.

Enzymes are proteins, and so are many of the structures in the cell. So if the proteins are denatured the enzymes and the cell structures will stop working and the cell will die. Whole organisms may survive for a time above 50 °C. Whether an organism dies depends on the temperature, the period of exposure and the proportion of its cells that are damaged.

Protein metabolism   The proteins you eat are broken down to amino acids by your digestive system (page 113). Your body cells re-assemble these amino acids to make the proteins it needs. Cells can also change one kind of protein into another by swapping amino acids.

Lipids

Lipids are oils or fats and substances related to or derived from them. Fat molecules contain carbon, hydrogen and oxygen atoms only. A molecule of fat is made up of three molecules of an organic acid, called a **fatty acid**, combined with one molecule of glycerol.

A common fat is tristearin (or glyceryl tristearate):

$$CH_2O\text{---stearic acid}$$
$$|$$
$$CHO\text{---stearic acid}$$
$$|$$
$$CH_2O\text{---stearic acid}$$

glycerol

Three molecules of a fatty acid, stearic acid, have combined with one molecule of glycerol to form the **triglyceride**, tristearin. The difference between one fat and another depends on which fatty acids are combined with the glycerol. The fatty acids in any one triglyceride are not necessarily the same. For example, another triglyceride is:

$$CH_2O\text{---stearic acid}$$
$$|$$
$$CHO\text{---oleic acid}$$
$$|$$
$$CH_2O\text{---palmitic acid}$$

Triglycerides are often combined with proteins to form **lipoproteins**. **Steroids** are also lipids. The structure of their molecules is complex and quite different from that of the triglycerides.

Lipid metabolism   Some of the fats and oils you digest are broken down to glycerol and fatty acids (page 116). Your body cells may then combine the glycerol and fatty acids in different ways to make the kinds of lipid they need.

Lipids form part of the cell membrane and the internal membranes of the cell such as the membrane round the nucleus. Droplets of fat or oil form a source of energy when stored in the cytoplasm.

Carbohydrates

These may be simple, soluble sugars or complex materials like starch and cellulose, but all carbohydrates contain carbon, hydrogen and oxygen only. A common simple sugar is **glucose**, whose chemical formula is $C_6H_{12}O_6$.

The glucose molecule is often in the form of a ring, represented as

$$CH_2OH$$

or merely

Two molecules of glucose can be combined to form a molecule of maltose $C_{12}H_{22}O_{11}$ or

> Sugars with a single carbon ring are called **monosaccharides**. Glucose and fructose are examples. Sugars such as maltose and sucrose, which have two carbon rings in their molecules, are called **disaccharides**. Mono- and di-saccharides dissolve easily in water.

Some carbohydrate molecules contain many glucose units joined together. These are called **polysaccharides**. **Glycogen** (Figure 2) is a polysaccharide which forms a food storage substance in many animal cells. The **starch** molecule is made up of hundreds of glucose molecules joined together to form long chains. Starch is an important storage substance in plant cells. **Cellulose** consists of even longer chains of glucose molecules. The chain molecules are grouped together to form microscopic fibres, which are laid down in layers to form the cell wall in plant cells.

Polysaccharides do not dissolve easily in water.

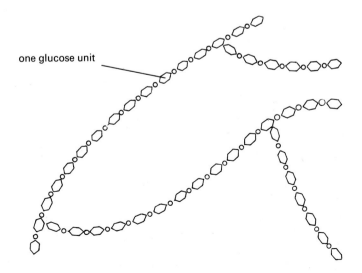

one glucose unit

Figure 2   Part of a glycogen molecule

Carbohydrate metabolism When you digest starch and glycogen, your digestive system breaks the long-chain molecules into glucose molecules (page 113). The glucose can be used as a source of energy (page 41), built up again to glycogen or converted to lipids. Human cells do not make cellulose and we cannot digest it without the aid of bacteria (page 250).

Salts

Salts are present in cells in the form of their ions. For example, sodium chloride in a cell exists as sodium ions (Na^+) and chloride ions (Cl^-). Some of the ions are free to move about in the water of the cell. Some are attached to other molecules such as the proteins or lipids (see also page 100).

Ions take part in and influence many chemical reactions in the cell. Phosphate ions (PO_4^{3-}), for example, are essential for energy-transfer reactions (see 'ATP', page 29). Calcium, potassium and sodium ions are particularly important in chemical changes related to the electrical activities of a cell. These include responding to stimuli and conducting nerve impulses. Having too many or too few ions in the cells upsets their physiology. The functioning of the whole organism is then disturbed.

Vitamins

These substances, in their chemical structure at least, have little in common. Plant cells can make their own vitamins. Animal cells have to be supplied with vitamins ready-made. Vitamins, or substances derived from them, play a part in chemical reactions in the cell. Examples are reactions in which energy is transferred from one compound to another. If cells are not supplied with vitamins or the substances needed to make them, the cell physiology is thrown out of order and the whole organism suffers (page 101).

QUESTIONS

1 Why do you think it is essential for us to eat proteins?
2 Which substances are particularly important in (a) forming the structures of the cell and (b) storing food in the cell?
3 Say which of the following are (a) carbohydrates, (b) salts, (c) lipids: sugar, butter, iron sulphate, starch, sodium chloride, olive oil, cellulose.
4 What elements do proteins contain that are not in carbohydrates?

> **5** What is the difference between a protein and a polypeptide?
> **6** In what ways does a protein molecule differ from a glycogen molecule?
> **7** How many different tripeptides could be made from the amino acids valine, serine and alanine?

Enzymes

Enzymes are proteins that act as **catalysts**. They are made in cells. A catalyst is a chemical substance which speeds up a reaction but does not get used up during the reaction. One enzyme can be used many times over (Figure 3).

Figure 4 (a) is a diagram of how an enzyme molecule might work to join two other molecules together and so form a more complicated molecule.

An example of an enzyme-controlled reaction such as this is the joining up of two glucose molecules to form a molecule of maltose:

$$C_6H_{12}O_6 \text{ glucose} + C_6H_{12}O_6 \text{ glucose} \xrightarrow{\text{enzyme}} C_{12}H_{22}O_{11} \text{ maltose} + H_2O \text{ water}$$

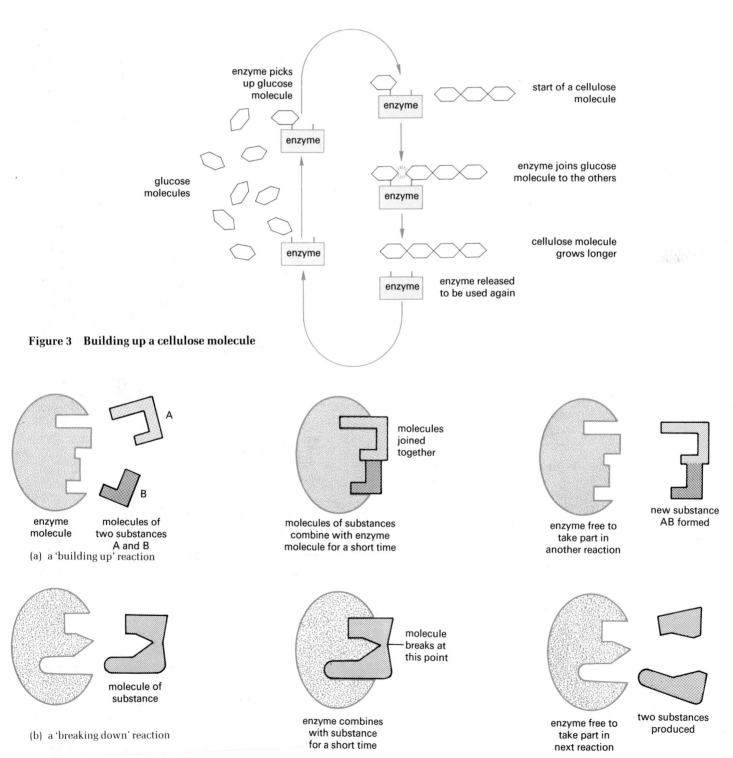

Figure 3   **Building up a cellulose molecule**

(a) a 'building up' reaction

enzyme molecule   molecules of two substances A and B

molecules joined together

molecules of substances combine with enzyme molecule for a short time

enzyme free to take part in another reaction

new substance AB formed

(b) a 'breaking down' reaction

molecule of substance

molecule breaks at this point

enzyme combines with substance for a short time

enzyme free to take part in next reaction

two substances produced

Figure 4   **A possible explanation of enzyme action**

Hundreds of glucose molecules might join together like this, end to end, to form a long molecule of glycogen to be stored in the liver. Protein molecules too are built up by enzymes which join together tens or hundreds of amino acid molecules. These proteins are added to the cell membrane, to the cytoplasm or to the nucleus of the cell. They may also become the proteins which themselves act as enzymes.

After the new substance has been formed, the enzyme is set free to start another reaction. Molecules of the two substances might have combined without the enzyme being present but they would have done so very slowly. By bringing the substances close together, the enzyme molecule makes the reaction much faster. A chemical reaction which would take hours or days to happen on its own takes only a few seconds when the right enzyme is present.

Figure 4 (b) shows an enzyme speeding up a chemical change but this time it is a reaction in which the molecule of a substance is split into smaller molecules. If starch is mixed with water it will break down very slowly to sugar, taking several years. In your saliva there is an enzyme called **amylase** which can break down starch to sugar in minutes or seconds. Inside a cell, many of the 'breaking-down' enzymes are helping to break down glucose to carbon dioxide and water in order to produce energy (see page 41).

Enzymes and temperature

A rise in temperature speeds up most chemical reactions. The rates of many reactions are doubled by a rise of 10 °C. This is equally true for enzyme-controlled reactions, but above 50 °C the enzymes, being proteins, are denatured and stop working.

Figure 4 shows how the shape of an enzyme molecule could be very important if it has to fit the substances on which it acts. Above 50 °C the shapes of enzymes are changed and the enzymes can no longer combine with the substances.

This is one of the reasons why organisms may be killed by high temperatures. The enzymes in their cells are denatured and the chemical reactions proceed too slowly to maintain life.

One way to test whether a substance is an enzyme is to boil it. If it can still carry out its reactions after this, it cannot be an enzyme. This technique is used as a 'control' (see page 25) in enzyme experiments.

Enzymes and pH

Acid or alkaline conditions alter the chemical properties of proteins, including enzymes. Most enzymes work best at a particular level of acidity or alkalinity (pH). The protein-digesting enzyme in your stomach, for example, works well at an acidity of pH 2. At this pH, the enzyme amylase, from your saliva, cannot work at all. Inside the cells, most

enzymes work best in neutral conditions (pH 7). The pH or temperature at which an enzyme works best is often called its **optimum** pH or temperature.

Although changes in pH affect the activity of enzymes, these effects are usually reversible. An enzyme whose activity disappears at a low pH will start working again when its optimum pH is restored. Very high or very low pH, however, may denature some enzymes irreversibly.

Enzymes are specific

This means simply that an enzyme which normally acts on one substance will not act on a different one. Figure 4 (a) shows how the shape of an enzyme could decide what substances it combines with. The enzyme in Figure 4 (a) has a shape which exactly fits the substances on which it acts, but would not fit the substance in (b). Thus, an enzyme which joins amino acids up to make proteins will not also join up glucose molecules to make starch. Where a reaction takes place in stages, such as:

protein → polypeptides (stage 1)
polypeptides → amino acids (stage 2)

a different enzyme is needed for each stage.

The names of enzymes usually end with **-ase**. The rest of the name is taken either from the substance on which they act, or from the reaction they speed up. For example, an enzyme that acts on proteins may be called a **protease**. One that removes hydrogen from a substance is a **dehydrogenase**.

The substance on which an enzyme acts is called its **substrate**. Thus the enzyme **sucrase** acts on the substrate **sucrose** to produce the monosaccharides glucose and fructose.

Intra- and extra-cellular enzymes

All enzymes are made inside cells. Most of them remain inside the cell to speed up reactions in the cytoplasm and nucleus. These are called **intra-cellular enzymes** ('intra-' means 'inside'). A few of the enzymes made in the cells are let out of the cell to do their work outside. These are **extra-cellular enzymes** ('extra-' means 'outside'). Fungi (page 255) and bacteria (page 249) release extra-cellular enzymes in order to digest their food. A mould growing on a piece of bread releases starch-digesting enzymes into the bread. The enzymes produce soluble sugars from the starch in the bread, and these are absorbed by the mould. In our digestive systems (page 112), extra-cellular enzymes are released into the stomach and intestines in order to digest the food.

Industrial use of enzymes

Enzymes have been used for hundreds of years to bring about changes in food and other organic products such as leather. These enzymes are not in a pure form, however. The processes use certain micro-organisms, such as fungi and bacteria, to produce the enzymes.

In brewing, barley is allowed to germinate (sprout). During germination the starch in the barley grains is converted to maltose (a sugar) by intra-cellular enzymes in the grains. The maltose is dissolved in water and mixed with yeast (a single-celled fungus). Extra-cellular enzymes from the yeast convert the maltose to alcohol (ethanol) and carbon dioxide. The mixture may be flavoured with hops and used to make beer. Sometimes the alcohol is distilled off for making spirits.

Sugar from sugar cane or beet may be fermented in this way to produce alcohol for the chemical industry or as fuel for motor cars.

Enzymes may also be extracted from organisms, partly purified, and used instead of the organism itself. For many years an enzyme called **rennin** has been extracted from the stomachs of calves and lambs. This enzyme clots the protein in milk and is used in cheese-making.

A protein-digesting enzyme is extracted from bacteria and included in some washing powders. When the dirty washing is soaked in a solution of the washing powder, the enzyme digests away organic stains such as blood or food.

Many other extracted enzymes are used industrially for the production of chemicals such as organic acids.

One promising way of using enzymes is to attach the extracted enzyme or the micro-organisms that produce it to an unreactive plastic material. Sometimes the enzyme is enclosed in the plastic. The substrate is then allowed to flow over the 'immobilized' enzyme. In this form, the enzyme is very stable and can be used over and over again.

PRACTICAL WORK

Tests for proteins, fats and carbohydrates are described on page 109. Experiments on the digestive enzymes amylase and pepsin are described on pages 121-2.

Methods of preparing the reagents for the following experiments are given on page 285.

1 Extracting and testing an enzyme from living cells

In this experiment, the enzyme to be extracted and tested is **catalase**, and the substrate (the substance on which it acts) is hydrogen peroxide (H_2O_2). Certain reactions in cells produce hydrogen peroxide, which is poisonous. Catalase makes the hydrogen peroxide harmless by breaking it down to water and oxygen:

$$2H_2O_2 \xrightarrow{\text{catalase}} 2H_2O + O_2$$

Grind a small piece of liver with about 20 cm^3 water and a little sand, in a mortar. This will break open the liver cells and release their contents. Filter the mixture and share it between two test-tubes, A and B (Figure 5). The filtrate will contain all sorts of substances dissolved out from the cytoplasm of the liver cells, including many enzymes. Enzymes are specific, however. Only one of these, catalase, acts on hydrogen peroxide. Add some drops of the filtrate from test-tube A to a few cm^3 hydrogen peroxide solution in a test-tube. You will see a vigorous

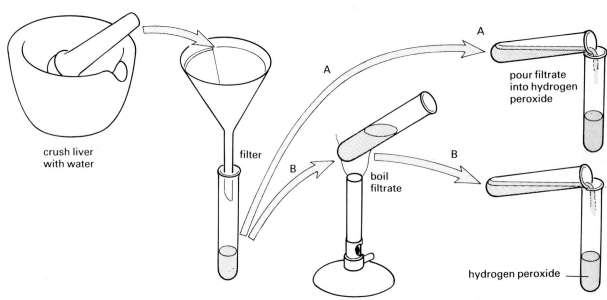

Figure 5   Extracting and testing living cells for catalase

reaction as the hydrogen peroxide breaks down to produce oxygen. (The oxygen can be tested for with a glowing splint.)

Now boil the filtrate in tube B for about 30 seconds. Add a few drops of the boiled filtrate to a fresh lot of hydrogen peroxide solution. There will be no reaction because boiling has denatured the catalase.

Next, shake a little manganese(IV) oxide powder in a test-tube with some water. Pour the mixture into some hydrogen peroxide solution. There will be a vigorous reaction, like the one with the liver extract. Now boil some manganese(IV) oxide with water and add this to hydrogen peroxide solution. The reaction will still occur. Manganese(IV) oxide is a catalyst but it is not an enzyme. You know this because heating has not altered its catalytic properties.

If you repeat the experiment with a piece of potato, you can compare its catalase content with that of the liver. The piece of potato should be about the same size as the piece of liver.

Controlled experiments

When biologists study a reaction they set up a **control experiment**. This is to ensure that the results of the experiment are due to the substance or the condition being investigated and not to some other unsuspected effect.

In Experiment 1, you were finding out whether liver contains an enzyme that can break down hydrogen peroxide. To make sure that an enzyme was causing the reaction (and not something else in a cell, perhaps a salt) you boiled some of the liver extract to denature any enzymes present. This was the control experiment. If you had still observed the reaction after boiling the extract, then it could not have been caused by an enzyme.

We cannot always define a 'control' consistently. It may depend on what the experiment is for. For example, if our experiment had been to study the effect of heat on catalase, the control would have been the experiment with the unboiled enzyme.

This is why some biologists prefer not to use the term 'control'. However, you need only remember that two parallel experiments are usually set up, differing from each other in only one respect. One of these will be the control, depending on the purpose of the experiment.

2 The effect of temperature on an enzyme reaction

Saliva contains a starch-digesting enzyme called **amylase**, which breaks down starch to a sugar (maltose). (If there is any objection to using saliva, use 2 cm³ diastase solution (5 per cent) instead.)

Collect about 30 mm (depth) of saliva in a clean test-tube. Label three test-tubes A, B and C and use a graduated pipette to place 1 cm³ saliva in each tube. Rinse the pipette.

Now label three test-tubes 1, 2 and 3, and use the pipette to place 5 cm³ of a 1 per cent starch solution, in each. To each of the test-tubes add 10 drops only of dilute iodine solution, using a dropping pipette.

Prepare three water baths by half-filling beakers or jars as follows:

1 ice and water, adding ice during the experiment to keep the temperature at about 10 °C;
2 water from the cold tap at about 20 °C;
3 warm water at about 35 °C by mixing hot and cold water from the tap.

Place tubes 1 and A in the cold water bath, tubes 2 and B in the water at room temperature, and tubes 3 and C in the warm water. Leave them for five minutes to reach the temperature of the water (Figure 6), then take the temperature of each water bath. Then pour the saliva from tube A into the starch solution in tube 1 and return tube 1 to the water bath. Repeat this with tubes 2 and B. Then repeat it with 3 and C.

As the amylase breaks down the starch, the blue colour will disappear. Make a note of how long this takes in each tube. Answer the following questions:

(a) At what temperature did the salivary amylase break down starch fastest?
(b) What do you think would have been the result if a fourth water bath at 90 °C had been used?

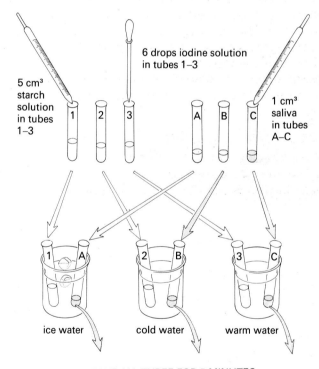

6 drops iodine solution in tubes 1–3

5 cm³ starch solution in tubes 1–3

1 cm³ saliva in tubes A–C

ice water   cold water   warm water

LEAVE ALL THREE FOR 5 MINUTES

NOTE THE TIME and add the saliva to the starch solution

Figure 6   The effect of temperature on an enzyme reaction

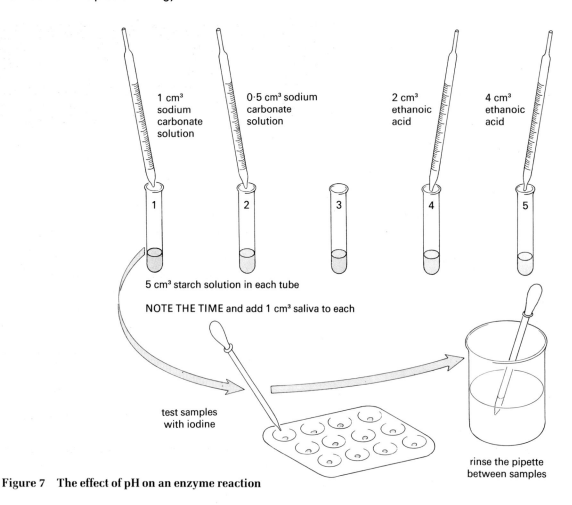

Figure 7   The effect of pH on an enzyme reaction

3 The effect of pH on an enzyme reaction

Label five test-tubes 1 to 5. Use a graduated pipette to place 5 cm³ of a 1 per cent starch solution in each tube. Add acid or alkali to each tube as shown in the table below. Rinse the pipette when changing from sodium carbonate to acid.

Place several rows of iodine solution drops in a cavity tile.

Tube	Chemical	Approximate pH	
1	1 cm³ sodium carbonate solution (0.05M)	9	(alkaline)
2	0.5 cm³ sodium carbonate solution (0.05M)	7–8	(slightly alkaline)
3	nothing	6–7	(neutral)
4	2 cm³ ethanoic (acetic) acid (0.1M)	6	(slightly acid)
5	4 cm³ ethanoic (acetic) acid (0.1M)	3	(acid)

Collect about 50 mm (depth) saliva in a clean test-tube and use a graduated pipette to add 1 cm³ saliva to each tube. If there is any objection to using saliva, use 5 cm³ diastase solution (5 per cent) instead. Shake the tubes and note the time (Figure 7).

Use a clean dropping pipette to remove a small sample from each tube in turn and let one drop fall on to one of the iodine drops in the cavity tile. Rinse the pipette in a beaker of water after each sample. Keep on sampling in this way.

When any of the samples fails to give a blue colour, this means that the starch in that tube has been completely broken down to sugar by the salivary amylase. Note the time when this happens for each tube and stop taking samples from that tube. Do not continue sampling for more than about 15 minutes. After that time, put a drop from each tube on to a piece of pH paper and compare the colour produced with a colour chart of pH values. Also find the pH of your own saliva.

Answer the following questions:

(a) At what pH did the enzyme, amylase, work most rapidly?

(b) Is this its optimum pH?

(c) Explain why you might have expected the result which you got.

(d) Your stomach pH is about 2. Would you expect starch digestion to take place in the stomach?

Further experiments   In the series *Experimental work in biology*, 17 experiments on food tests and 11 experiments on enzymes are described (see page 283).

QUESTIONS

8 Which of the following statements apply both to enzymes and to any other catalysts?
   (a) Their activity is stopped by high temperature.
   (b) They speed up chemical reactions.
   (c) They build up large molecules from small molecules.
   (d) They are not used up during the reaction.

9 How would you expect the rate of an enzyme-controlled reaction to change if the temperature was raised (a) from 20 °C to 30 °C, (b) from 35 °C to 55 °C? Explain your answers.

10 There are cells in your salivary glands which can make an extra-cellular enzyme, amylase. Would you expect these cells to make intra-cellular enzymes as well? Explain your answer.

11 Apple cells contain an enzyme which turns the tissues brown when an apple is peeled and left for a time. Boiled apple does not go brown (Figure 8). Explain why the boiled apple behaves differently.

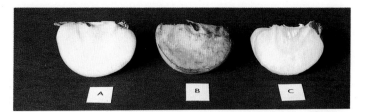

Figure 8   Enzyme activity in an apple. Slice A has been freshly cut. B and C were cut two days earlier, but C was dipped immediately in boiling water for one minute.

12 (a) What name would you give to an enzyme which converted a peptide to amino acids?
   (b) On what kind of substance would you expect a *lipase* to act?

13 Suppose that the enzyme in Figure 4 (a) is joining a glycine molecule to a valine molecule. Suggest why the same enzyme will not join glycine to serine.

CHECK LIST

- Living matter is made up of water, proteins, lipids, carbo-hydrates, salts and vitamins.
- Proteins are built up from amino acids joined together by peptide bonds.
- In different proteins the 20 or so amino acids are in different proportions and arranged in different sequences.
- Proteins are denatured by heat and some chemicals.
- Lipids include fats, oils, fatty acids and steroids.
- Fats are made from fatty acids and glycerol.
- Proteins and lipids form the membranes outside and inside the cell.

- Enzymes are proteins which catalyse chemical reactions in the cell.
- Enzymes are affected by pH and temperature and are denatured above 50 °C.
- Different enzymes may speed up reactions which build up or break down molecules.
- Each enzyme acts on only one substance (breaking down) or a pair of substances (building up).
- The substance on which an enzyme acts is called the substrate.

Energy from Respiration

Respiration

Definition. Aerobic and anaerobic respiration. Energy transfer with ATP. Metabolism.

Practical Work

Products of combustion of food. Anaerobic respiration. Muscle contraction with ATP. Hypothesis testing.

Respiration

Most of the processes taking place in cells need energy to make them happen. Building up proteins from amino acids and making starch from glucose both need energy. When muscle cells contract or when nerve cells conduct electrical impulses, they use energy. This energy comes from the food which cells take in. The food mainly used for energy in cells is glucose. The production of energy from food is called **respiration**.

Respiration is a chemical process that takes place in cells. Don't confuse it with the process of breathing, which is also sometimes called 'respiration'. To make the difference quite clear, the chemical process in cells is sometimes called **cellular respiration**, **internal respiration** or **tissue respiration**. Try not to use the word 'respiration' for breathing at all.

Aerobic respiration

The word **aerobic** means that oxygen is needed for this chemical reaction. The food molecules are combined with oxygen. We call the process **oxidation** and say that the food is **oxidized**. All food molecules contain carbon, hydrogen and oxygen atoms. Oxidation converts the carbon to carbon dioxide (CO_2) and the hydrogen to water (H_2O). At the same time, it sets free energy which the cell can use to drive other reactions.

Aerobic respiration can be summed up by the equation:

$$C_6H_{12}O_6 + 6O_2 \xrightarrow{\text{enzymes}} 6CO_2 + 6H_2O + 2830 \text{ kJ}$$

glucose   oxygen   carbon   water   energy
dioxide

The 2830 kilojoules (kJ) is the amount of energy you would get by completely oxidizing 180 grams of

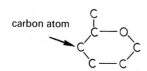

(a) Molecules of glucose (H and O atoms not all shown).

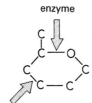

(b) The enzyme attacks and breaks the glucose molecule into two 3-carbon molecules.

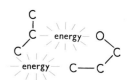

(c) This breakdown releases energy.

(d) Each 3-carbon molecule is broken down to carbon dioxide.

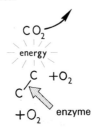

(e) More energy is released and carbon dioxide is produced.

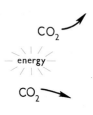

(f) The glucose has been completely oxidized to carbon dioxide (and water), and all the energy released.

Figure 1   Aerobic respiration

glucose to carbon dioxide and water. In the cells, the energy is not released all at once. The oxidation takes place in a series of small steps, not in one jump as the equation suggests. Each small step needs its own enzyme and at each stage a little energy is released (Figure 1).

Most of the aerobic respiration in cells takes place in mitochondria (page 12). The mitochondria are usually most plentiful in cells and regions of cells which are respiring rapidly. In effect, the mitochondria produce energy for the cell.

Whatever the energy is needed for, some of it always appears as heat. 'Warm-blooded' animals use some of the heat to keep up their body temperature. In 'cold-blooded' animals the heat may build up for a time and allow the animal to move about faster. In plants the heat is lost to the surroundings (by conduction, convection and evaporation) as fast as it is produced.

Anaerobic respiration

The word **anaerobic** means 'in the absence of oxygen'. Anaerobic respiration releases energy from food by breaking it down chemically. The reactions do not use oxygen, however, though they do often produce carbon dioxide. A common example is the action of yeast on sugar solution to produce ethanol (alcohol). This process is called **fermentation**. The following equation shows what happens:

$$\underset{\text{glucose}}{C_6H_{12}O_6} \xrightarrow{\text{enzymes}} \underset{\text{ethanol}}{2C_2H_5OH} + \underset{\substack{\text{carbon} \\ \text{dioxide}}}{2CO_2} + \underset{\text{energy}}{118 \text{ kJ}}$$

As with aerobic respiration, the reaction takes place in small steps and needs several different enzymes. The yeast uses the energy for its growth and living activities, but you can see from the equation that less energy is produced in anaerobic respiration than in aerobic respiration. This is because the ethanol still contains a great deal of energy which the yeast cannot use.

In animals, the first stages of respiration in muscle cells are anaerobic. These early stages produce **pyruvic acid** (the equivalent of the yeast's ethanol). Later on, the pyruvic acid is completely oxidized to carbon dioxide and water.

$$\underset{\substack{\text{enzymes} \\ \text{ANAEROBIC STAGE}}}{\text{glucose} \longrightarrow \text{pyruvic acid}} \xrightarrow[\text{AEROBIC STAGE}]{\substack{\text{enzymes} \\ \text{and oxygen}}} CO_2 + H_2O$$

During exercise pyruvic acid may build up in a muscle faster than it can be oxidized. In this case it is turned into **lactic acid** and removed in the bloodstream. When the lactic acid reaches the liver, some of it is oxidized to carbon dioxide and water, using up oxygen in the process. So the body goes on using up oxygen quite quickly, even after the exercise has stopped. We say that this build-up of lactic acid which is oxidized later creates an **oxygen debt**.

Energy transfer

The energy released when glucose is broken down is not used directly in the cell. Instead it is transferred to other chemicals which act as a store of readily available energy. One of these chemicals is **adenosine triphosphate** (ATP) (Figure 2).

Adenosine consists of a base combined with a sugar. The base is **adenine** and the sugar is **ribose**, which has five carbon atoms in its molecule. Adenosine may be combined with one, two or three phosphate groups.

At those stages in a glucose molecule's breakdown when energy is released, the energy is used to combine a phosphate group ($-PO_3$) with a molecule of adenosine diphosphate (ADP) to make a molecule of adenosine triphosphate (Figure 3).

Figure 3 seems to suggest that four molecules of ATP are made for every molecule of glucose broken down. The diagram leaves out many of the intermediate steps, however. In fact, 38 molecules of ATP can be built up when one molecule of glucose is completely oxidized to carbon dioxide and water.

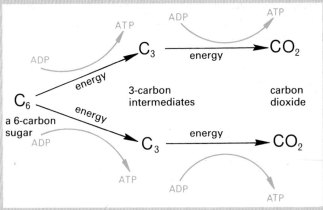

Figure 3 Energy transfer to ATP. The energy from the breakdown of glucose is used to build up ATP from ADP.

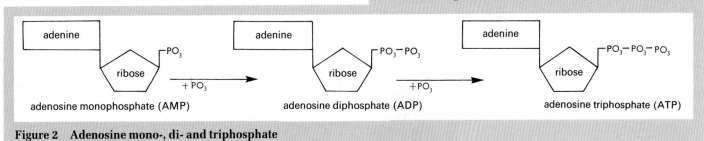

Figure 2 Adenosine mono-, di- and triphosphate

The cell's store of ATP is produced mainly by the mitochondria.

In the presence of the right enzyme, ATP breaks down to ADP, releasing energy and a phosphate ion. The energy can be used to drive other chemical reactions such as those producing muscle contraction:

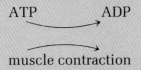

$$ATP \xrightarrow{\qquad} ADP$$

$$\xrightarrow{\qquad}$$

muscle contraction

ATP is thus a kind of energy store in the cell. It can be used directly for driving almost any reaction that needs energy. The breakdown of glucose to carbon dioxide and water is rather a slow process, with many intermediate steps and enzymes. ATP breakdown is rapid and needs only a suitable ATP-ase enzyme to bring it about. This is true in all cells – plant, animal or micro-organism.

We could compare the breakdown of glucose to burning coal, in order to generate steam, which drives a turbine and so charges a battery. All that is a fairly complex and long-winded business. The charged battery is like ATP, however. It can be used at a second's notice to do all kinds of things such as lighting a lamp, ringing a bell, driving a motor – whatever is needed at the time.

Metabolism

All the chemical changes taking place inside a cell or a living organism are called its **metabolism**. The minimum turnover of energy needed simply to keep an organism alive, without movement or growth, is called the **basal metabolism**. Basal metabolism maintains vital processes such as breathing, heart beat, digestion and excretion.

The reactions in which substances break down are sometimes called **catabolism**. In respiration, carbohydrates break down to carbon dioxide and water. So respiration is an example of catabolism. Chemical reactions that build up substances are called **anabolism**. Building up a protein from amino acids is an example of anabolism. The energy released by the **catabolic** process of respiration is used to drive the **anabolic** reactions which build up proteins.

You may have heard of 'anabolic steriods', in connection with drug-taking by athletes. These chemicals reduce the rate of protein breakdown and they may encourage the build-up of certain proteins. But their effects are complicated and not fully understood, they have undesirable side-effects and their use contravenes athletics' codes.

QUESTIONS

1 (a) Suppose that you had to say what respiration was about, in one word. Say which word you would choose from this list: breathing, energy, oxygen, cells, food.

(b) In which parts of a living organism does respiration take place?

2 What are the two main differences between aerobic and anaerobic respiration?

3 What chemical substances (a) from outside the cell, (b) from inside the cell, must be provided for aerobic respiration to take place? (c) What are the products of aerobic respiration?

4 Victims of drowning who have stopped breathing are sometimes revived by a process called 'artificial respiration'. Why wouldn't a biologist use this expression? ('Resuscitation' is a better word to use.)

5 Compare the equations for aerobic and anaerobic respiration on pages 28 and 29. How many molecules of ATP might you expect to be produced by the anaerobic fermentation of one molecule of glucose?

PRACTICAL WORK

1 The products of combustion of food

Make a combustion spoon by folding a piece of aluminium foil over a loop of wire (see Figure 4). Have a beaker of water ready.

Put a small piece of food in the spoon and hold it in a bunsen flame until it is burning. Hold the burning food under the mouth of an inverted, dry jam-jar (Figure 4), until the inside of the glass goes misty. Drop the spoon and burning food into the beaker of water and put the lid on the jar.

Use forceps to pick up a piece of cobalt chloride paper and hold it well above the bunsen flame till it goes blue. Remove the lid of the jar, drop the

Figure 4 Collecting the gases from burning food

cobalt chloride paper in and quickly replace the lid. Note any colour change in the cobalt chloride paper.

Remove the lid once more and pour a little clear lime water into the jar. Replace the lid as quickly as possible and shake the jar. Note any change in the lime water.

Result   The cobalt chloride changes colour from blue to pink. The lime water goes milky.

Interpretation   The 'mist' on the inside of the jar suggests that a liquid has condensed from a vapour produced in the burning. The colour change in the cobalt chloride paper confirms that the liquid is water.

Lime water going milky is evidence of the presence of carbon dioxide.

Control   To be sure that these gases came from the burning food and were not already present in the jar, you should take a clean, dry jar and test the air inside it with cobalt chloride paper and lime water as before.

2   Anaerobic respiration in yeast

Boil some water to expel all the dissolved oxygen. When cool, use the boiled water to make up a 5 per cent solution of glucose and a 10 per cent suspension of dried brewer's yeast. Place 5 cm^3 of the glucose solution and 1 cm^3 of the yeast suspension in a test-tube. Cover the mixture with a thin layer of liquid paraffin to keep out oxygen. Fit a delivery tube as shown in Figure 5 so that it dips into clear lime water.

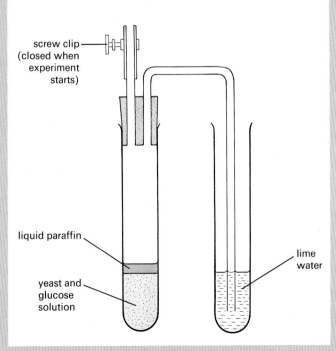

screw clip (closed when experiment starts)

liquid paraffin

yeast and glucose solution

lime water

Figure 5   Anaerobic respiration in yeast

Result   After 10–15 minutes there should be signs of fermentation in the yeast–glucose mixture. Bubbles of gas will escape through the lime water and should turn it milky. If the fermentation is slow to start, warm the test-tube gently.

Interpretation   The fact that the lime water goes milky shows that the yeast–glucose mixture is producing carbon dioxide. Let us assume that carbon dioxide production is evidence of respiration. Then it looks as if the yeast is respiring. In setting up the experiment, you took care to see that oxygen was removed from the glucose solution and the yeast suspension, and the liquid paraffin excluded air (including oxygen) from the mixture. Any respiration taking place must, therefore, be anaerobic (i.e. without oxygen). So if the yeast is respiring, it is doing so without oxygen. That is, the respiration is anaerobic.

Control   You may wonder whether the carbon dioxide came from a chemical reaction between yeast and glucose (as between chalk and acid) which had nothing to do with respiration or any other living process. You should therefore set up a control using the same procedure as before but with yeast which has been killed by boiling. The control will not produce any carbon dioxide. This is evidence that it was a living process in the yeast which produced the carbon dioxide in the first experiment.

3   Energy from adenosine triphosphate

Cut three very thin strips of fresh meat (muscle) as shown in Figure 6. Make your cuts along the strands of muscle tissue rather than across them. Keep cutting the strips until they are only about 1 mm wide but try to keep them at least 20 mm long. Put each strip on a slide in a drop of Ringer's solution. (Ringer's solution (see page 282) has a composition similar to tissue fluid.) Number the slides 1, 2 and 3 and measure the length of each muscle strip.

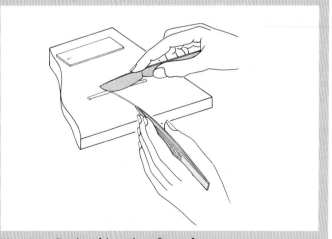

Figure 6   Cutting thin strips of muscle

Now add a drop of 1 per cent glucose solution to slide 1, ATP solution to slide 2 and boiled (and cooled) ATP solution to slide 3. After five minutes, measure the muscle strips again.

Result The muscle strips on slides 2 and 3 will have contracted.

Interpretation Slide 1: although glucose contains energy, the non-living muscle cannot use it for contraction.

Slide 2: ATP produced contraction probably because the non-living muscle still contained an active enzyme for breaking down ATP. This breakdown provided the necessary energy.

Slide 3: ATP is not affected by boiling. So it does not make muscle contract by acting like an enzyme to release energy from some other chemical.

Energy from food An experiment to compare the amounts of energy produced by burning sugar and burning oil is described on page 110.

Carbon dioxide in exhaled air An experiment to compare the carbon dioxide contents of inhaled and exhaled air is described on page 150.

Hypothesis testing

Science makes progress in many ways. One way is by putting forward a **hypothesis**, making predictions from the hypothesis, and then testing these predictions by experiments. A hypothesis tries to explain some event or observation using the information available at the time. If the results of an experiment do not confirm the predictions, the hypothesis has to be given up or altered.

For example, biologists observing that living organisms take up oxygen might put forward the hypothesis that 'Oxygen is used to convert food to carbon dioxide, so producing energy for move-ment, growth, reproduction, etc.' They could test their hypothesis by predicting that 'If the oxygen is used to oxidize food then an organism that takes up oxygen will also produce carbon dioxide.'

Looking at the equation for respiration on page 28 we might also predict that an organism which is respiring will produce carbon dioxide and take up oxygen. The experiment with yeast, however, does not fulfil this prediction. So the hypothesis cannot stand, because here is an organism producing carbon dioxide *without* taking up oxygen. The hypothesis will have to be modified. We might say, for example, 'Energy is released from food by breaking it down to carbon dioxide. Some organisms use oxygen for this process, others do not'.

By doing experiments, scientists can disprove a hypothesis. But they cannot prove it to be true. There might always be an alternative hypothesis which explains the facts better. Respiration, as a hypothesis to explain how most organisms obtain supplies of energy, has not been disproved. Many types of bacteria get their energy from quite different chemical reactions, however.

QUESTIONS

6 (a) In what way does Experiment 1 illustrate the process of respiration?

(b) In what ways does the release of energy in respiration differ from the release of energy by burning food?

7 Table 1 on page 145 shows you that ordinary air contains both carbon dioxide and water vapour. Explain why the control in Experiment 1 is still valid.

8 The experiment with yeast on page 31 supported the claim that anaerobic respiration was taking place. The experiment was repeated using unboiled water and without the liquid paraffin. Fermentation still took place and carbon dioxide was produced. Does this mean that the design or the interpretation of the first experiment was wrong? Explain your answer.

CHECK LIST

● Respiration is the process in cells which releases energy from food.

● The energy is used to drive other chemical reactions, generate nerve impulses and produce movement.

● Aerobic respiration needs oxygen. Anaerobic respiration does not.

● More energy is produced (per gram of glucose) from aerobic respiration than from anaerobic respiration.

● Both types of respiration may occur in active muscles.

● The oxidation of food produces carbon dioxide as well as releasing energy.

● Metabolism is the sum of all the chemical reactions which take place in cells.

● The energy from oxidation of food is transferred to ATP.

● ATP acts as a store of readily available energy.

5 How Substances get in and out of Cells

Diffusion
Explanation. Diffusion into and out of cells. Rates of diffusion. Controlled diffusion. Surface area. Endo- and exo-cytosis. **Active transport.**

Osmosis
Definition. Explanation. Artificial selectively permeable membranes. **The cell membrane.** Osmotic potential.

Practical Work
Experiments on diffusion of gases, diffusion in liquids, selective permeability, dialysis, osmotic flow.

Models
Use of 'models' to explain theories.

Cells need food materials which they can oxidize for energy or which they can use to build up their cell structures. They also need salts and water for the chemical reactions in the cell. On the other hand, substances such as carbon dioxide would upset some of the chemical reactions and even poison the cell if they were to build up in it. Cells need to get rid of substances like these.

Substances may pass in and out of the cell membrane either by diffusion, or by some form of active transport.

Diffusion

The molecules of a gas like oxygen are moving about all the time. So are the molecules of a liquid, or a substance such as sugar dissolved in water. As a result of this movement, the molecules spread themselves out evenly to fill all the available space (Figure 1). This process is called **diffusion**.

One effect of diffusion is that the molecules of a gas, a liquid or a dissolved substance will move from a region where there are a lot of them (high concentration) to regions where there are few of them (low concentration). This goes on until the concentration everywhere is the same. Figure 2 (a) is

a diagram of a cell with a high concentration of molecules (for example, oxygen) outside and a low concentration inside. The effect of this difference in concentration is to make the molecules diffuse into the cell until the concentration inside the cell is the same as the concentration outside (Figure 2 (b)).

Whether this will happen or not depends on whether the cell membrane will let the molecules through. Small molecules such as water (H_2O), carbon dioxide (CO_2) and oxygen (O_2) can pass through the cell membrane fairly easily. So diffusion tends to equalize the concentrations of these molecules inside and outside the cell all the time.

When a cell uses up oxygen for its aerobic respiration, the concentration of oxygen inside the cell falls. So oxygen molecules diffuse into the cell until the concentration is raised again. During tissue respiration, carbon dioxide is produced and so its concentration inside the cell goes up. Once again diffusion takes place, but this time the carbon dioxide molecules move out of the cell. So a cell takes in its oxygen by diffusion, and gets rid of its carbon dioxide in the same way.

(a) greater concentration outside cell

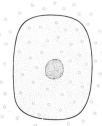

(b) concentrations equal on both sides of the cell membrane

Figure 2 Molecules entering a cell by diffusion

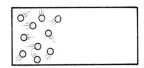

molecules moving about

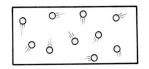

become evenly distributed

Figure 1 Diffusion

33

Rates of diffusion The speed with which a substance diffuses through a cell wall or cell membrane depends on the temperature and the pressure. It also depends on (1) the distance it has to diffuse, (2) its concentration inside and outside the cell and (3) the size of its molecules or ions.

1 Cell membranes are all about the same thickness (about 0.007 μm) but plant cell walls vary in their thickness: the thicker the wall, the slower the diffusion. Some cell walls are also more **permeable** than others are. This means that molecules can pass through them more easily.
2 The bigger the difference between the concentrations of a substance on the two sides of a membrane, the faster it will tend to diffuse across the membrane. The difference is called a **concentration gradient** or **diffusion gradient** (Figure 3). If a substance on one side of a membrane is steadily removed, the diffusion gradient is maintained. When oxygen molecules enter a red cell, for example, they combine with a chemical (haemoglobin) which takes them out of solution. Thus the concentration of free oxygen molecules inside the cell is kept very low, and the diffusion gradient for oxygen is maintained.

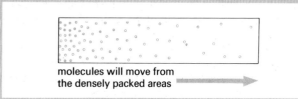

molecules will move from the densely packed areas

Figure 3   Diffusion gradient

3 In general, the larger the molecules or ions, the slower they diffuse. However, many ions and molecules in solution attract water molecules around them (see page 36). This means that they become effectively much bigger. We cannot always predict the rate of diffusion from the particle size alone.

Controlled diffusion For any one substance, the rate of diffusion through a cell membrane depends partly on the concentration gradient. But the rate is often faster or slower than we expect. Water diffuses more slowly and amino acids diffuse more rapidly through a membrane than we might expect. Sometimes this may happen because the ions or molecules can pass through the membrane only by means of special pores. These pores may be few in number, or they may open or close in different conditions.

The movement of other substances may be speeded up by an enzyme working in the cell membrane. So 'simple passive' diffusion, even of water molecules, may not be so simple or so passive after all, where cell membranes are concerned.

Surface area If 100 molecules diffuse through 1 mm² of a membrane in 1 minute, it is reasonable to suppose that an area of 2 mm² will allow twice as many through in the same time. Thus the rate of diffusion into a cell will depend on the cell's surface area. The greater the surface area, the faster is the total diffusion. Cells whose function is rapid absorption – for example, cells in the kidney or the intestine – often have their 'free' surface membrane formed into hundreds of tiny finger-like projections called **microvilli** (Figure 4). These greatly increase the absorbing surface.

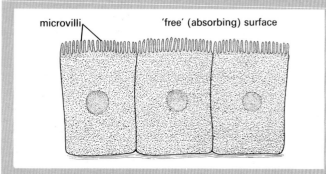

microvilli   'free' (absorbing) surface

Figure 4   Microvilli

The shape of a cell also affects its surface area. For example, the cell in Figure 5 (a) has a greater surface area than that in Figure 5 (b), even though they both have the same volume.

(a)   (b)

Figure 5   Surface area. The cells have the same volume, but (a) has a much greater surface area.

Endo- and exo-cytosis

Some cells can take in (**endocytosis**) or expel (**exocytosis**) solid particles or drops of fluid through the cell membrane. Endocytosis occurs in single-celled 'animals' such as *Amoeba* (page 256) when they feed. It also occurs in certain white blood cells (phagocytes, page 126) when they engulf bacteria. The process is then **phagocytosis**. Exocytosis takes place in the cells of some glands. A secretion, such as a digestive enzyme, forms vacuoles or granules in the cytoplasm. These are expelled through the cell membrane to do their work outside the cell (Figures 6 and 7).

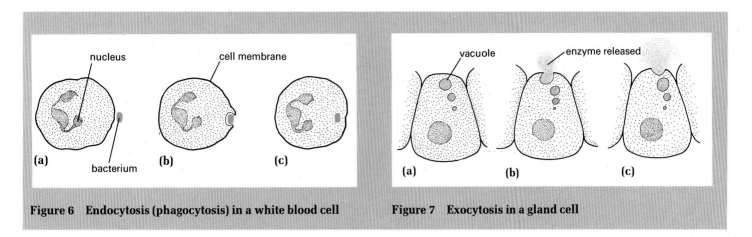

Figure 6   Endocytosis (phagocytosis) in a white blood cell

Figure 7   Exocytosis in a gland cell

Active transport

If a cell could take in substances only by diffusion it would have no control over what went in or out. Anything that was more concentrated outside the cell would diffuse into it, whether it was harmful or not. Food substances and essential salts would diffuse out as soon as their concentration inside rose above that outside the cell. But in fact the cell membrane has a great deal of control over the substances that enter and leave the cell.

Some substances are taken into or expelled from the cell against the concentration gradient. For example, sodium ions may continue to pass out of a cell even though the concentration outside is greater than inside. Biologists do not fully understand how this happens. There may be quite different processes for different substances. But all are generally described as **active transport** (Figure 8).

Anything that interferes with respiration, such as lack of oxygen, prevents active transport taking place. Thus it seems that active transport needs a supply of energy from respiration.

Sometimes active transport seems to be combined with controlled diffusion. For example, sodium ions are thought to get into a cell by diffusion through special pores in the membrane. They leave the cell by a form of active transport. The reversed diffusion gradient for sodium ions created in this way is very important for the conduction of nerve impulses in nerve cells.

QUESTIONS

1 Look at Figure 3 on page 126. If the symbol O_2 represents an oxygen molecule, explain why oxygen is entering the cells drawn on the left but leaving the cells on the right.

2 Look at Figure 10 on page 145. It represents one of the small air pockets (an alveolus) which form the lung.

(a) Suggest a reason why the oxygen and carbon dioxide are diffusing in opposite directions.

(b) What might happen to the rate of diffusion if the blood flow were to speed up?

3 List the ways in which a cell membrane might regulate the flow of substances into the cell.

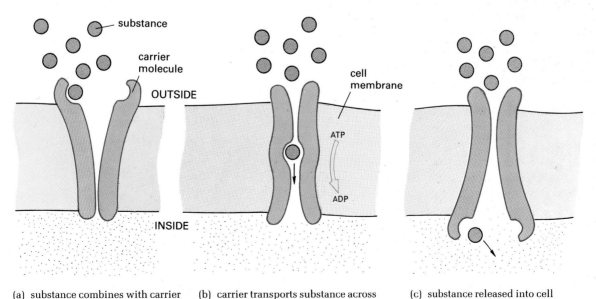

(a) substance combines with carrier molecule

(b) carrier transports substance across membrane using energy from ATP

(c) substance released into cell

Figure 8   Theoretical model to explain active transport

Osmosis

Osmosis is a special kind of diffusion. It is the diffusion of water across a membrane from a dilute solution to a more concentrated solution. The osmosis which biologists usually study is the diffusion of water into or out of cells.

Figure 3 showed that molecules will diffuse from a region where there are a lot of them to a region where they are fewer in number. That is, they will move from a region of highly concentrated molecules to a region of lower concentration.

Pure water has the highest possible concentration of water molecules. It is 100 per cent water molecules, all of them free to move (Figure 10 (a)).

Figure 9 shows a concentrated sugar solution, separated from a dilute solution by a membrane

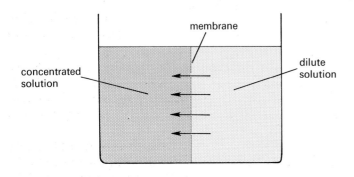

Figure 9   The effect of osmosis

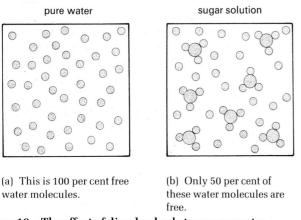

(a) This is 100 per cent free water molecules.

(b) Only 50 per cent of these water molecules are free.

Figure 10   The effect of dissolved substances on water concentration

which allows water molecules to pass through. The dilute solution, in effect, contains more water molecules than the concentrated solution. As a result of this difference in concentration, water molecules will diffuse from the dilute to the concentrated solution.

The level of the concentrated solution will rise. Or, if it is kept in a closed container and its level cannot rise, its pressure will increase.

The membrane separating the two solutions is often called **selectively permeable** or **semi-permeable**. This is because it appears as if water

molecules can pass through it more easily than sugar molecules can.

Osmosis, then, is the passage of water across a selectively permeable membrane from a dilute to a concentrated solution.

This is all you need to know in order to understand the effects of osmosis in living organisms. But a more complete explanation is given below.

Explanation of osmosis When a substance such as sugar dissolves in water, the sugar molecules attract water molecules and combine with them. The sugar molecules are said to be **hydrated**. The water molecules, now combined with sugar molecules, are no longer free to move and so the effective concentration of free water molecules in the solution has been reduced (Figure 10 (b)). The more sugar molecules there are in a solution, the more water molecules will be 'tied up'. In other words, the more concentrated a solution is, the fewer free water molecules it will contain.

Figure 11 represents a dilute sugar solution separated from a concentrated sugar solution by a thin membrane. The membrane stops the solutions from mixing freely. It does, however, let individual water molecules and sugar molecules pass through. There are more free water molecules on the left than on the right. So water molecules pass more rapidly through the membrane from left to right than from right to left.

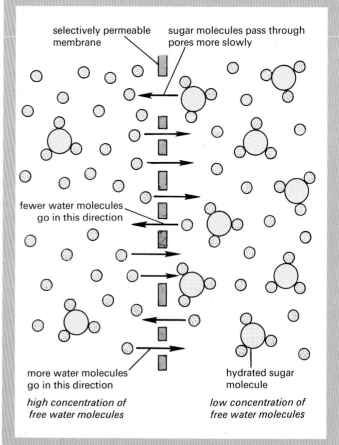

Figure 11   The diffusion theory of osmosis

In a similar way, there are more sugar molecules on the right of the membrane than on the left. So there will be a net movement of sugar molecules from right to left across the membrane. However, the sugar molecules are larger and move more slowly than the water molecules. Thus the most obvious effect is the flow of water molecules from the dilute to the concentrated sugar solution.

A membrane is called selectively permeable if it stops solutions from mixing freely but allows molecules below a certain size to pass through it.

The selectively permeable membrane The non-living membranes used in osmosis experiments are usually thin transparent sheets or tubes made of cellulose acetate. The membranes have tiny pores in them, too small to let liquids flow through freely but large enough to let individual molecules through. Very large molecules such as starch or protein molecules cannot get through the pores, but small molecules, such as those of water, salts or sugars, can do so. Selectively permeable membranes like these can be used for separating large molecules, such as starch, from smaller molecules in solution (see Experiment 3 on page 39).

The pores in the artificial membrane are large enough to allow sugar molecules and water molecules through. So the membrane is not selectively permeable with respect to these two kinds of molecule. Look again at the model shown in Figure 11. Here, as we have seen, water molecules diffuse from the dilute to the concentrated solution faster than sugar molecules diffuse in the opposite direction. This is why the membrane appears to be selectively permeable to water molecules while resisting the passage of sugar molecules.

The cell membrane behaves like a selectively permeable membrane to water and dissolved substances. The selective permeability may depend on pores in the cell membrane. But the processes involved are far more complicated than in an artificial membrane. They depend on the structure of the membrane and on living processes in the cytoplasm (see page 35). The cell membrane contains lipids and proteins. Anything which denatures proteins, such as heat, also destroys the structure and the selectively permeable properties of a cell membrane. If this happens, essential substances can diffuse out of the cell and harmful chemicals can diffuse in, and the cell will die.

Osmotic potential The osmotic potential of a solution is a measure of whether it is likely to lose or gain water molecules from another solution. A dilute solution has a high proportion of free water molecules. We say it has a higher osmotic potential than a concentrated solution, because water will flow from the dilute to the concentrated solution (from a high potential to a low potential). Pure water has the highest possible osmotic potential because water molecules will flow from it to any solution in water, however dilute it may be.

Animal cells

In Figure 12 an animal cell is shown very simply. The coloured circles represent molecules in the cytoplasm. They may be sugar, salt or protein molecules. The grey circles represent water molecules.

The cell is shown surrounded by pure water. Nothing is dissolved in the water; it has 100 per cent concentration of water molecules. So the concentration of free water molecules outside the cell is greater than that inside. Therefore, water will diffuse into the cell by osmosis.

The membrane allows water to go through either way. So in our example, water can move into or out of the cell.

The cell membrane is selectively permeable to most of the substances dissolved in the cytoplasm. So although the concentration of these substances inside may be high, they cannot diffuse freely out of the cell.

The water molecules move into and out of the cell, but because there are more of them on the outside, they will move in faster than they move out. The liquid outside the cell does not have to be 100 per cent pure water. As long as the concentration of water outside is higher than that inside, water will diffuse in by osmosis.

Water entering the cell will make it swell up. Unless the extra water is got rid of in some way the cell will burst. On the other hand, if the cells are surrounded by a solution which is more concentrated than the cytoplasm, water will move out of the cell by osmosis and the cell will shrink. So cells may be damaged if they either take up or lose too much water by osmosis.

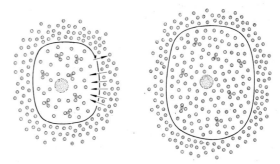

(a) There is a higher concentration of free water molecules outside the cell than inside, so water diffuses into the cell.

(b) The extra water makes the cell swell up. (Of course, molecules are really far too small to be seen at this magnification.)

Figure 12   Osmosis in an animal cell

This is why it is very important that the cells in an animal's body are surrounded by a liquid which has the same concentration as the liquid inside the cells. The outside liquid is called 'tissue fluid' (see page 130). Its concentration depends on the concentration of the blood. In vertebrate animals the blood's concentration is checked by the brain and adjusted by the kidneys, as described on page 153.

Since the blood concentration is kept fairly steady, the concentration of tissue fluid remains more or less constant (see pages 121 and 156). So the cells do not become bloated by taking in too much water, or dehydrated by losing too much.

QUESTIONS

4 A 10 per cent solution of copper sulphate is separated by a 'selectively permeable' membrane from a 5 per cent solution of copper sulphate. Will water diffuse from the 10 per cent to the 5 per cent solution, or from the 5 per cent to the 10 per cent solution?

5 If a fresh beetroot is cut up, the pieces washed in water and then left for an hour in a beaker of water, little or no red pigment escapes from the cells into the water. If the beetroot is boiled first, the pigment does escape into the water. Remembering the properties of a living cell membrane, explain this difference.

6 When doing experiments with animal tissues (for example, the experiment with muscle on page 31) they are usually bathed in Ringer's solution which has a concentration similar to that of blood or tissue fluid. Why do you think this is necessary?

7 Why does a dissolved substance reduce the number of 'free' water molecules in a solution?

PRACTICAL WORK

1 Diffusion of gases

Moisten eight small squares of red litmus paper with water. Push them into a wide glass tube, using a glass rod or piece of wire, so that they are equally spaced out. The squares will stick to the inside of the glass because they are wet.

Close both ends of the tube with corks, one of which contains a pad of cotton wool soaked in ammonia solution (Figure 13). Ammonia is an alkali which turns red litmus blue.

CAUTION Ammonia solution and ammonia vapour can be very harmful to the nose and eyes. The solutions must be made up and dispensed by the teacher.

Result The squares of litmus paper will gradually go blue, starting with the ones nearest the cotton wool containing ammonia.

Interpretation Molecules of ammonia must have passed down the tube to reach the litmus squares. They were not carried by air currents, because the ends of the tube are closed. So the ammonia molecules must have travelled by diffusion.

2 Diffusion in a liquid

Diffusion in a liquid is slow and liable to be affected by convection and other movements in the liquid. In this experiment the water is 'kept still', so to speak, by dissolving gelatin in it.

Half-fill a test-tube with a warm 10 per cent solution of gelatin. In a separate test-tube, colour a little of the liquid gelatin with methylene blue. When the first layer of gelatin has set, pour a little of the blue gelatin to make a thin layer on top of it. Once the blue layer is cold and firm, fill the rest of the test-tube with gelatin solution so that the blue layer is sandwiched between two clear layers (Figure 14). Leave it for a week.

Result After a week, the blue dye will have spread into the clear gelatin above and below the original blue layer.

Interpretation The methylene blue molecules have moved, by diffusion, into the clear gelatin. They have moved equally upwards and downwards, so gravity has not affected them.

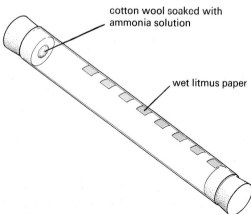

Figure 13 Diffusion of ammonia in air

cotton wool soaked with ammonia solution

wet litmus paper

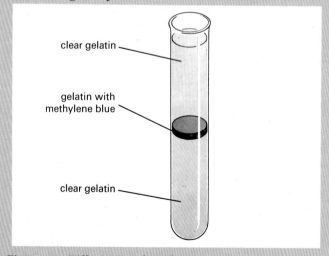

clear gelatin

gelatin with methylene blue

clear gelatin

Figure 14 Diffusion in a liquid

3 Selective permeability (dialysis)

The next two experiments use 'Visking' dialysis tubing. It is made from cellulose and is selectively permeable. It lets water and other small molecules diffuse through freely, but holds back dissolved substances with larger molecules. It is used in kidney machines because it lets the small molecules of harmful waste products out of the blood but retains the blood cells and large protein molecules.

Take a 15 cm length of dialysis tubing which has been soaked in water and tie a knot tightly at one end. Using a dropping pipette, partly fill the tubing with a 1 per cent starch solution. Put the tubing in a test-tube and hold it in place with an elastic band as shown in Figure 15. Rinse the tubing and test-tube under the tap to remove all traces of starch solution from the outside of the dialysis tube.

Fill the test-tube with water and add a few drops of iodine solution to colour the water yellow. Leave for 10–15 minutes.

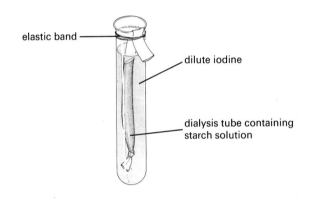

Figure 15   Dialysis

Result   The starch solution inside the dialysis tubing goes blue. The iodine solution outside stays yellow.

Interpretation   A blue colour always appears when starch reacts with iodine. The reaction is used as a test for starch (see page 109). So iodine molecules have moved through the dialysis tubing into the starch. But the starch molecules have not moved out into the iodine solution. This is what we would expect if the dialysis tubing is selectively permeable on the basis of its pore size. Starch molecules are very large (see page 21) and probably cannot get through the pores. Iodine molecules are much smaller and can therefore get through.

4 Osmosis and water flow

Tie a knot in one end of a piece of soaked dialysis tubing and use a dropping pipette to fill it with sugar solution. Then fit it over the end of a length of capillary tubing and hold it in place with an elastic band. Push the capillary tubing into the dialysis tubing until the sugar solution enters the capillary. Now clamp the capillary tubing so that the dialysis tubing is totally immersed in a beaker of water, as shown in Figure 16. Watch the level of liquid in the capillary tubing over the next 10 or 15 minutes.

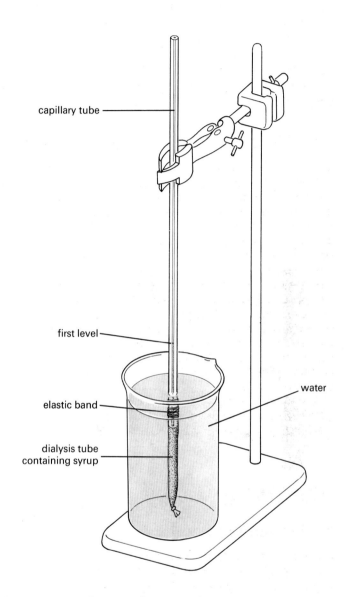

Figure 16   Experiment to show osmosis

Result   The level of liquid in the capillary tube will rise.

Interpretation   Water must be moving into the sugar solution from the beaker. This is what you would expect when a concentrated solution is separated from water by a 'selectively permeable' membrane.

These experiments and eleven others are described in greater detail in *Experimental work in biology* (see page 283).

QUESTIONS

8 In Experiment 1 (Figure 13) it may take 20 minutes for the last piece of litmus paper on the right to go blue. How could you change the design of the experiment in order to reduce this time interval?

9 In Experiment 4 (Figure 16), what do you think would happen (a) if a much stronger sugar solution was placed in the cellulose tube, (b) if the beaker contained a weak sugar solution instead of water, (c) if the sugar solution was in the beaker and the water was in the cellulose tube?

10 An alternative interpretation of the results of Experiment 3 on page 39 might be that the dialysis tubing allowed molecules (of any size) to pass in but not out. Describe an experiment to test this possibility. Say what results you would expect (a) if it were correct, and (b) if it were false.

11 In Experiment 4 on page 39, the column of liquid rising in the capillary tube exerts an ever-increasing pressure on the solution in the dialysis tube. Remembering this, at what stage would you expect the net flow of water from the beaker into the dialysis tubing to cease? (Assume the capillary tube is very long.)

Models

Sometimes scientists explain their theories by making 'models'. In this book we wanted to illustrate the way the cell membrane controls the water concentration in a cell. We used the dialysis tubing in Experiment 3 (page 39) as a model. This model leaves out most of what happens in a cell. It deals only with the selectively permeable membrane and the solution inside it. The model probably helped you to understand what might happen in a cell. But in many ways it is a poor model. For example, if you heated the dialysis tubing to 50 °C the experiment would still work. A cell membrane heated to this temperature would lose its selective properties. The dialysis tubing, therefore, does not model the cell membrane very well.

Some models are mathematical expressions or diagrams that represent the way a hypothesis might work in practice. Computer simulations are also models. Figure 8 on page 35 is a model to explain how the hypothesis of active transport might work. But we do not know for sure that it works like this. The carrier substance (if there is one) might not change its shape in order to push the substance through the membrane. Or more than one carrier substance might take part.

Since we cannot get inside cells to see what is happening, most of the explanations given at this level are in the form of models. The models become more detailed as more information comes to light. But we must not take a model to represent

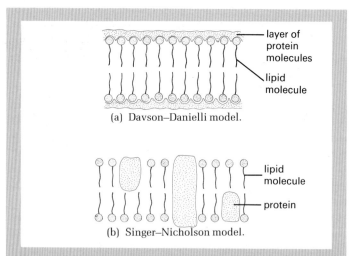

(a) Davson–Danielli model.

(b) Singer–Nicholson model.

Figure 17   Models of the cell membrane's structure

the 'truth'. For example, the most widely accepted model for the structure of the cell membrane has recently changed from Figure 17 (a) to Figure 17 (b). People who thought that Figure 17 (a) *was* the structure of the cell membrane were quite surprised to learn that it was just a model.

In a book of this kind it is rather boring to have to keep reading 'It is thought that . . .', 'There is evidence to show . . .', 'Some biologists believe . . .', and so on. So we have offered many explanations simply as if they were 'the truth'. Try to bear in mind that what we believe at any moment is based on what we actually know at the time.

Some explanations, such as the description of photosynthesis on page 41, have stood the test of time. Although details have been added, the hypothesis has not been seriously questioned. Others, such as the account of active transport on page 35, are quite likely to change greatly in the next few years.

CHECK LIST

- Diffusion is the result of molecules of liquid, gas or dissolved solid moving about.
- The molecules of a substance diffuse from a region where they are very concentrated to a region where they are less concentrated.
- Substances may enter cells by simple diffusion, controlled diffusion, active transport or endocytosis.
- Osmosis is the diffusion of water through a 'selectively permeable' membrane.
- Water diffuses from a dilute solution of salt or sugar to a concentrated solution. This is because the concentrated solution contains fewer free water molecules.
- Cell membranes are selectively permeable. Cytoplasm and cell sap contain many substances in solution.
- Cells take up water from dilute solutions but lose water to concentrated solutions because of osmosis.
- Scientists often explain their theories by using models.

6

Photosynthesis and Nutrition in Plants

Photosynthesis

The process; gaseous exchange.

The Plant's Use of Photosynthetic Products

Building other compounds from sugar.

Sources of Mineral Elements

Especially nitrates, phosphates and potassium.

Practical Work

Hypothesis testing. Experiments to test the need for light, chlorophyll and carbon dioxide, and the production of oxygen.

All living organisms need food. They need it as a source of raw materials from which to build new cells and tissues for growth. They also need food as a source of energy. Food is a kind of 'fuel' which drives essential living processes and brings about chemical changes (see pages 41 and 98). Animals take in food, digest it, and use the digested products to build their tissues or to produce energy. Plants, on the other hand, actually *make* the food they need. Then they use it for energy and growth. Plants make their food by a process called **photosynthesis** (*photos* means 'light'; *synthesis* means 'building-up').

Photosynthesis

Plants build sugars from carbon dioxide in the air, and water from the soil. A sugar molecule contains the elements carbon, hydrogen and oxygen (glucose, for instance, has the formula $C_6H_{12}O_6$). The carbon dioxide molecules, CO_2, provide the carbon and oxygen. The water molecules, H_2O, provide the hydrogen. From these simple compounds, CO_2 and H_2O, the plant can build sugar molecules, $C_6H_{12}O_6$. For this process it needs enzymes, which are present in its cells. It also needs energy, which it gets from sunlight.

The process takes place mainly in the cells of the leaves. It is summarized in Figure 1. Water is absorbed from the soil by the roots. Then it is carried in the water vessels of the veins, up the stem to the leaf. Carbon dioxide is absorbed from the air through the stomata (pores in the leaf). In the leaf cells, the carbon dioxide and water combine to make sugar.

The energy for this reaction comes from sunlight which is absorbed by the green pigment, **chlorophyll**. The chlorophyll is present in the **chloroplasts** of the leaf cells. The reaction takes place inside the chloroplasts.

Chloroplasts (Figure 1 (d)) are small, green structures in the cytoplasm of the leaf cells. Chlorophyll is the substance that gives leaves and stems their green colour. It can absorb energy from light and use it to split water molecules into hydrogen and oxygen. The oxygen escapes from the plant. The hydrogen molecules and the carbon dioxide molecules react to form sugar.

Chlorophyll, therefore, can change light energy into chemical energy.

We can define photosynthesis as **the build-up of sugars from carbon dioxide and water by green plants using energy from sunlight which is absorbed by chlorophyll.** A chemical equation for photosynthesis is

$$6CO_2 + 6H_2O \xrightarrow{\text{light energy}} C_6H_{12}O_6 + 6O_2$$

carbon dioxide   water   glucose   oxygen

But this really represents only the beginning and end of the process. It does not show the many steps in between.

Gaseous exchange in photosynthesis

You can see from the equation that one product of photosynthesis is oxygen. Therefore, in daylight, when photosynthesis is going on, green plants take in carbon dioxide and give out oxygen. In respiration, the opposite happens (page 141). Oxygen is taken in and carbon dioxide is given out. But you must not think that green plants do not respire. The energy they need for all their living processes – apart from photosynthesis – comes from respiration. And this is going on all the time, using up oxygen and producing carbon dioxide.

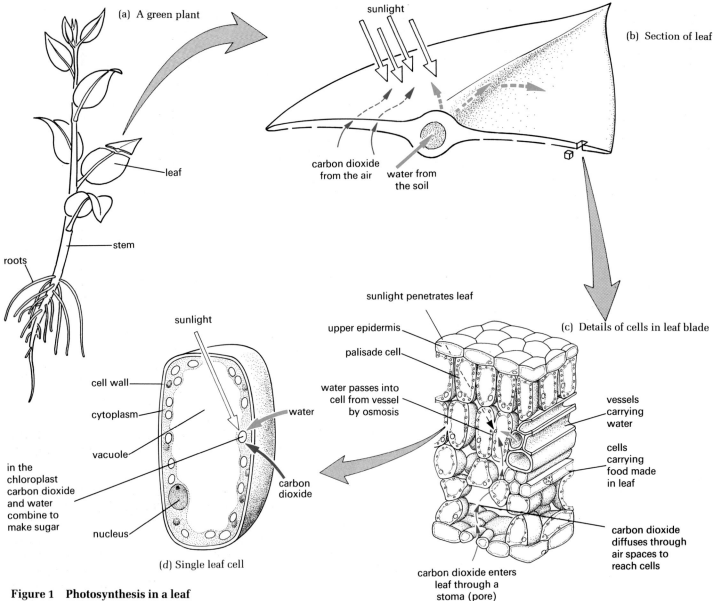

Figure 1   Photosynthesis in a leaf

During the daylight hours, plants are photosynthesizing as well as respiring, so that all the carbon dioxide produced by respiration is used up by photosynthesis. At the same time, all the oxygen needed by respiration is provided by photosynthesis. Only when the plant is photosynthesizing faster than it is respiring will it take in carbon dioxide and give out oxygen (Figure 2).

QUESTIONS

1 What is the essential difference between plants and animals in the way they obtain food?

2 What substances must a plant take in, in order to carry on photosynthesis? Where does it get these substances from?

3 What chemical process provides a plant with energy to carry on all its living activities?

4 Most leaves are thin. Why might this be an advantage? (See page 34.)

5 Measurements on a leaf show that it is giving out carbon dioxide and taking in oxygen. Does this prove that photosynthesis is *not* going on in the leaf? Explain your answer.

6 Using the equation on page 41, say what you would accept as experimental evidence that photosynthesis is taking place in a plant.

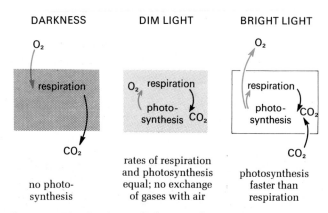

Figure 2   Respiration and photosynthesis

The Plant's Use of Photosynthetic Products

The glucose molecules produced by photosynthesis are quickly built up into starch molecules. These are added to the growing starch granules in the chloroplast. If the glucose concentration was allowed to increase in the cells of the leaf, it could disturb the osmotic balance between the cells (page 37). Starch is a fairly insoluble compound. So it does not alter the osmotic potential of the cell contents.

The starch, however, is steadily broken down to sucrose (page 21). This soluble sugar is transported out of the cell into the food-carrying cells of the leaf veins. These veins distribute the sucrose to all parts of the plant which do not photosynthesize. So the growing buds, the ripening fruits, the roots and the underground storage organs all receive a supply of sucrose.

The cells in these regions use the sucrose in various ways (Figure 3).

Respiration The sugar can be used to provide energy. It is oxidized by respiration (page 28) to carbon dioxide and water. The energy released is used to drive other chemical reactions such as the building up of proteins (this is described below).

Storage Sugar which is not needed for respiration is turned into starch and stored. Some plants store it as starch grains in the cells of their stems or roots. Other plants such as the potato and the parsnip have special storage organs (tubers) for holding the reserves of starch. Others store sugar in their fruits. Grapes, for example, contain a large amount of glucose.

Synthesis of other substances As well as sugars for energy and starch for storage, the plant needs other substances. These include – among many others – cellulose for its cell walls, lipids for its cell membranes, proteins for its cytoplasm and pigments for its flower petals. All these substances are built up (synthesized) from the sugar molecules and other molecules produced in photosynthesis.

By joining hundreds of glucose molecules together, the long-chain molecules of cellulose are built up and added to the cell walls. (Compare this with glycogen build-up, described on page 21.)

Amino acids (see page 19) are made by combining **nitrogen** with sugar molecules or smaller carbohydrate molecules. These amino acids then join together to make the proteins which form the enzymes and the cytoplasm of the cell. The nitrogen for this synthesis comes from **nitrates** (containing the NO_3^- ion) which are absorbed from the soil by the roots.

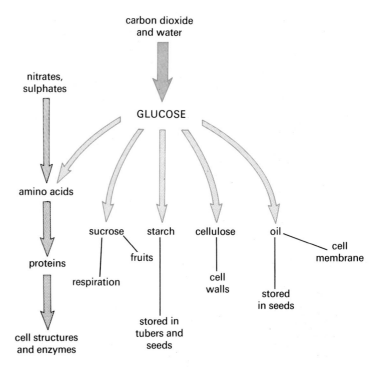

Figure 3   **Green plants can make all the substances they need from carbon dioxide, water and salts**

Proteins also need **sulphur**. This is absorbed from the soil in the form of sulphate ions (SO_4^{2-}).

Phosphorus is needed for the nucleus and for the energy-transfer reactions of ATP (page 29). It is taken up as phosphate ions (PO_4^{3-}).

The chlorophyll molecule needs **magnesium** (Mg). This metallic element is also obtained in salts from the soil. Many other elements are needed in very small quantities for healthy growth. These are often called **trace elements**. Iron, manganese and boron are examples of trace elements.

The metallic and non-metallic elements are all taken up in the form of their ions (page 21).

All of these chemical processes, such as the uptake of salts and the building up of proteins, need energy from respiration to make them happen.

QUESTIONS

7 What substances does a green plant need to take in, to make (a) sugar, (b) proteins? What must be present in the cells to make reactions (a) and (b) work?

8 A molecule of carbon dioxide enters a leaf cell at 4 p.m. and leaves the same cell at 6 p.m. What is likely to have happened to the carbon dioxide molecule during the two hours it was in the leaf cell?

9 If you grow plants in a greenhouse, you can at least partly control their environment. How could you alter external factors so that the plants' photosynthesis can be kept at a maximum?

The Sources of Mineral Elements

The mineral elements needed by plants are absorbed from the soil in the form of salts. For example, a plant might meet its needs for potassium (K) and nitrogen (N) by absorbing the salt **potassium nitrate** (KNO_3). Salts like this come originally from rocks which have been broken down to form the soil. All the time, plants are taking up salts from the soil, and rain is washing salts out of it. The salts are replaced partly from the dead remains of plants and animals. When these organisms die and their bodies decay, the salts they contain are released back into the soil. This process is explained in some detail, for nitrates, on page 57.

In arable farming, the ground is ploughed and whatever is grown is removed. No dead plants are left to decay and replace the mineral salts. The farmer must replace them by spreading animal manure, sewage sludge or artificial fertilizers in measured quantities over the land.

Three common artificial fertilizers are ammonium nitrate, superphosphate and compound NPK.

Ammonium nitrate (NH_4NO_3) The formula shows that ammonium nitrate is a rich source of nitrogen. It contains no other plant nutrients. It is sometimes mixed with calcium carbonate to form a compound fertilizer such as 'Nitrochalk'.

Superphosphates These fertilizers are mixtures of minerals. They all contain calcium and phosphate. Some have sulphate as well.

Compound NPK fertilizer 'N' is the chemical symbol for nitrogen, 'P' for phosphorus and 'K' for potassium. NPK fertilizers are made by mixing ammonium nitrate, ammonium phosphate and potassium chloride. They provide the ions of nitrate, phosphate and potassium. These are the ions most likely to be below the optimum level in farm soil.

PRACTICAL WORK

On page 41 the process of photosynthesis was described as if it were a proven fact. This account has stood the test of time and no one seriously questions it. All the same, photosynthesis is just a well-established hypothesis.

A **hypothesis** tries to explain certain observations (page 32). In this case the hypothesis is that plants make their food by photosynthesis. The equation given below is one way of stating the hypothesis.

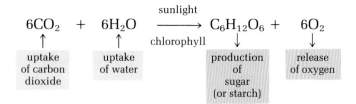

$$6CO_2 \ + \ 6H_2O \ \xrightarrow[\text{chlorophyll}]{\text{sunlight}} \ C_6H_{12}O_6 \ + \ 6O_2$$

uptake of carbon dioxide   uptake of water   production of sugar (or starch)   release of oxygen

This equation shows how the hypothesis might be tested.

A hypothesis can be tested by experiments. The experiments are designed to check certain predictions that can be made from the hypothesis. For example, one prediction is that if photosynthesis is going on in a plant, then the leaves should be producing sugars. In many leaves, as fast as sugar is produced, it is turned into starch. It is easier to test for starch than for sugar. So we use the production of starch in a leaf as evidence that photosynthesis has taken place.

The first three experiments described below are designed to see if the leaf can make starch without sunlight, chlorophyll or carbon dioxide, in turn. If the photosynthesis story is sound, then the lack of any one of these three should stop photosynthesis. Stopping photosynthesis will stop the production of starch. If a leaf without a supply of carbon dioxide can still produce starch, then the hypothesis is no good and must be altered or rejected.

Controls In designing the experiments, it is very important to make sure that only one condition is altered at a time. If, for example, the method of keeping light from a leaf also cuts off its carbon dioxide supply, we cannot decide whether it was the lack of light or lack of carbon dioxide which might stop the production of starch. To make sure that the experimental design has not altered more than one condition, a **control** is set up for each experiment. This is an identical situation, except that the condition missing from the experiment – either light, carbon dioxide or chlorophyll – is present in the control (see also page 25).

Destarching a plant If starch production is your evidence that photosynthesis is taking place, then you must make sure that the leaf does not contain any starch at the beginning of the experiment. You do this by **destarching** the leaves. You cannot remove the starch chemically without damaging the leaves, so a plant is destarched simply by keeping it in darkness.

Potted plants are destarched by leaving them in a dark cupboard for two or three days. In the darkness, any starch in the leaves will be changed to sugar and carried away from the leaves to other parts of the plant. For plants in the open, the experiment is set up on the day before the test. During the night, most of the starch will be removed from the leaves. Better still, wrap the leaves in aluminium foil for two days while they are still on the plant. Then test one of the leaves to see that no starch is present.

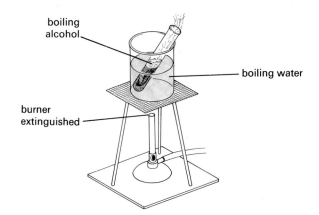

Figure 4   To remove chlorophyll from a leaf

Testing a leaf for starch   Iodine solution (yellow) and starch (white) form a deep blue colour when they mix. The test for starch, therefore, is to add iodine solution to a leaf to see if it goes blue. First however, the leaf has to be treated as follows:

1 Pick the leaf off the plant, and put it in boiling water for half a minute. This kills the cytoplasm and destroys the enzymes in it, so preventing any further chemical changes. It also makes the cell more permeable to iodine solution.
2 Boil the leaf in alcohol (ethanol), using a water bath (Figure 4), until all the chlorophyll is dissolved out. The leaf turns whitish. This makes any colour changes caused by iodine easier to see.
3 Alcohol makes the leaf brittle and hard. Soften it by dipping it once more into the hot water. Then spread it flat on a white surface such as a glazed tile.
4 Put a few drops of iodine solution on the leaf. Any parts that turn blue have starch in them. If no starch is present, the leaf is just stained yellow or brown by the iodine.

1 Is light necessary for photosynthesis?

Cut out a simple shape from a piece of aluminium foil to make a stencil. Attach the stencil to a destarched leaf (Figure 5 (a)). After four to six hours

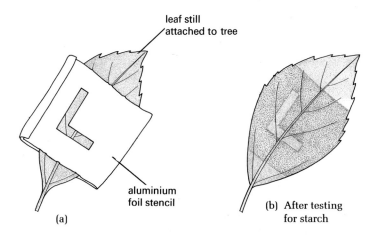

(a)

(b) After testing for starch

Figure 5   To show that light is necessary for photosynthesis

of daylight, remove the leaf from the plant and test it for starch.

Result   Only the parts of the leaf which had received light go blue with iodine.

Interpretation   Starch has not formed in the parts which received no light. So it seems that light is needed for starch formation and thus for photosynthesis.

> You could argue that the aluminium foil had stopped carbon dioxide from entering the leaf. In this case it might have been lack of carbon dioxide rather than absence of light that stopped photosynthesis taking place. You could design a further control, using transparent material instead of aluminium foil for the stencil.

2   Is chlorophyll necessary for photosynthesis?

You cannot remove chlorophyll from a leaf without killing it. So for this experiment you use a **variegated** leaf, which has chlorophyll only in

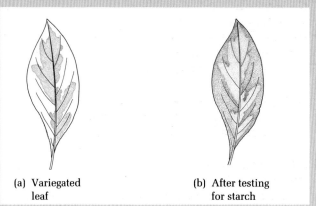

(a) Variegated leaf

(b) After testing for starch

Figure 6   To show that chlorophyll is necessary for photosynthesis

patches. A leaf of this kind is shown in Figure 6 (a). The white part of the leaf is the experiment, because it lacks chlorophyll. The green part with chlorophyll is the control. First, destarch the plant. Then keep it in daylight for a few hours. Remove the leaf from the plant, draw it carefully to show where the chlorophyll is (the green parts), and test it for starch as described above.

Result   Only the parts that were previously green turn blue with iodine. The parts that were white stain brown (Figure 6 (b)).

Interpretation   Starch is present only in the parts which originally contained chlorophyll. So it seems reasonable to suppose that chlorophyll is needed for photosynthesis.

Remember, however, that there are other possible interpretations which this experiment has not ruled out. For example, starch could be made in the green parts and sugar in the white parts. You could test these explanations by further experiments.

3 Is carbon dioxide needed for photosynthesis?

Destarch two potted plants. Put a dish of soda-lime on the soil of one pot. (Soda-lime is a chemical which absorbs carbon dioxide.) This pot is the experiment. Put a dish of sodium hydrogencarbonate solution, which provides carbon dioxide, on the soil of the other. This is the control. Water the pots, and enclose the shoots in polythene bags (Figure 7). Place both plants in the light for several hours. Remove a leaf from each and test it for starch.

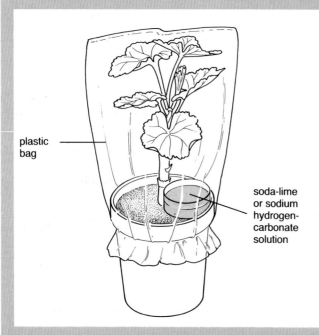

plastic bag

soda-lime or sodium hydrogen-carbonate solution

Figure 7 To show that carbon dioxide is necessary for photosynthesis

Result The leaf which had no carbon dioxide does not turn blue. The one from the polythene bag containing carbon dioxide does turn blue.

Interpretation Starch was made in the leaves which had carbon dioxide, but not in the leaves which had none. This suggests that carbon dioxide must be necessary for photosynthesis. The control shows that keeping a plant in a plastic bag does not prevent photosynthesis.

4 Is oxygen produced during photosynthesis?

Put some Canadian pondweed in a beaker of water. Place a short-stemmed funnel over the weed and put a test-tube filled with water upside down over the funnel stem (Figure 8). The funnel should be raised above the bottom of the beaker to allow the water to

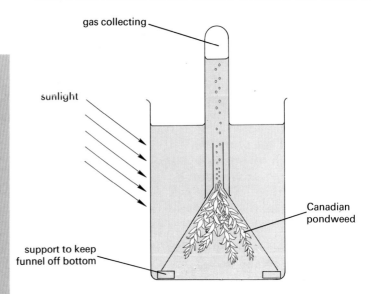

gas collecting

sunlight

Canadian pondweed

support to keep funnel off bottom

Figure 8 To show that oxygen is produced during photosynthesis

circulate. Place the apparatus in sunlight. Bubbles of gas will soon appear from the cut stems and collect in the test-tube.

Set up a control experiment in the same way but put it in a dark cupboard. Little or no gas will collect.

When the plant in the light has produced enough gas, remove the test-tube and hold a glowing splint in it.

Result The glowing splint bursts into flames.

Interpretation The relighting of a glowing splint does not prove that the gas collected in the test-tube is **pure** oxygen. But it does show that it contains extra oxygen. This must have come from the plant. The oxygen is given off only in the light.

Remember that water contains dissolved oxygen, carbon dioxide and nitrogen. These gases may diffuse in or out of the bubbles as they pass through the water and collect in the test-tube. The composition of the gas in the test-tube may not be the same as that in the bubbles leaving the plant.

In this experiment, we usually call the plant in darkness the 'control'. However, to be consistent with the other experiments, we should call the plant with one condition left out the 'experiment', and the plant with all conditions present is the control. But so long as the purpose of the control is clear, the inconsistency does not really matter.

The results of these four experiments support the hypothesis of photosynthesis stated on page 41. Starch formation (our evidence for photosynthesis) does not take place in the absence of light, chlorophyll or carbon dioxide. Oxygen is produced only in the light.

If starch or oxygen had been produced without light, chlorophyll or carbon dioxide, we should have to change our hypothesis about the way plants obtain their food. But although our results support the photosynthesis theory, they do not *prove* it. For example, we now know that many stages in the production of sugar and starch do not need light. These stages are often called the 'dark' reaction.

QUESTIONS

10 Say which of the following are needed for starch production in a leaf: (a) carbon dioxide, (b) oxygen, (c) nitrates, (d) water, (e) chlorophyll, (f) soil, (g) light.
11 What is meant by 'destarching' a leaf? Why do you need to destarch leaves before setting up some of the photosynthesis experiments?
12 Why do you think a pondweed, rather than a land plant, is used for Experiment 4 (concerning production of oxygen)? How might choosing pondweed make the results less useful?

13 In Experiment 2 (concerning the need for chlorophyll), why did you not need to set up a separate control experiment?
14 In Experiment 3 (concerning the need for carbon dioxide), what were the functions of (a) the soda-lime, (b) the sodium hydrogencarbonate, (c) the polythene bag?
15 A green plant makes sugar from carbon dioxide and water. Why do we not try the experiment of keeping a plant without water to see if that stops photosynthesis?
16 Does the method of destarching a plant take for granted the results of Experiment 1? Explain your answer.
17 In Experiment 1, an extra control was suggested to see whether the aluminium foil stencil had stopped carbon dioxide, as well as light, from getting into a leaf. If the stencil was made of clear plastic, should its effect differ from that of the aluminium foil stencil? What result would you expect (a) if the stencil *had* interfered with the supply of carbon dioxide, and (b) if it *had not*?

CHECK LIST

- Photosynthesis is the way plants make their food.
- They combine carbon dioxide and water to make sugar.
- To do this, they need energy from sunlight. The energy is absorbed by chlorophyll.
- Chlorophyll converts light energy to chemical energy.
- The equation to represent photosynthesis is

$$6CO_2 + 6H_2O \xrightarrow[\text{absorbed by chlorophyll}]{\text{energy from sunlight}} C_6H_{12}O_6 + 6O_2$$

- From the sugar made by photosynthesis, a plant can make all the other substances it needs, provided it has a supply of mineral ions like nitrate, phosphate and potassium.

- In daylight, respiration and photosynthesis will be taking place in a leaf. In darkness, only respiration will be taking place.
- In daylight a plant takes in carbon dioxide and gives out oxygen.
- In darkness a plant takes in oxygen and gives out carbon dioxide.
- Experiments to test photosynthesis are designed to keep out light, or carbon dioxide, or chlorophyll, to see if the plant can still produce starch.

Examination Questions

Do not write on this page. Where necessary copy drawings, tables or sentences.

Section 1   Some Principles of Biology

1 Man is classified as a mammal because the body possesses mammary glands and the young develop internally.

(a) Give *two* features which man has in common with all other mammals.

(b) Give *two* features by which man is classified as a primate.

(c) Give *two* ways in which animals differ from plants.   (S1)

2 The diagram below illustrates an experiment to test a leaf disc for starch. Discs were transferred in the directions shown by the arrows.

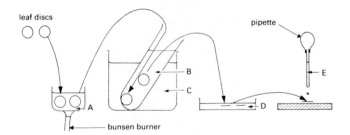

Which of the liquids A to E is

(a) iodine in potassium iodide solution,

(b) ethanol (alcohol),

(c) used to break down the cell walls of the leaf discs,

(d) used to soften the discs,

(e) used to decolorize the dead leaf cells?   (W1A)

3 The table below compares **respiration** and **photosynthesis**. Complete each line of the table by choosing suitable words from those given in brackets. Two lines have been completed for you.   (L1)

4 In an investigation to study the effect of temperature on the activity of a protein-digesting enzyme, six identical sets of apparatus were set up; one set is shown below. Each set was kept at a different temperature. After five minutes the enzyme was added to the egg-white, the tube shaken and returned to the same water bath. At first the solutions were cloudy because of the egg-white protein present. The time taken for the cloudiness to disappear was recorded as shown in the table below.

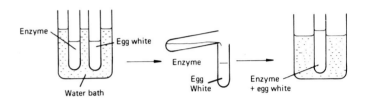

Results

Temperature/°C	5	15	25	40	50	60
Time for cloudiness to disappear/min	16	10	5	1	7	still cloudy

(a) Plot a line graph to show the results.

(b) At what temperature did the enzyme act most rapidly?

(c) Why were the enzyme and egg-white kept separately for five minutes before being mixed?

(d) The mixture at 60 °C remained cloudy. Could it be re-used in a similar experiment? Give a reason for your answer.

(e) Give a reason for the results at 5 °C.   (M3A)

5 (a) Give a word equation for photosynthesis.

(b) Explain why photosynthesis is essential for all life, including human life.

In your account include the terms producer, carnivore, herbivore, food chains to show that you know what they mean.   (W2B)

Process	Respiration	Photosynthesis
occurs in (plants/animals/plants and animals)	plants and animals	plants
occurs during (day/night/day and night)		
carbohydrate (used/produced)	used	produced
oxygen (used/produced)		
carbon dioxide (used/produced)		

48

SECTION 2
Humans in the Environment

7

The Interdependence of Living Organisms

Food Chains and Food Webs
Pyramids of numbers and biomass; dependence on sunlight.

Energy Flow in an Ecosystem

Recycling
Carbon cycle, nitrogen cycle, water cycle.

Agriculture
Principles of agriculture; conserving soil fertility.

'Interdependence' means the way in which living organisms depend on each other in order to remain alive, grow and reproduce. For example, bees depend for their food on pollen and nectar from flowers. Flowers depend on bees for pollination. Bees and flowers are, therefore, interdependent.

Food Chains and Food Webs

One important way in which organisms depend on each other is for their food. Many animals, such as rabbits, feed on plants. Such animals are called **herbivores**. Animals called **carnivores** eat other animals. A **predator** is a carnivore which kills and eats other animals. A fox is a predator which preys on rabbits. **Scavengers** are carnivores which eat the dead remains of animals killed by predators. These are not hard and fast definitions. Predators will sometimes scavenge for their food. Scavengers may now and then kill living animals.

Humans are **omnivores**. That means that they eat both animals and plants, and their products.

Food chains

In the long run, all animals depend on plants for their food. Foxes eat rabbits, but rabbits feed on grass. A hawk eats a lizard, the lizard has just eaten a grasshopper but the grasshopper was feeding on a grass blade. This relationship is called a **food chain** (Figure 1).

The organisms at the beginning of a food chain are usually present in large numbers. The animals at the end of the chain are often large, and only a few may be present. The **food pyramids** in Figure 2 show this

relationship. A pond will hold millions of tiny, single-celled green plants (Figure 3 (a)). It will also hold fewer, but larger, water-fleas and other crustacea. These will eat the tiny plants. In turn they will become the food of small fish, like minnow and stickleback. The hundreds of small fish may be able to provide enough food for only four or five large carnivores, like pike or perch.

The organisms at the base of the food pyramids in Figure 2 are plants. Plants produce food from carbon

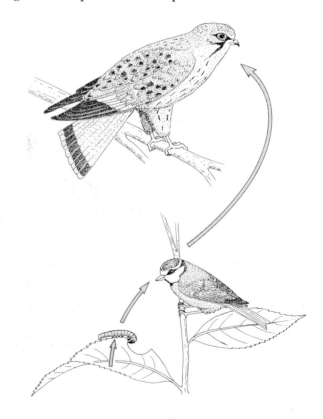

Figure 1   A food chain. The caterpillar eats the leaf. The blue tit eats the caterpillar but may itself be eaten by the kestrel.

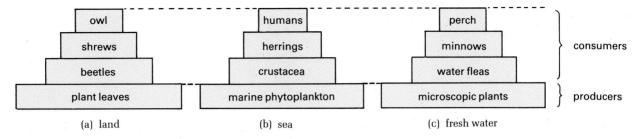

Figure 2 Examples of food pyramids

dioxide, water and salts (see 'Photosynthesis', page 41), and are therefore called **producers**. Animals such as grasshoppers that eat the plants are called **primary consumers**. Animals like shrews that prey on the plant-eaters are called **secondary consumers**. These may be eaten by **tertiary consumers** like weasels or kestrels.

The position of an organism in a food pyramid is sometimes called its **trophic level**.

Humans are primary consumers when they eat fruit, vegetables or cereals. They are secondary consumers when they eat meat or animal products such as eggs, milk or cheese. Since humans are not normally eaten by other animals, they are usually at the top of a food chain.

Food chains ending in humans are usually artificial. We grow the plants and rear the animals which we want to eat. For example:

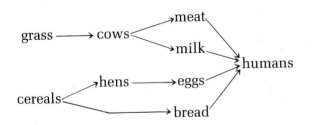

Pyramids of numbers and biomass

The widths of the bands in Figure 2 are related to the numbers of organisms at each trophic level. So the diagrams are sometimes called **pyramids of numbers**.

However, all pyramids of numbers are not the same shape. For example, a single sycamore tree may provide food for thousands of greenfly. One oak tree may feed hundreds of caterpillars. These pyramids of numbers are upside down.

The way round this is to forget the single tree. Think instead of the mass of the leaves that it produces in the growing season, and the mass of the insects which can live on them. We call the mass of living organisms **biomass**. We can draw pyramids of biomass, as in Figure 8 on page 54.

Or we can work out the energy available in a year's supply of leaves and compare this with the energy needed by all the insects feeding on the leaves. This would give us a **pyramid of energy**, with the producers at the bottom having the most energy. Each trophic level would show a smaller amount of energy than the one before it.

The chemical elements that make up living organisms are used over and over again. Energy is different. It always flows from producers to consumers. In the end it is lost to the atmosphere as heat.

(a) **Phytoplankton** (×100). These microscopic plants form the basis of a food pyramid in the water.

(b) **Zooplankton** (×30). These crustacea will eat microscopic plants.

Figure 3 Plankton. The microscopic organisms which live in the surface waters of the sea or fresh water are called, collectively, plankton. The single-celled plants are the phytoplankton. They are surrounded by water, salts and dissolved carbon dioxide. Their chloroplasts absorb sunlight and use its energy for making food by photosynthesis. The plankton is eaten by small animals in the zooplankton, mainly crustacea. Small fish will eat the crustacea.

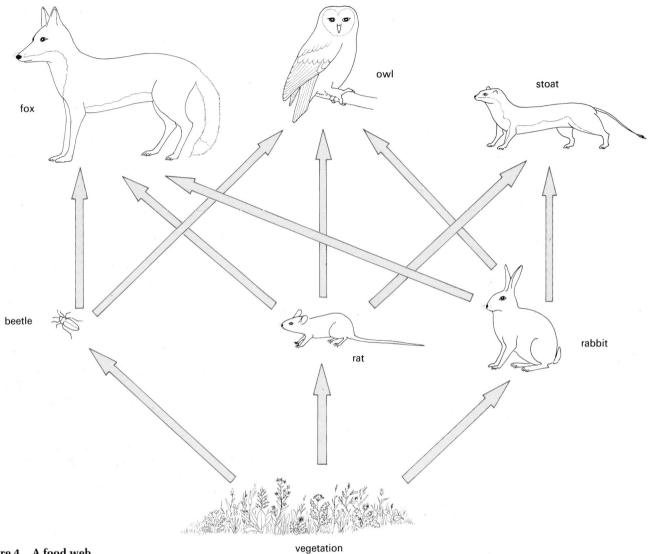

Figure 4   A food web

(a) Sheep have eaten any seedlings that grew under the trees.

(b) Ten years later, the fence has kept the sheep off and the tree seedlings have grown.

Figure 5   Effect of grazing

Food webs

Food chains are not really as simple as they sound. This is because most animals eat more than one type of food. A fox, for example, does not feed only on rabbits. It eats beetles, rats and voles too. A **food web** shows this more clearly than a food chain can (Figure 4).

The food webs for land, sea and fresh water, or for ponds, rivers and streams will all be different. Food webs also change with the seasons when the food supply changes.

If something alters a food web, all the organisms in it are affected. For example, if the rabbits in Figure 4 were to die out, the foxes, owls and stoats would eat more beetles and rats.

In 1954 a disease called myxomatosis wiped out nearly all the rabbits in England. Foxes ate more voles, beetles and even blackberries. They attacked more lambs and chickens. Even the vegetation changed, because the tree seedlings which the rabbits used to nibble off were able to grow. As a result, grassy downland began to change into woody scrub. Something like this has happened in Figure 5.

Some human communities do not practise agriculture. The Kalahari bushmen are an example. They live by catching wild animals and collecting plants and fruits. These humans fit into natural food webs.

Agricultural communities usually upset natural food webs. They may change the environment, perhaps by cutting down trees to make room for crops. Or they may use too much of one component of a food web – for example, by over-fishing.

Dependence on sunlight

Let us take the idea of food chains one step further. They show us that all living organisms depend on sunlight and photosynthesis (page 41). Green plants make their food by photosynthesis. Photosynthesis needs sunlight. All animals depend, in the end, on plants for their food. So all animals, including humans, depend indirectly on sunlight. Here are some examples.

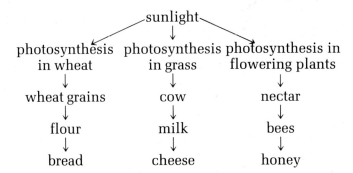

Nearly all the energy released on the Earth can be traced back to sunlight. Coal comes from tree-like plants, buried millions of years ago. These plants absorbed sunlight for their photosynthesis when they were alive. Petroleum (oil) was formed, also millions of years ago, probably from the partly decayed bodies of plants that lived in the sea. These too had absorbed sunlight for photosynthesis.

Today, mirrors and solar panels are used to collect energy from the Sun directly. But the best way, so far, to trap and store energy from sunlight is to grow plants and use their products. Starch, sugar, oil, alcohol and wood are all used, either for food or as energy sources for other purposes. For example, sugar from sugar cane can be fermented (page 29) to alcohol. Then the alcohol can be used as motor fuel instead of petrol.

QUESTIONS

1 Try to draw up a simple food web using the following: sparrow, fox, wheat seeds, cat, kestrel, mouse.
2 Write down all the possible ways in which the following might depend on each other: grass, earthworm, blackbird, oak tree, soil.
3 Explain how the following foodstuffs are produced as a result of photosynthesis: wine, butter, eggs, beans.
4 An electric motor, a car engine and a racehorse can all produce energy. Show how this energy could come, in the first place, from sunlight. What forms of energy on the Earth are *not* derived from sunlight?

5 How might you find evidence to help you to place animals such as a fox and a pigeon in a food web?

Energy Flow in an Ecosystem

An **ecosystem** is a community of living organisms and the habitat in which they live. A pond is an ecosystem consisting of plants, animals, water, dissolved air, minerals and mud. Energy from the Sun and a supply of water from rain is all that the pond community needs to keep going. A forest is an ecosystem. So is an ocean. You can think of the whole of the Earth's surface as one huge ecosystem.

Except for atomic energy and tidal power, all the energy released on Earth comes from sunlight (see above). If we want to work out just how much life the Earth can support, we must look at how efficiently the Sun's energy is used.

Use of sunlight

When the Sun's energy falls on to grassland, about 20 per cent is reflected by the plants, 39 per cent is used in evaporating water from the leaves (transpiration) and 40 per cent warms up the plants. This

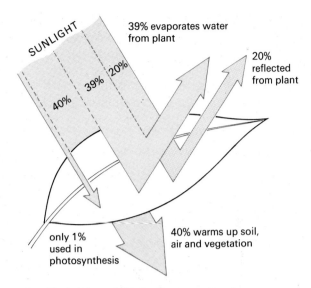

Figure 6 Absorption of the Sun's energy by plants

leaves only about 1 per cent to be used in photosynthesis for making new substances in the leaves of the plants (Figure 6).

This figure of 1 per cent depends on the type of plants on the land. It also depends on how much water is available and on the soil temperature. Sugar cane can convert up to 3 per cent of the Sun's energy into photosynthetic products. For sugar beet the figure is nearly 9 per cent. Tropical forests and swamps produce far more than grassland. But it is difficult to harvest and use their products. It may also harm the environment (page 66).

If crop plants are to use sunlight efficiently, they must have enough water and mineral salts. Farmers may need to irrigate the land and to put on artificial fertilizers (page 44).

Energy transfer between organisms

Producers to primary consumers We have looked at energy conversion from sunlight to plant products. The next step is to study energy transfer from plant products to primary consumers.

On land, primary consumers eat only a small part of the available plant material. In a deciduous forest as little as about 2 per cent is eaten. In grazing land, 40 per cent of the grass may be eaten by cows. In open water the producers are microscopic plants. They are swallowed whole by the primary consumers in the zooplankton, and 90 per cent or more may be eaten. In the land communities the parts of the plants not eaten by the primary consumers will die in time. The decomposers will then use them as a source of energy (page 55).

A cow is a primary consumer. Over 60 per cent of the grass it eats passes through its body without being digested. The cow uses another 30 per cent in its respiration to provide energy for its movement and other life processes. It uses less than 10 per cent of the plant material for growth (Figure 7). This figure depends on the diet and on the animal's age. In a fully grown animal all the digested food is used for energy and replacement and none is used for growth. This is why beef cattle and other primary consumers are usually killed before their rate of growth starts to fall off.

Primary to secondary consumers Energy transfer from primary to secondary consumers is usually more efficient. This is because, compared with plant material, a lower percentage of animal food passes undigested through the consumer's body.

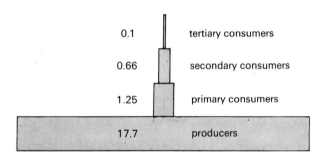

Figure 8 Biomass (dry weight) of living organisms in a shallow pond (in grams per square metre).
(After R.H. Whittaker, *Communities and ecosystems*, Macmillan, NY © 1975)

We can compare energy transfers at the different stages of a food chain by comparing the biomasses (page 51) of the producers and of the primary, secondary and tertiary consumers. We can do this by drawing a pyramid like the one in Figure 2, but using a more accurate scale. In Figure 8 the widths of the bands are proportional to the masses (dry weight) of the organisms in a shallow pond.

Energy transfer in agriculture

Human communities use plant products to feed animals which provide meat, eggs and dairy products. But this is wasteful. Only 10 per cent of the plant material is converted to animal products. It is more economical to eat bread made from wheat than to feed the wheat to hens and then eat the eggs and chicken meat. This is because eating the wheat as bread avoids using any part of its energy to keep the

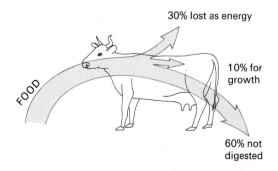

Figure 7 Energy transfer from plants to animals

chickens alive and active.

Less energy is lost if the hens are kept indoors in small cages. They then lose little heat to the atmosphere and cannot use much energy in movement. The same ideas are used in 'intensive' methods of rearing calves. However, many people feel that these methods are cruel. And the saving of energy is far less than if the humans ate the plant products themselves.

Energy flow in modern farming is inefficient in other ways. You would have to burn 5 tonnes of coal to get enough energy to make 1 tonne of nitrogen-containing fertilizer. More energy is needed to make fertilizer and to make a tractor and its fuel than we can get from the food these can produce.

QUESTIONS

6 'The Sun's energy is used indirectly to produce a muscle contraction in your arm.' Trace the steps in the transfer of energy which would justify this claim.

7 A group of explorers is wrecked on an island where there is no soil and no plants. From their stores they have saved some living hens and some wheat. To make these last as long as possible should they

(a) eat the wheat and, when it is finished, kill and eat the hens, or

(b) feed the wheat to the hens, collect and eat the eggs laid, and, when the wheat is gone, kill and eat the hens, or

(c) kill and eat the hens first and when they are finished, eat the wheat? Justify your answer.

8 What would be gained if humans tried to exploit a food chain nearer to its source, such as the plankton in Figure 3? What might be the drawbacks?

Recycling

Some organisms do not fit into the food webs or food chains described so far. Among these are the **saprophytes**. Saprophytes do not get their food by photosynthesis. Nor do they kill and eat living animals or plants. Instead they feed on dead and decaying matter such as dead leaves in the soil or rotting tree-trunks (see Figure 9). They include the fungi, such as mushrooms, toadstools or moulds, and the bacteria, especially those that live in the soil.

Saprophytes produce extra-cellular enzymes (page 23) which digest the decaying matter. Then they absorb the soluble products back into their cells. In so doing, they remove the dead remains of plants and animals which would otherwise collect on the Earth's surface. They also break these remains down into substances which other organisms can use. Some bacteria, for example, break down the protein of dead plants and animals and release nitrates. The nitrates are taken up by plant roots and there built into new amino acids and proteins (page 19). This use and re-use of materials in the living world is called **recycling**.

Figure 9 Saprophytes. These toadstools are getting their food from the rotting log.

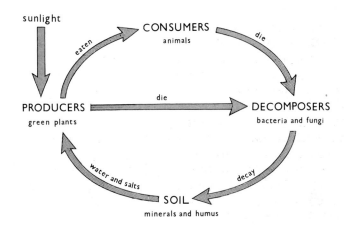

Figure 10   Recycling in an ecosystem

Figure 10 shows the general idea of recycling. The green plants are the producers. The animals which eat the plants and each other are the consumers. The bacteria and fungi, especially those in the soil, are called the **decomposers** because they break down the dead remains and release the chemicals for the plants to use again. Carbon recycling and nitrogen recycling are described below.

The same kind of cycling applies to nearly all the elements of the Earth. No new matter is created, but matter is rearranged over and over again. Many of the atoms of your body have, at one time, been part of other organisms.

THE CARBON CYCLE

All living organisms use the element carbon. Plants get their carbon from carbon dioxide in the air. Animals get their carbon from plants. The carbon cycle, therefore, is mainly to do with carbon dioxide and what happens to it (Figure 11).

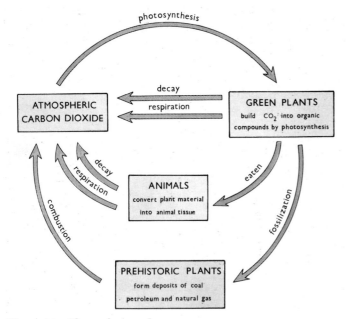

Figure 11   The carbon cycle

Removing carbon dioxide from the air

Photosynthesis   Green plants remove carbon dioxide from the air by their photosynthesis (page 41). The carbon of the carbon dioxide is built first into a sugar. Some of this is changed into starch or cellulose and the proteins, pigments and other compounds of a plant. When animals eat plants they digest and absorb the plant material and build it into the compounds making up their tissues. Thus carbon atoms from the plant become part of the animal.

The oceans   Carbon dioxide is absorbed by the sea. Some of it is used by the phytoplankton for photosynthesis and some of it reacts with the sea water itself. Sea water may absorb up to half of all the carbon dioxide that comes from burning fossil fuels, though we do not know exactly how this happens.

Adding carbon dioxide to the air

Respiration   Plants and animals obtain energy by oxidizing carbohydrates in their cells to carbon dioxide and water (page 28). The carbon dioxide and water are excreted. So the carbon dioxide returns to the air.

Decay   The organic matter of dead animals and plants is used by saprophytes, especially bacteria and fungi, as a source of energy. These decompose the plant and animal remains and turn the carbon compounds into carbon dioxide.

Combustion (burning)   When carbon-containing fuels such as wood, coal, oil and natural gas burn, the carbon is oxidized to carbon dioxide ($C + O_2 \rightarrow CO_2$). Fuels such as coal and oil come from ancient plants which have only partly decomposed over the

millions of years since they were buried. This is why we call them 'fossil fuels'.

So a carbon atom which today is in a molecule of carbon dioxide in the air may tomorrow be in a molecule of cellulose in a cell wall in a blade of grass. When the grass is eaten by a cow, the carbon atom may become part of a glucose molecule in the cow's bloodstream. If the cow uses glucose for respiration, it will breathe out the carbon atom into the air once again as carbon dioxide.

The balance of atmospheric carbon dioxide

Generally, carbon dioxide is removed from the air at much the same rate at which it is added. So the percentage of carbon dioxide in the air stays more or less constant. However, in the last hundred years or so, humans have burnt huge amounts of fossil fuels. At the same time, vast areas of tropical forests (which remove carbon dioxide by photosynthesis) have been cut down. As a result, the percentage of carbon dioxide in the air is now slowly rising. This may have long-term harmful effects on our climate and agriculture (see page 66).

QUESTIONS

9 (a) Why do living organisms need a supply of carbon?
   (b) Give three examples of carbon-containing compounds which occur in living organisms (see pages 19–21).
   (c) Where do (i) animals, (ii) plants get their carbon from?

10 Figure 12 is a graph showing the average daily change in the carbon dioxide concentration, 1 metre above an agricultural crop in July. From what you have learned about photosynthesis and respiration, try to explain the changes in the carbon dioxide concentration.

11 Construct a diagram, on the lines of the carbon cycle (Figure 11), to show the cycling process for hydrogen. (Start from the water used in photosynthesis.)

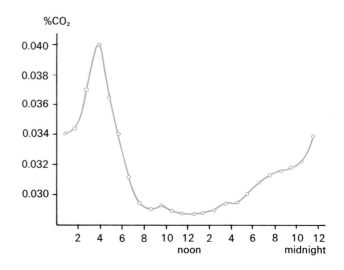

Figure 12   Daily changes in concentration of carbon dioxide one metre above a plant crop (Verma and Rosenberg, *Span*, 1979)

THE NITROGEN CYCLE

When a plant or animal dies, its tissues decompose. An important product of this decay is **ammonia** (NH_3, a compound of nitrogen), which is washed into the soil.

Animals excrete nitrogen-containing waste products such as ammonia, urea and uric acid (page 152). The organic matter in their droppings is also decomposed by soil bacteria.

Adding nitrates to the soil

Nitrifying bacteria   These are bacteria living in the soil. They use the ammonia from excretory products and decaying organisms as a source of energy (as we use glucose in respiration). In the process, the bacteria produce **nitrates**.

Although plant roots can take up compounds of ammonia, they take up nitrates more readily. So the nitrifying bacteria increase the fertility of the soil by making nitrates available to the plants.

Nitrogen-fixing bacteria   This is a special group of nitrifying bacteria. They can absorb nitrogen as a gas from the air spaces in the soil and build it into compounds of ammonia. Nitrogen gas cannot itself be used by plants. When it has been made into a compound of ammonia, however, it can easily be changed to nitrates by other nitrifying bacteria. The process of building nitrogen gas into compounds of ammonia is called **nitrogen fixation**.

Some nitrogen-fixing bacteria live freely in the soil. Others live in the roots of **leguminous plants** (peas, beans, clover), where they cause swellings called **root nodules** (Figure 13). These leguminous plants can thrive in soils where nitrates are scarce, because the nitrogen-fixing bacteria in their nodules make compounds of nitrogen available for them.

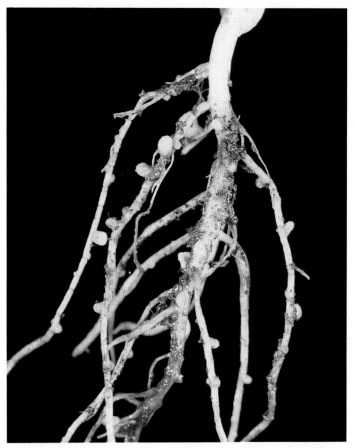

Figure 13   Root nodules on a pea plant. The nodules contain bacteria that can fix nitrogen.

Lightning   In the high temperature of lightning discharge, some of the nitrogen and oxygen in the air combine to form oxides of nitrogen. These dissolve in the rain and are washed into the soil as weak acids. Here they form nitrates. Although several million tonnes of nitrate may reach the Earth's surface in this way each year, this forms only a small part of the total nitrogen being recycled.

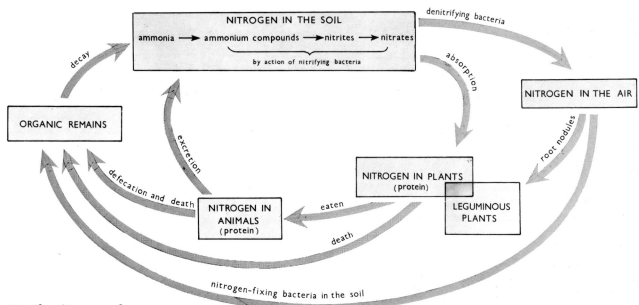

Figure 14   The nitrogen cycle

Removing nitrates from the soil

Uptake by plants   Plant roots absorb nitrates from the soil and combine them with carbohydrates to make proteins (page 43).

Leaching   Nitrates dissolve easily in water. As rain water passes through the soil it dissolves the nitrates and carries them away in the run-off or to deeper layers of the soil. This is called **leaching**.

Denitrifying bacteria   These are bacteria which obtain their energy by breaking down nitrates to nitrogen gas which then escapes from the soil into the atmosphere.

These processes are summed up in Figure 14.

THE WATER CYCLE

All the elements which make up living organisms are recycled, not just carbon and nitrogen. We could trace out cycles for hydrogen, oxygen, phosphorus, sulphur, iron and so on. The 'water cycle' is somewhat different, however. This is because only a tiny proportion of the water which is recycled passes through living organisms.

Animals lose water by evaporation, in faeces and urine, and when they breathe out. They gain water from their food and drink. Plants take up water from the soil and lose it by transpiration. Millions of tonnes of water are transpired. But only a tiny part of this has taken part in respiration or photosynthesis.

Most of the water is recycled without passing through animals or plants. The Sun shining on the oceans and the wind blowing over them evaporate water from their vast, exposed surfaces. The water vapour produced in this way enters the atmosphere. In time it forms clouds. The clouds release their water in the form of rain or snow. The rain collects in streams, rivers and lakes. In the end it finds its way back to the oceans. Humans take some of this water for drinking, washing, cooking, irrigation, hydro-electric schemes and other industrial purposes, before allowing it to return to the sea (Figure 15).

QUESTIONS

12 On a lawn growing on soil that is low in nitrogen, patches of clover often stand out as dark green and healthy against a background of pale green grass. Suggest a reason for this contrast. (See also page 43.)

13 Explain the difference between nitrifying, nitrogen-fixing and denitrifying bacteria.

Agriculture

For the greater part of the million or more years since humans evolved, they have fitted into the eco-systems where they chose to live. They got their food by collecting plants or their products and by catching animals. Thus, their effect on a balanced eco-system was much the same as that of any other omnivore.

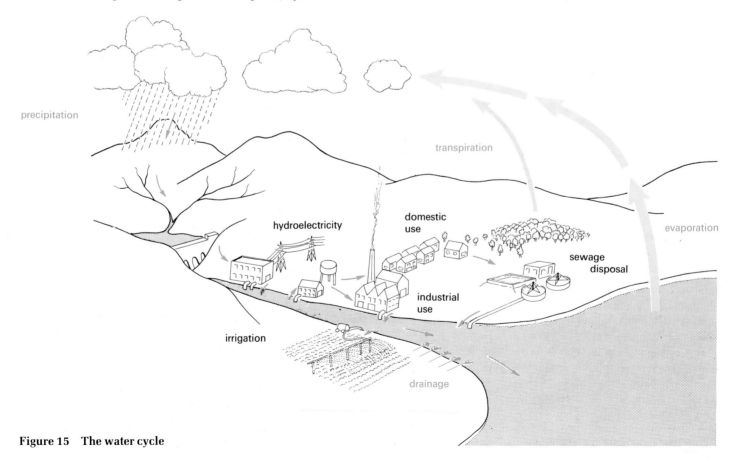

Figure 15   The water cycle

Probably 100 km² territory would support only three or four people who lived by hunting and gathering food. This may have been important in limiting the growth of the human population.

As agriculture developed, the population grew rapidly. In the last two or three hundred years the numbers of humans have become so large that their activities threaten to destroy the ecological balance.

This section looks at the principles of agricultural practice. The damaging effects of agriculture on the environment are discussed on pages 62-5.

Principles of agriculture

Arable farming In arable (crop) farming, the natural vegetation is first removed from the soil. Then (a) seeds of a single plant species are planted, (b) their growth is encouraged by improving the soil fertility and (c) plant competitors and (d) pests are controlled.

In this way, a field can produce far more edible plant material than if it were left to develop its natural vegetation, such as grass or trees.

(a) Improved crop plants
The plant species cultivated today must have had their origins in wild plants. Careful selection and cross-breeding over many hundreds of years have produced plants with large seeds (such as maize), edible fruits (tomato) or large root or stem tubers (carrot and potato).

Breeding and selection goes on even more intensively today. Now it is on a scientific basis. The breeders try to find plants that yield more food, or resist disease or drought.

Growing large numbers of a single species of plant on the same land year after year is called **monoculture**.

(b) Soil improvement
The soil used for agriculture is 'improved' by ploughing. This loosens the soil, lets in air, helps water to drain and makes penetration by plant roots easier. Minerals are added to the soil by adding natural fertilizers such as manure, or artificial fertilizers such as ammonium nitrate.

If water is in short supply, it can be added to the soil by irrigation. If the soil holds too much water, it can be drained by digging ditches or by placing pipes below the surface.

(c) Control of competitors
In the improved soil, plants other than crop plants will grow and compete with the crops for water, root space, minerals and light. We call such plants 'weeds'. The weeds are kept in check by ploughing the soil and then spraying chemicals, called **selective herbicides**, on the crops. These kill the weeds but do not harm the crop plants.

(d) Control of pests
Fungus diseases of the crop plants can partly be prevented by selecting resistant strains of plant.

Spraying crops with chemical **fungicides** kills the fungi. Spraying them with **insecticides** kills insect pests that eat or damage crop plants or their products.

Animal husbandry Animal protein contains more essential amino acids (page 99) than does plant protein. And humans particularly enjoy eating animal products. This is why humans use some of their crops to feed animals and then eat the animals or their produce, such as milk and eggs.

The principles of animal husbandry are much the same as those of growing crops. A small number of species is used and these have been bred and selected over many years so that they yield more food. Cows are bred to increase their milk yield. Sheep and pigs are bred to improve their lean/fat ratio. The animals are fed and kept in conditions in which they grow and make food products as fast as possible. Parasites and diseases are controlled. Even so, only about 10 per cent of the food given to animals appears as flesh or eggs or milk. The rest is used for energy to keep the animals alive, for movement, and for keeping their temperature steady.

Methods of conserving soil fertility

In natural conditions, soil fertility is maintained by the activity of the organisms living on it or in it. For example, the plant roots maintain the soil's structure and the burrows of earthworms improve its drainage. Although plants remove mineral salts, these are replaced by recycling of the dead and decaying plant and animal materials.

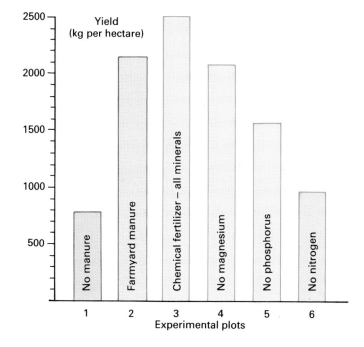

Figure 16   Average yearly wheat yields from 1852 to 1925. Broadbalk field, Rothamsted Experimental Station.
Plot 1 received no manure or chemical fertilizer for 73 years.
Plot 2 received an annual application of farmyard manure.
Plot 3 received chemical fertilizer with all necessary minerals.
Plots 4 to 6 received chemical fertilizer lacking one element.

Agriculture interrupts the natural cycles. Crops and animals are removed, and their remains and wastes are not returned to the soil. This practice, and the constant loss of soluble salts washed out of the soil by rain, greatly reduces the yield from crops.

Wheat has been grown and harvested on an experimental strip at Rothamsted Experimental Station for over 100 years without anything being added to the soil. In this time, the yield has dropped from 14.7 to 6.9 kg per 100 m^2. The soil nitrogen concentration, however, has remained steady for the last 80 years. This probably results from the activities of nitrogen-fixing bacteria and other soil micro-organisms (Figure 16).

To make good the losses from the soil, the farmer adds either manure or artificial fertilizers.

Manure   The straw bedding used for cattle and chickens collects their faeces and urine. When ploughed into the soil, it provides organic matter which (a) decays to give the salts needed by plants and (b) improves the soil structure by adding humus.

In 'factory farms', the manure often consists of a liquid 'slurry' which is washed out of the animal houses and milking parlours. This slurry is sprayed on the fields.

Untreated human sewage would help complete the nitrogen cycle. But it is not used on crops because of the dangers of spreading intestinal diseases. Treated sewage can be a safe and useful fertilizer for the soil, however. So can sewage sludge which has been fermented at a high temperature.

Artificial fertilizers   Small, mixed farms may produce enough manure to maintain soil fertility. Large-scale arable farms do not, and on their land the minerals must be replaced. The artificial fertilizers

Figure 17   Experimental plots of wheat. The rectangular plots have been treated with different fertilizers.

used are made in factories from sulphuric acid, ammonia, lime, slag from steel processing and other industrial waste.

Some examples of artificial fertilizers are given on page 44. Figure 17 shows some field trials of fertilizers.

QUESTIONS

14 To judge from Figure 16, which mineral element seems to have the most pronounced effect on the yield of wheat?
15 Draw up two columns headed 'Add' and 'Remove'. In the 'Add' column, list all the processes which add nitrates to the soil. In the 'Remove' column, list those which remove nitrates from the soil. How might human activities alter the normal balance of these processes?
16 List the ways in which a farmer might increase the yield of crops from the land.

CHECK LIST

- All animals depend, in the end, on plants for their source of food.
- Since plants need sunlight to make their food, all organisms depend, in the end, on sunlight for their energy.
- An ecosystem is a self-contained community of organisms.
- Only about 1 per cent of the Sun's energy which reaches the Earth is trapped by plants during photosynthesis.
- At each step in a food chain, only a small proportion of the food is used for growth. The rest is used for energy to keep the organism alive.
- Plants are the producers in a food web. Animals may be primary, secondary or tertiary consumers.
- The materials which make up living organisms are constantly recycled.

- Plants take up carbon dioxide during photosynthesis. All living organisms give out carbon dioxide during respiration. The burning of carbon-containing fuels produces carbon dioxide.
- Carbon dioxide uptake by plants and by the oceans balances carbon dioxide production from respiration and combustion.
- Soil nitrates are derived naturally from the excretory products of animals and the dead remains of living organisms.
- Nitrifying bacteria turn these products into nitrates which are taken up by plants.
- Nitrogen-fixing bacteria can make nitrogenous compounds from gaseous nitrogen.
- Agriculture aims to grow single, high-yielding species, eliminate competitors and pests and improve soil fertility.

8

The Human Impact on the Environment

Food Webs
Endangered species, agriculture, pesticides, eutrophication.

Forests
Erosion, flooding, greenhouse effect.

Soil
Erosion.

Water
Sewage, pollution, radioactive waste.

Air
Sulphur dioxide, oxides of nitrogen, lead, smog, carbon monoxide, chlorofluorocarbons.

Radiation

A few thousand years ago, most humans probably obtained their food by gathering leaves, fruits and roots and by hunting animals. The population was probably limited by the amount of food that could be collected in this way.

Human faeces, urine and dead bodies were left on or in the soil. They thus played a part in the nitrogen cycle (page 57). Life may have been short, and many babies may have died from starvation or illness. But humans fitted into the food web and nitrogen cycle like any other animal.

Once agriculture had been developed, it was possible to support much larger populations. The balance between humans and their environment was upset.

An increasing population has three main effects on the environment.

Intensification of agriculture Forests and woodland are cut down and the soil is ploughed up in order to grow more food. This destroys important wildlife habitats. It may even affect the carbon dioxide levels in the atmosphere.

Tropical rain forest is being cut down at the rate of 43 000 square miles per year. Since 1950, between 30 and 50 per cent of British deciduous woodlands have been felled to make way for farmland or conifer plantations.

Chemical fertilizers can damage the soil structure. They sometimes pollute rivers and streams. Pesticides often kill useful creatures as well as pests.

Urbanization The development of towns and cities makes less and less land available for wildlife. Crowded towns may have problems of waste disposal. The sewage and household waste from a town of several thousand people can cause disease and pollution if they are not dealt with effectively.

When fuels are burned for heating and transport, they produce gases which pollute the air.

Industrialization In some cases, an increasing population is accompanied by an increase in manufacturing industries which produce gases and other products which damage the environment.

The effects of the human population on the environment are complicated and difficult to study. They are even more difficult to forecast. In their ignorance, humans have destroyed many species of plants and animals and great areas of natural vegetation. We need to consume less of the Earth's resources, limit our own numbers and treat our environment with more care and understanding. Otherwise we could make the Earth's surface impossible to live on. Thus we would cause our own extinction.

The account which follows mentions just some of the ways in which humans damage the environment.

The Human Impact on Food Webs

Endangered species

The continued existence of many wild plants and animals is threatened by human activities. This threat comes from two main sources.

(a) Habitats are destroyed as the human population grows and uses up more land for agriculture,

Figure 1   One of the threats to wild animals. So long as some people are willing to buy products like these, other people will be prepared to kill the endangered species.

Figure 2   Barn owl. Between 1930 and 1960, the barn owl population fell by about half. One reason was that agriculture became more intensive during that time. As a result, suitable hunting areas and nesting sites became scarcer.

roads and buildings. (An organism's habitat is the place where it normally lives.)

(b) Animals are killed for food, sport or profit. Over-fishing has reduced some fish stocks to the point where they cannot reproduce fast enough to keep up their numbers.

Animals like the leopard and tiger have been reduced to dangerously low levels by hunting, in order to sell their skins (Figure 1). The blue whale's numbers have been cut from about 2 000 000 to 6000 as a result of intensive hunting. Rhinoceros populations in Africa are threatened by habitat destruction. They are also hunted for their horns, which are used for dagger handles and – mistakenly – as medicine. Probably fewer than 15 000 rhinos, of all species, are left in the world.

In Britain, the barn owl (see Figure 2), kingfisher, woodlark, horseshoe bat, otter, red squirrel, wood calamint, Snowdon lily and ghost orchid are some of the species that may not survive.

The world is losing species at the rate of 100 or more every year. Most people would agree that it is morally wrong for humans to cause the extinction of a species.

The destruction of a species may also mean the loss of a valuable resource. For example, many drugs were originally found in wild plants. Perhaps fewer than half the plant species in the world have been discovered and studied. Extinction of an undiscovered species means that we lose a possible source of new drugs.

To improve the disease resistance of a crop plant, the plant breeder often crosses a high-yielding crop plant with a wild relative. If a plant species becomes extinct we may lose a useful source of genes (page 86).

Agriculture

Monoculture   In crop farming, a mixed population of trees, shrubs, wild flowers and grasses is replaced with a dense population of only one species, such as wheat or beans (Figures 3 and 4). This is called a **monoculture**.

Figure 3   Uncultivated land carries a wide variety of plant species. How many different species can you see here?

Figure 4   A monoculture. Only oil-seed rape is allowed to grow. All competing plants are destroyed. Notice, however, the variety of wild flowers on this side of the fence.

Figure 5   Weed control by herbicide spraying. A young wheat crop is sprayed with herbicide to kill the weeds.

Figure 6   Effect of a herbicide spray. The crop has been sprayed except for a strip that the tractor driver missed.

Figure 4 (page 52) is a simplified diagram of a food web which can be supported by a meadow, wood or hedgerow. Similar food webs could be drawn up for other natural habitats. Clearly, a field of wheat could not support such a mixed population of creatures. Indeed, every attempt is made to destroy any organisms which try to feed on the crop plant, such as rabbits, insects or pigeons.

So the balanced life of a natural plant and animal community is displaced from farmland. It can survive only in small areas of woodland, heath or hedgerow. We have to balance the amount of land used for agriculture, roads or building with the amount of land left alone. This is the only way to keep a rich variety of wildlife on the Earth's surface.

Pesticides   This is a general name for any chemicals that destroy agricultural pests. For a monoculture to be maintained, plants which compete with the crop plant for root space, soil minerals and sunlight are killed by chemicals called **herbicides** (Figures 5 and 6). The crop plants are protected against fungus diseases by spraying them with chemicals called **fungicides** (Figure 7). To destroy insects that eat and damage the plants, the crops are sprayed with **insecticides**.

Pesticide	kills
insecticide	insects
fungicide	parasitic fungi
herbicide	'weed' plants

The trouble with nearly all these pesticides is that they kill the harmless or useful organisms as well as the harmful ones.

In about 1960, a group of insecticides, including one called **dieldrin**, were used to kill wireworms and other insect pests in the soil. Dieldrin was also used as a seed dressing. If seeds were dipped in the chemical before planting, it prevented certain insects from attacking the seedlings. This was thought to be better than spraying the soil with dieldrin, which would have killed all the insects in the soil. Unfortunately pigeons, rooks, pheasants and partridges dug up and ate so much of the seed that the dieldrin poisoned them. Thousands of these birds were poisoned. Because they were part of a food web, birds of prey and foxes, which fed on them, were also killed.

The concentration of insecticide often increases as it passes along a food chain (Figure 8). Clear Lake in California was sprayed with DDT to kill gnat larvae. The insecticide made only a weak solution of 0.015 parts per million (ppm) in the lake water. The microscopic plants and animals which fed in the lake water built up concentrations of about 5 ppm in their bodies. The small fish were eaten by larger fish, which in turn were eaten by birds called grebes. The grebes were found to have 1600 ppm of DDT in their body fat and this high concentration killed large numbers of them.

These new insecticides had been thoroughly tested in the laboratory. The tests showed that they

Figure 7   Control of fungus disease. The wheat on the left has been treated with a fungicide. The untreated wheat on the right has developed 'yellow rust'.

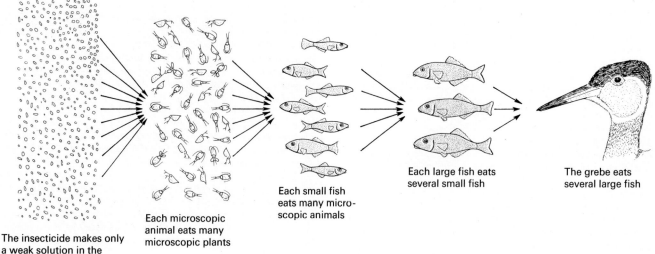

The insecticide makes only a weak solution in the water, but the microscopic plants take up the DDT

Each microscopic animal eats many microscopic plants

Each small fish eats many micro-scopic animals

Each large fish eats several small fish

The grebe eats several large fish

Figure 8   Pesticides become more concentrated as they move along a food chain. The intensity of colour represents the concentration of DDT.

were harmless to humans and other animals when used in low concentrations. No one guessed that the insecticides would become more and more concentrated as they passed along the food chain.

Insecticides like this are called **persistent** because they last a long time without breaking down. This makes them good insecticides. But they also persist for a long time in the soil, in rivers, lakes and the bodies of animals, including humans. This is a serious disadvantage. DDT is a persistent insecticide. Its general use in Britain was banned in 1984.

During the growing season, a field of wheat may be sprayed twice with herbicide, twice with insecticide and four times with fungicide. The resulting loss of insect and weed species upsets the food webs. For example, the population of grey partridge has dropped dramatically. This probably results from the loss of insects on which the chicks feed.

People also worry that some of the pesticides, sometimes as much as half, remain in the food products made from the crop.

Eutrophication

Plants need nitrates for making their proteins, and phosphates for many chemical reactions in their cells (page 29). The rate at which plants grow is often limited by how much nitrate and phosphate they can get. In recent years the amounts of nitrate and phosphate in our rivers and lakes has risen sharply. This leads to the speeding up of **eutrophication**.

Eutrophication is the enrichment of natural waters with nutrients such as phosphates and nitrates. When this happens the water can support an increasing amount of plant life. Eutrophication takes place naturally in many lakes, but usually very slowly. Human activities, especially those mentioned below, have greatly speeded up the eutrophication of rivers and lakes.

Discharge of treated sewage   In a sewage treatment plant, human waste is broken down by bacteria (page 76) and made harmless. The breakdown products include phosphates and nitrates. When the water leaves the sewage plant and goes into the rivers it still contains large quantities of phosphate and nitrate. These nutrients allow microscopic plants (algae) to grow and reproduce very rapidly (Figure 9).

Use of detergents   Some detergents contain a lot of phosphate. This is not removed by sewage treatment, so it is discharged into rivers. Again, the large amount of phosphate encourages the algae to grow.

Figure 9   Growth of algae in a canal. The water contains high levels of nitrate and phosphate from treated sewage and from farmland. These make the heavy growth of algae possible.

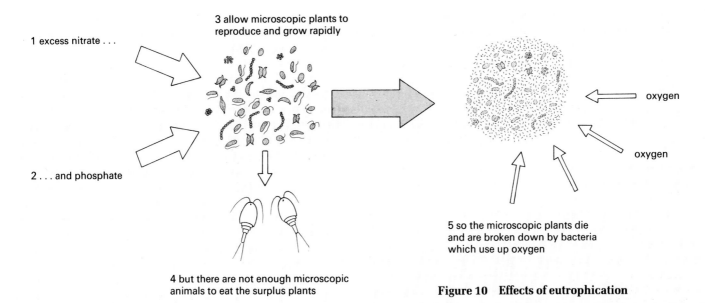

1 excess nitrate . . .

2 . . . and phosphate

3 allow microscopic plants to reproduce and grow rapidly

4 but there are not enough microscopic animals to eat the surplus plants

oxygen

oxygen

5 so the microscopic plants die and are broken down by bacteria which use up oxygen

Figure 10   Effects of eutrophication

Agriculture Intensive farming leads to excess nitrates being washed out of the soil by rain and finding their way into streams and rivers. Yet again, conditions are right for the growth of algae.

'Factory farming' Chickens, calves and pigs are often reared in large sheds instead of in open fields. Their urine and faeces are washed out of the sheds with water. If this mixture gets into streams and rivers it supplies still more nitrates and phosphates for the algae.

These four processes can lead to a level of eutrophication which damages fresh-water environments.

The extra nitrates and phosphates in the water allow the microscopic algae to grow and reproduce very rapidly. The tiny animals that eat the algae cannot keep pace with this rate of reproduction. So the uneaten algae eventually die and fall to the bottom of the river or lake. Here, their bodies are broken down by bacteria. The bacteria need oxygen to carry out this breakdown and take this oxygen from the water (Figure 10). So much oxygen is taken that the water becomes deoxygenated. It can then no longer support animal life. Fish and other organisms die from suffocation (Figure 11).

The pollution of river water is often measured by its **Biochemical Oxygen Demand (BOD)**. This is the amount of oxygen used up by a sample of water in a fixed period of time. The higher the BOD, the more polluted the water is likely to be.

Eutrophication can be reduced by using

1 detergents with less phosphates,
2 agricultural fertilizers that do not dissolve so easily,
3 animal wastes on the land instead of letting them reach rivers.

Figure 11   Fish killed by pollution. The water may look clear, but it is so short of oxygen that the fish have died from suffocation.

QUESTIONS

1 What might be the effect of the removal of foxes from the food web in Figure 4 on page 52?

2 Give five examples of a monoculture.

3 What might be the effect of an insecticide on the food web of figure 4 on page 52?

4 At one time, elm trees were sprayed with DDT to kill the beetles that carry Dutch elm disease. In the autumn, the sprayed leaves fell to the ground and were eaten by earthworms. Suggest what effects this might have had on other organisms.

5 Explain briefly why too much nitrate could lead to too little oxygen in river water.

Humans and Forests

Forests have far-reaching effects on climate, water supply and soil maintenance. For example, they break the force of heavy rainfall and release the water steadily and slowly to the soil beneath and to the streams and rivers that start in or flow through them. The tree roots hold the soil in place.

Figure 12   Cutting a road through a tropical rain forest. The road destroys the natural vegetation. It also opens up the forest to further exploitation.

At present, we are destroying forests, particularly tropical forests, at an alarming rate (a) for their timber, (b) to make way for agriculture, roads (Figure 12) and settlements, and (c) for firewood. Unless this destruction slows down, all tropical rain forests will vanish in the next 85 years.

Removal of forests allows soil erosion, silting up of lakes and rivers, floods and the loss for ever of thousands of species of animals and plants.

Trees can grow on hillsides even when the soil layer is quite thin. When the trees are cut down and the soil is ploughed, there is less protection from the wind and rain. Heavy rainfall washes the soil off the hillsides into the rivers. The hillsides are left bare and useless. The rivers become choked up with mud and silt which can cause floods (Figures 13 and 14).

For example, Argentina spends 10 million dollars a year on dredging silt from the River Plate estuary to keep the port of Buenos Aires open to shipping. Scientists found that 80 per cent of this sediment comes from a deforested and over-grazed region 1800 km upstream. Yet this region is only 4 per cent of the river's total catchment area. Similar sedimentation has halved the lives of reservoirs, hydro-electric schemes and irrigation programmes. The disastrous floods in India and Bangladesh in recent years were largely due to deforestation.

The soil of tropical forests is usually very poor in nutrients. Most of the organic matter is in the leafy canopy of the tree tops. For a year or two after felling and burning, the forest soil yields good crops. But the nutrients are soon used up and the soil eroded.

The agricultural benefit from cutting down forests is very short-lived, and the forest does not recover even if the humans leave the exhausted land.

The 'greenhouse effect' of carbon dioxide   In the last 100 years, the carbon dioxide concentration in the air has risen from about 0.027 per cent to over 0.033 per cent. This is a result of the increased combustion of coal and petroleum in our industries and motor vehicles.

Carbon dioxide is removed from the atmosphere by being dissolved in the sea and being taken up by photosynthesis. Destruction of large areas of tropical forest could significantly reduce the proportion of carbon dioxide removed by photosynthesis.

A higher level of atmospheric carbon dioxide may lead to 'trapping' the Sun's radiant energy, rather as a greenhouse does. This could result in a warming of the Earth's atmosphere, the melting of the polar ice-caps and a rise in sea level. There could also be climatic changes. These might interfere with food production all over the world.

It is hard to find good evidence about long-term changes in the average temperature of the atmosphere. But it does seem that there has been an overall increase in the last 100 years. However, apart from the dangers of the 'greenhouse effect', there are other, overwhelming reasons for preserving the forests.

Figure 13   Soil erosion. Removal of forest trees from the steep slopes in Madagascar has allowed the rain to wash away the topsoil.

Agriculture and the Soil

Soil erosion

Bad methods of agriculture lead to soil erosion. This means that the soil is blown away by the wind, or washed away by rain water. Erosion may occur for several reasons.

Deforestation   The soil cover on steep slopes is usually fairly thin. But often it can support the growth of trees. If the forests are cut down to make way for agriculture, the soil is no longer protected by a leafy canopy from the driving rain. So some of the soil is washed away. In the end it reaches streams and rivers (Figures 13 and 14).

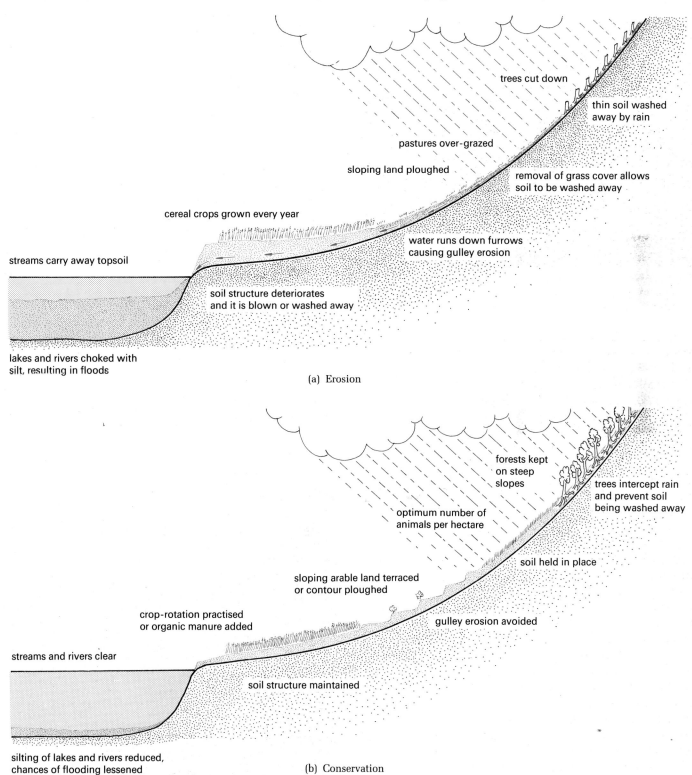

(a) Erosion

trees cut down

thin soil washed away by rain

pastures over-grazed

sloping land ploughed

removal of grass cover allows soil to be washed away

cereal crops grown every year

water runs down furrows causing gulley erosion

streams carry away topsoil

soil structure deteriorates and it is blown or washed away

lakes and rivers choked with silt, resulting in floods

(b) Conservation

forests kept on steep slopes

trees intercept rain and prevent soil being washed away

optimum number of animals per hectare

soil held in place

sloping arable land terraced or contour ploughed

gulley erosion avoided

crop-rotation practised or organic manure added

streams and rivers clear

soil structure maintained

silting of lakes and rivers reduced, chances of flooding lessened

Figure 14   Soil erosion and conservation
(From W.E. Shewell-Cooper, *The ABC of soils*, Hodder and Stoughton Educational)

Bad farming methods   If land is ploughed year after year and treated only with chemical fertilizers, the soil's structure may be destroyed. It may become dry and sandy. In strong winds it can be blown away as dust (Figure 15). This can lead to the formation of 'dust bowls', as in central USA in the 1930s, and even to deserts.

Over-grazing   If too many animals are kept on a pasture, they eat the grass down almost to the roots, and their hooves trample the surface soil into a hard layer. As a result, the rain water cannot soak into the soil and so it runs off the surface, carrying the soil with it.

Figure 15   Topsoil blowing in the wind. A dry sandy soil can easily be eroded by the wind.

QUESTIONS

6 In what ways might trees protect the soil on a hillside from being washed away by the rain?

7 A farmer ploughs a steeply sloping field. In what direction should the furrows run to help cut down soil erosion?

8 The graph in Figure 16 shows the change in the numbers of mites and springtails (tiny insects) in the soil after treating it with an insecticide. Mites eat springtails. How might you explain the changes in numbers over the 16-month period?

9 Apart from measurements of air temperature, what other evidence might point to a worldwide rise in temperature?

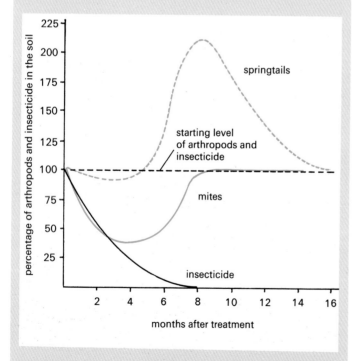

Figure 16   The effect of insecticide on some soil organisms
(From Clive A. Edwards, *Soil pollutants and soil animals*,
© *Scientific American* 1969)

Water Pollution

Human activity sometimes pollutes streams, rivers (Figure 17), lakes and even coastal water. It may also poison humans or infect them with disease.

Sewage   Diseases like typhoid and cholera are caused by certain bacteria when they get into the human intestine. People with these diseases pass faeces that contain the harmful bacteria. If the bacteria get into drinking water they may spread the disease to hundreds of other people. This is one reason why untreated sewage must not be emptied into rivers. It is treated at the sewage works so that all the solids are removed. The water poured from sewage works into rivers is free from harmful bacteria and poisonous chemicals.

Eutrophication   When nitrates and phosphates from farmland and sewage escape into water they cause over-growth of microscopic green plants. This may result in a serious oxygen shortage in the water (as explained on page 65).

Figure 17   River pollution. The river is badly polluted by the effluent from a paper mill.

Agriculture Intensification of agriculture has led to nitrates being washed out of the soil by rain. The nitrates will in time find their way into streams and rivers. Sometimes the amount of nitrates getting into drinking water is high enough to be dangerous, particularly for babies and young children. In areas of intensive farming, such as Lincolnshire, up to a million people are drinking water with levels of nitrate higher than the maximum laid down by the EEC (50 mg per litre). Not all this nitrate comes from agricultural fertilizers. However, a cut in the use of these might help towards a return to safe drinking water.

Chemical pollution Many industries produce poisonous waste products. Electroplating, for example, produces waste containing copper and cyanide.

Figure 18   Oil pollution. Oiled sea birds like this guillemot cannot fly to reach their feeding grounds. They also poison themselves by trying to clean the oil from their feathers.

If these chemicals are released into rivers they poison the animals and plants and could poison humans who drink the water. The River Trent may receive as much as 850 tonnes of zinc, 4000 tonnes of nickel and 300 tonnes of copper each year in industrial wastes (see Figure 3, page 75).

In 1971, 45 people in Minamata Bay in Japan died and 120 were seriously ill as a result of mercury poisoning. A compound of mercury had been released into the bay in factory waste. Although the mercury concentration in the sea was very low, its concentration rose as it passed through the food chain (see page 64). By the time it reached the people of Minamata Bay, who ate a great deal of fish and other sea food, it was concentrated enough to cause brain damage, deformity and death.

High levels of mercury have also been detected in the Baltic Sea and in the Great Lakes of North America.

Oil pollution of the sea is becoming common. In 1967, a tanker called the *Torrey Canyon* ran on to the rocks near Land's End and 100 000 tonnes of crude oil spilled into the sea. Thousands of sea birds were killed by the oil (Figure 18). Detergents were used to try and get rid of the oil. But these killed many more birds and sea creatures on the coast. Since then there have been even greater spillages of crude oil from tankers and off-shore oil wells.

Radioactive waste

Radioactive substances, unless very carefully controlled, can pollute land, sea, air and inland waters. In 1983, an accidental discharge of radioactive waste from the nuclear processing plant at Sellafield polluted the beaches and the sea in the area.

Nuclear (atomic) power stations and other industries use or process radioactive materials. The radiation from these materials can cause cancers such as leukaemia. The radioactivity cannot be destroyed by burning or any other means of disposal. Many of the compounds remain radioactive for thousands of years. The compounds have to be stored or transported in containers which do not allow the radiation to escape.

The wastes can be disposed of at sea or by burying on land or on the sea bed. At present, however, many people feel strongly that both these methods are unsafe.

QUESTIONS

10 What are the possible dangers of dumping and burying poisonous chemicals on the land?
11 Before most water leaves the waterworks, it is exposed for some time to the poisonous gas chlorine. What do you think is the point of this?

Air Pollution

Some factories and all motor vehicles release poisonous substances into the air. Factories produce smoke and sulphur dioxide. Cars produce lead compounds, carbon monoxide and the oxides of nitrogen which lead to smog (Figure 19).

Figure 19   Photochemical 'smog' over San Francisco.

Figure 20   Air pollution by industry. Tall chimneys keep pollution away from the immediate surroundings. But the air is still polluted.

Figure 21   Air pollution. The vegetation has been damaged by pollutants from the factory.

Smoke   This consists mainly of tiny particles of carbon and tar. The particles come from burning coal, either in power stations or in the home. The tarry drops contain chemicals which may cause cancer. When the carbon particles settle, they blacken buildings and damage the leaves of trees. Smoke in the atmosphere cuts down the amount of sunlight reaching the ground. For example, since the Clean Air Act of 1956, London has received 70 per cent more sunshine in December (page 74).

Smoke also caused the dense 'pea-soup' fogs of industrial towns. Inhaling the water droplets in these fogs was harmful to people with bronchitis, and many died. The Clean Air Acts of 1956 and 1968 stopped these deadly fogs in Britain. But they have not stopped pollution by sulphur dioxide and nitrogen oxides.

Sulphur dioxide and oxides of nitrogen ('acid rain')   Coal and oil contain sulphur. When these fuels are burned, they release sulphur dioxide (SO_2) into the air. Although the tall chimneys of factories (Figure 20) send smoke and sulphur dioxide high into the air, the sulphur dioxide dissolves in rain water and forms an acid. When this acid falls on buildings, it slowly dissolves the limestone and mortar. When it falls on plants, it reduces their growth and damages their leaves (Figure 21).

This form of pollution has been going on for many years and is getting worse. In North America, Scandinavia and Scotland, forests are being killed (Figure 22) and fish are dying in lakes, at least partly as a result of 'acid rain'.

Oxides of nitrogen from power stations and vehicle exhausts also play a part in air pollution and acid rain. The nitrogen oxides dissolve in raindrops and form nitric acid.

Oxides of nitrogen also react with other atmospheric pollutants to produce ozone. It may be the ozone and the nitrogen oxides which mainly cause the damage to forests.

One effect of acid rain is that it dissolves out the aluminium and magnesium salts in the soil. Without magnesium the plants cannot make chlorophyll (page 41). The aluminium salts are washed into rivers or lakes, where they poison the fish and other organisms living there.

Scientists are still arguing about the causes of acidification of lakes and damage to forests. But there is strong evidence pointing very clearly to the industrial areas of America, Britain and central Europe as the main sources of the pollutants that make acid rain.

Smog   This is a thin fog which forms in cities in certain climatic conditions (see Figure 19). Smog is irritating to the eyes and lungs and also damages plants. It is produced when sunlight and ozone (O_3) in the air act on the oxides of nitrogen and unburnt hydrocarbons released from vehicle exhausts. This

Figure 22   Effects of acid rain on conifers in the Black Forest.

type of smog is called 'photochemical smog' to distinguish it from the smoke plus fog that used to afflict British cities.

Carbon monoxide   This gas is also a product of combustion in the engines of cars and trucks. When inhaled, carbon monoxide combines with haemoglobin in the blood to form a fairly stable compound, carboxy-haemoglobin. The formation of carboxy-haemoglobin reduces the oxygen-carrying capacity of the blood. This can be harmful, particularly in people with heart disease or anaemia.

A smoker is likely to inhale far more carbon monoxide from cigarettes than from the air. But even so, the carbon monoxide levels produced by heavy traffic in towns can be harmful.

Chlorofluorocarbons (CFCs)   These are gases which easily liquefy when compressed. This makes them useful as refrigerants, as propellants in aerosol cans and in plastic foams. Chlorofluorocarbons are very stable and build up in the atmosphere, where they react with ozone (O_3).

Ozone is present throughout the atmosphere. Its peak concentration is at about 25 km above the Earth, where it forms what is called the 'ozone layer'. This layer filters out much of the ultraviolet radiation in sunlight.

The fear is that chlorofluorocarbons will destroy the ozone layer and allow more ultraviolet (u.v.) radiation to reach the Earth's surface. More u.v. radiation could cause more skin cancer, damage crops, interfere with the oxygen cycle and even alter weather patterns.

The reactions involved are very complex. There are also natural processes which destroy atmospheric ozone and some which produce ozone. The balance between destruction and creation is not known.

The use of chlorofluorocarbons in aerosol cans has fallen since 1974. But their use in other processes has risen, and the rate of their release is still rising by about 7.5 per cent each year.

In the Antarctic, scientists have recently discovered 'holes' in the ozone layer which appear each spring. After this discovery, some of the industrial countries agreed to a freeze on production of the most damaging CFCs at 1986 levels, followed by a 50 per cent reduction in output by the year 2000.

However, even at this level, the CFCs will continue to build up. About 16 per cent of the ozone layer could disappear in the next 80 years. Some scientists think that CFC production should be cut at once by 85 per cent to prevent further damage to the ozone layer.

Meanwhile, the chemical industries are working to produce other refrigerants and aerosol propellants which are less likely to damage the ozone layer.

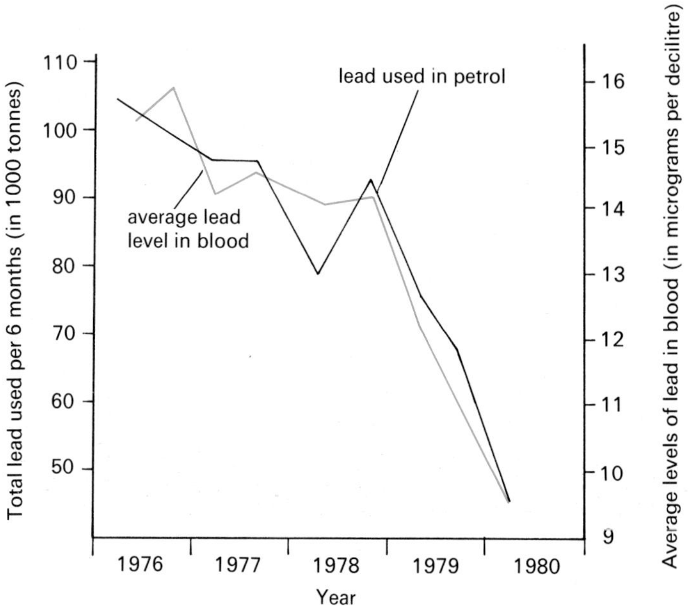

Figure 23   The effect of reducing lead in petrol. In 1975 the US government began to phase out the use of lead in petrol. This was later matched by a fall in the levels of lead in people's blood. This suggests (but does not prove) a close connection between lead in exhaust fumes and the lead in the body. (This first appeared in *New Scientist*, London)

Lead   Compounds of lead are mixed with petrol to improve the performance of motor cars. The lead is expelled with the exhaust gases into the air. In some areas of heavy traffic it may reach dangerous levels. These levels may cause brain damage in children.

There are other sources of lead pollution, such as some canned food, or water from lead pipes. But the main source of lead in the body is leaded petrol.

Laws have been passed to reduce the level of lead in petrol. The results of such legislation in America are shown in Figure 23. In 1985 in Britain the lead content in petrol was reduced from 0.4 to 0.15 grams per litre by law, and lead-free petrol is now widely available. Claims that cars do not run so well on lead-free petrol are not soundly based. Nor are claims that it increases engine wear. It is not difficult or expensive to do without leaded petrol altogether.

Radiation

Some kinds of radiation cause ions to form in living tissues and so can lead to tissue damage. Figure 24 shows the main sources of the ionizing radiation received by people in Britain.

Cosmic radiation comes from outer space. Gamma-radiation comes from minerals in the soil and in building materials. Internal radiation comes mainly from radioactive potassium and carbon in the body. Radon and thoron are radioactive

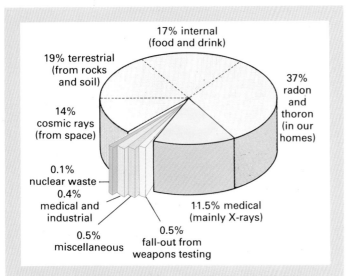

Figure 24   Sources of human exposure to radioactivity, as a percentage of the total. Thoron and radon are radioactive gases which escape from the soil and may build up in our homes. On average, 87 per cent of radiation comes from natural sources, but there are wide variations from place to place. (The sources shown in grey are collectively known as 'background radiation'.)
(National Radiological Protection Board)

gases given off by radium and thorium in the Earth's crust. The medical source of radiation is largely due to X-rays.

These sources of radiation differ in how easily they can pass through body tissues and in the damage they do. The amount of radiation received by the body is measured in sieverts (Sv). The 'effective dose' allows for the amount, the intensity and the type of radiation received by the body. X-rays and gamma-rays are less damaging than alpha-radiation.

On average, each person in Britain receives about 2 milli-sieverts (mSv) each year from natural sources. By law, workers exposed to radiation should not recieve more than 50 mSv in a year.

The main effects of ionizing radiation on the body are (a) an increased risk of cancer and (b) an increased chance of mutations (page 227) in the reproductive cells, giving rise to genetic defects in babies.

It is very hard to find clear evidence of the harm caused by radiation. It seems, however, that only 1–3 per cent of all cancers and 0.1–2 per cent of genetic deformities might be due to the low levels of background and medical irradiation. But we cannot say *which* cancers and *which* genetic defects are due to radiation. So these figures are not very reliable. However, our exposure to the present levels of radiation carries less risk of death or illness than, for example, smoking cigarettes or driving a car.

Some statisticians claim to have shown that background radiation could cause childhood cancers. If they are right, it is clearly important to keep exposure to additional, artificial radiation to an absolute minimum.

The cost of cleaning up

Most of the forms of pollution described in this chapter could be avoided, provided we were prepared to pay the cost of their prevention. Removing sulphur dioxide from the waste gases of power stations might increase our electricity bills by 5 per cent. It is probably essential to bear this extra cost if we are to preserve our environment. The British government has now made lead-free petrol cheaper than leaded petrol by lower taxation. When the costs of reducing pollution are compared with the costs of environmental damage and human ill-health, the difference may not be all that great.

Correlation and causation

Figure 23 shows what is called a correlation. As the percentage of lead in petrol falls, so does the lead level in people's blood. A correlation between two things, however, cannot usually *prove* that one of the effects causes the other.

All the same, if scientists find a strong correlation, they often suspect that a 'cause-and-effect' relationship exists and further research may follow. A correlation between deaths from lung cancer and number of cigarettes smoked led to research which found good evidence that cigarette smoking may be a major cause of lung cancer (see pages 148 and 149).

In the studies on lead pollution (Figure 23), it would be necessary to make sure, for example, that there had been no decrease in the use of other lead-containing substances over the same period which might have accounted for the decrease in blood levels of lead. An Italian study between 1977 and 1979 used special isotopes of lead in petrol. No other substances contained those particular isotopes. A correlation between the levels of the lead isotopes in petrol and in blood is strong evidence for causation (sometimes described as a 'causal relationship').

QUESTIONS

12 To what extent do tall chimneys on factories reduce atmospheric pollution?

13 What are thought to be the main causes of 'acid rain'?

14 If compounds of lead and mercury get into the body, they are excreted only very slowly. Why do you think this makes them dangerous poisons even when they are in low concentrations in the air or the water?

15 It costs money to prevent harmful chemicals escaping into the air from factories and cars. The effects of pollution also cost a great deal of money. List some of the ways in which the effects of pollution (a) affect our health and (b) cost us money.

CHECK LIST

- Hunting activities and farming upset the natural balance between other living organisms.
- Pesticides kill insects, weeds and fungi that could destroy our crops.
- Pesticides help to increase agricultural production. But they kill other organisms as well as pests.
- A pesticide or pollutant which starts off at a low, safe level can become dangerously concentrated as it passes along a food chain.
- Eutrophication of lakes and rivers results in over-growth of algae, followed by an oxygen shortage when the algae die and decay.
- Soil erosion results from removal of trees from sloping land, use of only chemical fertilizers on ploughed land and putting too many animals on pasture land.

- Tropical forests cannot usually be converted to agricultural land, because forest soils are poor in nutrients.
- Removal of forests can lead to erosion, to silting-up of lakes and rivers and to flooding.
- We pollute our lakes and rivers with industrial waste and sewage effluent.
- We pollute the sea with crude oil and factory wastes.
- We pollute the air with smoke, sulphur dioxide and nitrogen oxides from factories, and lead and nitrogen oxides from motor vehicles.
- The acid rain resulting from air pollution leads to poisoning of lakes and perhaps destruction of trees.
- Exposure to low levels of radiation does not seem particularly dangerous but evidence is hard to obtain.

Conservation and the Reduction of Pollution

Reduction of Pollution
Clean Air Acts, oxides of nitrogen and sulphur, lead, water pollution, sewage disposal.

Waste Disposal
Household waste, industrial waste, radioactive waste.

Recycling of Materials
Non-renewable resources, renewable resources, recycling.

Conservation
Environmental pressures, agriculture, habitats, reclamation, species conservation.

Reduction of Pollution

Pollution can be reduced either voluntarily or by passing laws that restrict polluting activities. Public opinion has sometimes persuaded a factory voluntarily to cut down its emission of polluting gases or liquids. However, to reduce pollution on a national scale, Parliament must pass laws which limit the amount of pollutants that may be released into the environment. The laws include penalties that may be applied if these limits are exceeded. The Clean Air Acts are examples of anti-pollution laws.

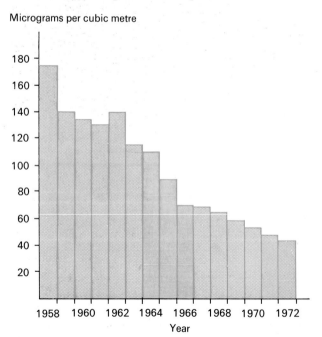

Micrograms per cubic metre

Figure 1   Average smoke concentration near ground level in the United Kingdom, 1958–72
(From John Barker, *Breathing space*, Unwin Hyman Ltd, 1975)

Control of air pollution

The Clean Air Acts of 1956 and 1968 By these Acts, certain city areas became 'smokeless zones'. Here no one could use coal to heat their homes and factories were not allowed to emit black smoke. This put an end to dense fogs in cities (Figure 1). But it did not stop the discharge of sulphur dioxide and nitrogen oxides in the country as a whole. Figure 23 on page 71 shows how a law to phase out lead in petrol cut pollution in the US.

Emission of sulphur dioxide and nitrogen oxides The concern over the damaging effects of acid rain has led several countries to press for regulations to reduce emissions of these acid gases. In 1983, nine European countries proposed a 30 per cent cut in sulphur dioxide emissions over 10 years. This move was blocked by Britain and France. In 1984, the EEC proposed a cut of 60 per cent in sulphur dioxide for large factories, and France announced an overall cut of 50 per cent in the next 10 years.

In 1986, the British government decided to build desulphurization plants for three of its power stations. By 1997, this should cut sulphur dioxide emissions from these stations by 90 per cent. But this will cut our *total* emission of sulphur dioxide by only 14 per cent. And by 1997, other power stations will have increased their emissions. We shall be back where we started – one of the biggest contributors to acid rain in Europe.

Sulphur dioxide and nitrogen oxides from our factories, particularly power stations, are seriously damaging our buildings, forests and fresh-water life. Moreover, the prevailing westerly winds carry 70 per cent of our polluting gases across the North Sea, to damage Scandinavian forests and lakes. We need to make drastic cuts in our emissions of these polluting gases from all sources.

Reduction of sulphur dioxide

This can be done partly by removing some of the sulphur from the coal before it is burned, and partly by removing sulphur dioxide from the flue gases before they are released into the air.

Both processes add to costs. The by-products can be sold, however, so reducing the extra expense.

A longer-term solution is to change the design of furnaces so that the fuel is burned at a lower temperature. This produces less acid gas.

Reduction of nitrogen oxides

Oxides of nitrogen come, almost equally, from industry and from motor vehicles. Flue gases from industry can be treated to remove most of the nitrogen oxides. Vehicles can have **catalytic converters** fitted to their exhaust systems. These converters remove most of the nitrogen oxides, carbon monoxide and unburned hydrocarbons. But they can add between £200 and £600 to the cost of a car and will work only if lead-free petrol is used (Figure 2).

Another solution is to re-design car engines to burn petrol at lower temperatures ('lean-burn' engines). These engines emit smaller amounts of nitrogen oxides but just as much carbon monoxide and hydrocarbons.

The EC is trying to cut car pollution in towns by 70 per cent in the next 15 years. For this reason it has set new limits on car exhaust emissions. After October 1993, all new cars will have to be fitted with catalytic converters.

Lead in petrol

The EC would like to move rapidly towards lead-free petrol but the member countries cannot agree on the timing of the measures. Germany planned to introduce lead-free petrol by 1986. Britain has reduced the lead in petrol from 0.4 to 0.15 grams per litre, and most British service stations now sell lead-free petrol.

Unfortunately, the additives in lead-free petrol are themselves a source of pollution. The most effective way of reducing pollution from motor vehicles would be to greatly reduce the volume of traffic.

Control of water pollution

The 1973 Water Act put the control of water supplies and sewage under ten Water Authorities. In 1989, when these authorities were 'privatised', the National Rivers Authority (NRA) was set up to oversee their activities.

The NRA is required to keep a check on the quality of water reaching rivers, estuaries and bathing beaches. It will exercise control over conservation of water, pollution, drainage, flood protection and inland fishing and navigation.

Figure 3   River pollution. Untreated industrial waste water being poured into one of the streams that feed the Mersey.

Responsibility for the quality of drinking water, however, rests with the Department of the Environment.

Under the current pollution laws, it is an offence to discharge water that has been used for any industrial purpose into a sewer or directly into a river without the consent of the appropriate water authority.

In practice, this may reduce pollution but does not stop it (Figure 3). The industries, the water authority and the NRA agree what levels of pollution are acceptable. These levels, in the past, have been too high. Even if they are exceeded, prosecutions are rare and any fines imposed are very small.

Figure 2   Pollutants from vehicles. The car is being monitored for its output of polluting gases while using unleaded petrol.

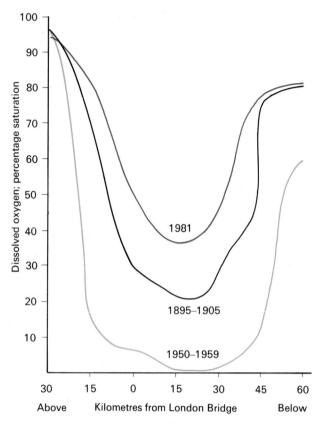

Figure 4   Improvement in the quality of water in the Thames
(Thames Water Authority)

Sewage disposal

Sewage contains bacteria from the human intestine which can be harmful (see page 262). These bacteria must be destroyed in order to prevent the spread of intestinal diseases. Sewage also contains substances from household wastes (such as soap and detergent) and chemicals from factories. These too must be removed before the sewage effluent is released into rivers. Rain water from the streets is also combined with the sewage.

Many coastal towns pour untreated sewage into the sea where it is thought to become diluted enough to be harmless. In practice, winds and tides sometimes carry it back to the shore, and it may become a health risk.

Figure 5   The Thames Bubbler. Heavy storms sometimes wash extra sewage effluent into the river. The bubbler injects oxygen into the water. This stops the oxygen level in the water falling to a point where fish would suffocate.

Inland towns have to make their sewage harmless in a sewage treatment plant before discharging the effluent into rivers. A sewage works removes solid and liquid waste from the sewage, so that the water leaving the works is safe to drink.

There are two main methods of large-scale sewage disposal. Most large towns (or groups of towns) use the activated sludge process (Figures 6 and 7). Most small towns use the percolating filter process.

The activated sludge process

(a)   Screening The sewage entering the sewage works is first 'screened'. That is, it is made to flow through a metal grid which removes solids like rags, plastics, wood and so forth. The 'screenings' are raked off and disposed of – by incineration, for example.

(b)   Grit The sewage next flows slowly through long channels. As it flows, grit and sand from roads and gardens settle down to the bottom and are removed from time to time. The grit is washed and used for landfill.

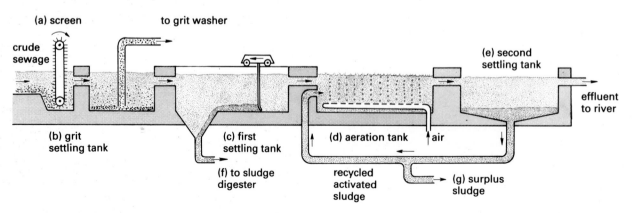

Figure 6   Sewage treatment – activated sludge

(c) First settling tanks The liquid continues slowly through another series of tanks. Here about 40 per cent of the organic matter settles out as crude sludge. The rest of the organic matter is in the form of tiny suspended particles which pass, with the liquid, to the aeration tanks.

The semi-liquid sludge from the bottom of the tank is pumped to the sludge digestion plant (see (f) below).

(d) Aeration tanks Oxygen is added to the sewage liquid, either by stirring it or by bubbling compressed air through it. Aerobic bacteria and protozoa (page 249) grow and reproduce rapidly in these conditions.

These micro-organisms cause the suspended organic particles to clump together (flocculate). The bacteria in the clumps (flocs) produce extra-cellular enzymes (page 23), which digest the organic solids. The soluble products are absorbed by the bacteria and used for energy and growth.

The bacteria also absorb the dissolved substances in the sewage and use them for their metabolism. Some bacteria turn urea (page 152) into ammonia. Others change ammonia to nitrates. Denitrifying bacteria change nitrates to nitrogen gas. The bacteria get energy from these chemical changes. They also absorb phosphates for use in their energy-transfer systems (see, for example, 'ATP' on page 29). The protozoa help in the flocculation process and they also eat the bacteria.

In this way, the suspended solids and dissolved substances in sewage are converted to nitrogen, carbon dioxide (from respiration) and the protoplasm of the bacteria and protozoa, leaving fairly pure water.

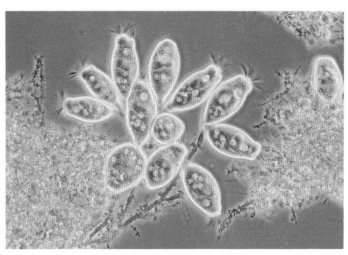

Figure 8   Protozoa in activated sludge. These single-celled organisms ingest bacteria in the liquid sewage.

(e) Second settling tanks In these tanks, the micro-organisms settle out. They form a fine sludge, which is returned to the aeration tanks to keep a high population of organisms there. This is the 'activated sludge' from which the process gets its name (Figure 8). Although the sewage stays in the aeration tanks for only six or eight hours, the recycling of activated sludge enables the micro-organisms to act on it for as much as 20–30 days.

When all the sludge has settled, the water is pure enough to put into a river.

(f) Sludge digesters The crude sludge from the first settling tanks is pumped into large containers, where anaerobic bacteria (page 249) 'digest' it. During this digestion methane gas is produced. The methane is used as fuel to drive the compressed air pumps and other machinery at the sewage works.

Figure 7   Sewage treatment – activated sludge method. In the foreground are the rectangular aeration tanks. Behind these are the circular settlement tanks. In the background are the sludge digesters.

Figure 9   Sewage treatment – percolating filter. Micro-organisms in the filter beds remove bacteria and organic matter from the effluent.

(g) Sludge disposal In Britain as a whole, about one-quarter of the sludge from the settling tanks and the digesters is pumped into ships and dumped at sea. About half is partially dried and used as an agricultural fertilizer. (It has to be free of harmful bacteria and poisonous metals for this use.) Most of the rest is used for landfill.

Percolating filter Stages (a) to (c) are much the same as for the activated sludge method.

(d) Clinker beds Instead of the liquid sewage passing into aeration tanks, it is sprayed over beds of clinker (Figure 9). You have probably seen these circular beds with the sprinkler arms going round and round over them. In the aerobic conditions of the clinker bed, bacteria, protozoa and algae grow, using the dissolved substances and suspended particles in the sewage.

The purified liquid is released into the river. The film of micro-organisms on the clinker bed falls away from time to time and collects as sludge at the bottom of the filter.

There are no sludge digesters because the process uses very little energy. The water flow and the sprinklers are driven by the pressure of the sewage.

Biodegradability It is important that factory wastes should contain no chemicals that might kill the micro-organisms in the activated sludge or the filter beds. And it is also important that the bacteria and protozoa should be able to digest any chemicals, such as detergents. That is, the chemicals should be **biodegradable**. If they are not biodegradable, the chemicals will pass unchanged into the river.

Eutrophication Although sewage effluent is 'pure' in that it contains no harmful bacteria or chemicals, it may still retain enough nitrates and phosphates to cause problems of eutrophication (page 64). Overloaded sewage works are the main source of river pollution.

QUESTIONS

1 Why have the Clean Air Acts not prevented atmospheric pollution?
2 How can (a) sulphur dioxide emissions, (b) nitrogen oxide emissions be reduced?
3 Study Figure 4 on page 76.
   (a) What was the concentration (as per cent saturation) of oxygen in Thames water at London Bridge in (i) about 1900, (ii) about 1955 and (iii) 1981?
   (b) Suggest reasons why all three graphs show a steep fall in oxygen concentration at about 20 miles downstream of London Bridge.
   (c) Why, do you think, did the water quality get worse between 1900 and 1950?
4 In what ways does sewage treatment (a) reduce pollution, (b) cause pollution?
5 In the long run, who pays the cost of reducing pollution?
6 What part do micro-organisms (bacteria and protozoa) play in sewage treatment?

Waste Disposal
Household waste

This consists of things like food residues, paper, fabrics, bottles and cans. Some householders sort these materials, take the waste glass to bottle banks and pass on the waste paper to collectors. The local authority (for example, the district council) is responsible for the collection and disposal of the household waste that ends up in the dustbin.

The waste may simply be taken to a landfill site (Figure 10), such as a disused gravel pit, tipped in, left to settle down to a compact mass and then covered with soil. Sometimes it is partially ground up and compressed before dumping. Sometimes the glass, metals and so on are sorted out before the residue is dumped. Once the landfill site is full and

Figure 10   Disposal of domestic waste by 'land-fill'. In this case, the rubbish is being used to 'reclaim' marsh-land.

the rubbish has compacted and been covered, the site may be reclaimed for agriculture or recreational use.

Landfill is usually the cheapest method of disposal, if the landfill sites are not too far away.

The organic materials, such as vegetables and paper, are decomposed by bacteria in the tip and they produce methane. If pipes are installed in the rubbish tip, this methane can be collected and used as fuel.

If the rubbish is not dumped, it may be burned in incinerators. In some cities the heat from incineration is used for district heating schemes (up to 7000 houses, shops and public buildings). But only four out of about 50 rubbish incinerators recover the energy in this way. Incineration is expensive if the heat is not used.

Some local authorities have set up installations which sort the rubbish and re-use nearly all of it (Figure 11).

Figure 11   Recycling domestic waste. This is an experimental plant for sorting and recycling household waste. The large drum on the left grades the garbage into coarse, medium and fine particles. The conveyor belts carry the graded material to other processes. Tin cans and other metals are removed and recycled; paper and plastic are pulverized and compressed into fuel pellets. Only the unusable residue goes for landfill.

Tin cans, other metals and glass are sorted mechanically from the rubbish and sent for recycling. The organic wastes are placed in fermenters where they decompose and produce methane. The methane is used as fuel to run the plant. The plastic waste may be recycled or it may be compacted with paper and rags to make fuel pellets.

Industrial waste

The least harmful waste products from industry may be mixed with household refuse and dumped in the same landfill sites. This is acceptable so long as the types and quantities of industrial waste are carefully controlled.

More hazardous waste may be deposited in separate sites, dumped at sea or burned in incinerators (see Figure 12).

Landfill   Many industrial wastes are poisonous or harmful in other ways, so the landfill tips must be sited with great care. They must not be in a place where substances leaking from the tip can find their way into ground water (the water beneath the soil) which might enter our water supplies. The tips must also be well fenced and manned so that no one dumps materials without permission and people cannot wander in (Figure 13).

Staff must make sure that only substances for which the tip is licensed are dumped and that reactive substances are not mixed (Figure 14).

Britain is unusual in that most of the tips are run by private companies, who compete with each other. The tips are licensed and inspected by the local authority. But the system is open to mismanagement and misuse. The Hazardous Wastes Inspectorate in 1985 was very critical of several badly managed

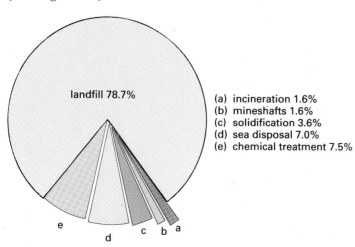

landfill 78.7%

(a) incineration 1.6%
(b) mineshafts 1.6%
(c) solidification 3.6%
(d) sea disposal 7.0%
(e) chemical treatment 7.5%

e   d   c   b   a

Figure 12   Disposal of hazardous waste in 1985. At the moment landfill is the cheapest method of disposal, but not always the safest.
This first appeared in *New Scientist*, London

Figure 13   Toxic waste from lead processing. The warning notice is clear enough but how many of them are there? Would the fence be effective in keeping people and animals out? This kind of dumping is no longer permitted.

Figure 14 Well-regulated disposal. The driver stops at the entrance to the site. His papers are checked to see what waste products the tanker is carrying and he will be directed to the correct disposal area.

sites. Competing waste disposal firms had 'cut corners', and the local authorities had not inspected and supervised the sites properly.

Landfill for industrial waste is become increasingly unpopular because of the dangers of poisonous chemicals seeping into ground water. Some waste disposal firms treat the waste to make it less harmful before dumping. Other methods of disposal are being sought. But while landfill is cheap and poorly regulated, firms will probably find it does not pay them to use other methods.

Incineration Industrial wastes may also be incinerated. But incineration plants are not very popular with the people who live near them. Incinerator ships overcome this problem, to some extent, by burning the wastes out at sea.

Incinerating some industrial wastes produces poisonous gases unless they are burned at high temperatures, or treated first to neutralize the acid content.

All these disposal methods have their disadvantages. To ensure safe disposal and to avoid pollution we will have to spend more on control measures and improved methods. We can also try to produce less waste by recycling materials. This will also help to conserve the sources of these materials.

Radioactive waste

Radioactive waste comes from nuclear power stations, reprocessing plants for nuclear fuel, research stations, the armed forces, and industries and hospitals that use radioactive substances. We cannot neutralize radioactivity. We have no way of burning or treating radioactive materials to make them harmless. We simply have to wait for the radioactivity to fall to a safe level. This may be tens, hundreds or thousands of years, depending on the nature of the radioactive waste. Meanwhile, the waste has to be kept in containers which do not let the radioactivity

escape. These must be stored or dumped in places where the containers will not corrode or release their contents into the air or into water supplies.

Radioactive waste is classified into low-level, intermediate-level and high-level waste, according to the amount and type of its radioactivity. This is not a very good classification because each class may contain a wide range of materials with different types of radioactivity.

Low-level waste includes things like worn-out equipment, glassware, protective clothing and air filters. Its radioactivity is very low. It does not need to be sealed in containers but it can remain potentially harmful for about 300 years. The policy so far has been to bury solid waste in trenches lined with concrete. When the trenches are full they are sealed off with a concrete capping.

It is essential that the storage trenches do not leak and so allow radioactive substances to get into the surrounding soil and water supplies. In the past, shallow burial in unlined trenches has not always been successful in preventing leaks or trench fires.

Liquid low-level waste is put into the sea. This practice has been strongly criticized by environmental organizations, and the levels of radioactivity in these discharges is being cut.

Intermediate-level waste consists of fuel cladding (the magnesium alloy containers which surround the fuel rods in nuclear power stations), reactor components, gas filters and chemical sludges. They do not produce heat but they do need shielding (that is, they must be kept in containers that will not let radiation pass through). They are stored in special containers, mostly at Sellafield. In the end they will be embedded in concrete for storage or dumping.

Intermediate-level waste with short-lived radio-

Figure 15 Vitrified waste. The glass block represents the amount of high-level waste, solidified into glass, that would result from one person's life-time use of nuclear energy.

activity may be 'diluted' with less active material. Then it can be buried in shallow trenches with low-level waste. Long-lived intermediate-level waste may eventually be buried in disused mines or specially dug deep pits.

High-level waste comes from 'spent' nuclear fuel or reprocessed fuel. It produces heat and is dangerously radioactive for thousands of years. At the moment reprocessed fuel is stored at Sellafield in double-lined stainless steel tanks encased in concrete.

One plan is to evaporate the liquid from the waste and make the solid residue into glass blocks. The glass blocks (Figure 15) will need to be stored in air-cooled buildings for 50 years or more, to allow the heat to escape. The glass resists corrosion and should prevent water from reaching the waste.

The volume of this high-level waste is not very great and it can be stored at the site of production.

The final resting place of all these radioactive wastes is in doubt at the moment (1987). The London Dumping Convention, representing 56 countries, regulates dumping at sea but does not forbid it. However, all dumping at sea has now stopped while scientific studies are carried out to try and predict the likely effects of sea dumping. People dislike low-level dumps being set up near their homes. Sites for deep burial of high-level waste are nearly as unpopular. The nuclear industry is considering, among other possibilities, deep burial in suitable rock formations on land, and burial in the sea bed.

One of the main problems is that we do not know whether the proposed methods of disposal will safely hold these wastes for the hundreds or thousands of years needed for the radiation levels to become fairly safe. We cannot be sure that corrosion or some disturbance such as mining or earthquakes will not crack open the containers and allow the radioactive material to escape.

At the moment, the volume of intermediate- and high-level waste produced from nuclear power stations is small enough to be stored on the site. This is perhaps the best policy until more is known about the risks of disposal.

Reprocessing At Sellafield, the 'spent' fuel is dissolved in acid and chemically treated to recover some of the uranium and plutonium. The uranium, after 'enrichment', can be used again. The plutonium is stored. Some may be used in atomic weapons. Some is for future use in 'fast breeder' reactors which may be built when stocks of uranium run out.

Unfortunately, reprocessing produces very large volumes of low- and intermediate-level waste, as well as the high-level waste mentioned above. Environmental groups such as Friends of the Earth and Greenpeace suggest that reprocessing is unnecessary at the moment. They say it would be better simply to store the spent fuel until we are better able to use it or dispose of it safely.

QUESTIONS

7 List the advantages and disadvantages of landfill and incineration as methods of disposing of household waste.
8 What are the possible dangers of uncontrolled tipping of industrial waste?
9 How can (a) useful materials, (b) energy be recovered from household waste?
10 Why can radioactive waste *not* be disposed of by incineration?

Recycling of Materials

Non-renewable resources

Mineral resources such as coal, oil and metals cannot be renewed once they are used up. It is difficult to work out how long these resources may last. However, the following predictions were made some years ago. They assume that no new deposits will be found. They also assume that we will not increase our use of these resources, but in fact we are almost certain to do so.

World resources	Years' supply
Oil and gas	50
Coal	300
Aluminium	100
Iron	360
Lead	26
Tin	17

Some of these estimates have proved to be unduly gloomy. For example, known oil and gas reserves have increased by 50% or more since 1973. Even so, sooner or later we will have to find other sources of energy and recycle as much material as possible (see below).

Renewable resources

These are either materials derived from plants, or sources of energy that do not come from fossil fuels or uranium (hydro-electric power, for example).

By photosynthesis (page 41), plants can make a wide variety of substances from carbon dioxide, water and mineral salts, which are recycled, rather than being used up.

As well as food, we can obtain the following materials from plants:

wood, and paper made from it,

sugar, which can be fermented to alcohol,

alcohol, which can be used as a fuel or for making other chemicals,

oils, such as sunflower oil, palm oil. These may become important as fuels one day.

At the moment, fuel from plants is more expensive than fuel from coal or petroleum.

Figure 16   Wind generators in the Canary Islands. On otherwise unproductive land, these generators can make a small but useful input to the electricity supply.

Renewable sources of energy (other than plant products) are:

hydro-electric power,
wind power (Figure 16),
tidal power,
wave power.

Apart from hydro-electric power, none of these is yet adding much to our energy supplies. Some of them are still in the experimental stage. All of them damage the environment to some extent.

Recycling

As minerals and other resources become scarcer, they also become more expensive. It then pays to use them more than once. The recycling of materials may

Figure 17   Bottle bank. Recycling glass can save on raw materials.

also reduce the amount of energy used in manufacturing. In turn this helps to conserve fuels and reduce pollution.

For example, producing aluminium alloys from scrap uses only 5 per cent of the energy that would be needed to make them from aluminium ores. In 1986, Britain used 31 700 tonnes of aluminium scrap.

We also recycle 56 per cent of the lead used in Britain. This seems quite good until you realize that it also means that 44 per cent of this poisonous substance enters the environment.

Manufacturing glass bottles uses about three times more energy than if they were collected, sorted, cleaned and re-used. Recycling the glass from bottles does not save energy but does reduce the demand for sand used in glass manufacture. In 1985, 200 000 tonnes of glass were recycled (Figure 17).

Waste paper can be pulped and used again, mainly for making paper and cardboard. Newspapers are de-inked and used again for newsprint. One tonne of waste paper is equivalent to perhaps 17 trees. (Paper is made from wood-pulp.) So collecting waste paper may help to cut our import bill for timber and spare a few more hectares of moorland from the spread of commercial forestry.

QUESTIONS

11 Explain why some renewable energy sources depend on photosynthesis.
12 In what ways does the recycling of waste help to save energy and conserve the environment?
13 Explain why some of the alternative and renewable energy resources are less likely to cause pollution than coal and oil.

Conservation

Conservation aims to protect individual species of plants and animals and to preserve their habitats (the places where they normally live).

In practice, these two aims cannot be separated. There is little point in preserving plants and animals if their habitats have been destroyed.

A case for preserving species was made on page 62. The same arguments apply to habitats. Quite apart from economic reasons, few people want to live in a world consisting of towns, roadways, factory farms and agricultural prairies, with just a handful of over-visited national parks and nature reserves.

Pressures on the environment

Habitats are destroyed by building, road construction, mineral extraction, commercial forestry, reservoirs and agricultural development. There are laws controlling many of these activities but when there is

Figure 18 Destruction of a hedgerow. Once an area has been declared an SSSI, damage like this can be prevented. But there are still loopholes in the law. Some land-owners have destroyed SSSIs.

a clash of interests, the commercial firms usually win the day. This is often because the people wanting to protect the environment do not have as much money or power as the 'developers' have.

Harmful effects of agriculture The countryside which many of us enjoy and wish to preserve is not 'natural'. It is the product of hundreds of years of farming and forestry. Left to itself, most countryside would revert to forests of oak, ash and beech. Farming activities have produced the variety of habitats that support communities of birds, plants, insects, fungi and so on.

It is not agriculture which threatens the countryside but the *intensification* of agriculture. Since the Second World War, governments have encouraged farmers to increase their production. They gave grants for clearing woodland, ploughing pastures, grubbing up hedgerows and draining wetlands. These incentives, plus the farmers' natural wish to

make more money, have led to the following estimated losses or damage since 1949:

Chalk grassland: 80 per cent loss or damage
Lowland heaths: 40 per cent loss
Ancient woodlands: 30–50 per cent loss
Hedges: 28 per cent loss (224 000 km of hedgerow)
Wetlands: 50 per cent loss or damage
Moorland: 30 per cent loss or serious damage.

In addition, the herbicides used to kill weeds have also destroyed the wild plants of the hedgerows. Insecticides for controlling insect pests have killed butterflies, dragonflies and the insects on which many birds feed.

On large farms, hedgerows are often removed (Figure 18) to increase the area for cultivation, to allow large agricultural machines to be used, and to reduce 'pests' such as rabbits and weed plants.

On the other hand, hedgerows do act as windbreaks, offering shelter to farm animals and reducing wind erosion of topsoil.

Hedgerows are also a valuable habitat for wild flowers, small mammals, birds and insects. For example, one study showed that five hectares of arable land supported five species of birds. Adding a ditch increased the number to seven species. With a low hedge, the number went up to twelve species and increased to seventeen species with a tall hedge. Also, the total number of organisms of each species increased.

Changes in agricultural practice have upset wildlife communities. Planting a single grass species for silage instead of cutting hay from meadows has left 95 per cent of lowland meadows with little wildlife interest (Figures 19 and 20). The early cut of silage also disrupts the breeding cycle of birds that used to nest in hayfields.

The outcome of these changes is a drastic fall in the numbers of species of wild flowers, birds, butterflies and other insects. And the numbers of

Figure 19 Grass for silage. There is no variety of plant life and, therefore, an impoverished population of insects and other animals.

Figure 20 Traditional hay meadow. The variety of wild flowers will attract butterflies and other insects.

organisms of different species have also fallen. Some species have been reduced to the verge of extinction.

Yet many of these changes have been encouraged by the support prices (subsidies) paid by the EC for cereals. But we are producing more cereals than we can eat or sell. So farmers are paid grants to destroy valuable habitats in order to grow wheat which we do not want, and which costs us £40 per tonne to store in the 'grain mountain'. Over-production of farm produce in 1980 cost the British tax-payers around a billion pounds.

Farming and conservation The Farming and Wildlife Advisory Group offers an advisory service to farmers. The Group will send scientists to work out plans, with the farmer, to help preserve the wildlife habitats on the farm without seriously affecting the farm's income.

In the last ten years or so, there have been some welcome changes of policy. Grants are no longer given for grubbing up hedgerows. In fact, grants are now paid for planting hedges and trees as shelter for crops or animals. Even so, between 1980 and 1985 only 4000 km of new hedgerows were planted, compared with 37 600 km that were removed.

EC grants can now be used for conservation of farmland as well as for increasing production. As a result, £6 million was made available to support six 'Environmentally Sensitive Areas' in England and Wales (see below). This figure did not compare with the £2 billion set aside for agricultural support, but at least it was a start.

By 1989 there were 19 ESAs in Britain. It is now clear that agricultural production must be reduced. This may benefit the environment, provided that the 'surplus' agricultural land is not used for extensive building. Two possibilities, depending on the quality of the land are as follows:

(a) Low input/low output farming
Cutting down the use of chemical fertilizers and pesticides (input) reduces the farmers' yields (output). But their costs are also reduced. The environment benefits because pollution from nitrates and pesticides is cut, while the land is left in production. The practice may also help to keep more people on the land and increase the number of jobs in farming.

An example of the 'low input/low output' method is seen in 'organic farming'. Here only organic manure and 'natural' pesticides are used. This policy could also encourage a return to 'mixed farming', with cattle or sheep as well as arable crops on the same farm. Organically produced food is more expensive, however.

(b) Afforestation
Conifers grow large enough to be felled and sold in 20–30 years, but conifer plantations are poor habitats for wildlife. Broad-leaved woodland takes longer to yield a profit but is a much better wildlife habitat. Farmers who plant broad-leaved trees need to be helped by government grants.

Figure 21   A National Nature Reserve at Scolt Head, Norfolk. The reserve attracts shore birds and provides a nesting site for large numbers of terns.

Conservation of habitats

The Nature Conservancy Council (NCC) was set up in 1949 to establish and maintain nature reserves, to protect threatened habitats and to carry out research into conservation matters. The NCC established 195 national nature reserves (Figure 21). It was also responsible for notifying planning authorities of Sites of Special Scientific Interest.

The NCC has now been split up into regional conservation bodies for England, Scotland and Wales.

Sites of Special Scientific Interest (SSSIs) These are privately owned lands which include important habitats or rare species (Figure 22). The NCC arranged management agreements with the owner so that the site was not destroyed by felling trees, ploughing land or draining marshes or fens. There are now 4150 SSSIs.

Land-owners have to be paid for giving up their right to develop their land in the most profitable way. This means that some farmers are paid for *not*

Figure 22   A Site of Special Scientific Interest (SSSI). This land in Bedfordshire is privately owned but protected by a management agreement with the land-owner.

doing something that might damage the environment. There is, however, nothing to stop land-owners from claiming compensation for not doing something which they never meant to do anyway.

In 1983, for example, a commercial forestry company bought an SSSI and applied for permission to plant it with conifers (which would have destroyed or damaged the site). If their application was granted, the company would get grants and tax help covering 75 per cent of their costs. If their application was turned down, they could claim compensation. Either way, the tax-payer would foot the bill.

In the end, the NCC bought the site and the forestry company made a profit of £130 000 at our expense.

One snag in the SSSI system is that it depends on voluntary agreement. If a land-owner is determined to damage a site, or if the compensation money runs out, there is little that can be done.

Environmentally Sensitive Areas (ESAs)
In 1986, six areas in England and Wales were given this status. They include the Pennine Dales, the Cambrian Mountains in Wales, the Norfolk Broads, the Somerset Levels (water meadows) and the South Downs (chalk grassland).

Farmers are encouraged, by a system of payments, to avoid intensification of farming and thus preserve the environment. Hedges, dry stone walls and farm buildings will be maintained. Grazing will continue to follow traditional patterns.

The number of ESAs in England has since been increased to 22.

National Parks
The National Parks Commission has set up ten national parks, covering some 9 per cent of England and Wales, such as Dartmoor, Snowdonia and the Lake District. Although the land is privately owned, the park authorities are responsible for protecting the landscape and wildlife, and for planning public recreation such as walking, climbing or gliding.

Voluntary organizations
Several non-governmental organizations have also set up reserves and help to conserve wildlife. The Nature Conservation Trust Reserve has about 1400 reserves. The Royal Society for Protection of Birds (RSPB) has 93. The Woodland Trust has 102 and about 160 other reserves are managed by other organizations.

All those reserves, however, cover only 1 per cent of the country.

Reclamation of derelict land

There are probably more than 10 000 hectares of derelict land in Britain. Some are abandoned industrial sites. Others are the result of excavations and dumping of waste from the coal, limestone and steel industries. Government grants can be paid for reclaiming some of these derelict areas. Spoil heaps are levelled and excavations are filled in. Topsoil and sewage sludge are added. Then grass and trees are planted.

In this way, the land may become a public amenity or be restored to agriculture.

The margins of clay and gravel pits may be replanted and restored to attract aquatic habitats or developed for water sports such as sailing.

In spite of reclamation schemes, the area of derelict land is probably increasing at the rate of 1400 hectares per year.

Figure 23 (a) and (b) show the reclamation of a colliery site near Merthyr Tydfil in South Wales. The Mid-Glamorgan Land Reclamation Unit removed derelict buildings, capped several mine shafts and re-contoured the spoil heap to make a new river valley and lakes. The site is now being developed for recreation. There will be caravan and camping sites, with fishing in the lakes.

(a) **Before:** the spoil heap fills the valley.

(b) **After:** the spoil has been removed or re-contoured, covered with topsoil and grassed over.

Figure 23   Reclamation of an old colliery site: the Darren Valley Project

Conservation of species

According to some estimates, the world is losing 100 species a year, and within 20 years at least 25 per cent of all forms of wildlife could be extinct. There are laws in Britain which protect wildlife. For example, it is an offence to capture or kill almost any species of wild bird or to take eggs from their nests. Wild flowers in their natural habitat may not be uprooted. Badgers, otters and bats are three of the protected species of mammal (Figure 24).

Animals and plants cannot be conserved unless their habitats are protected. Thus, the organizations mentioned above are concerned with habitats as well as with endangered species. Other organizations are particularly concerned with endangered species. Three examples are given below.

Figure 24 **The otter.** A protected species.

CITES (Convention on International Trade in Endangered Species) gives protection to about 1500 animals and thousands of plants. It works by persuading governments to restrict or ban trade in endangered species or their products, such as snake skins or rhino horns. About 70 countries are party to the Convention.

The World Wide Fund for Nature (WWF) is represented in 25 countries. The WWF raises money for conservation projects in all parts of the world. It has particular interest in endangered species and habitats (Figure 25).

The WWF calls on advice from the International Union for the Conservation of Nature (IUCN), a group of experts from governments and conservation agencies in over 100 countries.

The International Whaling Commission (IWC) was set up to try and avoid the extinction of whales as a result of uncontrolled whaling. It has 40 members.

Figure 25 **Trying to stop the trade in endangered species.** A representative of the WWF checks an illegal cargo impounded at an Indian customs post.

The IWC sets quotas of whales that member countries may catch. But it has no powers to enforce its decisions, so it cannot prevent countries from exceeding their quotas. For example, a ban on catching sperm whales in 1982 was ignored by Japan. In 1985, the IWC declared a complete ban on all commercial whaling. However, some countries have used a loop-hole which permits whales to be killed for 'scientific purposes'.

Conservation of genes

Crossing a wild grass with a strain of wheat can produce an improved variety (page 244). Many such crosses have succeeded in improving yield, drought resistance and disease resistance in food plants. Some 25 000 plant species are threatened with extinction at the moment. This would mean a huge loss of hereditary material (genes, see page 224) and a reduction of about 10 per cent in the genes available for crop improvement. 'Gene banks' have been set up to preserve a wide range of plants. But these banks could fail because of accidents, disease or human error. The only secure way of preserving the full range of genes is to keep the plants growing in their natural environments.

QUESTIONS

14 (a) What are the differences between the Nature Conservancy Council and the National Parks Commission?

(b) In what ways do both organizations contribute to conservation?

15 What are the differences between an SSSI, an ESA and a nature reserve?

16 Discuss whether habitat conservation would automatically result in species conservation.

17 What schemes exist in your district for (a) conservation of habitats, (b) reclamation of waste land?

CHECK LIST

- Sulphur dioxide emissions can be reduced by removing sulphur compounds from coal.
- Sulphur dioxide and nitrogen oxides can be removed from flue gases.
- Nitrogen dioxide, carbon monoxide and hydrocarbons can be removed from vehicle exhausts by fitting catalytic converters.
- Removal of lead from petrol reduces lead pollution of the air.
- The EEC is pressing for regulations to reduce discharge of all these pollutants.
- Water pollution of rivers is regulated by regional water authorities.
- Household and industrial waste is disposed of mainly by landfill and incineration.
- Raw materials and energy can be saved by recycling processes.
- Alternative sources of energy must be used, as coal and oil stocks run out.
- No form of energy production can entirely avoid causing some environmental damage or problems of waste disposal.
- It is urgently necessary to stop the destruction of wildlife and their habitats.
- The Joint Nature Conservancy Council has responsibility for this in Britain.
- Many voluntary organizations help to conserve wildlife and habitats.

10

The Human Population

Limits to Population Growth

Hunter-gatherers, African bushmen.
Shifting cultivation, Amazonian Indians.
Pastoralism.
Agriculture.

Population growth, increase in life expectancy,
reduction in death rate.
Stability and growth.
Population pressures.

In AD 1000, the world population was probably about 300 million. In the early nineteenth century it rose to 1000 million (1 billion), and by 1984 it had reached 4.7 billion. The United Nations expect this number to increase to 6.1 billion by the year 2000. And the population might stabilize at 10 billion by 2100 – about twice its present level. The graph in Figure 1 shows that the greatest population surge has taken place in the last 300 years.

Remember, however, that there are no reliable figures for population size before about 1650. The estimates are based on interpretations of archaeological data and calculations of how many people could be supported by the environment before agriculture was practised.

If these figures, known and estimated, are plotted in a different way (using log scales for time and

numbers), three upsurges of population appear (Figure 2). The first of these may have followed the development of stone and metal tools one million years ago. The second surge happened at the time of the change to agricultural communities 10 000 years ago. The third fits in with our scientific and industrial revolution about 300 years ago.

Clearly an agricultural community can produce more food than it needs, and can support a larger population than one that depends on hunting and gathering. But which is the cause and which the effect? Some scientists think that the development of agriculture allowed a rapid growth of the population. Others think that a growing population forced nomadic (wandering) hunters to become settled farmers.

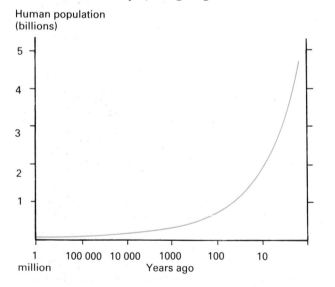

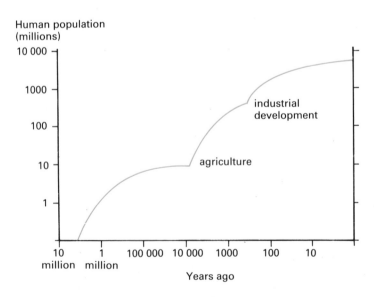

Figure 1   World population growth. The time scale (horizontal axis) is logarithmic. The right-hand space (0–10) represents only 10 years, but the left-hand space (100 000–1 million) represents 900 000 years. The greatest population growth has taken place in the last 300 years.

Figure 2   World population growth. When both the time and the population are plotted on a logarithmic scale, two growth spurts show up. The first corresponds to the development of agriculture. The second matches the beginning of industrialization.

(Reproduced with permission from James Bonner, *The world's people and the world's food supply*, 1980. Carolina Biology Readers Series. © Carolina Biological Supply Company, Burlington, North Carolina, USA)

Limits to Population Growth

About 15 years ago, the human population was increasing at the rate of 2 per cent a year. This may not sound very much. But it means that the world population was doubling every 35 years. This doubles the demand for food, space and other resources. Recently, the growth rate has slowed to 1.7 per cent. But it is not the same everywhere. Kenya's population is growing by 3.9 per cent each year, but western Europe's grows at only 0.1 per cent.

Traditionally, it is assumed that population growth is limited by famine, disease or war. Famine and disease are obvious limiting factors in some parts of Africa at the moment. Here the environment cannot support the increasing demands of an expanding population.

Diseases such as malaria (spread by mosquitoes), and sleeping sickness (spread by tsetse flies) have for many years limited the spread of people into areas where these insects carry the infections. Diseases such as bubonic plague and influenza have checked population growth from time to time.

It seems unlikely, however, that famine and war and disease have always been limiting factors. Let us look at the four main types of human community.

Hunter-gatherers

We believe that early humans lived in harmony with their environment. They collected leaves, fruits and nuts, and they killed animals for meat. Their numbers were low and they moved from place to place so that the environment was not damaged and food species were not endangered.

We do not know what factors limited the population growth. Famine affects agricultural communities rather than hunter-gatherers. Epidemics of disease seem unlikely to affect small, isolated groups of nomadic people. Tribal clashes might have inflicted casualties, but not on a large scale. The population density was probably about 1 person per 25 km^2, but early humans should have been able to find enough food in 2–4 km^2.

The life expectancy may have been little more than 25 years, which would limit the family size. There may also have been a high death rate among the new-born babies. It seems likely, however, that there were social customs which controlled the population. Until a few years ago, some Australian aboriginals and some Eskimo groups killed unwanted children. If a woman felt that she could not support an additional child, the new baby was left to die. There have probably always been some forms of voluntary birth control, supported by tribal customs related to 'marriage'.

African bushmen Some human communities still depend, almost entirely, on hunting and gathering. These communities are rapidly changing to agriculture, however.

The bushmen live in the Kalahari desert in southern Africa. There are only about 50 000 of them today, but probably they once occupied the whole of southern Africa. Although the Kalahari is hot and dry, only parts of it are truly desert. Most of it is a grassy plain with trees and shrubs.

The women collect edible roots, nuts and berries plus firewood for cooking. The men use poisoned arrows to hunt antelope and other game (Figure 3). The life-style of the bushmen depends on the tribe and the region where they live. Most are nomadic, camping together in groups of about 25 people but with families dispersing for food collecting. Each group may use a territory of up to 1000 km^2 in the course of a year.

In good conditions, bushmen may spend only about two hours per day in food collecting. This leaves plenty of time for their social life, which includes games, religious rituals, music-making and visiting other groups. One of the strongest forces holding the groups together is the custom of food sharing. No matter how successful the different families may have been in their hunting or collecting, food is always shared between the families according to strict rules.

Although the bushmen still follow a pattern of life similar to that of early humans, they are not 'primitive'. They have their own culture and

Figure 3 Hunting and gathering communities. This Kalahari bushman gets his meat by hunting rather than by herding animals.

traditions, passed on by word of mouth rather than by a written language. However, their way of life is changing rapidly as they are influenced by neighbouring cattle herders and ranchers. It seems unlikely that they will preserve their traditional way of life for much longer.

Shifting cultivation

The development of tools made it possible to cut down trees and to break up the soil so that edible plants could be cultivated. In the tropical forests where this took place, the soils are poor. Most of the nutrient salts have been taken up into the plants' tissues. Where forest dwellers clear and burn the trees and undergrowth, the ash provides enough nutrients for crop plants for about two or three years only. When the soil becomes too poor to crop well, the group moves on to a fresh part of the forest. The old vegetable patch goes back to forest in about eight years.

This 'slash and burn' cultivation works well where population density is low, and where the exhausted 'gardens' can be left for long enough to recover their fertility (Figure 4).

Amazonian Indians   The Indians of the Amazon basin now use steel tools rather than stone axes, but they can still clear only small areas of forest. They live in settled villages within easy reach of their cultivated 'gardens'. When all the nearby forest has been used the village may move to a new area. The men do the work of clearing the forest and the women do the planting. The crops include cassava (tapioca), sweet potatoes, maize and bananas. They also grow cotton for making cloth or string, and plants that produce poisons for

Figure 4   Slash and burn agriculture. Some Amazonian tribes clear areas of jungle to plant their crops. When the soil is depleted of nutrients, the garden is allowed to revert to jungle.

tipping the arrows used in hunting and fishing.

The fish, game and nuts obtained by hunting and gathering are important sources of protein. The staple diet, cassava, is almost entirely carbohydrate.

This way of life does no permanent damage to the environment. But the communities and the environment are now threatened by the commercial felling of timber and extraction of minerals, and by attempts (often disastrous) at large-scale agriculture.

Pastoralism

Archaeologists believe that goats, sheep, pigs and cattle were domesticated by humans at least 10 000 years ago. But we do not know the steps by which humans changed from hunters to herders.

Figure 5   Pastoralism. The Masai tribe herd cattle, moving them to the most productive areas.

In the temperate regions, there are grassy plains which support the grazing herds. In Africa, the cattle can graze in the savanna regions. Many African tribes, such as the Masai of East Africa, use the natural grassland to feed their cattle, simply driving them to fresh areas as the grasses are eaten down (Figure 5). The only form of 'management' is the burning of the dry grass each year, to encourage the growth of new shoots when the rains come.

Management may be more intensive. Trees may be cut down and the land ploughed. Grass species that make good fodder for the animals are planted, and the grazing area fenced off.

Pastoralism can damage the environment if too many animals are grazed, or if trees are removed from hillsides. Both of these can lead to severe soil erosion (page 66).

Agriculture

Agriculture probably started (with wheat) about 10 000 years ago in the 'Fertile Crescent' of the Middle East (Figure 6). Central America (maize) and south-east Asia (rice) are also suggested as

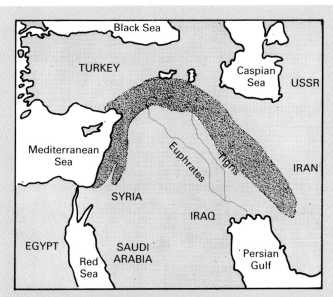

Figure 6   The 'Fertile Crescent'. This was one of the first areas to develop agriculture, 10 000 years ago.

early sites for agricultural development. Agriculture had spread to Europe by about 4500 BC and to Britain by 3000 BC.

The development of agriculture may have reduced the land area needed to support one person by about 500 times. This would have allowed the population to rise considerably.

Now that food was produced in one place, people no longer had to move about, searching for food. Also, now that one person could produce enough food to feed many others, there was no need for everyone to work in agriculture or even to remain on the land.

Between 4000 and 2000 BC, cities started to appear in the valleys of the Tigris, Euphrates, Nile and Indus. The city dwellers could be fed with the surplus produce from the agricultural lands. This still happens, of course. At the present rate at which cities are growing, over one-third of the world population will soon be living in cities with populations of 100 000 or more.

Agriculture may also have seen the beginning of divisions in society, such as those between landowner, manager and worker.

Agriculture always changes the environment. But, if methods are suited to the climate and the soil conditions, the changes need not be damaging. The deserts of North Africa and the 'dust bowls' of America are evidence of mistaken agricultural practice in the distant and not-so-distant past. There are plenty of signs today that we have not learned much from these lessons.

QUESTIONS

1 Suggest reasons why the development of (a) stone implements, (b) agriculture, could have led to an increase in population.
2 If a population of 500 people increases by 4 per cent per year, how big will the population be at the end of four years?

3 Suggest reasons why (a) hunting-gathering communities, (b) 'slash and burn' communities did not cause permanent environmental damage.
4 What is the likely connection between the development of agriculture and the rise of cities?

Population growth

If a population is to grow, the birth rate must be higher than the death rate. But if the birth rate is higher than the death rate, the population does not automatically grow.

Suppose a population of 1000 people produces 100 babies each year but only 50 people die each year. This means that 50 new individuals are added to the population each year and the population will double in 20 years (or less if the new individuals start reproducing at 16).

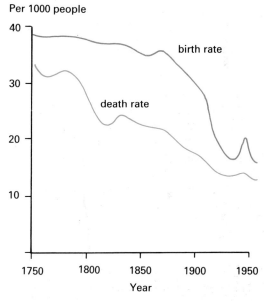

Figure 7   Birth and death rates in England and Wales from 1750 to 1950. Although the birth rate fell during this period, so did the death rate. As a result, the population continued to grow. Note the 'baby boom' after the Second World War.
(Reproduced with permission from James Bonner, *The world's people and the world's food supply*, 1980. Carolina Biology Readers Series. © Carolina Biological Supply Company, Burlington, North Carolina, USA)

However, if half the babies die before reaching their first birthday, the population will remain stable. Populations in the Third World are growing, not because of an increase in the number of babies born per family, but because more babies are surviving to reach reproductive age. Infant mortality is falling and more people are living longer. That is, **life expectancy** is increasing.

Increase in life expectancy   The life expectancy is the average age to which a new-born baby can be expected to live. In Europe between 1830 and 1900 the life expectancy was 40–50 years. Between 1900 and 1950 it rose to 65 and it now stands at 72–3 years.

In the Third World, the life expectancy has increased since 1950 from 40 years to 58 years (Figure 8).

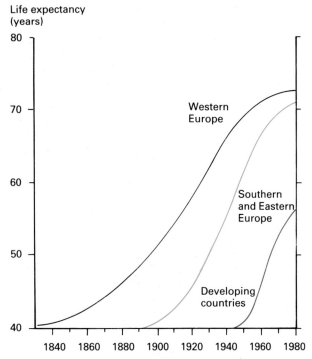

Figure 8 Increase in life expectancy. In western Europe this began in the mid-19th century. In eastern and southern Europe it started later but proceeded faster. In the developing countries, improvement in life expectancy started only in the 1950s and still has some way to go to match that of the developed countries.

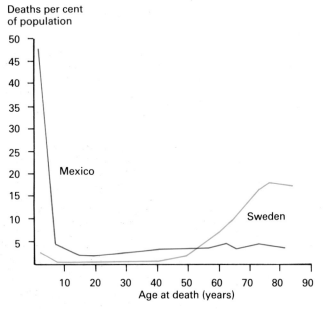

Figure 9 Age distribution of deaths. In Mexico (a developing country) the highest death rate occurs in children less than five years old. In Sweden (a developed country) the death rate for this group is only about 3 per cent. Why, do you think, is the death rate for the 70–80 age group higher in Sweden than it is in Mexico?
(Figures 8 and 9 are from D.R. Gwatkin and S.K. Brandel, *Life expectancy and population growth in the Third World*, © Scientific American, 1982)

These figures are averages. They do not mean, for example, that everyone in the Third World will live to the age of 58. In the Third World, 40 per cent of the deaths are of children younger than 5 years and only 25–30 per cent are deaths of people over 60. In Europe, only 5–20 per cent of deaths are those of children below the age of 5, but 70–80 per cent are of people over 60 (Figure 9).

An increase in the number of people over the age of 60 does not change the rate of population growth much, because these people are past child-bearing age. On the other hand, if the death rate among children falls and the extra children survive to reproduce, the population will continue to grow. This is the main reason for the rapid population growth in the Third World since 1950.

Causes of the reduction in death rate The causes are not always easy to identify and vary from one community to the next. In nineteenth-century Europe, agricultural development and economic expansion led to improvements in nutrition, housing and sanitation, and to clean water supplies. These improvements reduced the incidence of infectious diseases in the general population. And better-fed children could resist these infections when they did meet them. The drop in deaths from infectious diseases probably accounted for three-quarters of the total fall in deaths.

The social changes probably affected the population growth more than did the discovery of new drugs or improved medical techniques. Because of these techniques, particularly immunization, diphtheria, tuberculosis and polio are now rare. And by 1977 smallpox had been wiped out by the World Health Organization's vaccination campaign.

In the Third World, sanitation, clean water supplies and nutrition are improving slowly. The surge in the population since 1950 is likely to be at least 50 per cent due to modern drugs, vaccines and insecticides (see Figures 10 and 11).

Stability and growth

Up to 300 years ago, the world population was relatively stable. Fertility (the birth rate) was high and so was the mortality rate (death rate). Probably less than half the children born lived to have children of their own. Many died in their first year (infant mortality). And many mothers died during childbirth.

No one saw any point in reducing the birth rate. If you had a lot of children, you had more help on your land and a better chance that some of them would live long enough to care for you in your old age.

In the past 300 years, the mortality rate has fallen but the birth rate has not gone down to the same extent. As a result the population has expanded rapidly.

In eighteenth-century Europe, the **fertility rate**

Figure 10   **Village water pump being installed in Chad.** The pump may look old-fashioned, but it is a considerable advance on walking for miles to collect water from a polluted river.

Figure 11   **Immunization.** These children in Swaziland are receiving a polio vaccine.

was about 5. This means that, on average, each woman would have five children. When the death rate fell, the fertility rate lagged behind so that the population increased. However, the fertility rate has now fallen to somewhere between 1.4 and 2.6, and the European population is more or less stable.

A fall in the fertility rate means that young people will form a smaller proportion of the population. There will also be an increasing proportion of old people for the younger generation to look after. In Britain it is predicted that between 1981 and 1991, the number of people aged 75–84 will increase by 16 per cent. The number of those over 85 may increase by 46 per cent (Figure 14).

In the Third World, the fertility rate has dropped from about 5.8 to 4.7. But this is still very much higher than the mortality rate. An average fertility rate of 2.1 is necessary to keep the population stable.

Breast-feeding babies is unfashionable in some parts of the world. The process of breast-feeding prevents ovulation (page 166), particularly if the baby is fed frequently. If breast-feeding continues for

two years or more, later births are spaced out and the family size is limited. A woman who does not breast-feed her babies could conceive every year. So breast-feeding helps to keep the birth rate down.

In industrial countries, women who go out to work usually have to start bottle-feeding after the first few months. This is not very satisfactory, for several reasons (page 173). However, most women have modern methods of contraception available, and are not likely to conceive more often than they wish.

In the Third World, however, milk substitutes have been advertised by some manufacturers as a 'modern' or 'superior' form of infant feeding (Figure 12). Once a mother changes to bottle-feeding, her own milk supply stops and the baby must depend on

Figure 12   **A misleading advertisement for manufactured baby food.** 'The better milk for infant feeding'? Better than cows' milk, maybe, but certainly not better than human breast milk. 'Proper nutrition and economy'? Mother's milk is the 'proper' nutrition and it is far more economical than buying manufactured products.

Figure 13   **Family planning.** A health worker in Bangladesh explains the use of a condom.

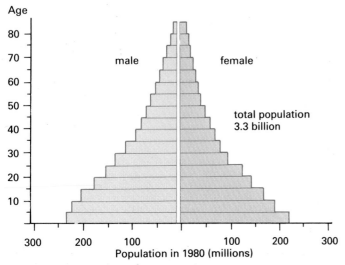

Age

300 200 100   100 200 300
Population in 1980 (millions)

(a) The developing regions. The tapering pattern is characteristic of a
population with a high birth rate and a low average life expectancy. The
bulk of the population is under 25.

Figure 14   Age distribution of population in 1980

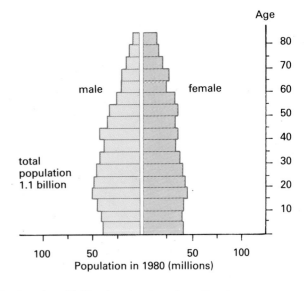

Age

100   50   50   100
Population in 1980 (millions)

(b) The developed world. The almost rectangular pattern is
characteristic of an industrialized society, with a steady birth rate and a
life expectancy of about 70. (The horizontal scale is not the same as in
(a).)

the milk substitutes. Thus her fertility is restored,
and one limit on an over-high birth rate is removed.

As a community grows wealthier, the birth rate
goes down. There are believed to be four reasons.

Longer and better education   Marriage is post-
poned and a better educated couple will have
learned about methods of family limitation.

Better living conditions   Once people realize that
half their offspring are not going to die from disease
or malnutrition, family sizes fall.

Agriculture and cities   Modern agriculture is no
longer labour-intensive. Farmers do not need large
families to help out on the land. City dwellers do not
depend on their offspring to help raise crops or herd
animals.

Application of family planning methods, either
natural methods of birth control or the use of
contraceptives.

It takes many years for social improvements to
produce a fall in birth rate. Some countries are trying
to speed up the process by encouraging couples to
limit their family size (Figure 13), or by penalizing
families who have too many children.

Meanwhile the population goes on growing. The
United Nations expect that the birth rate and death
rate will not be in balance until the year 2100. By
that time the world population may have reached 10
billion, assuming that the world supply of food will
be able to feed this population.

In the past few decades, the world has produced
enough food to feed, in theory, all the extra people.
But the extra food and the extra people are not
always in the same place. As a result, 72 per cent of
the world's population has a diet which lacks
energy, as well as other nutrients.

Every year between 1965 and 1975, food production in the developed nations rose by 2.8 per cent,
while the population rose by 0.7 per cent. In the
developing nations during the same period, food
production rose by only 1.5 per cent each year, while
the annual population rise was 2.4 per cent.

The western world can produce more food than its
people can consume. Meanwhile people in the drier
regions of Africa face famine due to drought and
population pressure on the environment. Even if the
food could be taken to the Third World, people there
are often too poor to buy it. Ideally, each region
needs to grow more food or reduce its population
until the community is self-supporting. Some countries grow tobacco, cotton, tea and coffee (cash crops)
in order to obtain foreign currency for imports from
the western world. This is fine, so long as they can
also feed their people. But when food is scarce,
people cannot live on the cash crops.

Population pressures

More people, more agriculture and more industrialization will put still more pressure on the
environment unless we are very watchful (see
Chapters 8 and 9). If we damage the ozone layer
(page 71), increase atmospheric carbon dioxide (page
66), release radioactive products or allow farmland
to erode, we may meet with additional limits to
population growth.

QUESTIONS

5 Look at the graphs in Figure 7.
   (a) When did the post-war 'baby-boom' occur?
   (b) What was the growth rate of the population in 1800?
6 Look at the graph in Figure 8.
   (a) Which of the three regions has shown the most rapid increase in life expectancy in the last 30 years?
   (b) What were the differences in life expectancy between the three regions in 1970?
7 Which of the following causes of death are likely to have most effect on the growth rate of a population?

smallpox, tuberculosis, heart disease, polio, strokes, measles.

Give reasons for your answer.

8 Suggest some reasons why the birth rate tends to fall as a country becomes wealthier.
9 Give examples of the kind of demands that an increasing population makes on the environment. In what ways can these demands lead to environmental damage?

CHECK LIST

- The world population is increasing by about 2 per cent per year.
- This means that it doubles every 35 years.
- The rate of increase is slowing down and the population may stabilize at 10 billion by the year 2100.
- The limits to population growth may include famines, epidemics and wars.
- Until the beginning of agriculture, humans lived in harmony with their environment.
- The extra food resulting from agriculture allowed rapid population growth and the development of cities.
- A population grows when the birth rate exceeds the death rate, provided the offspring live to reproduce.
- In the developed countries, the birth rate and the death rate are now about the same.
- In the developing countries, the birth rate exceeds the death rate and their populations are growing. This is not because more babies are born, but because more of them survive.
- The increased survival rate may be due to improved social conditions, such as clean water, efficient sewage disposal, better nutrition and better housing.
- It is also the result of vaccination, new drugs and improved medical services.
- As a population becomes more wealthy, its birth rate tends to fall.
- Food production in the developed countries has increased faster than the population growth.
- Food production in the developing countries has not kept pace with population growth.

Examination Questions

Do not write on this page. Where necessary copy drawings, tables or sentences.

Section 2 Humans in the Environment

1 In an investigation of a Lapp community in Northern Scandinavia the following information about feeding was obtained. The Lapp people were eating reindeer meat and berries from various bushes. The reindeer fed on the bushes and lichens. Mosquitoes were feeding on blood from the Lapps and the reindeer. Draw a food web for this community. (N1)

2 (a) Look at the table below.

Habitat	Mass of new growth/ grams per square metre per year
Salt marsh	3000
Pine forest	2800
Oak forest	1200
Grassland	600

(i) Make a bar chart from the above table.
(ii) Why would the salt marsh feed the largest population of animals?
(b) In the oak forest, the trees lose their leaves each autumn. Name *two* organisms which make the leaves rot. (N2P)

3 (a) Set out below is a simple food chain:

microscopic plants → shrimps → baleen whale

(i) Which organisms are the producers?
(ii) Which organisms are the consumers?
(iii) By what process does the producer make its food?
(iv) Write a word equation for the process you have named in (iii).
(b) The baleen whale is in danger of extinction because it is eaten by Man. In order to conserve the whale it has been suggested that Man should eat shrimps instead. Explain the possible results of following this suggestion. (M2)

4 Lake Victoria, in East Africa, used to contain a large population of crocodiles which ate lung fish (not used as food by Man). The lung fish ate *Tilapia* fish (very important as food for Man). *Tilapia* eat plankton. The crocodiles were eliminated by hunting.
(a) From the food chain described name the following: (i) a producer, (ii) a secondary consumer.
(b) It was thought that the removal of crocodiles from the lake would benefit the human population living near the lake. Suggest why this view was incorrect. (W2A)

5 The graph below shows the nitrate levels in the River Lee over 50 years.

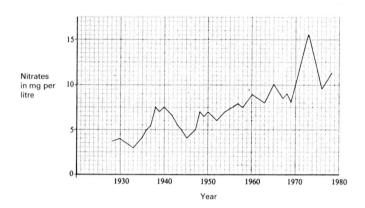

(a) In what year were nitrogen levels highest?
(b) (i) How many times greater was the nitrate level in 1970 compared with 1936?
(ii) What human activities could have led to the increase in nitrate levels over the 50 years shown in the graph?
(iii) State *one* effect on humans of excess nitrate in drinking water.
(c) High nitrate levels in river water are one example of water pollution.
(i) Name one other water pollutant.
(ii) How does this pollutant get into the water?
(iii) State *one* harmful effect of this pollutant on living organisms in the water. (L1)

6 In the carbon cycle, which *one* of the following processes removes carbon dioxide from the atmosphere?
A combustion
B decay
C diffusion
D photosynthesis
E respiration

7 The table shows the estimated population of the world since the year AD 1.

Year (AD)	Population/ millions
1	200
1000	300
1500	400
1800	1000
1900	2000
1950	3000

(a) Use these figures to plot a graph on the paper provided.
(b) Suggest two possible factors which since 1800 have caused the change in the rate of population increase. (W1B)

SECTION 3
Human Physiology

11

Food and Diet

Classes of Food
Carbohydrates, proteins and fats.

Diet
Mineral salts, vitamins, fibre and water.

Balanced Diets
Energy needs and proteins. Special needs. Western diets.

Preserving and Processing
Additives.

Practical Work
Food tests. Energy from food.

The Need for Food

All living organisms need food. An important difference between plants and animals is that the green plants can make food in their leaves but animals have to take it in 'ready-made'.

Plants can build up (synthesize) all the organic compounds they need from inorganic substances, such as carbon dioxide, water and salts (see page 41). Animals cannot do this. Therefore animals, including humans, have to obtain their organic compounds, such as sugars and proteins, from plants or from animals that eat plants.

In all animals, food is used as follows:

For growth It provides the substances needed for making new cells and tissues.

As a source of energy for the chemical reactions which keep living organisms alive. When food is broken down during respiration (see page 28), the energy from the food is used for reactions such as building complex molecules (page 19). The energy is also used for activities such as movement, heart beat and nerve impulses.

For replacement of worn and damaged tissues The substances provided by food are needed to replace – for example – the millions of our red blood cells that break down each day, to replace the skin which is worn away, and to repair wounds.

Classes of Food

The components of food can be classed as **macronutrients** or **micronutrients**. Macronutrients are needed in bulk to provide energy and the raw materials for growth. Micronutrients are needed in small quantities to enable certain chemical reactions to take place in the body.

The principal macronutrients are carbohydrates, proteins and fats. Their chemical structures are described on pages 19-21.

Micronutrients are salts and vitamins.

Carbohydrates

Sugars and **starch** are important carbohydrates in our diet. There is a lot of starch in potatoes, bread, maize, rice and other cereals. We eat sugars mainly as **sucrose** (table sugar) which is added to drinks and many prepared foods such as jam, biscuits and cakes. Glucose and fructose are sugars which occur naturally in many fruits and some vegetables.

Although all foods provide us with energy, carbohydrates are the cheapest and most readily available source of energy. They contain the elements carbon, hydrogen and oxygen (for example, glucose is $C_6H_{12}O_6$). When carbohydrates are oxidized to provide energy by respiration they are broken down to carbon dioxide and water (see page 28). One gram of carbohydrate can provide, on average, 16 kilojoules (kJ) of energy.

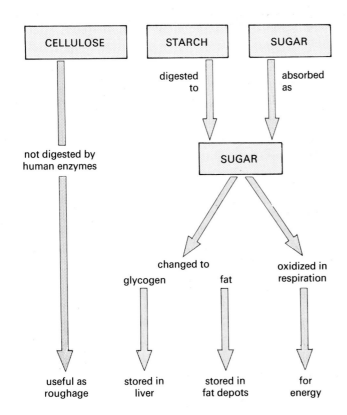

Figure 1   Digestion and use of carbohydrate

ala—gly—gly—leu—val—cys—gly
                              |
                              s
                              |
                              s
                              |
glu—val—lys — cys—ala
                         leu
                          |
                         leu

Part of a plant protein of 14 amino acids

ala gly val cys val
         gly   ala gly
  cys   gly leu   lys
      glu   leu

Digestion breaks up protein into its amino acids
and . . .

glu—val—cys—gly
              |
              s
              |
              s
              |
     ala—leu—cys—val—gly
    leu
     |
    lys
     ala—leu—gly

. . . our body builds up the same 14 amino acids but
into a protein that it needs

ala=alanine   gly=glycine   leu=leucine
cys=cysteine   glu=glutamine   lys=lysine   val=valine

Figure 2   Digestion and use of a protein molecule

If we eat more carbohydrates than we need for our energy requirements, the excess is converted in the liver to either glycogen (see page 120) or fat. The glycogen is stored in the liver and muscles. The fat is stored in fat depots in the abdomen, round the kidneys or under the skin (Figure 1).

The **cellulose** in the cell walls of all plant tissues is a carbohydrate. We probably cannot get much nourishment from cellulose but it is important in the diet as **fibre** (see page 102), which helps to keep the digestive system healthy.

Proteins

All plants contain some protein, but beans or cereals like wheat and maize are the best sources. Lean meat, fish, eggs, milk and cheese are important sources of animal protein.

Proteins, when digested, provide the chemical substances needed to build cells and tissues, such as skin, muscle, blood and bones. Neither carbohydrates nor fats can do this. So it is essential to include some proteins in the diet.

Protein molecules consist of long chains of **amino acids** (see page 19). When proteins are digested, the chains are broken up into the constituent amino acids. The amino acids are absorbed into the bloodstream and used to build up different proteins. These proteins form part of the cytoplasm and enzymes of cells and tissues. Figure 2 shows such a rearrangement of amino acids.

The amino acids which are not used for making new tissues cannot be stored, but the liver removes their amino (—NH_2) groups and changes the residue to glycogen. The glycogen can be either stored or oxidized to provide energy (page 120).

When proteins are used for energy, they yield 17 kJ of energy per gram.

Chemically, proteins differ from both carbohydrates and fats because they contain nitrogen and sulphur as well as carbon, hydrogen and oxygen.

Essential amino acids   Although humans and other animals cannot make amino acids, they can change one amino acid into another. But there are at least eight amino acids that the body cannot produce in this way. These are called **essential amino acids** and they must be included in the diet. Lysine, valine and leucine are examples of essential amino acids.

Some plant proteins do not contain enough essential amino acids to supply the needs of the body. Protein from cereals, for example, has too little lysine. A diet that was almost entirely made up of rice or maize could lead to a protein-deficiency disease. Beans are a rich source of lysine, however. A diet containing beans need not be short of lysine.

Most animal proteins contain all the essential amino acids (see Table 1 in question 4, below). But they are more expensive than plant proteins.

Fats

Animal fats are found in meat, milk, cheese, butter and egg-yolk. Plant fats occur as oils in fruits (palm oil is an example) and seeds (sunflower seed oil). They are used for cooking and making margarine. Fats and oils are sometimes collectively called **lipids**.

Lipids are used in the cells of the body to form part of the cell membrane and other membrane systems (page 12). Lipids can also be oxidized in respiration, to carbon dioxide and water. When used to provide energy in this way, 1 g fat gives 37 kJ of energy. This is more than twice as much energy as can be obtained from the same weight of carbohydrate or protein.

Fats are stored in the body as *adipose tissue* in fat depots. The principal fat depots are in the abdomen and under the skin.

QUESTIONS

1 What sources of protein-rich foods are available to a vegetarian who (a) will eat animal products but not meat itself, (b) will eat only plants and their products?
2 Why must all diets contain some protein?
3 In what sense can the fats in your diet be said to help 'keep you warm'?

4 The table below shows the number of milligrams of four essential amino acids provided by a fixed amount of protein. It also shows how much of these the body needs to get from that amount of protein. Of the seven proteins shown,
  (a) which one is the best source of essential amino acids?
  (b) which is the best plant source?
  (c) which combinations of plant products will provide an adequate supply of essential amino acids?

Table 1   Four essential amino acids

		Amino acid/mg		
	try	lys	leu	val
Body needs	90	270	300	270
Protein in these foods provides:				
Meat	80	510	490	330
Milk	90	490	630	440
Eggs	110	420	560	450
Wheat	80	170	400	270
Rice	90	220	510	370
Beans	60	450	530	370
Potatoes	65	230	290	270

(try = tryptophan; lys = lysine; leu = leucine; val = valine.)

Diet

In addition to proteins, carbohydrates and fats, the diet must include salts, vitamins, water and vegetable fibre (roughage). These substances are present in a balanced diet and do not normally have to be taken in separately.

Salts

These are sometimes called 'mineral salts' or just 'minerals'. Proteins, carbohydrates and fats provide the body with carbon, hydrogen, oxygen, nitrogen, sulphur and phosphorus. But there are several more elements which the body needs and which occur as salts in the food we eat.

Iron   Red blood cells contain the pigment haemoglobin (page 125). Part of the haemoglobin molecule contains iron and this plays an important part in carrying oxygen round the body. Millions of red cells break down each day. Their iron is stored by the liver and used to make more haemoglobin. Some iron is lost, however, and adults need to take in about 15 mg each day. Iron is needed also in the muscles and for enzyme systems in all the body cells.

Red meat, especially liver and kidney, contains a high proportion of iron. Eggs, beans and cereals are also rich in iron. However, it is not clear how much of the iron in these foodstuffs can be absorbed. In green vegetables and cereals, other chemicals are present which may prevent the iron being taken up.

Nevertheless, if these iron-containing foods are missing from your diet, you may develop some form of anaemia. Your body cannot make enough haemoglobin, and the oxygen-carrying capacity of the blood is reduced.

Calcium   Calcium, in the form of calcium phosphate, is deposited in the bones and the teeth and makes them hard. It is present in blood plasma and plays an essential part in normal blood clotting (page 134). Calcium is also needed in the muscles for the chemical changes which make muscles contract.

The richest sources of calcium are milk (liquid, skimmed or dried) and cheese. Calcium is present in most foods in small quantities and also in 'hard' water.

Many calcium salts are not soluble in water and may pass through the digestive system without being absorbed. Simply increasing the calcium in the diet may not have much effect unless the calcium is in the right form, the diet is balanced and the intestine is healthy. Vitamin D and bile salts (page 116) are needed for efficient absorption.

The level of calcium in the blood is controlled by a gland in the neck, called the **parathyroid**.

Iodine   This is needed in only small quantities, but it forms an essential part of the molecule of **thyroxine**. Thyroxine is a hormone (page 214) produced by the thyroid gland in the neck.

Specially rich sources of iodine are sea-fish and shellfish. It is also present in most vegetables, provided that the soil in which they grow contains enough iodine. In some parts of the world, where soils have little iodine, potassium iodide may be added to table salt to bring the iodine in the diet to a satisfactory level.

Sodium and potassium   These elements occur in all the cells and fluids of the body. Sodium is mainly in the blood and tissue fluid, while most of the potassium is inside the cells. Salts of sodium and potassium are needed to keep the blood and tissue fluids at the correct osmotic concentration (see page 36) so that the tissues do not become waterlogged or dehydrated. Both sodium and potassium salts are excreted in the urine, and sodium is lost in the sweat. We need about 2–4 g of each of these salts every day.

Most diets contain enough sodium and potassium. The extra salt added during cooking, or shaken over the food, is probably unnecessary. It may even be harmful for some people. Only people who lose a lot of sodium chloride in sweat may need a high intake.

Fluoride   Fluoride occurs naturally, in small quantities, in drinking water. It plays a part in the formation of teeth and helps teeth to resist decay, particularly in children. (Tooth decay, however, results mainly from the continuous presence of sugar or other carbohydrate in the mouth – see page 193.) For this reason, some toothpastes have fluoride added to them and some people dissolve fluoride tablets in their drinking water.

Vitamins

All proteins have similar chemical structures. So have all carbohydrates. Vitamins, on the other hand, are a group of organic substances whose chemical

Table 2 Vitamins

Name and sources of vitamin	Diseases and symptoms caused by lack of vitamin	Notes
Retinol (vitamin A; fat-soluble): Liver, cheese, butter, margarine, milk, eggs. **Carotene** (vitamin A precursor; water-soluble): Fresh green leaves and carrots.	Reduced resistance to disease, particularly those which enter through the epithelium. Poor night vision. Cornea of eyes becomes dry and opaque leading to **keratomalacia** and blindness.	The yellow pigment carotene, present in green leaves and carrots, is turned into retinol by the body. Retinol forms part of the light-sensitive pigment in the retina (page 199). Retinol is stored in the liver.
Folic acid (water-soluble): Liver, spinach, fish, beans, peas.	**Vitamin-deficiency anaemia:** not enough red blood cells are made.	Deficiency is likely to affect pregnant women on poor diets.
Ascorbic acid (vitamin C; water-soluble): Oranges, lemons, grapefruit, tomatoes, fresh green vegetables, potatoes.	Fibres in connective tissue of skin and blood vessels do not form properly. This leads to bleeding under the skin, particularly at the joints. The gums swell and bleed, and wounds heal badly. These are all symptoms of **scurvy**.	Possibly acts as a catalyst in cell respiration. Scurvy is only likely where fresh food is not available. Cow's milk and milk powders contain little ascorbic acid so babies may need additional sources. Cannot be stored in the body; daily intake needed.
Calciferol (vitamin D; fat-soluble): Butter, milk, cheese, egg-yolk, liver, oily fish (herring, mackerel, pilchard).	Calcium is not deposited properly in the bones. This leads to **rickets** in young children because the bones remain soft and are deformed by the child's weight. Deficiency in adults causes **osteomalacia**; fractures are likely.	Calciferol helps the absorption of calcium from the intestine and the deposition of calcium salts in the bones. Natural fats in the skin are converted to a form of calciferol by sunlight.

The B vitamins   There are ten or more water-soluble vitamins which occur together, particularly in whole cereals, peas and beans. A deficiency of any one of these vitamins is likely only in communities living on restricted diets such as maize or milled rice.

Several other substances are classed as vitamins, including **riboflavin** (B_2), **tocopherol** (E), **phylloquinone**. But these are either unlikely to be missing from the diet, or not known to be important in the human diet.

structures are quite different. But they do have certain things in common:

1 They are not digested or broken down for energy.
2 Mostly, they are not built into the body structures.
3 They are essential in very small quantities for normal health.
4 They are needed for chemical reactions in the cells, working in association with enzymes.

Plants can make these vitamins in their leaves, but animals have to take them in ready-made either from plants or from other animals.

If any one of the vitamins is missing from your diet, or at a low level, you will develop a vitamin-deficiency disease. These diseases can be cured, at least in the early stages, simply by adding the vitamin to the diet.

Scientists know of fifteen or more vitamins. They are sometimes grouped into two classes: water-soluble vitamins and fat-soluble vitamins. The fat-soluble vitamins are found mostly in animal fats or vegetable oils, which is one reason why our diet should include some of these fats. The water-soluble vitamins are present in green leaves, fruits and cereal grains.

Table 2 (page 101) describes vitamins, and gives examples of foods that contain them and of the vitamin-deficiency diseases that result from their absence.

Dietary fibre (roughage)

When we eat vegetables and other fresh plant material, we take in a lot of plant cells. The cell walls of plants consist mainly of cellulose, but we do not have enzymes for digesting this substance. The result is that the plant cell walls reach the large intestine (colon) without being digested. This un-digested part of the diet is called **fibre** or roughage. The colon contains many bacteria which can digest some of the substances in the plant cell walls to form fatty acids (see page 20). Vegetable fibre, therefore, may supply some useful food material. But it has other important functions too.

The fibre itself, with the bacteria which multiply from feeding on it, adds bulk to the contents of the colon and helps it to retain water. This softens the faeces (page 118) and reduces the time needed for the undigested residues to pass out of the body. Both these effects help to prevent constipation and keep the colon healthy.

Most vegetables and whole cereal grains contain fibre, but white flour and white bread do not contain much. Good sources of dietary fibre are wholemeal bread and bran.

Water

About 70 per cent of most tissue consists of water. It is an essential part of cytoplasm. The body fluids, such as blood, lymph and tissue fluid (Chapter 13), are composed mainly of water.

Digested food, salts and vitamins are carried round the body as a watery solution in the blood (page 133). Waste substances such as excess salt and urea are excreted in solution by the kidneys (page 152). Water thus acts as a solvent and as a transport medium for these substances.

Digestion is a process which uses water in a chemical reaction to break down insoluble sub-stances to soluble ones (page 113). These products then pass, in solution, into the bloodstream. In all cells there are many reactions in which water plays an essential part as a reactant and a solvent.

Water also plays a part in regulating our tempera-ture when we sweat (page 162).

We lose water by evaporation, sweating, urinating and breathing. We have to make good this loss by taking in water with the diet. (See also page 155.)

QUESTIONS

5 Which tissues of the body need (a) iron, (b) glucose, (c) calcium, (d) protein, (e) iodine?

6 Figure 3 shows some examples of the food that would give a balanced diet. Consider each sample in turn and say what class of food or item of diet is mainly present. For example, the meat is mainly protein but also contains some iron.

7 What is the value of leafy vegetables, such as cabbage and lettuce, in the diet?

8 Why is a diet consisting mainly of one type of food, such as potatoes, likely to be unsatisfactory even if it meets our energy needs?

Figure 3 Healthy diet. A diet made up from the correct proportions of these food samples would be balanced and healthy.

Balanced Diets

A balanced diet must contain enough carbohydrates and fats to meet the body's energy needs. It must also contain enough protein of the right kind to provide the essential amino acids to make new cells and tissues for growth or repair. The diet must also contain vitamins and mineral salts, plant fibre and water. Figure 4 shows the composition of four food samples.

Vegetarians can obtain all their nutrients from a diet containing no meat. Their proteins come from cereals, beans, eggs and cheese. Similarly **vegans**, who eat no animal products at all, can obtain all essential nutrients, provided that their vegetable diet is varied.

Energy requirements

Energy can be obtained from carbohydrates, fats and proteins. The cheapest energy-giving food is usually carbohydrate. Fats give as much energy as carbohydrates but are expensive. Whatever mixture of carbohydrate, fat and protein makes up the diet, the total energy must be sufficient (1) to keep our internal body processes working (for example, to

(1 megajoule = 1000 kJ)

Figure 5   Energy needs according to age, sex and occupation

keep the heart beating), (2) to keep up our body temperature and (3) to meet the needs of work and other activities.

The amount of energy that can be obtained from food is measured in calories or joules. One gram of carbohydrate or protein can provide us with up to 17 kJ (kilojoules). A gram of fat can give 37 kJ. We need to obtain about 12 000 kJ of energy each day from our food. Table 3 shows how this figure is made up. However, the figure will vary greatly according to our age, sex, occupation and activity (Figure 5). It is fairly obvious that a person who does hard manual work, such as digging, will use more energy than someone who sits in an office.

People living in tropical climates do not lose so much heat as those living in temperate countries. So they do not need as much energy from their food.

Table 3 Energy requirements in kJ

8 hours asleep	2400
8 hours awake; relatively inactive physically	3000
8 hours physically active	6600
Total	12 000

The 2400 kJ used during 8 hours' sleep represents the energy needed for **basal metabolism** (page 30). This is the energy required for the circulation, breathing, body temperature, brain function and essential chemical processes in the liver and other organs.

If more food is eaten than is needed to supply the energy demands of the body, the surplus food is stored either as glycogen in the liver (see page 120) or as fat below the skin and in the abdomen.

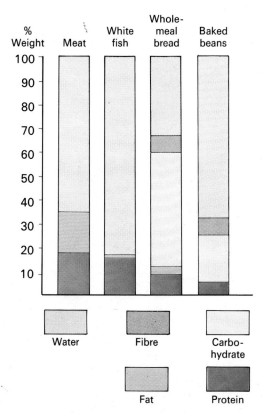

Figure 4   An analysis of four food samples. The percentage of water includes any salts and vitamins. The composition of any given food sample depends on its source and on any method of preservation and cooking that has been used. 'White fish' (such as cod, haddock or plaice) contains only 0.5 per cent fat while herring and mackerel contain up to 14 per cent. White bread contains only 2–3 per cent of fibre. Frying the food adds greatly to its fat content.

Protein requirements

As explained on page 99, proteins are an essential part of the diet because they supply the amino acids needed to build up the body structures. Ideas of how much protein we need have changed over the last few years. A recent FAO/WHO report recommended that an average person needs 0.57 g protein daily for every kilogram of body weight. That is, a 70 kg person would need $70 \times 0.57 = 39.9$ g – about 40 g protein per day. This could be supplied by about 200 g (7 ounces) lean meat or 500 g bread. But 2 kg potatoes would be needed to supply this much protein, and potato protein does not contain all the essential amino acids.

In practice, a diet with the minimum recommended level of protein would be rather unattractive. A more acceptable target is an intake of protein which represents about 10 per cent of the total energy intake. That means between 60 and 70 g of protein per day for an average adult.

Special needs

Pregnancy   A woman who is already receiving an adequate diet needs to take in little extra food when she becomes pregnant. Her metabolism will adapt to the demands of the growing baby. But if her diet is low in protein, calcium, iron or vitamin D, she will need to increase her intake of these substances to meet the baby's needs.

The baby needs protein for making tissues. It also needs calcium and vitamin D for bone development, and iron to make the haemoglobin in its blood.

Lactation   'Lactation' means the production of breast milk for feeding the baby. The production of milk, rich in proteins and minerals, makes a large demand on the mother's body. If her diet is already adequate, her metabolism will adjust to these demands and she will not need much extra food. Otherwise, she may need to increase her intake of proteins, vitamins and calcium to produce enough milk of good quality.

Growing children   Most children up to the age of about 12 years need less food than adults, but they need more in proportion to their body weight. For example, an adult may need 0.57 g protein per kg body weight, but a 6–11 month baby needs 1.53 g per kg, and a 10-year-old needs 0.8 g per kg. Children need the extra protein for making new tissues as they grow.

As well as protein, children need extra calcium for their growing bones, iron for their red blood cells, vitamin D to help calcification of their bones and vitamin A for disease resistance.

Western diets

In the rich societies of the USA, USSR and Europe, there is no general shortage of food. Most people can afford a diet with an adequate energy and protein content.

Many people's diets are not balanced, however. This may lead to **malnutrition** or illnesses in middle age and old age. Malnutrition is not simply the result of not getting enough food. It can also be caused by eating too much food of the wrong kind, or by not getting enough vitamins or minerals.

Too much sugar   White sugar (sucrose) is made by refining (purifying) the sugar from sugar cane or sugar beet. Refined sugar is used in sweets, jam, biscuits and soft drinks. It is also added to many other processed foods.

Sugar is an important cause of tooth decay (page 193). But refined sugar also affects us in many other ways. It is a very concentrated source of energy. You can absorb a lot of sugar from biscuits, ice-cream, sweets, soft drinks, tinned fruits and sweet tea without ever feeling 'full up' so you tend to eat more sugar than your body needs. Eating a lot of refined sugar, therefore, causes some people to become overweight.

Too much fat   In some people, a fatty layer forms in the lining of arteries and leads to coronary heart disease (page 138). This layer contains lipids and a substance called cholesterol. The more lipid and cholesterol you have in your blood, the more likely you are to have a coronary heart attack. Many doctors and scientists think that if you eat too much fat, you raise the level of fats and cholesterol in your

Figure 6   Margarine made from sunflower oil. Notice that the cholesterol content is low and the unsaturated fatty acids (polyunsaturates) are high.

blood and so put yourself at risk. There is still a good deal of argument about this, but until more is known, it seems to be a good idea to keep a low level of fats in your diet. For example, some doctors think that no more than 30 per cent of your energy intake should come from fat. There is rather less argument about the correlation between a high-fat diet and the incidence of gallstones and of cancer of the large intestine.

There are reasons to believe that animal fats such as butter, cream, some kinds of cheese, egg-yolk and the fat present in meat might be more harmful than some vegetable oils. Animal fats are digested to give what are called **saturated** fatty acids (because of the structure of their molecules). Many of the fats and oils from plants, such as the oil from sunflower seeds, contain **unsaturated** fatty acids (Figure 6). These are thought to be less likely to cause fatty deposits in the arteries. It may thus be better to fry food in vegetable oil and to use margarine from certain vegetable oils rather than butter. This is still a matter for debate, however.

Too much salt? To replace the salt lost in sweat we need to take in about 3 g sodium chloride a day. Many communities seem perfectly healthy with less, however. On average, we take in about 10 g a day (Table 4). We excrete the excess in urine and sweat.

Table 4 Our average daily intake of salt

Salt occurring in food	3.0 g
Salt added to processed food	3.8 g
Salt added in cooking or afterwards	3.2 g

Some studies show a correlation between a high salt intake and an increase in blood pressure, particularly over a long period of time. (High blood pressure can lead to strokes and heart attacks.) Communities whose life styles are very different but whose salt intake is low show little or no increase in blood pressure with age.

Not all scientists agree, however, that a high salt intake, over a long period, *causes* a rise in blood pressure. (One difficulty is in deciding how much salt people actually eat.) Some believe that the animal studies prove nothing about humans, and that only people already predisposed to high blood pressure are affected by salt.

But if we need only 3 g or less salt per day, it seems unnecessary to take in more. You can cut your salt intake by not adding it to food either before or after cooking. Another way is to avoid processed foods, some of which contain large amounts of salt.

Too little fibre Most of us eat too many processed foods, such as sugar, which have been purified from their vegetable sources. And we eat too much white bread, from which the bran has been removed. Unprocessed foods such as potatoes, vegetables and fruit contain a large amount of fibre. Fibre prevents

constipation and probably other disorders and diseases of the intestine, including cancer. Eating a diet with a lot of fibre makes you feel 'full up' and so stops you from over-eating. A 100 g portion of boiled potato provides only 340 kJ. (A potato about the size of an egg weighs 50–70 g.) You could feel quite full after eating 300 g of potatoes but would have taken in only 1000 kJ. A 100 g bar of milk chocolate will give you 2400 kJ, but it is not filling. So a high-fibre diet helps to keep your weight down without leaving you feeling hungry all the time.

Too much 'junk food' Mass-produced processed food often contains too much sugar and fat and too many additives. It is also low in vitamins and fibre. Eaten once in a while it is harmless enough. But a diet containing a lot of these products would be very unbalanced.

Too much of everything If you eat more food than your body requires for its energy needs or for building tissues, you are likely to store the surplus as fat and so become over-weight (Figure 7). An over-weight person is much more likely to suffer from high blood pressure, coronary heart disease and diabetes than someone whose weight is about right. Being fat also makes you less willing to take exercise because you have to carry the extra weight around.

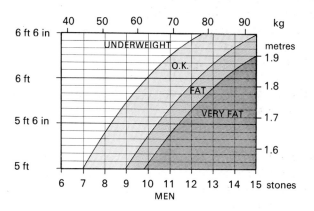

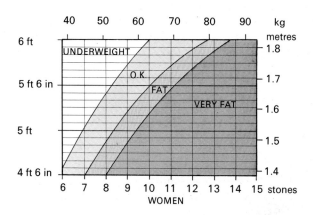

Figure 7   Height and weight. These tables are intended for adults who have reached their full height. They would find their height on the vertical scales and look along the horizontal lines until they reach their weight.
(By permission of the Health Education Authority, London)

Whether you put on weight or not depends to some extent on genetics. You may inherit the tendency to get fat. Some people seem able to 'burn off' their excess food as heat and never get fat, no matter how much they eat. You can't change your genetics but you can avoid putting on too much weight by controlling your diet. This may not mean eating less, but simply eating differently. Avoid sugar and all processed food with a high sugar level, such as sweets, cakes and biscuits. Eat more vegetables, fruit and wholemeal bread. Your teeth, waistline, intestines and health in general will benefit from such a change in diet.

Controversies about diet

Apart from malnutrition, allergies and deficiency diseases, the evidence which links diet to the degenerative diseases of middle and old age (see page 261) is largely circumstantial. Some evidence comes from experiments on animals, which may give results that do not apply to humans. Some consists of comparisons between death rates from diseases (such as heart attacks), or the incidence of certain illnesses (such as cancer of the large intestine), in communities whose diets are significantly different.

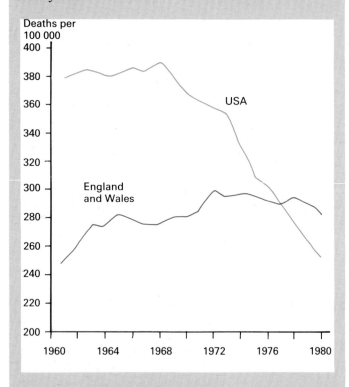

Figure 8   Deaths from coronary heart disease in England and Wales, compared with those in the USA. Between 1957 and 1976 the proportion of butter, lard and beef fat in American diets fell from 46 per cent to 18 per cent of total fat intake. The proportion of vegetable oils rose from 54 per cent to 82 per cent. There may have been other reasons why deaths from heart disease fell. For example, people may have been smoking less or exercising more.
(This first appeared in *New Scientist*, London)

The evidence can be interpreted in different ways. Most experimental trials on humans have not produced convincing results. Critics say that, for example, saturated fats or salt are harmful only to people whose metabolism is already faulty. They point out that there are other differences between populations, besides their diet.

All the same, the circumstantial evidence is quite strong. More and more, well-informed advisers recommend us to eat less saturated fat, refined sugar and salt, and to eat more fibre. If you can follow these suggestions without become over-anxious or a 'food fanatic', it seems sensible to do so.

Slimming

If you are over-weight, you can reduce your body weight by (a) eating less and (b) taking more exercise. If your body weight is steady the energy value of the food you eat must equal your energy expenditure. To lose weight, you must either take in food of less energy value than you are using, or increase your energy output until it exceeds the energy value of your food.

The energy value of body fat (which contains some protein) is about 32 kJ per g. Therefore, to lose 1 kg of adipose tissue (fatty tissue) in a week, you would need to reduce the energy content of your diet to 32 000 kJ below your average weekly output. That means taking in about 5000 kJ per day less than you need. The shortfall is made up by using some of your surplus adipose tissue for energy.

A man who walks for one hour uses up 1250 kJ. This is equivalent to only 40 g adipose tissue. So eating less food seems to be more effective than taking exercise in reducing weight. A combination of both is probably best. Short-term weight losses which result from vigorous dieting probably represent loss of water, glycogen and protein rather than adipose tissue. The best solution is a long-term change in diet and pattern of exercise.

A 'slimming diet' must always contain enough energy to keep basal metabolism going and for all normal activity. It must also include the necessary proteins, vitamins and salts. The diet should reduce sugar and fat, though some fat, such as margarine or vegetable oil, is essential. Green vegetables are usually filling without containing much energy. But if you want to lose weight you must get used to leaving the table while still feeling hungry.

It is worth consulting diet sheets from your local health centre in order to work out a diet which is both nutritious and palatable. Commercially marketed 'slimming formulae' are no more effective than a carefully regulated diet of natural food. 'Slimming' drugs have not been shown to be effective and may be harmful.

Anorexia nervosa

This is a neurosis (page 273) which sometimes affects adolescent girls. They develop a dislike of food and take in so little that they lose a great deal of weight. They can even die from starvation. They sometimes claim that they are dieting because they are over-weight. This is usually a rationalization of a much deeper psychological cause, which has little to do with diet or food but may be associated with 'coming to terms' with maturation and sexuality. The sufferer usually needs treatment by a doctor or a psychiatrist.

Alcohol

Alcohol in drinks such as beer, wine and spirits can be used as a source of energy (29 kJ per g). Alcohol can also be converted to fats. However, it is not a desirable food source. It lacks other nutrients and has harmful effects on the body (see page 270).

QUESTIONS

9 Make a list of the food and other substances that are needed to make up a balanced diet.
10 Why is it better to take in regular, small amounts of protein rather than to eat a large amount of protein at one meal? (Revise page 99.)
11 Select one food class and one mineral salt which are particularly important in the diet of *all three* of the following: pregnant woman, woman breast-feeding a baby, growing child.
12 (a) If you feel 'peckish' between meals, why is it better to eat an apple than a bar of chocolate?
  (b) If you are going to do a long-distance walk, why is it better to take chocolate bars than apples?
13 One hundred grams of boiled potato will give you 340 kJ of energy, but 100 grams of chips give you 900 kJ. Why do you think there is such a big difference?
14 Why should a 'high-fibre' diet help to stop you putting on weight?
15 It is sometimes believed that a person who does hard, physical work needs to eat a lot of protein. Try to explain why this is not true.
16 How much protein would a 5 kg baby need each day?
17 From Table 3 on page 103, work out the approximate minimum amount of energy needed each day to maintain your basal metabolism.

18 In comparing communities for salt intake and high blood pressure, the text speaks of 'communities whose life styles are very different'. Why do you think this proviso is made?

Preserving and Processing

Food preservation

If food is kept for any length of time before it is eaten it may start to 'go off'. This may be because it is attacked by its own enzymes, oxidized by the air or – more important – decomposed by bacteria and fungi. All these processes make the food taste and smell unpleasant. But the greatest harm is likely to result from the fungi and bacteria.

Both kinds of organism may produce poisonous compounds (toxins) which make us ill if we eat them. For example, bacteria cause **Salmonella** poisoning. Cooking the food may kill the organisms but may not destroy the toxins they have already produced.

Methods of food preservation try to prevent the food's own enzymes from working and to stop the growth of fungi and bacteria.

Pasteurization Milk is heated to 72 °C for 15 seconds (or to 60 °C for 30 minutes) and then cooled rapidly. This does not sterilize the milk, but does destroy the bacteria which might cause diseases like tuberculosis.

Refrigeration Most refrigerators are kept at 4 °C. At this temperature, bacteria reproduce very slowly but they are not killed. The activity of any enzymes in the food is also slowed down.

Food which has been refrigerated should be eaten cold or thoroughly heated. If it is simply warmed up, any bacteria which are present will be able to multiply rapidly.

Both pasteurization and refrigeration are short-term methods of food preservation. They keep food fresh for several days. The following examples are long-term methods of preservation, and last for months.

Freezing A 'deep-freeze' cabinet keeps food at a temperature of −18 °C or below. Bacteria are not killed but they cannot grow or reproduce. Food may be kept for between three and twelve months.

After frozen food has been thawed it must not be re-frozen. This is because, during thawing, any bacteria which are present may multiply rapidly and re-freezing will not kill them.

Drying (dehydration) Removal of water stops the enzymes from working and prevents the growth of bacteria and fungi. The food is usually dried under low air pressure. This makes the water evaporate without raising the food to a temperature at which it would start to cook. The dehydrated food is sealed in packets and kept at room temperature until it is reconstituted by adding water.

Canning Food is enclosed in cans which are sealed and heated to 120 °C to destroy enzymes and bacteria. Bacteria cannot enter the cans. So canned food can remain good to eat for years, provided the cans are not damaged or corroded.

Salting Impregnating food with salts, such as sodium chloride or sodium nitrate, lowers its osmotic potential. Any bacteria that land on the food will be killed because the salt extracts water from them by osmosis (page 36).

Syrup Food soaked in concentrated sugar solutions has the same osmotic effect on bacteria as salted food.

Pickling The ethanoic (acetic) acid in vinegar lowers the pH so far that bacteria cannot grow and enzymes are inhibited.

Ultra-high temperature (UHT) Milk is heated under pressure to 132 °C for one second and sealed in cartons or plastic bottles. All the bacteria are killed and so the milk will keep for months. There is a slight change of flavour.

Irradiation If food is packed in sealed plastic wrapping and exposed to X-rays or gamma-rays, any bacteria present are killed. The wrapping then prevents any more bacteria getting in. The food does not become radioactive because the radiation dose is too low.

The flavour, texture and colour of some foods are altered by radiation, however, and the vitamin content may be reduced. At present, the sale of irradiated food is not permitted in Britain except under licence.

Food additives

About 3500 different chemicals may be used by the processed food industry. These chemicals have no food value but are added to food (1) to stop it going bad, (2) to 'improve' its colour or (3) to alter or enhance its flavour.

Preservatives There is always a time lag between harvesting a perishable food, processing it, packaging it and sending it to the food shops. The food also spends time on the shelf in the shop and in the kitchen. Thus, except for dried or frozen food, some chemical method of preservation is needed to stop bacterial growth.

Two chemical preservatives are sodium nitrite (E250) and sulphur dioxide (E220). Sodium nitrite is added to cured meat (ham or bacon, for example). It prevents the growth of bacteria, particularly *Clostridium botulinum* which causes a deadly form of food poisoning called botulism. Sulphur dioxide is added to jams, fruit juices, beer and wine. It suppresses the growth of bacteria and fungi in these products.

Other additives Of the 3500 additives, only about 1 per cent are preservatives. The rest are flavourings, colourings, stabilizers and bulking agents (Figure 9).

Flavouring

One widely used flavouring is monosodium glutamate, made from sugar beet pulp and wheat protein. It is described as a 'flavour enhancer', and may achieve its effect by promoting the flow of saliva or stimulating the taste receptors on the tongue.

Sugar is a widely used flavouring agent. We expect to find it in cakes and biscuits. But it turns up in many unexpected places too – in instant baby cereal (34 per cent in certain brands), tomato sauce (14 per cent), frozen peas (7 per cent) and baked beans (5 per cent).

Colouring

Many substances (for example chlorophyll, saffron and turmeric) used for colouring food are from natural sources. This does not necessarily mean that they are harmless. Others are synthetic dyes. For example, tartrazine, sunset yellow and carmoisine are 'azo' dyes, and are known to cause allergic reactions in some people.

'Bulking agents'

Some substances, such as sodium polyphosphate (E450), are added to meat (ham and poultry particularly) as so-called 'tenderizers'. In fact they serve mainly to promote the absorption of water into the meat by osmosis, so that it weighs more.

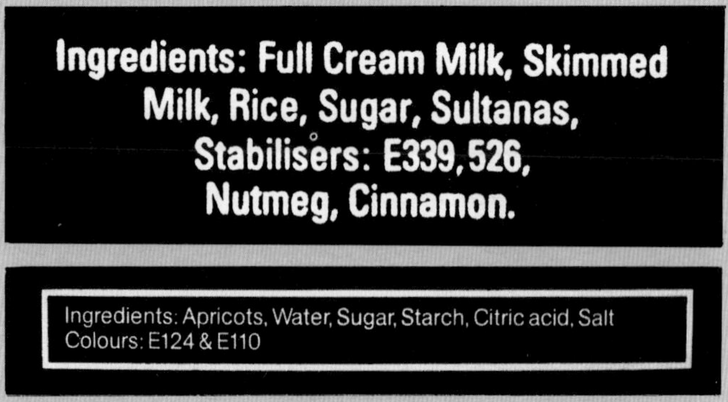

Ingredients: Full Cream Milk, Skimmed Milk, Rice, Sugar, Sultanas, Stabilisers: E339, 526, Nutmeg, Cinnamon.

Ingredients: Apricots, Water, Sugar, Starch, Citric acid, Salt Colours: E124 & E110

Figure 9 Additives. E339 is sodium dihydrogen phosphate, E526 is calcium hydroxide; these keep the pH steady and keep the liquid components in a stable emulsion (stop them separating out). E124 and E110 are azo dyes (red and yellow); these may cause allergic reactions, especially in asthmatics and in people who react badly to aspirin.

Possible harmful effects Only about 300 of the additives are regulated by law. But the food industry tests all the additives, usually by feeding them in large doses to animals. The results need not necessarily apply to humans, however. Some workers, for example, believe that animal tests may be only 37 per cent successful in detecting cancer-causing properties.

There is little widely accepted evidence to show that food additives are harmful. Most allergic reactions are caused by naturally occurring substances in food (such as strawberries and shellfish) rather than by additives.

However, the yellow dye tartrazine (E102) does cause asthma and skin rashes in a few people. Eczema in some children has been relieved by keeping artificial colour and flavouring out of their diets.

Some studies have linked behavioural problems in children with additives in food. The results have been questioned, however. The school work of 800 000 children in New York significantly improved when colourings, flavourings and some preservatives were left out of their school meals. But other improvements were made in their diet as well (less sugar, fat and salt, and more vitamins and minerals).

Most of us unwittingly eat a kilogram or more of additives each year with no obvious harm, but it is hard to tell if the additives have a long-term effect. The risks of cancer from eating cured meat are far lower than the risk of serious bacterial poisoning from eating unprocessed meat.

Nevertheless, only a tiny proportion of all the additives eaten are used to make the food safe. Many people question the wisdom of using so many unregulated additives that have no food value, raise the cost of food and are not essential for a safe and healthy diet.

QUESTIONS

19 What biological principles (relating to enzymes, bacteria and osmosis) are applied in food preservation?
20 Give some examples of foods in your home which are (a) dehydrated, (b) frozen, (c) canned and (d) pickled.
21 Which methods of preservation make food sterile (that is, free from all bacteria)?
22 Look at cans and packets of food in your home. Make a list of the additives. Are there any nutrients in a can of soft drink?
23 What kind of evidence can help people decide whether a food additive is harmful or not?

PRACTICAL WORK

1 Food tests

See page 285 for the preparation of iodine and Benedict's solutions.

(a) Test for starch Shake a little starch powder in a test-tube with some cold water and then boil it to make a clear solution. When the solution is cold, add three or four drops of **iodine solution**. A dark blue colour should be produced.

(b) Test for glucose Heat a little glucose with some **Benedict's solution** in a test-tube. Do this by placing the test-tube in a beaker of boiling water (see Figure 10). The solution will change from clear blue to cloudy green, then yellow and finally to a red precipitate (deposit) of copper(I) oxide.

(c) Test for protein (biuret test) To a 1 per cent solution of albumen (the protein of egg-white) add 5 cm³ dilute sodium hydroxide (*CARE*: this solution is caustic). Then add 5 cm³ 1 per cent copper sulphate solution. A purple colour means that protein is present.

(d) Test for fat Shake 2 drops of cooking oil with about 5 cm³ alcohol (ethanol) in a dry test-tube until the fat dissolves. Pour the alcoholic solution into a test-tube containing a few cm³ water. A cloudy white emulsion will form. This shows that the solution contained some fat or oil.

Alternatively, drop a little of the alcoholic solution on to a piece of white paper and allow it to evaporate. It will leave a translucent spot (grease spot) on the paper, showing that fat is present.

(e) Test for vitamin C Draw up 2 cm³ fresh lemon juice into a plastic syringe. Add this juice drop by drop to 2 cm³ of a 0.1 per cent solution of PIDCP (a blue dye) in a test-tube. The PIDCP will become colourless quite suddenly as the juice is added. The amount of juice added from the syringe should be noted down. Repeat the experiment but with orange juice in the syringe. If it takes more orange juice than lemon juice to decolorize the PIDCP, the orange juice must contain less vitamin C.

2 Application of the food tests

The tests can be used on samples of food such as milk, potato, raisins, onion, beans, egg-yolk, peanuts, to find what food materials are present. Crush the solid samples in a mortar and shake the product with warm water to extract the soluble products. Test separate samples of the watery mixture of crushed food for starch, glucose or protein as described above. To test for fats, crush the food first in ethanol, not water, and then filter the mixture. Pour the clear filtrate into water to see if it goes cloudy, meaning that fats are present. (See Figure 10.)

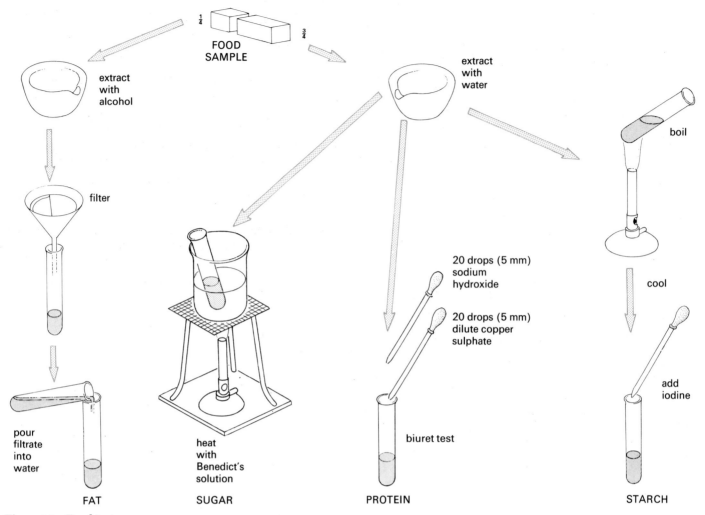

Figure 10   Food tests

3   Energy from food

Arrange the apparatus as shown in Figure 11. Use a measuring cylinder to place 100 cm³ cold water in the can. With a thermometer, find the temperature of the water and make a note of it. In a nickel crucible or tin lid place 1 g sugar and heat it with the bunsen flame until it begins to burn. As soon as it starts burning, slide the crucible under the can so that the flames heat the water. If the flame goes out, do not apply the bunsen burner to the crucible while it is under the can, but return the crucible to the bunsen

flame to start the sugar burning again. Replace the crucible beneath the can as soon as the sugar catches light. When the sugar has finished burning and cannot be ignited again, gently stir the water in the can with the thermometer and record its new temperature. Calculate the rise in temperature by subtracting the first temperature from the second. Work out the quantity of energy transferred to the water from the burning sugar as follows.

4.2 joules raise 1 g water 1 °C
100 cm³ cold water weighs 100 g
Let the rise in temperature be T °C

To raise 1 g water 1 °C needs 4.2 joules
∴To raise 100 g water 1 °C needs 100×4.2 joules
∴To raise 100 g water T °C needs $T \times 100 \times 4.2$ joules
∴1 g burning sugar produced $420 \times T$ joules

The experiment may now be repeated using 1 g vegetable oil instead of sugar and replacing the warm water in the can with 100 cm³ cold water.
(**Note**   The experiment is very inaccurate because much of the heat from the burning food escapes into the air without reaching the water. But since the errors are about the same for both samples, the results can at least be used to compare the amounts of energy released from sugar and oil.)

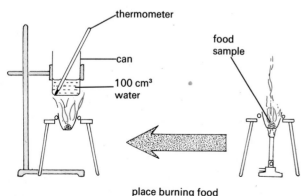

Figure 11   Energy from food

CHECK LIST

- Our diets must contain proteins, carbohydrates, fats, minerals, vitamins, fibre and water.
- Fats, carbohydrates and proteins provide energy.
- Proteins provide amino acids for the growth and replacement of the tissues.
- Mineral salts like calcium and iron are needed in tissues such as bone and blood.
- Vegetable fibre helps to keep the intestine healthy.
- Adolescents and adults need about 10–12 thousand kilojoules of energy each day from their food.
- Vitamins are essential in small quantities for chemical reactions in cells.
- The fat-soluble vitamins A and D occur mainly in animal products.
- Most cereals contain vitamins of the B group.
- Vitamin C occurs in certain fruits and in green leaves.
- Lack of vitamin A can lead to blindness. Shortage of vitamin C causes scurvy. Shortage of vitamin D causes rickets.
- Growing children have special dietary needs.
- Western diets often contain too much sugar and fat and too little fibre.
- Methods of food preservation aim to stop enzymes working and to suppress growth of fungi and bacteria.

12 Digestion, Absorption and Use of Food

The Alimentary Canal
Structure, function, peristalsis.

Digestion
Definition. Mouth, stomach, small intestine.

Absorption
Absorption in the small and large intestine.

Use and Storage of Digested Food
Glucose, fats, amino acids.

The Liver
Functions.

Practical Work
Experiments on digestion. Salivary amylase and pepsin.

When we eat we take food into the mouth, chew it and swallow it down into the stomach. This satisfies our hunger, but for food to be of any use to the whole body it has first to be **digested** and **absorbed**. This means that the food is dissolved, passed into the bloodstream and carried by the blood all round the body. In this way, the blood takes dissolved food to the living cells in all parts of the body such as the muscles, brain, heart and kidneys. This chapter describes how the food is digested and absorbed. Chapter 13 describes how the blood carries it round the body.

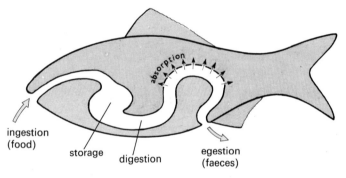

Figure 1　The alimentary canal (generalized)

The Alimentary Canal

The **alimentary canal** is a tube, running through the body. Food is digested in the alimentary canal. The soluble products are absorbed and the undigested residues expelled (egested). Figure 1 shows a simplified diagram of an alimentary canal.

The inside of the alimentary canal is lined with layers of cells, forming what is called an **epithelium**. New cells in the epithelium are being produced all the time to replace the cells worn away by the movement of the food. There are also cells in the lining which produce **mucus**. Mucus is a slimy liquid that makes the lining of the canal slippery and protects it from wear and tear. Mucus may also protect the lining from attack by the **digestive enzymes** which are released into the alimentary canal.

Some of the digestive enzymes are produced by cells in the lining of the alimentary canal, as in the stomach lining. Others are produced by **glands** which are outside the alimentary canal but pour their enzymes through tubes (called **ducts**) into the alimentary canal. The **salivary glands** (shown in Figure 6) and the **pancreas** (Figure 9) are examples of such digestive glands.

The alimentary canal has a great many blood vessels in its walls, close to the lining. These bring oxygen needed by the cells and take away the carbon dioxide they produce. They also absorb the digested food from the alimentary canal.

Peristalsis

The alimentary canal has layers of muscle in its walls (Figure 2). The fibres of one layer of muscles run round the canal (**circular muscle**) and the others run along its length (**longitudinal muscle**). When the circular muscles in one region contract, they make the alimentary canal narrow in that region.

A contraction in one region of the alimentary canal

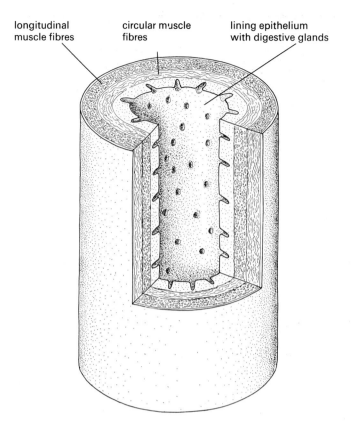

Figure 2   The general structure of the alimentary canal

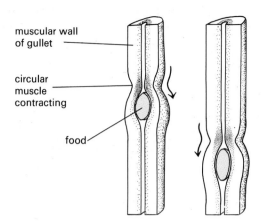

Figure 3   Diagram of peristalsis in the gullet

is followed by another contraction just below it so that a wave of contraction passes along the canal pushing food in front of it.

The wave of contraction, called **peristalsis**, is illustrated in Figure 3.

QUESTIONS

1 What three functions of the alimentary canal are shown in Figure 1?
2 Into what parts of the alimentary canal do (a) the pancreas, (b) the salivary glands, pour their digestive juices?
3 Starting from the inside, name the layers of tissue that make up the alimentary canal.

Digestion

Digestion is a chemical process. It is the breaking down of large molecules to small molecules. Most of the large molecules are not soluble in water, while the smaller ones are. The small molecules can pass through the epithelium of the alimentary canal, through the walls of the blood vessels and into the blood.

Some food can be absorbed without digestion. The glucose in fruit juice, for example, can pass through the walls of the alimentary canal and enter the blood vessels. Most food is solid, however, and cannot get into blood vessels. Digestion is the process by which solid food is dissolved to make a solution.

The chemicals that dissolve the food are enzymes, described on page 22. These digestive enzymes are extra-cellular (see page 23). They are made inside the cells of the digestive glands, and then pass out of the cells into the cavity of the alimentary canal.

Digestive enzymes speed up digestion. A protein might take 50 years to dissolve if just placed in water. Enzymes can digest it completely in a few hours. All the solid starch in foods such as bread and potatoes is digested to **glucose**, which is soluble in

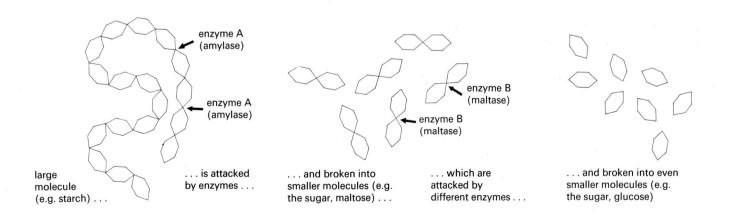

Figure 4   Enzymes acting on starch

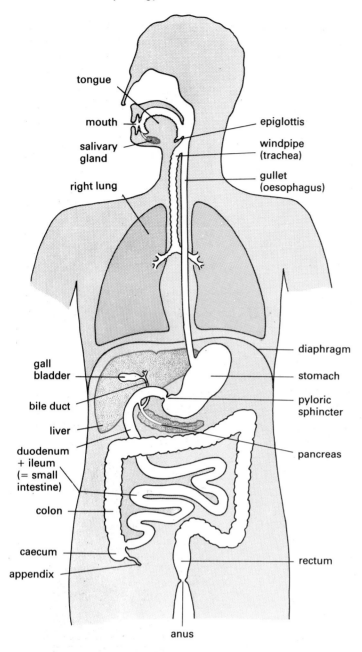

Figure 5 The digestive system

water. The solid proteins in meat, egg and beans are digested to soluble **amino acids**. Fats are digested to two soluble products called **glycerol** and **fatty acids** (see page 20).

The chemical breakdown usually takes place in stages. For example, the starch molecule is made up of hundreds of carbon, hydrogen and oxygen atoms. The first stage of digestion breaks it down to a sugar containing 12 carbon atoms in its molecule, called **maltose**. The last stage of digestion breaks the maltose molecule into two 6-carbon sugar molecules called glucose (Figure 4). Protein molecules are digested first to smaller molecules called **peptides** and finally into the soluble amino acids:

$$starch \rightarrow maltose \rightarrow glucose$$

$$protein \rightarrow peptide \rightarrow amino\ acid$$

These stages take place in different parts of the alimentary canal.

The progress of food through the canal and the stages of digestion will now be described (Figures 5 and 6).

The mouth

The act of taking food into the mouth is called **ingestion**. In the mouth, the food is chewed and mixed with **saliva**. The chewing breaks the food into pieces which can be swallowed and it also increases the surface area for the enzymes to work on later. Saliva is a digestive juice produced by three pairs of glands whose ducts lead into the mouth (Figure 6). It helps to lubricate the food and make the small pieces stick together. Saliva contains one enzyme, **salivary amylase**, which acts on cooked starch and begins to break it down into maltose.

> Strictly speaking, the 'mouth' is the opening between the lips. The space inside, containing the tongue and teeth, is called the **buccal cavity**. Beyond the buccal cavity is the 'throat' or **pharynx**.

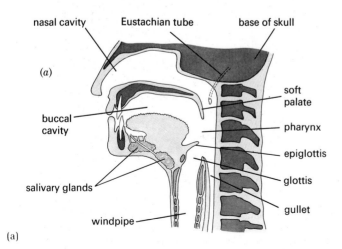

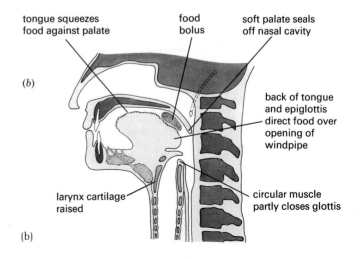

Figure 6 Section through the head, to show swallowing action

Swallowing

Figure 6 (a) shows that for food to enter the gullet (oesophagus), it has to pass over the windpipe. All the complicated movements of swallowing ensure that food does not enter the windpipe and cause choking.

1 The tongue presses upwards and back against the roof of the mouth, forcing a pellet of food, called a **bolus**, to the back of the mouth.
2 The soft palate closes the nasal cavity at the back.
3 The larynx cartilage round the top of the windpipe is pulled upwards so that the opening of the windpipe (the **glottis**) lies under the back of the tongue.
4 The glottis is also partly closed by the contraction of a ring of muscle.
5 The **epiglottis**, a flap of cartilage (page 182), helps to prevent the food from going down the windpipe instead of the gullet.

The beginning of the swallowing action is voluntary. But once the food reaches the back of the mouth, swallowing becomes an automatic or reflex action. The food is forced into and down the gullet by peristalsis. This takes about 6 seconds with solid food, and rather less with liquids. Then the food enters the stomach.

The stomach

The stomach has elastic walls which stretch as the food collects in it. The **pyloric sphincter** is a circular band of muscle at the lower end of the stomach which stops solid pieces of food from passing through. The stomach stores the food from a meal, turns it into a liquid and releases it in small quantities at a time to the rest of the alimentary canal.

Glands in the lining of the stomach (Figure 7) produce **gastric juice** containing the enzyme **pepsin**.

Pepsin is a **protease** (or proteinase). It acts on proteins and breaks them down into soluble compounds called peptides (page 20). The stomach lining also produces hydrochloric acid, which makes a weak solution in the gastric juice. This acid provides the best degree of acidity for pepsin to work in (see page 23). It also kills many of the bacteria taken in with the food.

The regular, peristaltic movements of the stomach, about once every 20 seconds, mix up the food and gastric juice into a creamy liquid. How long food remains in the stomach depends on its nature. Water may pass through in a few minutes; a meal of carbohydrate such as porridge may be held in the stomach for less than an hour, but a mixed meal containing protein and fat may be in the stomach for an hour or two.

The pyloric sphincter lets the liquid products of digestion pass, a little at a time, into the first part of the small intestine called the **duodenum**.

The pyloric sphincter closes as each wave of peristalsis passes down the stomach and also when the acid contents of the stomach enter the duodenum. It then remains closed until the duodenal contents are partially neutralized.

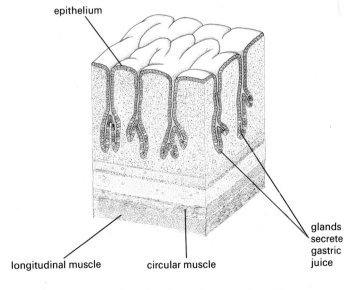

Figure 7 Diagram of section through stomach wall

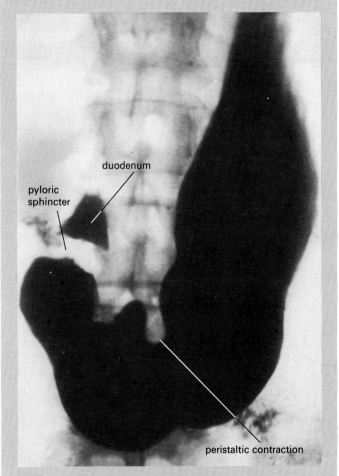

Figure 8 X-ray of stomach containing barium meal. The barium meal, which appears black, has started to enter the duodenum. The clear gap in this region represents the pyloric sphincter.

The stomach contractions can be followed by swallowing a small balloon attached to a long tube. The balloon is inflated and the pressure changes are monitored by connecting the tube to a manometer.

The peristaltic movements of the alimentary canal in general can be followed by observing the passage of a barium-containing meal by using X-rays (Figure 8). Barium sulphate is opaque to X-rays. So the meal can be watched travelling along the alimentary canal by using an X-ray screen.

The small intestine

A digestive juice from the pancreas (**pancreatic juice**) and bile from the liver pour into the duodenum to act on food there. The pancreas is a digestive gland lying below the stomach (Figure 9). It makes several enzymes, which act on all classes of food. There are several proteases which break down proteins to peptides and amino acids. **Pancreatic amylase** attacks starch and converts it to maltose. **Lipase** digests fats (lipids) to fatty acids and glycerol.

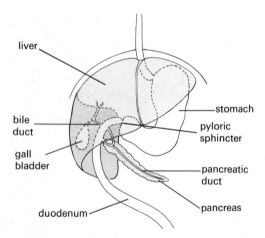

Figure 9   Relationship between stomach, liver and pancreas

Pancreatic juice contains sodium hydrogencarbonate, which partly neutralizes the acid liquid from the stomach. This is necessary because the enzymes of the pancreas do not work well in acid conditions.

Bile is a green, watery fluid made in the liver, stored in the gall bladder and delivered to the duodenum by the bile duct (Figure 9). Bile contains no enzymes. Its green colour is caused by bile pigments, such as **bilirubin**. These are formed in the liver from the breakdown of haemoglobin from worn-out red blood cells. Bile also contains bile salts which act on fats rather like a detergent. The bile salts **emulsify** the fats. That is, they break them up into small drops which are more easily digested by lipase.

All the digestible material is thus changed to soluble compounds. These can pass through the lining of the intestine and into the bloodstream. The final products of digestion are:

food	final products
starch	→ glucose
proteins	→ amino acids
fats (lipids)	→ fatty acids and glycerol

The small intestine itself does not appear to liberate digestive enzymes. The structure labelled 'crypt' in Figure 12 is not a digestive gland, though some of its cells do produce mucus and other secretions. The main function of the crypts is to produce new epithelial cells to replace those lost from the tips of the villi (see 'Absorption', below).

The epithelial cells of the villi contain enzymes in their cell membranes. These enzymes complete the breakdown of sugars and peptides, before they pass through the cells on their way to the bloodstream. For example, the enzyme **maltase** converts the disaccharide maltose into the monosaccharide glucose.

Prevention of self-digestion   The gland cells of the stomach and pancreas make protein-digesting enzymes (proteases). Yet the proteins of the cells that make these enzymes are not digested. One reason for this is that the proteases are secreted in an inactive form. Pepsin is produced as **pepsinogen** and does not become the active enzyme until it encounters the hydrochloric acid in the stomach. The lining of the stomach is protected from the action of pepsin, probably by the layer of mucus.

Similarly **trypsin**, one of the proteases from the pancreas, is secreted as the inactive **trypsinogen**. It is activated by **enterokinase**, an enzyme secreted by the lining of the duodenum.

Control of secretion

The sight, smell and taste of food set off nerve impulses from the sense organs to the brain. These impulses are relayed by the brain to the stomach, and make the gastric glands start to secrete. When the food reaches the stomach, it stimulates the stomach lining to produce a hormone (page 214) called **gastrin**. This hormone circulates in the blood. When it returns to the stomach in the bloodstream, it stimulates the gastric glands to continue secretion. Thus gastric secretion goes on all the time food is present.

In a similar way, the pancreas is affected first by nervous impulses and then by the hormone **secretin**. Secretin is released into the blood from cells in the duodenum when they are stimulated by the acid contents of the stomach. When secretin reaches the pancreas, it stimulates it to produce pancreatic juice.

Caecum and appendix

In humans, the caecum and appendix are small structures, possibly without digestive functions. (The appendix functions as a lymphoid organ (page 132), however.) In grass-eating animals (herbivores), like the cow and the rabbit, the caecum and appendix are much larger. This is where digestion of the cellulose in plant cell walls takes place, largely as a result of bacterial activity.

QUESTIONS

4 Why can't you breathe while you are swallowing?
5 Why is it necessary for our food to be digested? Why don't plants need a digestive system? (See page 41.)
6 In which parts of the alimentary canal is (a) starch, (b) protein digested?
7 Study the characteristics of enzymes on pages 22-4.
    (a) Suggest a more logical name for pepsin.
    (b) In what ways does pepsin show the characteristics of an enzyme?

Absorption

The small intestine consists of two parts: the duodenum and the **ileum**. Nearly all the absorption of digested food takes place in the ileum. It absorbs efficiently for the following reasons:

1 It is fairly long and presents a large absorbing surface to the digested food.
2 Its internal surface is greatly increased by circular folds (Figure 10) bearing thousands of tiny projections called **villi** (singular = villus) (Figures 11 and 12). The villi are about 0.5 millimetre long. They may be finger-like or flattened in shape.
3 The lining epithelium is very thin and the fluids can pass rapidly through it. The outer membrane of each epithelial cell carries microvilli (page 34). These increase by 20 times the exposed surface of the cell.
4 There is a dense network of blood capillaries (tiny blood vessels, see page 130) in each villus (Figure 12).

The small molecules of the digested food, such as glucose and amino acids, pass into the epithelial

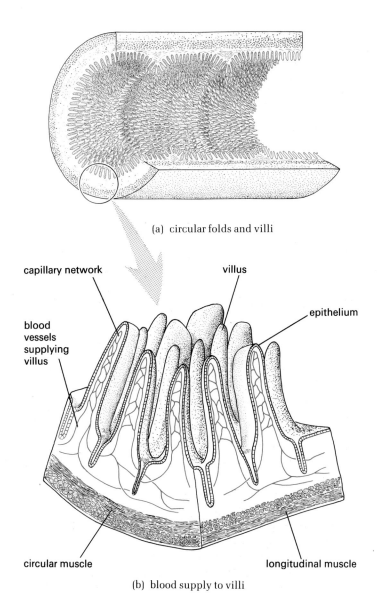

(a) circular folds and villi

(b) blood supply to villi

Figure 10   The absorbing surface of the ileum

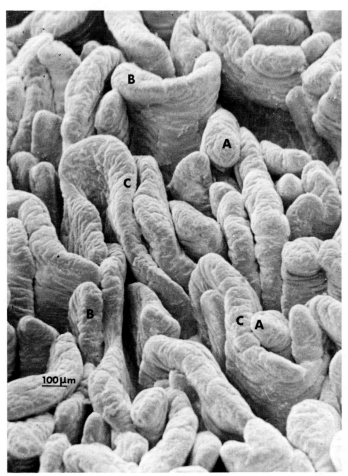

Figure 11   Scanning electron micrograph of the human intestinal lining (×60). The villi are about 0.5 mm long. In the duodenum most villi are leaf-shaped (C). Further towards the ileum they become narrower (B), and in the ileum most are finger-like (A). This micrograph shows the lining of the duodenum.

cells. They move through the wall of the capillaries in the villus and into the bloodstream. They are then carried away in the capillaries which join up to form veins. These veins join up to form one large vein, the **hepatic portal vein** (see Figure 10 on page 129). This vein carries all the blood from the intestine to the liver, which may store or alter any of the digestion products. When these products are released from the liver, they enter the general blood circulation.

Some of the fatty acids and glycerol from the digestion of fats enter the blood capillaries of the villi. However, much of the fatty acids and glycerol may combine to form fats again in the intestinal epithelium. These fats then pass into the **lacteals** (Figure 12). The fluid in the lacteals flows into the **lymphatic system** which forms a network all over the body. Finally, the contents of the lymphatic system are emptied into the bloodstream (see page 132).

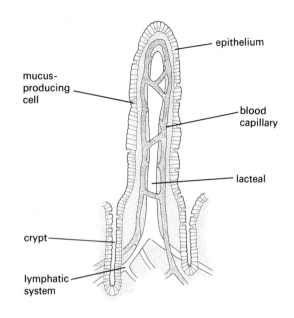

Figure 12   Structure of a single villus

The products of digestion and other dietary items are not absorbed just by simple diffusion, except perhaps for alcohol and, sometimes, water. The mechanisms for transport across the intestinal epithelium have not been fully worked out. The most likely seems to be some form of active transport (page 35). Even water can cross the epithelium against an osmotic gradient (page 34). Amino acids, sugars and salts are, almost certainly, taken up by active transport. Glucose, for example, crosses the epithelium faster than fructose although their rates of diffusion would be about the same.

Water-soluble vitamins may diffuse into the epithelium. Fat-soluble vitamins are carried in the microscopic fat droplets that enter the cells. The ions of mineral salts are probably absorbed by active transport. Calcium ions need vitamin D for their effective absorption.

The epithelial cells of the villi are constantly being shed into the intestine. Rapid cell division in the epithelium of the crypts (Figure 12) replaces these lost cells. In effect there is a steady procession of epithelial cells moving up from the crypts to the villi.

The large intestine (colon and rectum)

The material passing into the large intestine consists of water with undigested matter (largely cellulose and vegetable fibres), mucus and dead cells from the lining of the alimentary canal. The large intestine secretes no enzymes but the bacteria in the colon digest part of the fibre to form fatty acids which the colon can absorb. Bile salts are absorbed and returned to the liver by the blood circulation. The colon also absorbs much of the water from the undigested residues. About 7 litres of digestive juices are poured into the alimentary canal each

day. If the water from these was not absorbed by the ileum and colon, the body would soon be dehydrated.

The semi-solid waste, the **faeces** or 'stool', is passed into the rectum by peristalsis and is expelled at intervals through the anus. The residues may spend from 12 to 24 hours in the intestine. The act of expelling the faeces is called **egestion** or **defecation**.

QUESTIONS

8 What are the products of digestion of (a) starch, (b) protein, (c) fats, which are absorbed by the ileum?
9 What characteristics of the small intestine enable it to absorb digested food efficiently?

Use of Digested Food

The products of digestion are carried round the body in the blood. From the blood, cells absorb and use glucose, fats and amino acids. This uptake and use of food is called **assimilation**.

Glucose   During cell respiration, glucose is oxidized to carbon dioxide and water (see page 28). This reaction provides energy to drive the many chemical processes in the cells.

Amino acids   These are absorbed by the cells and built up, with the aid of enzymes, into proteins. Some of the proteins will become plasma proteins in the blood (page 127). Others may form structures such as the cell membrane. Still others may become enzymes, controlling the chemical activity within the cell. Amino acids not needed for making cell proteins are converted by the liver into glycogen, which can then be used for energy (see below).

Fats   These are built into cell membranes and other cell structures. Fats also form an important source of energy for cell metabolism. Fatty acids, produced from stored fats or taken in with the food, are oxidized in the cells. Carbon dioxide and water are formed, together with energy for processes such as muscle contraction. A gram of fat can provide twice as much energy as a gram of sugar.

QUESTIONS

10 State briefly what happens to a protein molecule in food, from the time it is swallowed to the time its products are built up into the cytoplasm of a muscle cell.

11 List the chemical changes which a starch molecule undergoes, from the time it reaches the duodenum to the time its carbon atoms become part of carbon dioxide molecules. Say where in the body these changes occur.

Storage of Digested Food

If more food is taken in than the body needs for energy or for building tissues, such as bone or muscle, it is stored in one of the following ways:

Glucose   The sugar not required immediately for energy in the cells is changed in the liver to glycogen. The glycogen molecule is built up by combining many glucose molecules into a long-chain molecule, rather like that of starch (see page 21). Some of this insoluble glycogen is stored in the liver and the rest in the muscles. When the blood sugar falls below a certain level, the liver changes its glycogen back to glucose and releases it into the bloodstream. The muscle glycogen is not returned to the blood. It is used by muscle cells as a source of energy during muscular activity.

The glycogen in the liver is a 'short-term' store, enough for only about six hours. Excess glucose not stored as glycogen is converted to fat and stored in the fat depots.

Amino acids   Amino acids are not stored in the body. Those not used in protein formation are **de-aminated** (see page 120). The protein of the liver and other tissues can act as a kind of protein store to maintain the protein level in the blood. But absence of protein in the diet soon leads to serious disorders.

Fat   Unlike glycogen, there is no limit to the amount of fat stored. Because of its high energy value (page 100), it is an effective 'long-term' store. The fat is stored in adipose tissue in the abdomen, round the kidneys and under the skin. These are the **fat depots**. Figures 1–3 on page 159 show the adipose tissue of the skin.

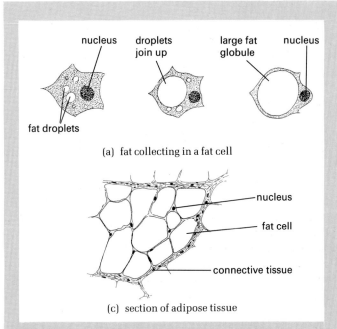

(a) fat collecting in a fat cell

(c) section of adipose tissue

Figure 13   Adipose tissue

In certain cells, drops of fat can collect in the cytoplasm. As these drops increase in size and number, they join together to form one large globule of fat in the middle of the cell, pushing the cytoplasm into a thin layer and the nucleus to one side (Figure 13). Groups of fat cells form **adipose tissue**.

All these conversions of one substance to another need specific enzymes to make them happen.

Body weight

The rate at which glucose is oxidized or changed into glycogen and fat is controlled by hormones (page 214). When intake of carbohydrate and fat is more than enough to meet the energy requirements of the body, the surplus will be stored mainly as fat. Some people never seem to get fat no matter how much they eat. Others start to lay down fat when their intake only just exceeds their needs. Putting on weight is certainly the result of eating more food than the body needs, but it is not clear why people should differ so much in this respect. The explanation probably lies in the balance of hormones. This, to some extent, is determined by heredity.

QUESTIONS

12 List the ways in which the body can store an excess of carbohydrates taken in with the diet.

13 If you ate no food for several days, how would your body meet the demands for energy by your heart and other organs?

The Liver

The liver has been mentioned several times in connection with the digestion, use and storage of food. This is only one aspect of its many important functions, some of which are described below. It is a large, reddish-brown organ which lies just beneath the diaphragm and partly overlaps the stomach. All the blood from the blood vessels of the alimentary canal passes through the liver, which adjusts the composition of the blood before releasing it into the general circulation (Figure 14).

Regulation of blood sugar After a meal, the liver removes excess glucose from the blood and stores it as glycogen. In the periods between meals, when the glucose concentration in the blood starts to fall, the liver converts some of its stored glycogen into glucose and releases it into the bloodstream. In this way, the concentration of sugar in the blood is kept fairly steady.

The concentration of glucose in the blood of a person who has not eaten for eight hours is usually between 90 and 100 mg/100 cm^3 blood. After a meal containing carbohydrate, the blood sugar level may rise to 140 mg/100 cm^3. But two hours later, the level returns to about 95 mg. The liver has converted the excess glucose to glycogen.

About 100 g glycogen is stored in the liver of a healthy man. If the concentration of glucose in the blood falls below about 80 mg/100 cm^3 blood, some of the glycogen stored in the liver is converted by enzyme action into glucose and it enters the circulation. If the blood sugar level rises above 160 mg/100 cm^3, glucose is excreted by the kidneys. A blood glucose level below 40 mg/100 cm^3 is harmful to the brain cells, leading to convulsions and coma. By helping to keep the glucose concentration between 80 and 150 mg/100 cm^3, the liver prevents these harmful effects and so helps in the homeostasis (see page 156) of the body. (The blood supply to the liver is shown in Figure 10 on page 129.)

Production of bile Cells in the liver make bile continuously. Bile is stored in the gall bladder until it is discharged through the bile duct into the duodenum.

The bile also contains bile salts which assist the digestion of fats as described on page 116. Most of the bile salts are re-absorbed in the ileum, along with the fats they have helped to emulsify. Bile salts are also absorbed in the colon.

De-amination The amino acids not needed for making proteins are converted to glycogen in the liver. During this process, the nitrogen-containing, amino part (–NH_2) of the amino acid is removed and changed to **urea**. Urea is later excreted by the kidneys (see page 152).

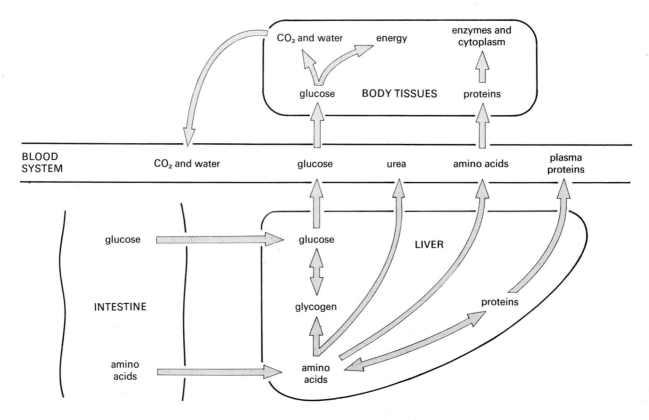

Figure 14   Some functions of the liver

When the –NH$_2$ group is removed from certain amino acids it forms ammonia, NH$_3$ (or, more strictly, the ammonium ion, NH$_4^+$). Ammonia is very poisonous to the body cells, and the liver converts it at once to urea, (NH$_2$)$_2$CO, which is a comparatively harmless substance.

Storage of iron   Millions of red blood cells break down every day. The iron from their haemoglobin (page 125) is stored in the liver.

Manufacture of plasma proteins   The liver makes most of the proteins found in blood plasma. These include fibrinogen, which plays an important part in the clotting action of the blood (page 134).

Detoxication   Poisonous compounds are produced in the large intestine by the action of bacteria on amino acids. These enter the blood, but on reaching the liver are converted to harmless substances, later excreted in the urine. The liver also modifies many other chemical substances normally present in the body or introduced as drugs. They too are then excreted by the kidneys. Hormones, for example, are converted to inactive compounds in the liver, so limiting their period of activity in the body.

Alcohol is one of the poisonous compounds which is detoxified by the liver. Enzymes in the liver oxidize 90 per cent of any alcohol taken into carbon dioxide and water. It takes about three hours to completely oxidize the alcohol in a pint of beer.

Storage of vitamins   The fat-soluble vitamins A and D are stored in the liver. This is why animal liver is a valuable source of these vitamins in the diet.

Heat production   NOTE Contrary to statements made in the 1988 impression, the liver is not a net producer of heat. Although some of its chemical reactions release heat energy, many require an input of energy.

QUESTION

14 Explain how the liver exercises control over the substances coming from the intestine and entering the general blood circulation.

Homeostasis

A complete list of the functions of the liver would be a very long one. Remember, however, that the one vital function of the liver is that it helps to keep a steady concentration and composition of the body fluids, particularly the blood.

Within reason, the kind of food eaten will not produce changes in the composition of the blood.

If this **internal environment**, as it is called, were not so constant, the chemical changes that keep life

going would become erratic and unpredictable. With quite slight changes of diet or activity, the whole organization might break down. This maintenance of the internal environment is called **homeostasis**. It is discussed again on pages 133 and 156.

PRACTICAL WORK

1   The action of salivary amylase on starch

Rinse the mouth with water to remove traces of food. Collect saliva in two test-tubes, labelled A and B, to a depth of about 15 mm (see Figure 15). (If there is any objection to using saliva, use 5 cm^3 of a 5 per cent diastase solution instead.)

Heat the saliva in tube B over a small flame. Let it boil for about 30 seconds. Cool the tube under the tap.

Add about 2 cm^3 of a 2 per cent starch solution to each tube. Shake each tube and leave them for 5 minutes.

Share the contents of tube A between two clean test-tubes. To one of these add some iodine solution. To the other add some Benedict's solution and heat in a water bath as shown in Figure 17. Test the contents of tube B in exactly the same way.

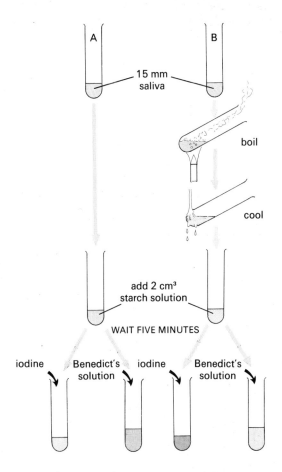

Figure 15   Salivary amylase acting on starch

Results   The contents of tube A give no blue colour with iodine, showing that the starch has gone. The other half of the contents gives a red or orange precipitate with Benedict's solution, showing that sugar is present.

The contents of tube B still give a blue colour with iodine. They do not form a precipitate on heating with Benedict's solution.

Interpretation   The results with tube A suggest that something in saliva has converted starch into sugar. But the boiled saliva in tube B fails to do this. This suggests that an enzyme in saliva brought about the change (see page 23), because enzymes are proteins and are destroyed by boiling. If the boiled saliva had changed starch to sugar, an enzyme could not have been responsible.

This interpretation assumes that it is something in saliva which changes starch into sugar. However, the results could equally well support the hypothesis that starch can turn unboiled saliva into sugar. Our knowledge of (1) the chemical composition of starch and saliva and (2) the effect of heat on enzymes makes the first interpretation more likely.

2   The action of pepsin on egg-white protein

A cloudy suspension of egg-white is prepared by stirring the white of one egg into 500 cm³ tap water, heating it to boiling point and filtering it through glass wool to remove the larger particles.

Label four test-tubes A, B, C and D and place 2 cm³ egg-white suspension in each of them. Then add pepsin solution and/or dilute hydrochloric acid to the tubes as follows (Figure 16):

A   Egg-white suspension + 1 cm³ pepsin solution (1%)
B   Egg-white suspension + 3 drops dilute hydrochloric acid (HCl)
C   Egg-white suspension + 1 cm³ pepsin + 3 drops HCl
D   Egg-white suspension + 1 cm³ boiled pepsin + 3 drops HCl.

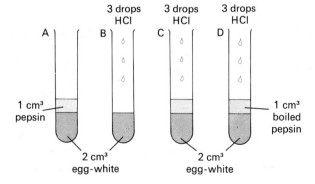

Figure 16   Pepsin acting on egg-white

Place all four tubes in a beaker of warm water at 35 °C for 10–15 minutes.

Result   The contents of tube C go clear. The rest remain cloudy.

Interpretation   The change from a cloudy suspension to a clear solution shows that the solid particles of egg protein have been digested to soluble products. The failure of the other three tubes to give clear solutions shows that:

A   pepsin will work only in acid solutions,
B   it is the pepsin and not the hydrochloric acid which does the digestion, and
D   pepsin is an enzyme, because its activity is destroyed by boiling.

3   The effect of temperature and pH on digestion by amylase

See Experiments 2 and 3 on pages 25-6.

4   A 'model' for digestion and absorption

Put about 30 mm 3 per cent starch solution in a test-tube. Take a 15 cm length of dialysis tubing which has been soaked in water. Tie a knot securely in one end. Use a dropping pipette to fill the dialysis tubing with the starch solution and place the tubing in a test-tube labelled A. Secure the tubing to the rim of the test-tube with an elastic band as shown in Figure 17. Wash away all traces of starch solution from the outside of the tube by filling the test-tube with water and emptying it several times. Finally, fill the test-tube with water and leave it in the rack.

Now add about 2 mm saliva (or, if preferred, diastase solution) to the remaining starch solution. Shake the mixture and fill a second dialysis tube, exactly as before. Wash it thoroughly and secure it in a test-tube of water, labelled B.

After 24 hours pour about 30 mm of water from tube A into each of two clean test-tubes. Add 5 drops of iodine to one of these tubes. Test the other for sugar by heating it in a water bath with an equal volume of Benedict's solution.

Repeat this procedure for the water taken from tube B.

Result   The water from tube A should not give a blue colour with iodine, nor should it give a red precipitate with Benedict's solution.

The water from tube B also should not give a blue colour with iodine but it should give a red precipitate with Benedict's solution.

Interpretation   In tube A, the starch has been confined to the dialysis tubing and has not diffused out into the surrounding water. In tube B, starch has not diffused through the dialysis tubing. However, in tube B, salivary amylase has turned some of the

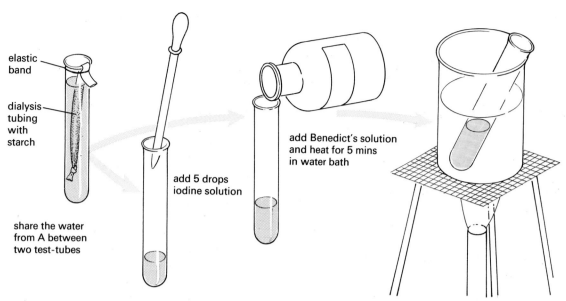

elastic band

dialysis tubing with starch

share the water from A between two test-tubes

add 5 drops iodine solution

add Benedict's solution and heat for 5 mins in water bath

Figure 17   A model for digestion and absorption

starch into maltose which diffused through the dialysis tubing into the water.

This is an acceptable model for the digestion of starch. But it is a poor model for absorption in the ileum. Probably little, if any, absorption in the ileum takes place by passive diffusion. The epithelial cell membranes play an active part in both the digestion and absorption of food in the ileum.

More rapid results can be obtained by placing a mixture of 3 per cent starch and 30 per cent glucose solutions in the dialysis tubing. The glucose can be detected in the dialysate (the liquid in the test-tube) after about 15 minutes. But the model is even less satisfactory than before, because no digestion is taking place. It could also be argued that the glucose, being 10 times more concentrated than the starch, would be expected to diffuse faster.

QUESTIONS

15 In experiments with enzymes, the control often uses the boiled enzyme. Suggest why this type of control is used.

16 In Experiment 2, why does the change from cloudy to clear suggest that digestion has occurred?

17 How would you modify Experiment 2 if you wanted to find the optimum (best) temperature for the action of pepsin on egg-white?

18 It was suggested that an alternative interpretation of the result in Experiment 1 might be that starch has turned saliva into sugar. From what you know about starch, saliva and the design of the experiment, explain why this is a less acceptable interpretation.

19 Write down the menu for your breakfast and lunch (or supper). State the main food substances present in each item of the meal. State the final digestion product of each.

CHECK LIST

- Digestion is the process which changes insoluble food into soluble substances.
- Digestion takes place in the alimentary canal.
- The changes are brought about by chemicals called digestive enzymes.

Region of alimentary canal	Digestive gland	Digestive juice produced	Enzymes in the juice	Class of food acted upon	Substances produced
Mouth	salivary glands	saliva	salivary amylase	starch	maltose
Stomach	glands in stomach lining	gastric juice	pepsin	proteins	peptides
Duodenum	pancreas	pancreatic juice	proteases	proteins and peptides	peptides and amino acids
			amylase	starch	maltose
			lipase	fats	fatty acids and glycerol

- Maltose and sucrose are changed to glucose by enzymes in the epithelium of the villi.

- The ileum absorbs amino acids, glucose and fats.
- These are carried in the bloodstream first to the liver and then to all parts of the body.
- Internal folds, villi and microvilli greatly increase the absorbing surface of the small intestine.
- The digested food is used or stored in the following ways:
  Glucose is (1) oxidized for energy or (2) changed to glycogen or fat and stored.
  Amino acids are (1) built up into proteins or (2) de-aminated to urea and glycogen and used for energy. Fats are (1) oxidized for energy or (2) stored.
- Glycogen in the liver and muscles acts as a short-term energy store. Fat in the fat depots acts as a long-term energy store.
- The liver stores glycogen and changes it to glucose and releases it into the bloodstream to keep a steady level of blood sugar.

- The liver exercises control over many other aspects of blood composition and so helps maintain chemical stability in the body.

13

The Blood Circulatory System

Blood Composition
Blood cells and plasma.

The Heart
Structure and function.

Circulation
Arteries, veins and capillaries.

Lymphatic System
Spleen and thymus.

Functions of the Blood
Homeostasis, transport and defence.

Antibodies and Immunity
Vaccines. Graft rejection.

Blood Groups and Transfusions
ABO blood groups. Rhesus factor.

Coronary Heart Disease
Possible causes.

Correlation and Cause

Diffusion (page 33) is a fairly slow process. But in a single cell, the distances are so small that diffusion is fast enough to supply all parts of the cell with oxygen and nutrients.

In large, active animals, diffusion is too slow to provide all the cells with food and oxygen. Most animals have transport systems which carry these essential substances to the body cells and remove the cell's excretory products.

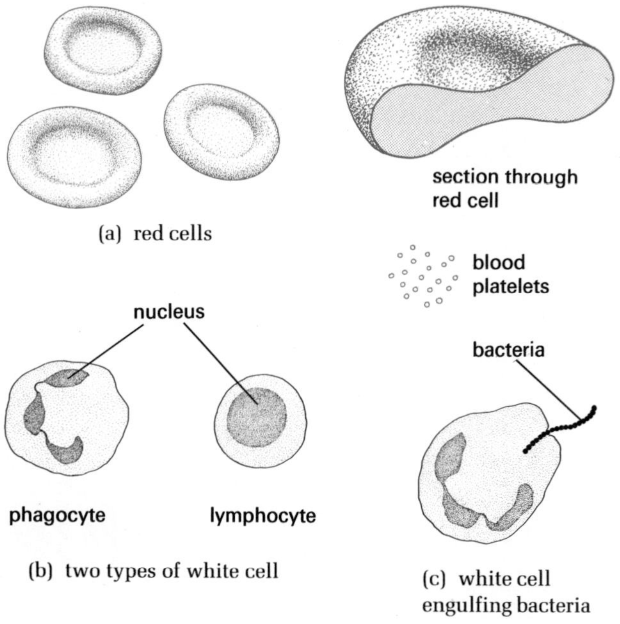

In mammals and some invertebrates, the transport is provided by a circulatory system containing blood. A heart pumps blood through the blood vessels, which reach every living part of the body.

In humans, the blood picks up digested food from the intestine and oxygen from the lungs, and carries these substances round the body. The same blood collects carbon dioxide and urea from the body and takes these to the lungs and kidneys respectively.

Composition of Blood

Blood consists of red cells, white cells and platelets floating in a liquid called **plasma**. There are between 5 and 6 litres of blood in the body of an adult.

Red cells

These are tiny, disc-like cells (Figures 1 (a) and 2) which do not have nuclei. They are made of spongy cytoplasm enclosed in an elastic cell membrane. In their cytoplasm is the red pigment, **haemoglobin**, a protein containing iron. Haemoglobin combines with oxygen in the lungs, where there is a high concentration of oxygen, to form **oxy-haemoglobin**. Oxy-haemoglobin is unstable. It breaks down and

(a) red cells

section through red cell

blood platelets

nucleus

phagocyte   lymphocyte

(b) two types of white cell

bacteria

(c) white cell engulfing bacteria

Figure 1 Blood cells

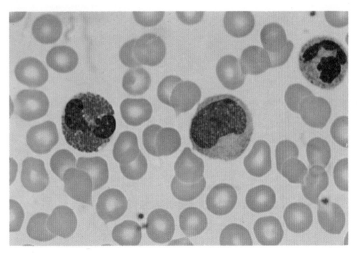

Figure 2 Red and white cells from human blood (×2000). The large nucleus (stained purple) in the white cells shows up clearly.

White cells

There are several different kinds of white cell (Figures 1 (b) and 2). Most are larger than the red cells, and they all have a nucleus. There is one white cell to every 600 red cells, and they are made in the same bone marrow that makes red cells. Many of them undergo part of their development in the thymus gland, lymph nodes or spleen (page 133). The two most numerous types of white cell are **phagocytes** and **lymphocytes**.

Phagocytes can move about by a flowing action of their cytoplasm. They can escape from the blood capillaries into the tissues by squeezing between the cells of the capillary walls. They collect at the site of an infection, engulfing (**ingesting**) and digesting harmful bacteria and cell debris (Figure 1 (c)). In this way they prevent the spread of infection through the body.

The lymphocytes' function is to produce antibodies (page 134).

Platelets

These are pieces of special blood cells budded off in the red bone marrow. They help to clot the blood at wounds and so stop the bleeding (page 134).

Plasma

The liquid part of the blood is called plasma. It is water with a large number of substances dissolved in it. The ions of sodium, potassium, calcium, chloride

releases its oxygen in tissues where the oxygen concentration is low.

Blood which contains mainly oxy-haemoglobin is said to be **oxygenated**. Blood with little oxy-haemoglobin is called **deoxygenated**.

Red cells are made by the red bone marrow of certain bones in the skeleton, such as the ribs, vertebrae and breastbone. Each red cell lives for about four months, after which it breaks down. The red haemoglobin changes to a yellow pigment, bilirubin, which is excreted in the bile. The iron from the haemoglobin is stored in the liver. About 200 000 million red cells wear out and are replaced each day. This is about 1 per cent of the total.

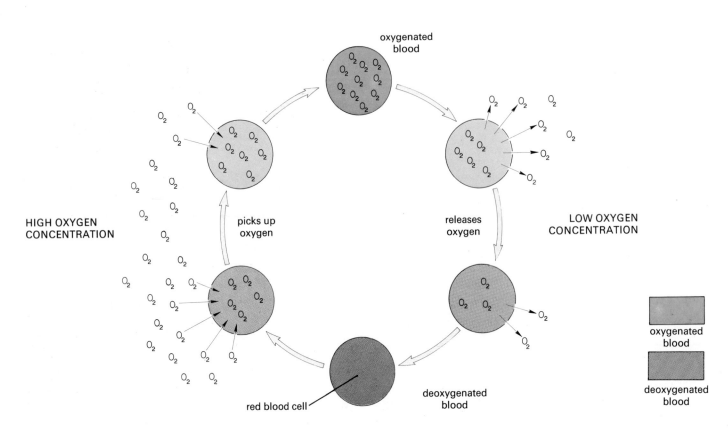

Figure 3 The function of the red cells

HIGH OXYGEN CONCENTRATION

LOW OXYGEN CONCENTRATION

oxygenated blood

deoxygenated blood

picks up oxygen

releases oxygen

red blood cell

oxygenated blood

deoxygenated blood

and hydrogencarbonate, for example, are present. Proteins such as fibrinogen, albumin and globulins are an important part of the plasma. Fibrinogen is needed for clotting (page 134). The globulin proteins include the antibodies that combat bacteria and other foreign matter (page 134). The plasma also contains varying amounts of food substances such as amino acids, glucose, lipids (fats) and vitamins. Hormones (page 214) may also be present, depending on the activities taking place in the body. The excretory product, urea, is dissolved in the plasma.

The liver and kidneys keep the composition of the plasma more or less constant. But the amounts of digested food, salts and water will vary a little, according to food intake and body activities.

QUESTIONS

1 In what ways are white cells different from red cells in (a) their structure, (b) their function?
2 (a) Where in the body would you expect haemoglobin to be combining with oxygen to form oxy-haemoglobin?
   (b) In what parts of the body would you expect oxy-haemoglobin to be breaking down to oxygen and haemoglobin?

3 Why is it important for oxy-haemoglobin to be an unstable compound (that is, easily changed to oxygen and haemoglobin)?
4 What might be the effect on you if your diet contained too little iron?

The Heart

The heart pumps blood through the circulatory system all round the body. Figure 4 shows its appearance from the outside, Figure 5 shows the left side cut open, while Figure 6 is a diagram of a vertical section to show its internal structure. The diagrams show the heart as if in a dissection of a person facing you (the left side is drawn on the right).

If you study Figure 6 you will see that the heart has four chambers. The upper, thin-walled chambers are the **atria** (singular = atrium). Each of these opens into a thick-walled chamber, the **ventricle**, below.

Blood enters the atria from large veins. The **pulmonary vein** brings oxygenated blood from the lungs into the left atrium. The **vena cava** brings deoxygenated blood from the body tissues into the right atrium. The blood passes from each atrium to its corresponding ventricle, and the ventricle pumps it out into the arteries.

The artery carrying oxygenated blood to the body from the left ventricle is the **aorta**. The **pulmonary artery** carries deoxygenated blood from the right ventricle to the lungs.

In pumping the blood, the muscle in the walls of

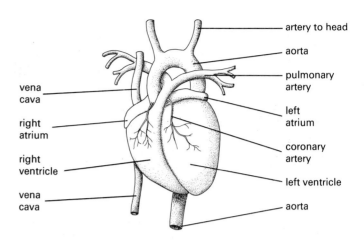

Figure 4   External view of the heart

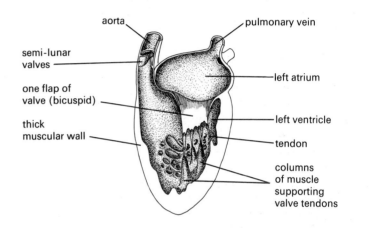

Figure 5   Diagram of heart cut open (left side)

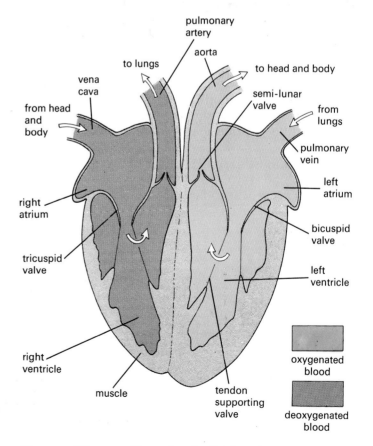

Figure 6   Diagram of heart, longitudinal section

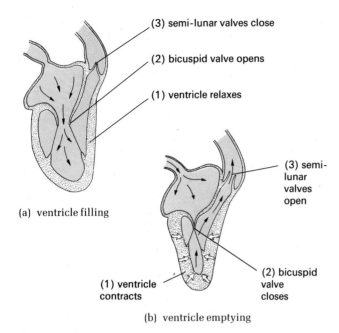

(a) ventricle filling

(3) semi-lunar valves close
(2) bicuspid valve opens
(1) ventricle relaxes

(3) semi-lunar valves open
(2) bicuspid valve closes
(1) ventricle contracts

(b) ventricle emptying

Figure 7   Diagram of heart beat (only the left side is shown)

the atria and ventricles contracts and relaxes (Figure 7). The walls of the atria contract first and force blood into the two ventricles. Then the ventricles contract and send blood into the arteries. The blood is stopped from flowing backwards by four sets of valves. Between the right atrium and the right ventricle is the **tricuspid** (= three flaps) valve. Between the left atrium and the left ventricle is the **bicuspid** (= two flaps) valve. The flaps of these valves are shaped rather like parachutes, with 'strings' called **tendons** or **cords** to prevent their being turned inside out.

In the pulmonary artery and aorta are the **semi-lunar** (= half-moon) valves. These each consist of three pockets which are pushed flat against the artery walls when blood flows one way. If blood tries to flow the other way, the 'pockets' fill up and meet in the middle to stop the flow of blood (Figure 8).

When the ventricles contract, blood pressure closes the bicuspid and tricuspid valves and these prevent blood returning to the atria. When the ventricles relax, the blood pressure in the arteries

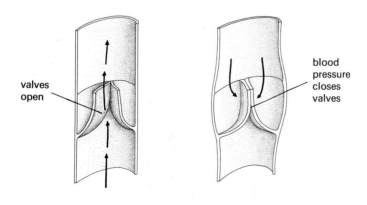

valves open

blood pressure closes valves

Figure 8   Action of the semi-lunar valves

closes the semi-lunar valves so preventing the return of blood to the ventricles.

The heart contracts and relaxes 60–80 times a minute. During exercise, this rate goes up to over 100 and increases the supply of oxygen and food to the tissues.

The heart muscle is supplied with food and oxygen by the **coronary arteries** which can be seen in Figure 4.

From the description above, it may seem that the ventricles are filled with blood as a result of the contraction of the atria. In fact, when the ventricles relax, their internal volume increases. So they draw in blood from the pulmonary vein or vena cava through the relaxed atria. Atrial contraction then forces the final amount of blood into the ventricles just before ventricular contraction.

Control of the heart beat

At rest, the normal heart rate may lie between 50 and 100 beats per minute, according to age, sex and other factors. During strenuous exercise, the rate may increase to 200 per minute.

The heart beat is initiated by the '**pace-maker**', a small group of specialized muscle cells at the top of the right atrium. The pace-maker receives two sets of nerves from the brain. One group of nerves speeds up the heart rate and the other group slows it down. In this way, the heart rate is adjusted to meet the needs of the body at times of rest, exertion and excitement.

QUESTIONS

5 Which parts of the heart (a) pump blood into the arteries, (b) stop blood flowing the wrong way?
6 Put the following in the correct order: (a) blood enters arteries, (b) ventricles contract, (c) atria contract, (d) ventricles relax, (e) blood enters ventricles, (f) semi-lunar valves close, (g) tri- and bi-cuspid valves close.

7 Why do you think that (a) the walls of the ventricles are more muscular than the walls of the atria and (b) the muscle of the left ventricle is thicker than that of the right ventricle? (Look at Figure 10.)
8 Which important veins are not shown in Figure 4?
9 Why is a person whose heart valves are damaged by disease unable to take part in active sport?

The Circulation

The blood, pumped by the heart, travels all round the body in blood vessels. It leaves the heart in arteries and returns in veins. Figure 9 shows the route of the circulation as a diagram. The blood passes twice through the heart during one complete circuit: once on its way to the body and again on its way to the lungs. The circulation through the lungs is called the **pulmonary** circulation. The circulation round the rest of the body is called the **systemic** circulation. On average, a red cell goes round the whole circulation in 45 seconds. Figure 10 is a more detailed diagram of the circulation.

Arteries

These are fairly wide vessels (Figures 11 (a) and 12) which carry blood from the heart to the limbs and organs of the body (Figure 13 (a)). The blood in the arteries, except for the pulmonary arteries, is oxygenated.

Arteries have elastic tissue and muscle fibres in their thick walls.

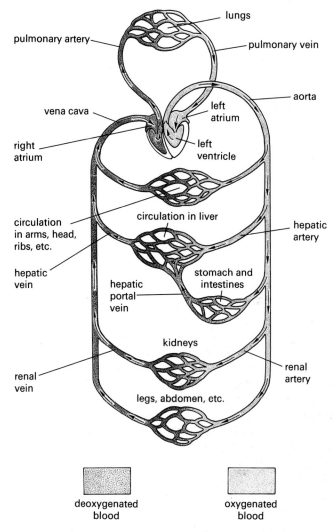

Figure 10   Diagram of human circulation

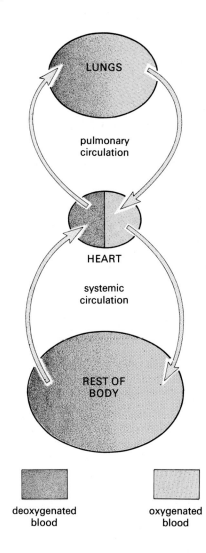

Figure 9   Blood circulation

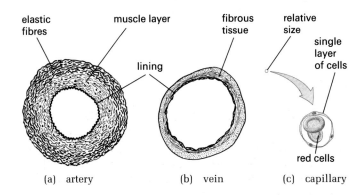

Figure 11   Blood vessels, transverse sections

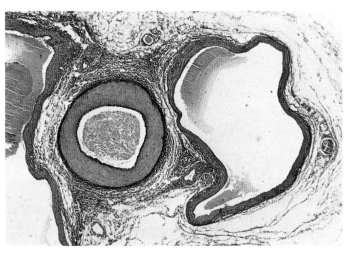

Figure 12   Transverse section through a vein and an artery. The vein is on the right, the artery on the left. The wall of the artery is much thicker than that of the vein. The material filling the artery is formed from coagulated red blood cells. These can also be seen in two regions of the vein.

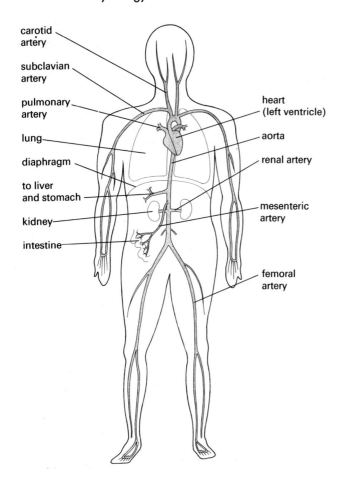

Figure 13 (a)   Diagram of the arterial system

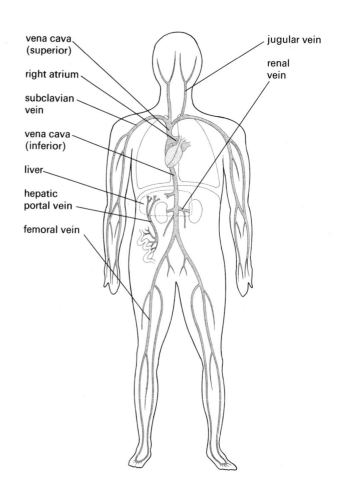

Figure 13 (b)   Diagram of the venous system

The walls of the large arteries, near the heart, have a greater proportion of elastic tissue. This allows these vessels to stand up to the surges of high pressure caused by the heart beat. The ripple of pressure which passes down an artery as a result of the heart beat can be felt as a 'pulse' when the artery is near the surface of the body. You can feel the pulse in your radial artery if you press the finger-tips of one hand on the wrist of the other (Figure 14).

The region where a pulse can be felt is called a **pressure point**. There are several pressure points in the body.

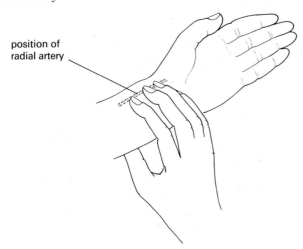

Figure 14   Feeling the pulse on the wrist (radial pulse)

The arteries divide into smaller vessels called **arterioles**. The small arteries and the arterioles have, in proportion, less elastic tissue and more muscle fibres than the great arteries. When the muscle fibres of the arterioles contract, they make the vessels narrower and restrict the blood flow. In this way, the distribution of blood to different parts of the body can be regulated. (See page 162 for an example of this.)

The arterioles divide repeatedly to form a branching network of microscopic vessels. These final branches pass between the cells of every living tissue. They are called **capillaries**.

Capillaries

These are tiny vessels, often as little as 0.001 mm in diameter and with walls only 1 cell thick (Figures 11 (c) and 15). Although the blood as a whole cannot escape from the capillary, the thin capillary walls allow some liquid to pass through. That is, they are permeable. Blood pressure in the capillaries forces part of the plasma out through the walls. The fluid that escapes is neither blood nor plasma, but **tissue fluid**. Tissue fluid is similar to plasma but contains less protein. This fluid bathes all the living cells of the body. Since it contains dissolved food and oxygen from the blood, it supplies the cells with their needs (Figures 16 and 17). The tissue fluid

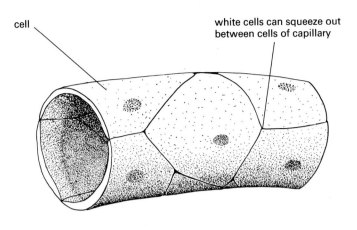

Figure 15   Diagram of blood capillary

eventually seeps back into the capillaries, having given up its oxygen and dissolved food to the cells. It has now received the waste products of the cells, such as carbon dioxide. The bloodstream carries these away.

The capillary network is so dense that no living cell is far from a supply of oxygen and food. The capillaries join up into larger vessels, called **venules**, which then join to form **veins**.

Veins

Veins return blood from the tissues to the heart (Figure 13 (b)). The blood pressure in them is steady and is less than that in the arteries. They are wider and their walls are thinner, less elastic and less

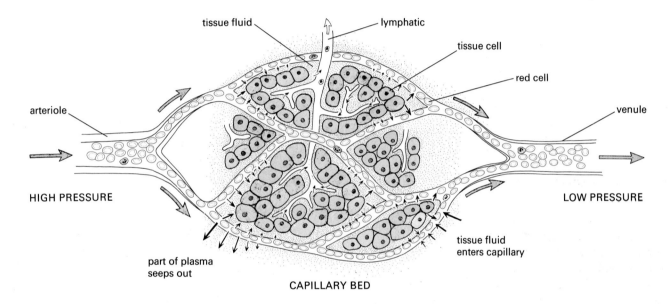

Figure 16   Relationship between capillaries, cells and lymphatics

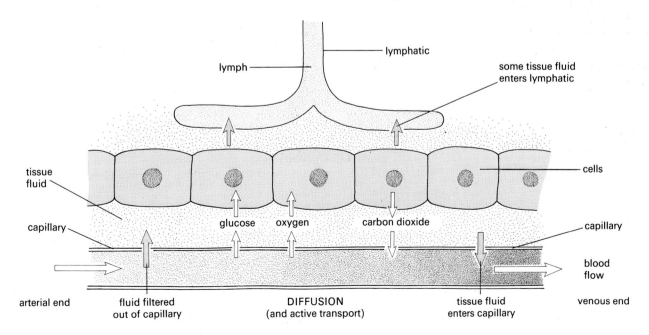

Figure 17   Blood, tissue fluid and lymph

muscular than those of the arteries (Figures 11 (b) and 12). They also have valves in them similar to the semi-lunar valves (Figure 8).

Contraction of body muscles, particularly in the limbs, compresses (squeezes) the thin-walled veins. The valves in the veins prevent the blood flowing backwards when the vessels are compressed in this way.

The blood in most veins is deoxygenated. It contains less food but more carbon dioxide than the blood in most arteries. This is because respiring cells have used the oxygen and food and produced carbon dioxide. The pulmonary veins, which return blood from the lungs to the heart, contain oxygenated blood.

Blood pressure

The pumping action of the heart produces a pressure which drives blood round the circulatory system. In the arteries, the pressure goes up and down with the heart beat, and the pressure wave can be felt as a pulse. The millions of tiny capillaries offer resistance to the blood flow and, by the time the blood enters the veins, the surges due to the heart beat are lost and the blood pressure is greatly reduced.

Doctors use the words 'blood pressure' to mean the two pressures, as measured in the arteries, when the heart is contracting and relaxing.

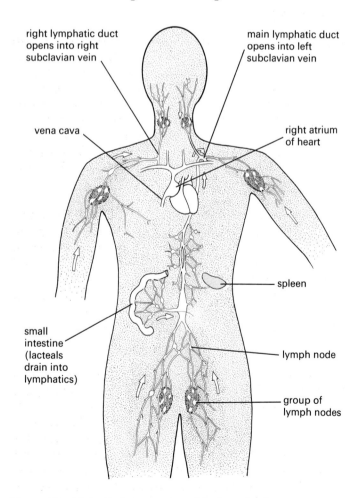

Figure 18   **Main drainage routes of the lymphatic system**

QUESTIONS

10 Starting from the left atrium, put the following in the correct order for circulation of the blood: (a) left atrium, (b) vena cava, (c) aorta, (d) lungs, (e) pulmonary artery, (f) right atrium, (g) pulmonary vein, (h) right ventricle, (i) left ventricle.
11 Why is it not correct to say that all arteries carry oxygenated blood and all veins carry deoxygenated blood?
12 How do veins differ from arteries in (a) their function, (b) their structure?
13 How do capillaries differ from other blood vessels in (a) their structure, (b) their function?
14 Describe the path taken by a molecule of glucose, from the time it is absorbed in the small intestine, and the path taken by a molecule of oxygen absorbed in the lungs, to the time when they both meet in a muscle cell of the leg. (Use Figure 10.)

The Lymphatic System

Not all the tissue fluid returns to the capillaries. Some of it enters blindly-ending, thin-walled vessels called **lymphatics** (Figure 16). The lymphatics from all parts of the body join up to make two large vessels which empty their contents into the blood system, as shown in Figure 18.

The lacteals from the villi in the small intestine (page 118) join up with the lymphatic system. So most of the fats absorbed in the intestine reach the circulation by this route. The fluid in the lymphatic vessels is called **lymph** and is similar in composition to tissue fluid.

Some of the larger lymphatics can contract, but most of the lymph flow results from the vessels being compressed from time to time when the body muscles contract in movements such as walking or breathing. There are valves in the lymphatics (Figure 19) like those in the veins, so that when the lymphatics are squashed, the fluid in them is forced in one direction only: towards the heart.

Figure 18 shows that at certain points in the lymphatic vessels, there are swellings called **lymph nodes**. Lymphocytes are stored in the lymph nodes and released into the lymph. In time, they reach the blood system. There are also phagocytes in the lymph nodes. If bacteria enter a wound and are not

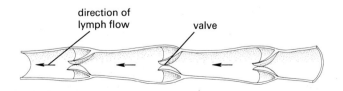

Figure 19   **Lymphatic vessel cut open to show valves**

ingested by the white cells of the blood or lymph, the lymph will carry them to a lymph node and white cells there will ingest them. The lymph nodes thus form part of the body's defence system against infection.

Other lymphoid organs which contain lymphocytes are the spleen, thymus and appendix.

Spleen

The spleen is the largest organ in the adult lymphatic system. It is a solid, deep red body about 12 cm long and lies in the left side of the upper abdomen, between the lower ribs and the stomach. It contains lymphatics and blood vessels. Its main functions are to (1) remove worn-out red cells, bacteria and cell fragments from the blood, (2) produce lymphocytes and antibodies (page 134).

The spleen contains many phagocytes which ingest the spent red cells and turn their haemoglobin into the compounds **bilirubin** and **ferritin**. These are released into the blood circulation. The yellow pigment, bilirubin, is excreted in the bile (page 116). Ferritin, a protein, contains the iron from the haemoglobin and is used by the red bone marrow to make more haemoglobin.

If bacteria or their antigens (page 134) reach the spleen, the lymphocytes there start to make antibodies against them.

Thymus

The thymus gland lies at the top of the thorax, partly over the heart and lungs. It is an important lymphoid organ, particularly in new-born babies, in whom it controls the development of the spleen and lymph nodes. The thymus produces lymphocytes and is the main centre for providing immunity against harmful micro-organisms.

After puberty (page 175), the thymus becomes smaller but is still an important immunological organ. White cells from the bone marrow are stored in the thymus. Here they divide, producing a large population of lymphocytes which can be 'programmed' to make antibodies against specific micro-organisms.

QUESTIONS

15 List the things you would expect to find if you analysed a sample of lymph.
16 Describe the course taken by a molecule of fat from the time it is absorbed in the small intestine to the time it reaches the liver to be oxidized for energy. (Use Figure 12 on page 118, Figure 10 on page 129 and Figure 18 on page 132.)

Functions of the Blood

The blood has three main functions: (1) as the agent replenishing the tissue fluid surrounding the cells (its role in homeostasis, page 156), (2) as a circulatory transport system and (3) as a defence mechanism against harmful bacteria, viruses and foreign proteins.

Homeostatic functions

All the cells of the body are bathed by tissue fluid which is derived from plasma. Tissue fluid supplies the cells with the food and oxygen necessary for their living chemistry, and removes the products of their activities. Some of these products would poison the cell if they were allowed to build up.

The composition of the blood plasma is controlled by the liver and kidneys so that the living cells are soaked in a liquid of almost unvarying composition. This provides them with the environment they need, so they can live and grow in the best possible conditions. By carrying oxygen and nutrients to the tissue fluid and carrying away the excretory products, the blood helps in homeostasis (page 121), maintaining the constancy of the internal environment. (See page 156 for further details.)

Transport

Transport of oxygen from the lungs to the tissues   In the lungs, the concentration of oxygen is high and so the oxygen combines with the haemoglobin in the red cells, forming oxy-haemoglobin. The blood is now said to be **oxygenated**. When this oxygenated blood reaches tissues where oxygen is being used up, the oxy-haemoglobin breaks down and releases its oxygen to the tissues. Oxygenated blood is a bright red colour. **Deoxygenated** blood is dark red.

Transport of carbon dioxide from the tissues to the lungs   The blood picks up carbon dioxide from actively respiring cells and carries it to the lungs. In the lungs, the carbon dioxide escapes from the blood and is breathed out (see page 145).

The carbon dioxide is carried in the form of hydrogencarbonate ions (HCO_3^-). Some of the hydrogencarbonate is carried in the red cells, but most of it is dissolved in the plasma.

Transport of digested food from the intestine to the tissues   The soluble products of digestion pass into the capillaries of the villi lining the small intestine (page 117). They are carried in solution by the plasma and, after passing through the liver, enter the main blood system. Glucose, salts, vitamins and some proteins pass out of the capillaries and into the tissue fluid. The cells bathed by this fluid take up the substances they need for their living processes.

Transport of nitrogenous waste from the liver to the kidneys   When the liver changes amino acids into glycogen (page 120), the amino part of the molecules ($-NH_2$) is changed into the nitrogenous waste product, urea. This substance is carried away in the blood circulation. When the blood passes through the kidneys, much of the urea is removed and excreted (page 153).

Transport of hormones   Hormones are chemicals made by certain glands in the body (see page 214). The blood carries these chemicals from the glands which make them to the organs ('target organs' on which they act. For example, a hormone called **insulin** is made in the pancreas. It is carried by the blood to the liver and controls how much glucose is stored as glycogen (page 120).

Transport of heat   The limbs and head lose heat to the surrounding air. Chemical changes elsewhere in the body produce heat. The blood carries the heat from the warm places to the cold places and so helps to keep an even temperature throughout the body. The blood vessels in the skin also help to control the body temperature, by opening when warm and closing when cold (page 162).

Table 1   Transport by the blood system

Substance	From	To
Oxygen	lungs	whole body
Carbon dioxide	whole body	lungs
Urea	liver	kidneys
Hormones	glands	target organs
Digested food	intestine	whole body
Heat	abdomen and muscles	whole body

Note that the blood is not directed to a particular organ. A molecule of urea may go round the circulation many times before it enters the renal artery, by chance, and is removed by the kidneys.

QUESTION

17 What substances would the blood (a) gain, (b) lose, on passing through (i) the kidneys, (ii) the lungs, (iii) an active muscle? Remember that respiration (page 28) is taking place in all these organs.

Defence against infection

Clotting   When tissues are damaged and blood vessels cut, platelets clump together and block the smaller capillaries. The platelets and damaged cells at the wound also produce a substance which acts on the plasma protein called **fibrinogen**. A series of enzymes then change the fibrinogen into **fibrin**, which forms a network of fibres across the wound. Red cells become trapped in this network and so

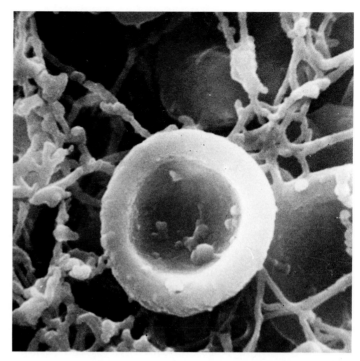

Figure 20   A red cell trapped in a fibrin network ($\times 8800$)

form a blood clot. The clot not only stops further loss of blood, but also stops harmful bacteria from entering the wound (Figures 20 and 21).

White cells   White cells, either at the site of the wound, in the blood capillaries or in lymph nodes, may ingest harmful bacteria and so stop them entering the general circulation. This process of ingestion is called **phagocytosis**. White cells can squeeze through the walls of capillary vessels and so attack bacteria which get into the tissues, even though the capillaries themselves are not damaged.

Antibodies   The surfaces of bacteria and viruses carry chemical substances called **antigens**. Certain types of white cells, lymphocytes, produce chemicals called **antibodies** which attack the antigens of bacteria and other foreign proteins which get into the body. Antibodies are themselves proteins, released into the plasma by the lymphocytes. They may become attached to the surface of the bacteria or viruses and make them easier for the phagocytes to ingest. Sometimes they simply neutralize the poisonous proteins (toxins) produced by the bacteria.

Each antibody is very **specific**. This means that an antibody which attacks a typhoid bacterium will not affect a pneumonia bacterium. Figure 22 shows this in the form of a diagram.

Active immunity   Once an antibody has been made by the blood, it may remain in the circulation for some time. This means that the body has become **immune** to the disease, because the antibody will attack the bacteria or viruses as soon as they get into the body. Even if the antibodies do not remain for long in the circulation, the lymphocytes can usually

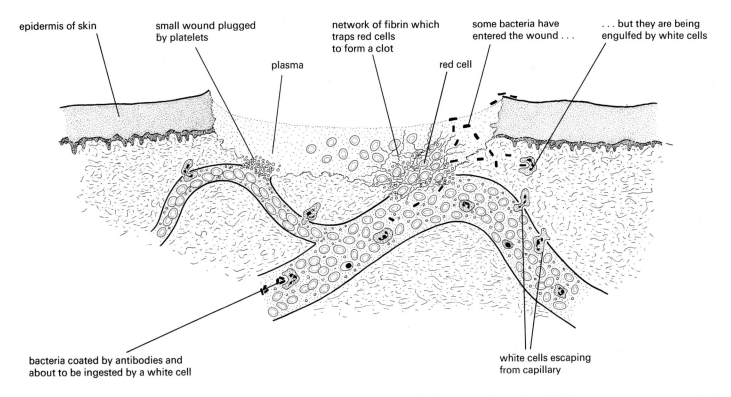

epidermis of skin

small wound plugged by platelets

plasma

network of fibrin which traps red cells to form a clot

red cell

some bacteria have entered the wound . . .

. . . but they are being engulfed by white cells

bacteria coated by antibodies and about to be ingested by a white cell

white cells escaping from capillary

Figure 21   The defence against infection. Part of the skin has been damaged and two capillaries have broken open.

make them again very quickly, so giving the person some degree of immunity, called **natural immunity**. This is why you are very unlikely to catch a disease like measles or chicken-pox more than once.

When you are **inoculated** (vaccinated) against a disease, a harmless form of the bacteria or viruses is introduced into your body. The white cells make the correct antibodies, so that if the real micro-organisms get into the blood, the antibody is already present or very quickly made by the blood.

The material which is injected or swallowed is called a **vaccine** and is either

1 a harmless form of the micro-organism, as in the BCG inoculation against tuberculosis and the Sabin oral vaccine against polio (oral, in this

context, means 'taken by mouth'), or
2 the killed micro-organisms, as in the whooping cough vaccine, or
3 a **toxoid** (the inactivated toxin from the bacteria). The diphtheria and tetanus vaccines are of this kind. (A toxin is the poisonous substance produced by certain bacteria and which causes the disease symptoms.)

The immunity produced by a vaccine is called **artificial immunity**. You are said to be **immunized** against the disease.

Immunity which results from either a natural infection or from inoculation is called **active immunity**. The lymphocytes actively produce antibodies to the disease organisms.

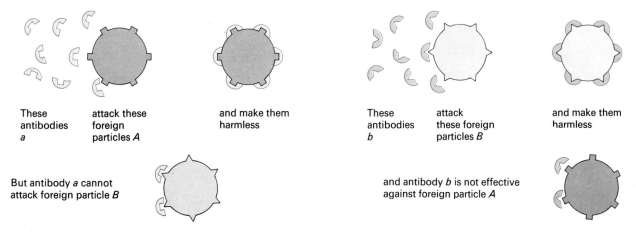

These antibodies a

attack these foreign particles A

and make them harmless

These antibodies b

attack these foreign particles B

and make them harmless

But antibody a cannot attack foreign particle B

and antibody b is not effective against foreign particle A

Figure 22   Antibodies are specific

Passive immunity is acquired when a person receives an injection of blood serum which already contains antibodies against a disease. This preparation is called an **antiserum**.

Serum is blood plasma with the fibrinogen removed. Sera are prepared from plasma given by blood donors. For example, people who have recently had an anti-tetanus inoculation will have made anti-tetanus antibodies in their blood. Some of these people offer to donate more blood than usual. The plasma is separated from the red cells, which are then returned to the donor's circulation. The anti-tetanus antibodies are extracted from the plasma and used to treat patients who are at risk of developing tetanus.

If a wound is likely to have soil or dust in it, the person may be given an injection of anti-tetanus antibodies. The antibody (an anti-toxin) will neutralize any tetanus toxin in the circulation before the toxin can affect the nervous system.

There are also antisera for chicken-pox and rabies.

Graft rejection If skin has been badly burnt, it can be repaired by grafting skin from another part of the body on to the damaged area. If the skin is from the patient's own body, blood vessels grow into it and the graft survives. If the graft is from another person, blood vessels do not grow and the grafted skin falls away in a few days. The graft has been rejected.

Graft rejection is one aspect of the body's immune response. The cells of the foreign tissue carry antigens on their surface. Lymphocytes in the patient's circulation recognize these antigens as foreign, and attack the tissue.

Kidney and heart transplants may also be rejected. To avoid this, the patient is given drugs which suppress the immune response. The problem with using **immuno-suppressive** drugs is that they prevent the patient from responding to any other foreign substance or organism. The patient therefore cannot resist infection by bacteria or viruses. However, the drug cyclosporine selectively suppresses the immune response to the graft tissue, while leaving the defence against most bacteria and some viruses intact. Since this drug was developed in the 1970s, organ transplants have been more successful.

QUESTIONS

18 What part do white cells play in the defence of the body against infection?

19 Why is it necessary to inoculate a person against a disease before he catches it, rather than wait until he catches it?

Blood Groups and Transfusions

ABO blood groups

If somebody loses a lot of blood as a result of an injury or surgical operation, a blood transfusion can be given. Blood taken from a healthy person, the **donor**, is fed into one of the patient's veins. For a transfusion to be successful the blood type of the donor has to match the blood of the patient. If the two blood types do not match, the donor's red cells will clump together in the patient's blood vessels and cause serious harm. Red cells carry antigens on their cell membranes. If the blood types do not match, the antibodies in the patient's blood will act on the donor's red cells and clump them together.

For the purposes of transfusion, people can be put into one of four groups called group A, group B, group AB and group O.

Groups A and B can receive blood from their own group and from group O. AB people can receive blood from any group. Group O can receive blood only from people of their own group.

A donor gives 420 cm³ of blood from a vein in the arm (Figure 23). The blood is led into a sterilized bag containing sodium citrate which prevents clotting. The blood can then be stored at 4 °C for 10 days, or longer if glucose is added (Figure 24). Before blood is transfused, even though both groups are known, it is carefully tested against the patient's blood to make sure of a good match. Then it is fed into one of the patient's arm veins at the correct rate and temperature. In a few hours, the donor will have made up his or her blood to the normal volume and in a week or two the red cells will have been replaced.

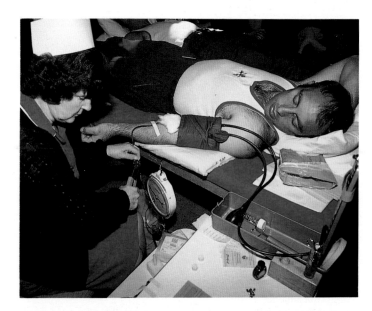

Figure 23 Blood donor. The veins in the upper arm are compressed by using an inflatable 'cuff'. The donor's blood is then tapped from a vein near the inside of the elbow. It takes 5–10 minutes to fill the plastic bag.

Figure 24   Donated blood. The plastic bag, containing blood from a donor, is about to be placed in a refrigerated blood bank.

The red cells of group A people have antigen A on their cell membranes and the plasma contains anti-B antibodies. Since antibodies are specific, as explained on page 134, the anti-B antibodies do not attack the A antigens on the red cells.

The red cells of group B people carry the B antigen and their plasma has the anti-A antibody. So if group A cells are introduced into a group B person, they will be clumped by the anti-A antibody. Group AB people have both A and B antigens on their cells but no antibodies in their plasma. The red cells of group O people have neither A nor B antigens but their plasma contains both anti-A and anti-B antibodies (Table 2).

Table 2   Antigens and antibodies

Group	Antigen on cells	Antibody in plasma
A	A	anti-B
B	B	anti-A
AB	A and B	neither
O	neither	anti-A and anti-B

The red cells from group O people can be given to any other group. This is because they have neither A nor B antigens and so cannot be clumped. Group O people, on the other hand, can receive blood only from their own group because their plasma contains both anti-A and anti-B antibodies.

Group AB people, having neither anti-A nor anti-B antibodies in their plasma, can receive blood from any group. Table 3 shows the acceptable pattern of giving and receiving for the four groups.

Table 3   Blood transfusion

Group	Can donate blood to	Can receive blood from
A	A and AB	A and O
B	B and AB	B and O
AB	AB	all groups
O	all groups	O

A person's blood group is found by mixing a drop of his or her blood with anti-A serum and anti-B serum (Figure 25). Group AB cells will clump in both anti-sera. Group O cells will clump in neither. A cells will clump only in anti-A serum, and B cells only in anti-B.

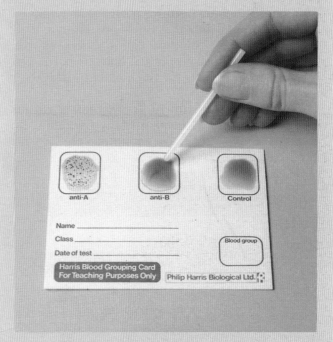

Figure 25 (a)   ABO blood grouping. A blood sample is mixed with the dried serum on the card. Clumping has occurred in anti-A but not in anti-B serum, so the sample is from a group A person. The control ensures that clumping was not caused by some other factor.

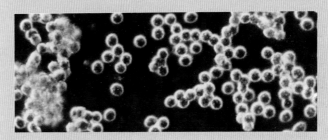

Figure 25 (b)   The red cells are being clumped (×800).

The rhesus factor

The red cells of rhesus-positive people carry the Rh+ antigen, sometimes called the D antigen. (The rhesus factor is so called because it was first studied in rhesus monkeys.) Rhesus-negative people have no antigen. If the Rh+ antigen gets into the blood of a rhesus-negative person, it does not cause clumping because there are no antibodies to it in the rhesus-negative plasma. However, the rhesus-negative recipient does then make antibodies. If he or she later receives a second transfusion of rhesus-positive blood, there is a serious reaction. The first transfusion is said to have sensitized the rhesus-negative person to the Rh+ antigen.

Something similar may happen when a rhesus-negative woman has a child by a rhesus-positive man. If the embryo is rhesus-positive, its Rh+ antigens may get into the mother's blood at the time of birth. She will then produce anti-Rh+ antibodies – that is, she will be sensitized. If she has a second rhesus-positive baby, her anti-Rh+ antibodies may attack her embryo's red cells. The baby would then be born with severe anaemia.

If the parents' blood groups are known to be incompatible, the mother can be de-sensitized when the first rhesus-positive baby is born. This will prevent problems for the next baby, if it too is rhesus-positive.

About 1 marriage in 10 is between a rhesus-positive man and a rhesus-negative woman. But only 1 in 40 of these couples are rhesus-incompatible.

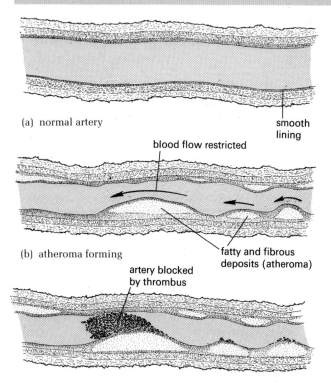

(a) normal artery   smooth
                                                 lining

blood flow restricted

(b) atheroma forming

fatty and fibrous
deposits (atheroma)

artery blocked
by thrombus

(c) thrombus forming

Figure 26   Atheroma and thrombus formation

QUESTIONS

20 One of the ABO blood groups is sometimes called the 'universal donor'. Which group do you think this is and why?

21 A drop of a person's blood shows clumping in anti-B serum but not in anti-A. What is his blood group?
22 A drop of blood from a donor is clumped in serum taken from a group B person. What blood groups might the donor be?

Coronary Heart Disease

In the lining of the large and medium arteries, deposits of a fatty substance, called **atheroma**, are laid down in patches. This happens to everyone and the patches get more numerous and larger with age. But until a patch actually blocks an important artery, the effects are not noticed. It is not known how or why the deposits form. Some doctors think that fatty substances in the blood pass into the lining. Others believe that small blood clots form on damaged areas of the lining and are covered over by the atheroma patches. The patches may join up to form a continuous layer which reduces the internal diameter of the vessel (Figure 26).

The surface of a patch of atheroma sometimes becomes rough. Fibrinogen in the plasma then deposits fibrin on it, so causing a blood clot (a **thrombus**) to form. Sometimes the blood clot blocks the **coronary artery** (see Figure 4), which supplies the muscles of the ventricles with blood. It then starves the muscles of oxygenated blood and the heart may stop beating. This is a severe heart attack from **coronary thrombosis**. A thrombus can form anywhere in the arterial system, but its effects in the coronary artery and in parts of the brain are the most drastic.

In the early stages of coronary heart disease, the atheroma may partially block the coronary artery and reduce the blood supply to the heart. This can lead to **angina**, which is a pain in the chest during exercise or exertion. This is a warning that the person is at risk and should take precautions to avoid a coronary heart attack.

Causes of heart disease

Atheroma and thrombus formation are the immediate causes of a heart attack. But we do not fully understand why atheroma or a thrombus should form.

A tendency towards the disease can be inherited. But the death rate from heart disease has increased markedly in some of the richer countries in recent years. This makes us think that some features of 'western' diets or life-styles might be causing it. Although there is very little direct evidence, the main factors are thought to be smoking, fatty diet, stress and lack of exercise.

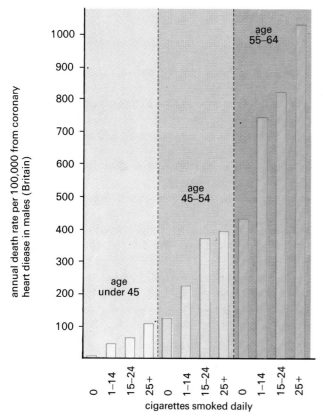

Figure 27 Smoking and heart disease. Obviously, older people are more likely to die from a heart attack than younger people. The diagram shows that in any age group, the more you smoke, the higher are your chances of dying from heart disease.
(From *Smoking or health: a report of the Royal College of Physicians*, Pitman Medical Publishing Co. Ltd)

Smoking Statistical studies suggest that smokers are two or three times more likely to die from a heart attack than are non-smokers of the same age (Figure 27). The carbon monoxide and other chemicals in cigarette smoke may damage the lining of the arteries, allowing atheroma to form, but there is not much direct evidence for this.

Carbon monoxide is known to combine with haemoglobin, to form the compound carboxy-haemoglobin (page 70). Carboxy-haemoglobin is stable and does not break down again to carbon monoxide and haemoglobin. Nor can it take up oxygen. Carbon monoxide therefore reduces the oxygen-carrying capacity of the blood. This may not cause heart attacks, but an oxygen shortage could make their effects worse.

Fatty diet Atheroma deposits contain cholesterol, which is normally present in the blood combined with proteins. Cholesterol plays an essential part in our physiology, but people with high levels of blood cholesterol are more likely to have a heart attack than people with low cholesterol levels.

Blood cholesterol can be influenced, to some extent, by the amount and type of fat in the diet. Many doctors and dieticians believe that animal fats (milk, cream, butter, cheese, egg-yolk, fatty meat) are more likely to raise the blood cholesterol than are vegetable oils, which contain a high proportion of

unsaturated fatty acids (page 105). This is still a matter for argument, however.

Stress Emotional stress often leads to a raised blood pressure. High blood pressure may increase the rate at which atheroma is formed in the arteries.

Lack of exercise There is some evidence that regular, vigorous exercise reduces the chances of a heart attack. This could be the result of an improved coronary blood flow. A sluggish blood flow, resulting from lack of exercise, may allow atheroma to form in the arterial lining. But once again, the direct evidence for this is slim.

Correlation and cause

We cannot conduct experiments on humans to find out more precisely the causes of heart attack. The evidence has to be collected from long-term studies on populations of individuals, for example, comparing smokers and non-smokers. Statistical analysis of these studies will often show a **correlation**. For example, more smokers, within a given age band, suffer heart attacks than do non-smokers of the same age.

This correlation does *not* prove that smoking *causes* heart attacks. Perhaps people who are already prone to heart attacks for other reasons (such as high blood pressure) are more likely to take up smoking. This may strike you as improbable. But until substances in tobacco smoke can be shown to cause an increase in atheroma, the correlation cannot be used on its own to prove a cause and effect.

However, there are so many other correlations between smoking and ill-health (bronchitis, emphysema, lung cancer) that the circumstantial evidence against smoking is very strong.

Another example of correlation is that people who have a television set are more likely to develop heart disease than people who don't. Nobody would seriously claim that television sets cause heart attacks. The correlation probably reflects a way of life associated with over-eating, fatty diets, lack of exercise and other factors which may play a part in causing coronary heart disease.

QUESTIONS

23 (a) What positive steps could you take, and (b) what things should you avoid, to reduce your risk of coronary heart disease in later life?

24 About 95 per cent of patients with disease of the leg arteries are cigarette-smokers. Arterial disease of the leg is the most frequent cause of leg amputation.
  (a) Is there a correlation between smoking and leg amputation?
  (b) Does smoking cause leg amputation?
  (c) In what way could smoking be a possible cause of leg amputation?

CHECK LIST

- Blood consists of red cells, white cells and platelets suspended in plasma.
- Plasma contains water, proteins, salts, glucose and lipids.
- The red cells carry oxygen. The white cells attack bacteria.
- The heart is a muscular pump with valves, which sends blood round the circulatory system.
- The left side of the heart pumps oxygenated blood round the body.
- The right side of the heart pumps deoxygenated blood to the lungs.
- Blood pressure is essential in order to pump blood round the body.
- Arteries carry blood from the heart to the tissues.
- Veins return blood to the heart from the tissues.
- Capillaries form a network of tiny vessels in all tissues. Their thin walls allow dissolved food and oxygen to pass from the blood into the tissues, and carbon dioxide and other waste substances to pass back into the blood.
- All cells in the body are bathed in tissue fluid which is derived from plasma.
- Lymph vessels return tissue fluid to the lymphatic system and finally into the blood system.
- One function of the blood is to carry substances round the body. For example, it carries oxygen from the lungs to the rest of the body, food from the intestine to the body, and urea from the liver to the kidneys.
- Lymph nodes, the spleen and the thymus are important immunological organs.
- Antibodies are chemicals made by white cells in the blood. They attack any micro-organisms or foreign proteins which get into the body.
- In blood transfusions, it is essential to match the ABO blood group of donor and recipient.
- Blockage of the coronary arteries in the heart leads to a heart attack.
- Smoking, fatty diets, stress and lack of exercise may contribute to heart disease.

Lung Structure
Air passages and alveoli.

Ventilation of the Lungs
Inhaling, exhaling, lung capacity.

Gaseous Exchange
Uptake of oxygen; removal of carbon dioxide.

Respiratory Surfaces
Characteristics.

Diseases of the Respiratory System

Smoking
Effect of smoking on the lungs and circulatory system.

Practical Work
The composition of exhaled air. Lung volume.

Everything the body does, such as movement, growth and reproduction, requires energy. Animals can obtain this energy only from the food they eat. Before the energy can be used by the cells of the body, it must be set free from the chemicals of the food by respiration (see page 28). Respiration needs a supply of oxygen and produces carbon dioxide as a waste product. All cells, therefore, must be supplied with oxygen and must be able to get rid of carbon dioxide.

Humans and other mammals obtain their oxygen from the air by means of the lungs. In the lungs, the oxygen dissolves in the blood and is carried to the tissues by the circulatory system (page 129).

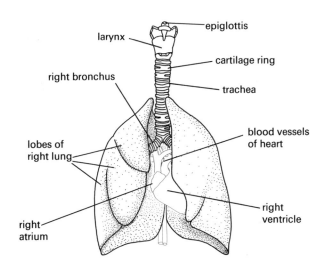

Figure 1 Diagram of lungs showing position of heart

Lung Structure

The lungs are enclosed in the thorax (chest region) (see Figure 5 on page 114). They have a spongy texture and can be expanded and compressed by movements of the thorax in such a way that air is sucked in and blown out. The lungs are joined to the back of the mouth by the windpipe or **trachea** (Figure 1). The trachea divides into two smaller tubes, **bronchi** (singular = bronchus). These enter the lungs and divide into even smaller branches. When these branches are only about 0.2 mm in diameter, they are called **bronchioles** (Figure 2 (a)). These fine branches end up in a mass of little, thin-walled, pouch-like air sacs called **alveoli** (Figures 2 (b), 2 (c) and 3).

Rings of cartilage stop the trachea and bronchi collapsing when we breathe in. The **epiglottis** and other structures at the top of the trachea stop food and drink from entering the air passages when we swallow (see page 115).

The epithelium which lines the inside of the trachea, bronchi and bronchioles consists of ciliated cells (page 15). There are also cells which secrete mucus. The mucus forms a thin film over the internal lining. Dust particles and bacteria become trapped in the sticky mucus film and the mucus is carried upwards, away from the lungs, by the flicking movements of the cilia. In this way, harmful particles are prevented from reaching the alveoli. When the mucus reaches the top of the trachea, it passes down the gullet during normal swallowing.

The alveoli have thin elastic walls, formed from a

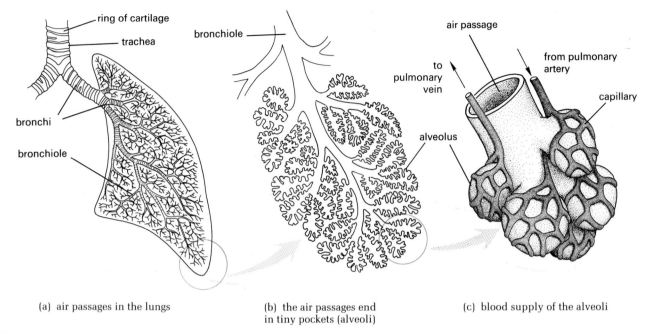

(a) air passages in the lungs

(b) the air passages end in tiny pockets (alveoli)

(c) blood supply of the alveoli

Figure 2   Lung structure

single cell layer or **epithelium**. Beneath the epithelium is a dense network of capillaries (Figure 2 (c)) supplied with deoxygenated blood (page 126). This blood, from which the body has taken oxygen, is pumped from the right ventricle, through the pulmonary artery (see Figure 10 on page 129). In humans, there are about 350 million alveoli, with a total absorbing surface of about 90 m². This large absorbing surface makes it possible to take in oxygen and give out carbon dioxide at a rate to meet the body's needs.

QUESTIONS

1 Place the following structures in the order in which air will reach them when breathing in: bronchus, trachea, nasal cavity, alveolus.
2 One function of the small intestine is to absorb food (page 117). One function of the lungs is to absorb oxygen. Point out the basic similarities in these two structures which help to speed up the process of absorption.

Ventilation of the Lungs

The movement of air into and out of the lungs is called **ventilation**. This movement renews the oxygen supply in the lungs and removes the surplus carbon dioxide from them. The lungs contain no muscle fibres and are made to expand and contract by movements of the ribs and diaphragm.

The diaphragm is a sheet of tissue which separates the thorax from the abdomen (see Figure 5 on page 114). When relaxed, it is domed slightly upwards.

The ribs are moved by the **intercostal muscles** which run from one rib to the next (Figure 4). Figure

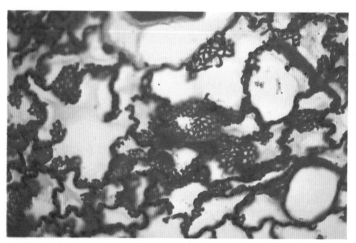

Figure 3   Small piece of lung tissue (×100). The capillaries have been injected with a red dye. The capillary networks round two or three alveoli can be seen.

5 shows how the contraction of the intercostal muscles makes the ribs move upwards.

Inhaling

1 The diaphragm muscles contract and pull it down (Figure 7 (a)).
2 The intercostal muscles contract and pull the rib cage upwards and outwards (Figure 6 (a)).

These two movements make the space in the thorax bigger, so forcing the lungs to expand and draw air in through the nose and trachea.

During vigorous exercise, it may be easier to breathe through the mouth rather than through the nose. Normally, however, it is better to breathe through the nose because then the cilia and mucus in the lining of the nasal passages can remove some of the dust particles and bacteria. Also, the air is warmed up and moistened before it reaches the lungs.

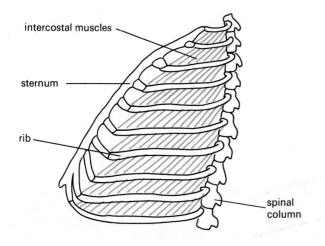

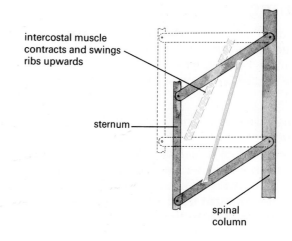

Figure 4   Rib cage seen from left side, showing the intercostal muscles

Figure 5   Model to show the action of the intercostal muscles

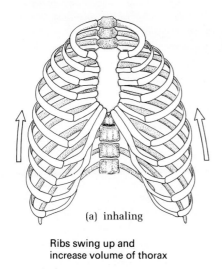

(a) inhaling

Ribs swing up and increase volume of thorax

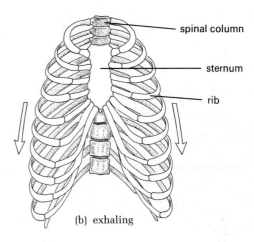

(b) exhaling

Ribs swing down and reduce volume of thorax

Figure 6   Movement of rib cage during breathing

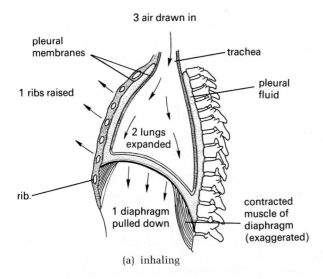

(a) inhaling

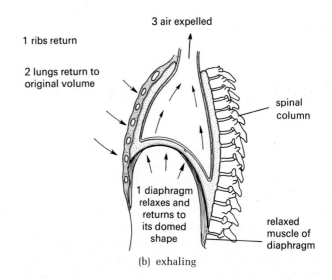

(b) exhaling

Figure 7   Diagrams of thorax to show mechanism of breathing

Exhaling

1 The diaphragm muscles relax, allowing the diaphragm to return to its domed shape (Figure 7 (b)).
2 The intercostal muscles relax, allowing the ribs to move downwards under their own weight (Figure 6 (b)).

The lungs are elastic and shrink back to their relaxed size, forcing air out again.

The outside of the lungs and the inside of the thorax are lined with a smooth membrane called the **pleural membrane**. This produces a thin layer of liquid called **pleural fluid** which reduces the friction between the lungs and the inside of the thorax.

Controlled expiration

When we speak, sing, blow a whistle, cough or sneeze, we contract the muscles in the front of the abdomen. This puts pressure on the stomach and intestines. They, in turn, push the diaphragm upwards and compress the lungs. The glottis at the top of the windpipe can be closed to control the rate at which air escapes.

Lung capacity and breathing rate

Lung capacity   In an adult, the total volume of the lungs when fully inflated is about 5 litres. However, during quiet breathing, when at rest or asleep, you normally exchange only about 500 cm^3 (Figure 8). This is called the **tidal volume**.

During exercise you breathe more deeply. In fact, you can take in an extra 2 litres and expel an extra 1 litre. The thorax cannot collapse completely, so there is about 1.5 litres of air which can never be exhaled. This is called the **residual air**. It exchanges carbon dioxide and oxygen by diffusion with the tidal air that sweeps into the bronchioles.

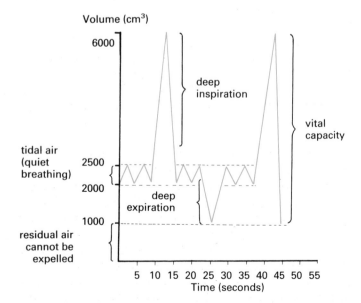

Figure 8   **Volume of air exchanged in the lungs**

Your **vital capacity** is the maximum volume of air which can be exchanged, that is, the volume of air which can be expelled by a forced expiration after a deep inspiration (Figure 9 and Experiment 3).

A person with a large vital capacity might be able to exercise more vigorously and for longer periods than someone with a small vital capacity. It seems unlikely, on the basis of present evidence, that training can increase a person's vital capacity.

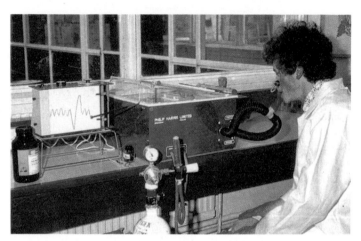

Figure 9   **A spirometer.** This instrument measures the volume of air breathed in and out of the lungs. The first part of the chart shows quiet breathing. In the middle, the chart shows a deep breath in and a deep breath out.

Breathing rate   At rest, you normally inhale and exhale about 16 times per minute. During exercise, the rate and depth of breathing both increase. Your breathing rate may rise to 20 or 30 breaths per minute, and you may exchange an extra 3 litres of air with each breath.

When you take exercise, your muscles require extra oxygen for their increased rate of respiration (page 28). The active muscles also produce more carbon dioxide. Your increased rate and depth of breathing during exercise helps to meet the muscles' demand for extra oxygen and to remove the extra carbon dioxide they are producing.

The oxygen from the lungs is carried to the muscles by the blood. Even at rest, the blood from the lungs is almost saturated with oxygen. So if extra oxygen is to reach the muscles, the blood supply must be increased. This is achieved by a rise in the heart rate (see page 188).

QUESTIONS

3 What are the two principal muscular contractions which cause air to be inhaled?
4 Place the following in the correct order: lungs expand, ribs rise, air enters lungs, intercostal muscles contract, thorax expands.
5 During inhalation, which parts of the lung structure would you expect to expand most?

Gaseous Exchange

Ventilation refers to the movement of air into and out of the lungs. **Gaseous exchange** refers to the exchange of oxygen and carbon dioxide between the air and the blood vessels in the lungs.

The 1.5 litres of residual air in the alveoli is not exchanged during ventilation and the oxygen has to reach the blood capillaries by the slower process of diffusion. Figure 10 shows how oxygen reaches the red blood cells and how carbon dioxide escapes from the blood.

The oxygen combines with the haemoglobin in the red blood cells, forming oxy-haemoglobin (page 125). The carbon dioxide in the plasma is released when the hydrogencarbonate ions (HCO_3^-) break down to CO_2 and H_2O.

The capillaries carrying oxygenated blood from the alveoli join up to form the pulmonary vein (see Figure 10 on page 129). This is the vein that returns blood to the left atrium of the heart. From here it enters the left ventricle and is pumped all round the body, so supplying the tissues with oxygen.

The gaseous exchange in the alveoli does not remove all the oxygen from the air. The air breathed in contains about 21 per cent of oxygen. The air breathed out still contains 16 per cent of oxygen (see Table 1).

Table 1   Changes in the composition of breathed air

	Inhaled %	Exhaled %
Oxygen	21	16
Carbon dioxide	0.04	4
Water vapour	variable	saturated

The remaining 79 per cent of the air consists mainly of nitrogen. The proportion of nitrogen hardly changes during breathing.

The lining of the alveoli is coated with a film of moisture, in which the oxygen dissolves. Some of this moisture evaporates into the alveoli and saturates the air with water vapour. The air you breathe out therefore always contains a great deal more water vapour than the air you breathe in. The exhaled air is warmer as well, so in cold and temperate climates you lose heat to the air by breathing.

Sometimes the word **respiration** or **respiratory** is used in connection with breathing. The lungs, trachea and bronchi are called the **respiratory system**. Your rate of breathing may be called your **respiration rate**. Do not confuse this use of the word with the biological meaning of respiration. This always refers to the release of energy in cells (page 28). This chemical process is sometimes called **tissue respiration** or **internal respiration** to distinguish it from breathing. Gaseous exchange and ventilation are sometimes called **external respiration**.

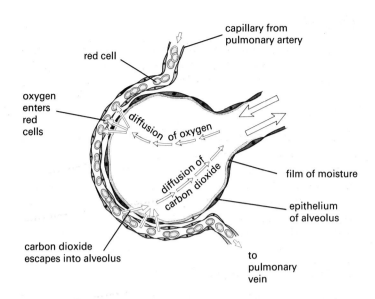

Figure 10   Gaseous exchange in the alveolus

Characteristics of respiratory surfaces

The exchange of oxygen and carbon dioxide across a respiratory surface, as in the lungs, depends on the diffusion of these two gases. Diffusion is faster if (1) there is a large surface exposed to the gas, (2) the distance across which diffusion has to take place is small, (3) there is a big difference in the concentrations of the gas at two points brought about by ventilation and (4) there is a rich supply of blood capillaries.

Large surface   The presence of millions of alveoli in the lungs provides a very large surface for gaseous exchange.

Thin epithelium   There is only a two-cell layer, at the most, separating the air in the alveoli from the blood in the capillaries (Figure 10). So the distance for diffusion is very short.

Ventilation   Ventilation of the lungs helps to maintain a steep diffusion gradient (page 34) between the air at the end of the air passages and the alveolar air. The concentration of the oxygen in the air at the end of the air passages is high, because the air is constantly renewed by the breathing actions.

Capillary network   The blood in the capillaries lining the alveoli is removing oxygen from the alveolar air all the time. Thus the oxygen concentration is kept low, and a steep diffusion gradient is maintained. So oxygen diffuses quickly from the air passages to the alveolar lining.

At the same time, blood brings carbon dioxide to the alveoli, and ventilation removes it from the air passages. Again, a diffusion gradient is maintained, and carbon dioxide diffuses quickly from the alveolar lining into the bronchioles.

QUESTIONS

6 Try to make a clear distinction between 'respiration' (page 28), 'gaseous exchange' and 'ventilation'. Say how one depends on the other.

7 Describe the path taken by a molecule of oxygen from the time it is breathed in through the nose, to the time it enters the heart in some oxygenated blood.

8 Figure 10 shows oxygen and carbon dioxide diffusing across an alveolus. Why do they diffuse in opposite directions? (See page 34.)

9 In 'mouth-to-mouth' resuscitation, air is breathed from the rescuer's lungs into the lungs of the person who has stopped breathing. How can this 'used' air help to revive the person?

Diseases of the Respiratory System

Tuberculosis (TB)

A bacterium, *Mycobacterium tuberculosis*, causes this disease. It usually enters the body through the respiratory system and infects mainly the lungs (**pulmonary tuberculosis**), though it may spread to other parts of the body. The bacteria are killed by sunlight. In dark, damp places, however, they can survive in droplets (page 261) for hours and in dust for weeks. Over-crowded, badly lit and poorly ventilated places increase the chances of the bacteria spreading.

The incidence of TB has dropped sharply in western societies. But it is still common in the developing countries where poor nutrition and chronic illnesses, such as malaria, predispose people to the disease. The World Health Organization believes that each year there are 1–2 million deaths from tuberculosis and 2–3 million new cases.

The bacteria first attack a small patch of lung tissue. This often produces no symptoms and may heal up in a week or two. Many people have had an attack of tuberculosis and recovered from it without ever being aware of the fact. The only trace left is a scar on the lung, shown up on X-ray examination.

If the disease persists and spreads in the lungs, it causes an obstinate cough, slightly raised temperature and loss of weight. These are very vague symptoms. TB is only diagnosed accurately by (1) an X-ray examination of the lungs, (2) finding the bacteria in a sample of coughed-up mucus (**sputum**) and (3) a skin test to see if the person is making antibodies to the disease. In chronic cases of the disease, the sputum may contain blood. If the disease is not stopped, it may spread from the lungs through the lymphatic system or blood, and affect many other parts of the body.

Tuberculosis can be cured by certain modern drugs such as streptomycin, *para*-amino-salicylic acid (PAS), isoniazid or thiacetazone. These drugs all have side-effects which may make the treatment unpleasant. But they do kill the bacteria effectively.

Babies and young people can be immunized against tuberculosis by injecting them with a harmless form of the tuberculosis bacteria. This is the **BCG vaccine**, named after the two Frenchmen who developed it (Bacillus Calmette–Guérin).

The long-term prevention of TB requires good standards of nutrition and housing, together with programmes of immunization and early detection of infection.

Common cold

At least 80 different strains of virus cause the common cold. You may develop a few weeks' immunity to one strain but this is no use if you are then infected with a different strain. This is why it is possible to catch one cold after another.

The virus attacks the lining of the nasal passages and pharynx, giving a runny nose, watery eyes and sneezing. Colds are spread by droplet infection (page 261) and usually get better in a few days unless followed by a bacterial infection. No drug can cure the common cold, but antibiotics may be used to prevent a secondary bacterial infection in someone who is very liable to get bronchitis.

Bronchitis

Acute tracheobronchitis   A virus infection of the nose and throat, such as a common cold, may spread to the trachea and bronchi. This is often followed by a bacterial infection which inflames the trachea (**tracheitis**) and the bronchi (**bronchitis**). There is a dry cough, sore throat and raised temperature. There is nothing to be done about the virus infection, but antibiotics are sometimes used to reduce the bacterial infection which follows. Inhaling steam has a soothing effect on the irritated membranes of the airways.

Chronic bronchitis   This is not an infection but a result of persistent irritation of the bronchi by polluted air or cigarette smoke. It is commonest in densely populated industrial cities where the air is polluted. The underlying cause seems to be an over-production of mucus which is made much worse by cigarette smoke or chemicals in the air.

In chronic bronchitis, the cilia lining the airways do not work properly and the mucus is not removed. This gives rise to a persistent cough ('smoker's cough'), and a constant production of mucus (sputum). Over a long period, chronic bronchitis damages the lungs because the alveoli break down (Figure 11). This is called **emphysema**, and it causes breathlessness because the absorbing surface of the lungs is greatly reduced.

Chronic bronchitis is not caused by infection. But it does make the patient more likely to suffer from infections of the bronchi, which can be treated with antibiotics. The chronic condition can be eased only

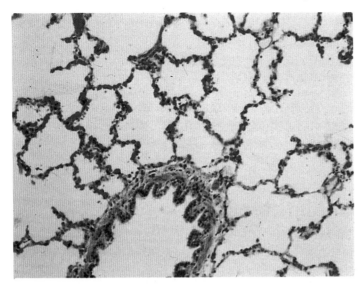

(a) Normal lung tissue showing a bronchiole and about 25 alveoli (×200).

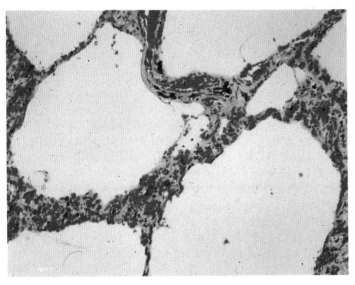

(b) Lung tissue from a person with emphysema. This is the same magnification as (a). The alveoli have broken down, leaving only about five air sacs which provide a much reduced absorbing surface.

Figure 11   Emphysema

by giving up smoking, and avoiding, as far as possible, polluted air.

Bronchial asthma

In an attack of asthma, the circular muscles in the walls of the bronchi contract and so make the airway narrower. This makes breathing difficult for the patient, particularly breathing out. In some cases, the lining of the bronchi may swell up and produce a lot of mucus which is difficult to cough up. The attacks may last a few minutes or several hours. In between attacks the patient probably feels quite well, though he or she may still 'wheeze' when breathing.

People with asthma seem to have bronchial tubes which are unusually sensitive to certain foreign substances. These may be smoke or irritants, but are just as likely to be substances like household dust, pollen, and dust from cats' or horses' hair. Certain kinds of food such as eggs, cows' milk or wheat may even bring on an attack. This reaction is known as an **allergy** and the person is said to be **allergic** to the substance. An allergic reaction is something like an antigen–antibody reaction. The patient's bronchial tubes respond vigorously to the antigen.

The family of an asthmatic person often has a history of allergic reactions, not necessarily asthmatic ones.

Asthmatic attacks may happen during infections such as bronchitis. But it is not clear whether bronchitis may set off an attack of asthma, or whether an asthmatic is more likely than other people to develop bronchitis.

In many cases of asthma there is a strong, but not easily identifiable, psychological cause. The first attack may be brought on by anxiety or emotional stress. Similar situations may provoke further attacks.

Although asthma attacks are distressing they are not usually dangerous. Most asthmatic children stop having attacks after puberty (page 175).

There are modern drugs that help to relax the bronchial muscles. They can be taken by mouth or sprayed into the airways. Some of these drugs are dangerous if used too often and must be provided by a doctor.

There is no long-term cure for asthma. But the frequency of attacks can be reduced by avoiding the substances known to bring on an attack, such as dust and animal fur, by avoiding – if possible – nervous tension and anxiety and by taking care to avoid infections of the bronchial passages.

Atmospheric pollutants

The lungs can be damaged by chemicals and particles in the air we breathe. The sulphur dioxide and nitrogen oxides produced by industry and motor vehicles irritate the lungs and may cause bronchitis if exposure to these gases is prolonged. People already suffering from respiratory illness are particularly likely to be affected. The 1952 'smog' in London is thought to have caused 4000 extra deaths in one week.

The nasal epithelium traps particles larger than about 7 μm. Smaller particles are trapped by the bronchial epithelium or are ingested by white cells living in the respiratory passages. These defences can be overwhelmed, however, when people are exposed for many years to high levels of dust. In some industrial workers, breathing in certain types of dust leads in time to lung diseases known generally as **pneumoconiosis**. These dusts are produced during mining or other industrial activities such as processing asbestos, china clay or cotton.

Just how pneumoconiosis is produced is not known for certain. The dust particles may irritate the lungs and cause bronchitis and emphysema. The white cells which ingest the particles may die and release toxic substances. In the long term, the dust causes fibrous tissue to develop in the lungs. This reduces their elasticity and their absorbing surface and leads to breathlessness.

Silica dust, from mining and quarrying, and asbestos dust are particularly harmful. Long exposure to asbestos may also lead to a form of lung cancer.

Diseases associated with particular industrial processes are called **occupational diseases**. The occupational lung diseases can be reduced by using powerful extractor fans in the place of work. Workers often wear face masks which filter out the suspended particles.

QUESTIONS

10 What are the possible causes of a persistent cough? How would a doctor try to find out if the cause was tuberculosis?

11 If antibiotics are not effective against viruses, why are they sometimes used in cases of bronchitis?

12 Suggest a reason why it is possible to acquire immunity to tuberculosis but not to the common cold.

Smoking

In the short term, smoking causes the bronchioles to constrict and the cilia lining the air passages to stop beating. The smoke also makes the lining produce more mucus. The long-term effects may take many years to develop but they are severe and disabling. And they often kill. Probably 100 000 people per year, in Britain alone, die prematurely as a result of smoking.

Lung cancer

All forms of air pollution are likely to increase the chances of lung cancer. But many scientific studies show clearly that the vast increase in lung cancer (4000 per cent in the last century) is almost entirely due to cigarette-smoking (Figure 12).

At least 17 substances in tobacco smoke are known to cause cancer in animals. It is now thought that 90 per cent of lung cancer is caused by smoking. Table 2 shows the relationship between smoking cigarettes and the risk of developing lung cancer.

Table 2   Cigarette-smoking and lung cancer

Number of cigarettes per day	Increased risk of lung cancer
1–14	×8
15–24	×13
25+	×25

Emphysema

Emphysema is a breakdown of the alveoli. The action of one or more of the substances in tobacco smoke weakens the walls of the alveoli. The irritant substances in the smoke cause a 'smoker's cough' and the coughing bursts some of the weakened alveoli. In time, the absorbing surface of the lungs is greatly reduced (Figure 11). Then the smoker's blood cannot be oxygenated properly and the least exertion brings on breathlessness and exhaustion.

Chronic bronchitis

Smoke stops the cilia in the air passages from beating. So the irritant substances in the smoke and the excess mucus collect in the bronchi. This leads to bronchitis. Over 95 per cent of people suffering from bronchitis are smokers. They have a 20 times greater chance of dying from bronchitis than non-smokers.

Heart disease

Coronary heart disease is the leading cause of death in most developed countries. It results from a blockage of coronary arteries by fatty deposits. This reduces the supply of oxygenated blood to the heart muscle and sooner or later leads to heart failure (see page 138). High blood pressure, diets with too much animal fat, and lack of exercise may also be causes of heart attack. But about a quarter of all deaths from coronary heart disease are thought to be caused by smoking (Figure 27 on page 139).

The nicotine and carbon monoxide from cigarette smoke make blood more likely to clot and so block the coronary arteries, already partly blocked by fatty deposits. The carbon monoxide may increase the rate at which the fatty material is laid down in the arteries.

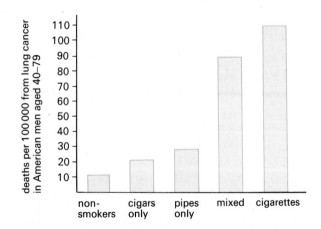

Figure 12   Smoking and lung cancer. Cigar- and pipe-smokers are probably at less risk than cigarette-smokers because they often do not inhale the smoke. But their death rate from lung cancer is still twice that of non-smokers.

(From *Smoking and health now: a report of the Royal College of Physicians*, Pitman Medical Publishing Co. Ltd)

Other risks

About 95 per cent of patients with disease of the leg arteries are cigarette-smokers. This condition is the most frequent cause of leg amputations.

Strokes due to arterial disease in the brain are more frequent in smokers than in non-smokers.

Cancer of the bladder, ulcers in the stomach and duodenum, tooth decay, gum disease and tuberculosis all occur more frequently in smokers.

Babies born to women who smoke during pregnancy are smaller than average, probably as a result of reduced oxygen supply caused by the carbon monoxide in the blood. In smokers, there is twice the frequency of miscarriages and a 50 per cent higher stillbirth rate. Their babies have a 26 per cent higher death rate (Figure 13).

In 1976 two famous doctors predicted that one in every three smokers will die as a result of their smoking habits. Those who do not die young will probably be seriously disabled by one of the conditions described above.

Passive smoking It is not only the smokers themselves who are harmed by tobacco smoke. Non-smokers in the same room are also affected. In a family where both parents smoke, the children may breathe in as much nicotine as if they were themselves smoking 80 cigarettes a year.

Statistical studies indicate that non-smokers who live with smokers have an increased chance of developing the above smoking-related diseases.

Figure 13 Cigarette smoke can harm an unborn baby. Pregnant women who smoke may have smaller babies. They have a higher risk of miscarriage or stillbirth.

Reducing the risks

Suppose you smoked up to 20 cigarettes a day. If you gave up smoking today you would, after ten years, be at no greater risk than a non-smoker of your own age. If you smoked a pipe or cigars (without inhaling) you would be at less risk than a cigarette-smoker, but still at greater risk than a non-smoker. You could reduce your risk of disease or death by changing to low-tar cigarettes, leaving longer stubs, inhaling less and taking fewer puffs.

Correlations and causes

As explained on page 139, a correlation between two variables does not prove that one of the variables causes the other. The fact that a higher risk of dying from lung cancer is correlated with heavy smoking does not actually prove that smoking causes lung cancer. It may be that people who become heavy smokers are, in some way, exposed to other possible causes of lung cancer. They may live in areas of high air pollution or they may have an inherited tendency to cancer of the lung. These hypotheses are not very convincing, particularly when such an extensive list of ailments is associated with smoking.

This is not to say that smoking is the only cause of lung cancer. Nor does everyone who smokes eventually develop lung cancer. People's lifestyles, environments and genetic backgrounds may interact in some complex way that leads, in some cases, to lung cancer. Smoking may be only a part, but a very important part, of these interactions.

QUESTIONS

13 What are (a) the immediate effects and (b) the long-term effects of tobacco smoke on the trachea, bronchi and lungs?
14 Why does a regular smoker get out of breath sooner than a non-smoker of similar age and build?
15 If you smoke 20 cigarettes a day, by how much are your chances of getting lung cancer increased?
16 Apart from lung cancer, what other diseases are probably caused by smoking?

PRACTICAL WORK

1 Oxygen in exhaled air

Place a large screw-top jar on its side in a bowl of water (Figure 14 (a)). Put a rubber tube in the mouth of the jar. Then turn the jar upside down, still full of water and with the rubber tube still in it. Start breathing out and when you feel your lungs must be about half-empty, breathe the last part of the air down the rubber tubing so that the air collects in the upturned jar and fills it (Figure 14 (b)). Put the screw top back on the jar under water. Remove the jar from the bowl and place it upright on the bench.

Light the candle on the special wire holder (Figure 14 (c)). Remove the lid of the jar, lower the burning candle into the jar and count the number of seconds the candle stays alight.

Now relight the candle. Take a fresh jar, with ordinary air. See how long the candle stays alight in this.

Results The candle will burn for about 15–20 seconds in a large jar of ordinary air. In exhaled air it will go out in about 5 seconds.

Interpretation Burning needs oxygen. When the oxygen is used up, the flame goes out. It looks as if exhaled air contains much less oxygen than atmospheric air.

(a) Lie the jar on its side under the water

(b) Breathe out through the rubber tube and trap the air in the jar

(c) Lower the burning candle into the jar until the lid is resting on the rim

Figure 14   Testing exhaled air for oxygen

2 Carbon dioxide in exhaled air

Prepare two large test-tubes as shown in Figure 15, each containing a little clear lime water. Put the ends of both rubber tubes at the same time in your mouth. Breathe in and out gently through the tubes for about 15 seconds. Notice which tube is bubbling when you breathe out and which one bubbles when you breathe in.

If after 15 seconds there is no difference in the appearance of the lime water in the two tubes, continue breathing through them for another 15 seconds.

Results The lime water in tube B goes milky. The lime water in tube A stays clear.

Interpretation Carbon dioxide turns lime water milky. Exhaled air passes through tube B. Inhaled air passes through tube A. Exhaled air must, therefore, contain more carbon dioxide than inhaled air.

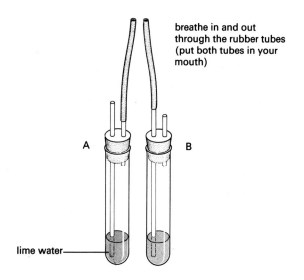

breathe in and out through the rubber tubes (put both tubes in your mouth)

A   B

lime water

Figure 15   Comparing the carbon dioxide content of inhaled and exhaled air

3 Vital capacity and tidal volume

Calibrate a large (5 litre) plastic bottle by filling it with water, half a litre at a time, and marking the water levels on the outside. Fill the bottle with water and put on the stopper. Put about 50 mm depth of water in a large plastic bowl. Hold the bottle upside down with its neck under water and remove the screw top. Some of the water will run out but this does not matter. Push a rubber tube into the mouth of the bottle to position A (shown on Figure 16). Take a deep breath and then exhale as much air as possible down the tubing into the bottle. The final water level inside the bottle will tell you your vital capacity.

Now push the rubber tubing further into the bottle, to position B (Figure 16), and blow out any water left in the tube. Support the bottle with your hand and breathe quietly in and out through the tube, keeping the water level inside and outside the bottle the same. This will give you an idea of your tidal volume.

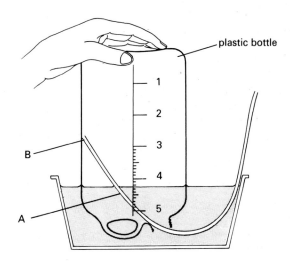

Figure 16 Measuring the vital capacity and tidal volume. 'A' shows the position of the tube when measuring the vital capacity. 'B' is the position for measuring the tidal volume.

CHECK LIST

- Ventilation is inhaling and exhaling air.
- The ribs, rib muscles and diaphragm make the lungs expand and contract. This causes inhaling and exhaling.
- Air is drawn into the lungs through the trachea, bronchi and bronchioles.
- The vast number of air pockets (alveoli) give the lungs an enormous internal surface area. This surface is moist and lined with capillaries.
- The blood in the capillaries picks up oxygen from the air in the alveoli and gives out carbon dioxide. This is called gaseous exchange.
- Ventilation exchanges the air in the air passages but not in the alveoli.
- Exchange of oxygen and carbon dioxide in the alveoli takes place by diffusion.
- The oxygen is carried round the body by the blood and used by the cells for their respiration.
- During exercise, the rate and depth of breathing increase. This supplies extra oxygen to the muscles and removes their excess carbon dioxide.
- Tobacco smoke causes the bronchioles to constrict, the cilia in their lining to stop beating and excessive mucus to be produced.
- Smoking is correlated with heart disease, bronchitis, emphysema and lung cancer.

Excretion
Definition.

Excretory Organs
Lungs, kidneys, liver.

Kidneys
Structure. Function. Selective re-absorption.

Osmo-regulation
Controlling the blood concentration.

The Dialysis Machine

Homeostasis
The stability of the internal environment.

A great many chemical reactions take place inside the cells of an organism in order to keep it alive. The products of some of these reactions are poisonous and must be removed from the body. For example, the breakdown of glucose during respiration (page 28) produces carbon dioxide. This is carried away by the blood and removed in the lungs. Excess amino acids are de-aminated in the liver to form glycogen and **urea**, as explained on page 120. The urea is removed from the tissues by the blood, and expelled by the kidneys.

Urea and similar waste products from the breakdown of proteins, like **uric acid**, contain the element nitrogen. For this reason they are often called **nitrogenous waste products**.

During feeding, more water and salts are taken in with the food than are needed by the body. So these excess substances need to be removed as fast as they build up.

The hormones produced by the endocrine glands (page 214) affect the rate at which various body systems work. Adrenalin, for example, speeds up the heart beat. When hormones have done their job, they are modified in the liver and excreted by the kidneys.

The nitrogenous waste products, excess salts and spent hormones are excreted as a watery solution called **urine**.

Excretion is the name given to the removal from the body of

1 the waste products of its chemical reactions,
2 the excess water and salts taken in with the diet, and
3 spent hormones.

Excretion also includes the removal of drugs or other foreign substances taken into the alimentary canal and absorbed by the blood. The term 'excretion' should not usually be applied to the passing out of faeces (page 118). This is because most of the contents of the faeces, apart from the bile pigments, have not taken part in reactions in the cells of the body.

QUESTIONS

1 Write a list of the substances that are likely to be excreted from the body during the day.
2 Why do you think that urine analysis is an important part of medical diagnosis?

Excretory Organs

Lungs The lungs supply the body with oxygen. But they are also excretory organs because they get rid of carbon dioxide. They also lose a great deal of water vapour, but this loss is not a method of controlling the water content of the body.

Kidneys The kidneys remove urea and other nitrogenous waste from the blood. They also expel excess water, salts, hormones (page 214) and drugs.

Liver The yellow-green bile pigment bilirubin is a breakdown product of haemoglobin (see page 126). Bilirubin is excreted with the bile into the small intestine and expelled with the faeces. The pigment undergoes changes in the intestine and is largely responsible for the brown colour of the faeces.

Skin Sweat consists of water, with sodium chloride and traces of urea dissolved in it. When you sweat, you will expel these substances from your body. So, in one sense, they are being excreted. However, sweating is a response to a rise in temperature and not to a change in the blood composition. In this sense, therefore, skin is not an excretory organ like the lungs and kidneys.

The Kidneys

Structure

The two kidneys are fairly solid, oval structures. They are red-brown, enclosed in a transparent membrane and attached to the back of the abdominal cavity (Figure 1). The **renal artery** branches off from the aorta and brings oxygenated blood to them. The **renal vein** takes deoxygenated blood away from the kidneys to the vena cava (see Figure 10 on page 129). A tube, called the **ureter**, runs from each kidney to the bladder in the lower part of the abdomen.

The kidney tissue consists of many capillaries and tiny tubes, called **renal tubules**, held together with connective tissue. If the kidney is cut down its length (sectioned), it is seen to have a dark, outer

region called the **cortex** and a lighter, inner zone, the **medulla**. Where the ureter joins the kidney there is a space called the **pelvis** (Figure 2).

The conical projections of the medulla into the pelvis are called **pyramids**.

The renal artery divides up into a great many arterioles and capillaries, mostly in the cortex (Figure 3). Each arteriole leads to a **glomerulus**. This is a capillary repeatedly divided and coiled, making a knot of vessels (Figure 4). Each glomerulus is

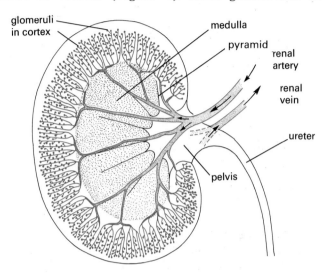

Figure 3 **Section through kidney to show distribution of glomeruli**

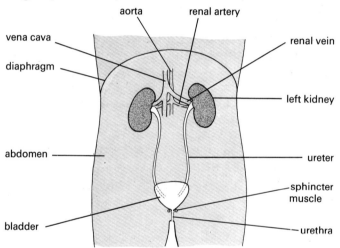

Figure 1 **Position of the kidneys in the body**

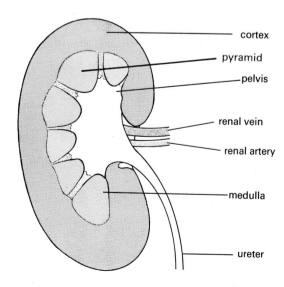

Figure 2 **Section through the kidney to show regions**

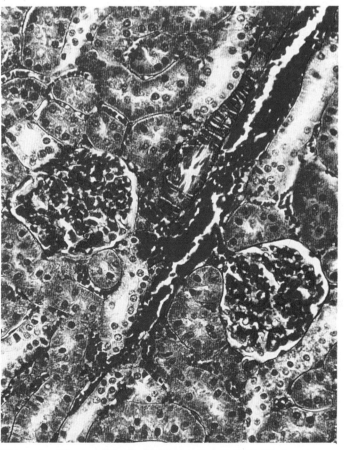

Figure 4 **Glomeruli in the kidney cortex** ($\times 300$). The two glomeruli are surrounded by kidney tubules cut across at different angles. The light space around each glomerulus represents the Bowman's capsule.

almost entirely surrounded by a cup-shaped organ called a **Bowman's capsule**, which leads to a coiled renal tubule. This tubule, after a series of coils and loops, joins a **collecting duct**. The ducts pass through the medulla to open into the pelvis (Figure 5). There are thousands of glomeruli in the kidney cortex and the total surface area of their capillaries is very great.

A single glomerulus with its Bowman's capsule, renal tubule and blood capillaries is called a **nephron** (see Figure 6).

Function of the kidneys

The blood pressure in a glomerulus causes part of the blood plasma to leak through the capillary walls. The red blood cells and the plasma proteins are too big to pass out of the capillary, so the fluid that does filter through is plasma without the protein. (It is very like tissue fluid – see page 130.) The fluid thus consists mainly of water with dissolved salts, glucose, urea and uric acid. The process by which the glomerulus filters the fluid out of the blood is called **ultra-filtration**.

The filtrate from the glomerulus collects in the Bowman's capsule and trickles down the renal tubule (Figure 6). As it does so, the capillaries around the tubule absorb back into the blood those substances which the body needs. First, all the glucose is re-absorbed, with much of the water. Then some of the salts are taken back, to keep the correct concentration in the blood. The process of absorbing back the substances needed by the body is called **selective re-absorption**.

Salts not needed by the body are left to pass on down the kidney tubule together with the urea and uric acid. So these nitrogenous waste products, excess salts and water continue down the renal tube into the pelvis of the kidney. The watery solution is now called **urine**.

The walls of the ureters contain circular muscle fibres (page 183). Contraction of these fibres produces peristaltic waves which carry the urine down the ureters to the bladder.

Table 1 shows some of the differences in composition between the blood plasma and the urine. The

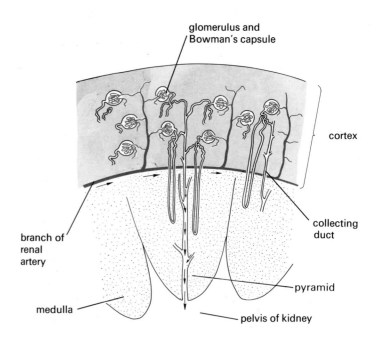

Figure 5   Section through cortex and medulla

figures represent average values, because the composition of the urine varies a great deal. The diet, activity, temperature and intake of liquid all affect it.

The **bladder** can expand to hold about 400 cm³ urine. The urine cannot escape freely from the bladder because a band of circular muscle, called a sphincter, is normally contracted, so shutting off the exit. When this sphincter muscle relaxes, the muscular walls of the bladder expel the urine through the **urethra**. Adults can control this sphincter muscle and relax it only when they want to urinate. In

Table 1   Composition of blood plasma and urine

	Plasma %	Urine %
Water	90–93	95
Urea	0.03	2
Uric acid	0.003	0.05
Ammonia	0.0001	0.05
Sodium	0.3	0.6
Potassium	0.02	0.15
Chloride	0.37	0.6
Phosphate	0.003	0.12

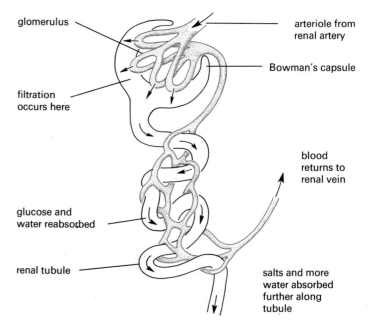

Figure 6   Part of a nephron (glomerulus, Bowman's capsule and renal tubule)

babies, the sphincter relaxes by a reflex action (page 209), set off by pressure in the bladder. Most children can control the sphincter by the time they are three years old.

Water balance and osmo-regulation

Your body gains water from food and drink. It loses water by evaporation, urination and defecation (page 118). Evaporation from the skin takes place all the time but is particularly rapid when we sweat. Air from the lungs is saturated with water vapour, which is lost to the atmosphere every time we exhale. Despite these gains and losses of water, the concentration of body fluids is kept almost constant by the kidneys, which adjust the concentration of the blood flowing through them.

If the blood is too dilute (contains too much water), less water is re-absorbed from the renal tubules. So more is left to enter the bladder. Thus, after you drink a lot, you produce a large volume of dilute urine.

If the blood is too concentrated, more water is absorbed back into the blood from the kidney tubules. So, if the body is short of water (as it may be after sweating a lot), only a small quantity of concentrated urine is produced.

This regulatory process keeps the blood at a steady concentration. It is called **osmo-regulation**, because it regulates the osmotic potential (see page 37) of the blood. Osmo-regulation is one example of the process of **homeostasis**, which is described on page 156.

Changes in the concentration of the blood are detected by a part of the brain called the **hypothalamus**. If the blood passing through the brain is too concentrated, the hypothalamus stimulates the pituitary gland, which lies beneath it. The pituitary gland then secretes into the blood a hormone (page 214) called **anti-diuretic hormone (ADH)**. When this hormone reaches the kidneys, it causes the kidney tubules to absorb more water from the glomerular filtrate back into the blood. Thus the urine becomes more concentrated and the further loss of water from the blood is reduced. If blood passing through the hypothalamus is too dilute, production of ADH from the pituitary gland is suppressed and less water is absorbed from the glomerular filtrate.

Scientists do not fully understand what makes us feel thirsty. However, the feeling of thirst certainly helps to control the intake of water and so to keep the concentration of the blood steady.

QUESTIONS

3 Why should a fall in blood pressure sometimes lead to kidney failure?

4 In what ways would you expect the composition of blood in the renal vein to differ from that in the renal artery? (Remember that the cells in the kidney will be respiring.)

5 State where, in the urinary system, the following take place (answer as precisely as possible): filtration, re-absorption, storage of urine, transport of urine, osmo-regulation.

6 In hot weather, when you sweat a great deal, you urinate less often and the urine is a dark colour. In cold weather, when you sweat little, you urinate more often and the urine is pale in colour. Use your knowledge of kidney function to explain these observations.

7 Trace the path taken by a molecule of urea from the time it is produced in the liver to the time it leaves the body in the urine (see also page 129).

The dialysis machine ('artificial kidney')

Kidney failure may be the result of an accident involving a drop in blood pressure, or of a disease of the kidneys. In an accident victim the kidneys usually recover without treatment. But if this takes longer than two weeks, the patient may die as a result of a potassium imbalance in the blood, which causes heart failure. A person with kidney disease can survive with only one kidney. If both fail, however, the patient's blood composition has to be controlled by a dialysis machine. Similarly, the accident victim can be kept alive on a dialysis machine until his or her blood pressure is normal again.

In principle, a dialysis machine consists of a long cellulose tube coiled up in a water bath. The patient's blood is led from a tube in the radial artery in the forearm and pumped through the cellulose (dialysis) tubing (Figures 7 and 8). The tiny pores in the dialysis tubing allow small molecules, such as those of salts, glucose and urea, to leak out of the tubing. Blood cells and protein molecules are too large to get through the pores (see Experiment 3, page 39). This stage is similar to the filtration process in the glomerulus.

To prevent a loss of glucose and essential salts from the blood, the liquid around the tubing consists of a solution of salts and sugar of the correct composition. So only the substances above this concentration can diffuse out of the blood into the bathing solution. Thus urea, uric acid and excess salts are removed.

The bathing solution is kept at body temperature. It is constantly changed as the unwanted blood solutes build up in it. The blood is then returned to the patient through a vein in the arm.

A patient with total kidney failure has to spend two or three nights each week connected to the machine (Figure 8). With this treatment and a carefully controlled diet, the patient can lead a fairly

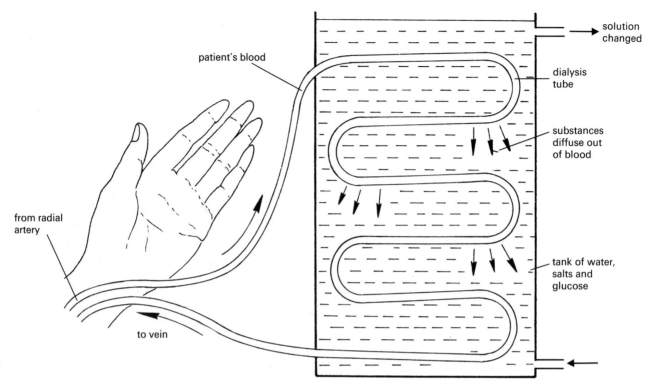

Figure 7   The principle of the kidney dialysis machine

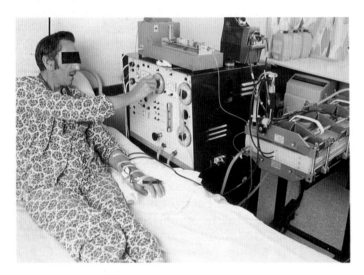

Figure 8   Kidney dialysis machine. The patient's blood is sent by the pump (top right) to the dialyser (bottom right). The patient is adjusting the control box which regulates the temperature and concentration of the dialysing liquid.

normal life. A kidney transplant, however, is a better solution because the patient is not obliged to return to the dialysis machine every three days or so.

The problems with kidney transplants are, firstly, to find enough suitable donors of healthy kidneys and, secondly, to prevent the transplanted kidney from being rejected.

The donor may be a close relative who is prepared to donate one of his or her kidneys (you can survive quite well with one kidney). Or the donated kidney may be taken from a healthy person who has died, for example, as a result of a road accident. Unless the accident victim is carrying a kidney donor card giving permission for his or her kidneys to be used, the relatives must give their permission.

The problem with rejection is that the body reacts to any transplanted cells or tissues as it does to all foreign proteins. It produces lymphocytes which attack and destroy them (see page 134). This rejection can be overcome by (1) choosing a donor whose tissues are as similar as possible to those of the patient, such as a close relative, and (2) using immuno-suppressive drugs. These suppress the production of lymphocytes and their antibodies against the transplanted organ.

Homeostasis

Homeostasis (it means 'staying similar') is the way in which the composition of the tissue fluid (page 130) in the body is kept within narrow limits. Its concentration, acidity and temperature are being adjusted all the time to prevent any big changes.

In living cells, all the chemical reactions are controlled by enzymes. The enzymes are very sensitive to the conditions in which they work. A slight fall in temperature or a rise in acidity (page 23) may slow down or stop an enzyme from working. The change could thus prevent an important reaction from taking place in the cell.

The cell membrane controls the substances which enter and leave the cell. But the tissue fluid supplies or removes these substances, and it is therefore important to keep the composition of the tissue fluid as steady as possible. If the tissue fluid were too

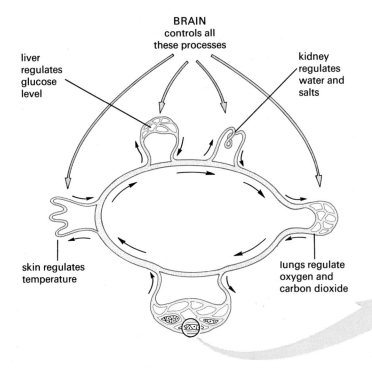

BRAIN
controls all
these processes

liver
regulates
glucose
level

kidney
regulates
water and
salts

skin regulates
temperature

lungs regulate
oxygen and
carbon dioxide

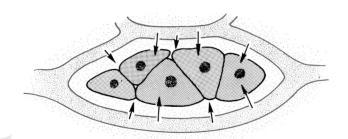

This tissue fluid, with its carefully controlled
composition, provides the best conditions for
the cell's enzymes to work in

Figure 9   The homeostatic mechanisms of the body

concentrated, it would withdraw water from the cells by osmosis (page 36) and the body would be dehydrated. If the tissue fluid were too dilute, the cells would take up too much water from it by osmosis and the tissues would become waterlogged and swollen.

Many systems in the body help in homeostasis (Figure 9). The obvious example is the kidney, which removes substances that might poison the enzymes and also controls the level of salts, water and acids in the blood. The composition of the blood affects the tissue fluid which, in turn, affects the cells.

Another example of a homeostatic organ is the liver, which regulates the level of glucose in the blood (page 120). The liver stores the excess glucose as glycogen. It also turns glycogen back into glucose if the concentration in the blood gets too low. The brain cells are very sensitive to the glucose concentration in the blood. If the level drops too far, they stop working properly and the person becomes unconscious and will die unless glucose is injected into the blood system. This shows how important homeostasis is to the body.

The lungs (page 141) play a part in homeostasis by keeping the concentrations of oxygen and carbon dioxide in the blood at the best level for the cell's chemical reactions, especially respiration.

The next chapter describes the way in which the skin regulates the temperature of the blood. If cells were to get too cold, the chemical reactions would become too slow to maintain life. If they became too hot, the enzymes would be destroyed.

The brain has overall control of the homeostatic processes in the body. It checks the composition of the blood flowing through it. If the blood is too warm, too cold, too concentrated or has too little glucose, nerve impulses or hormones are sent to the organs concerned, causing them to make the necessary adjustments.

QUESTION

8 Where will the brain send nerve impulses or hormones if the blood flowing through it (a) has too much water, (b) contains too little glucose, (c) is too warm, (d) has too much carbon dioxide?

CHECK LIST

- Excretion is getting rid of unwanted substances from the body.
- The lungs excrete carbon dioxide.
- The kidneys excrete urea, unwanted salts and excess water.
- Part of the blood plasma entering the kidneys is filtered out by the capillaries. Substances which the body needs, like glucose, are absorbed back into the blood. The unwanted

substances are left to pass down the ureters into the bladder.
- The bladder stores urine, which is discharged at intervals.
- The kidneys help to keep the blood at a steady concentration by excreting excess salts and by adjusting the amount of water (osmo-regulation).
- The kidneys, lungs, liver and skin all help to keep the blood composition the same (homeostasis).

16 The Skin, and Temperature Control

Functions of the Skin
Protection, sensitivity, temperature control, vitamin D production. Immunological function.

Structure of the Skin
Epidermis, dermis, hair, sweat glands.

Heat Balance
Gain and loss of heat.

Temperature Control
Vaso-dilation, vaso-constriction, sweating.

Hypothermia

The skin forms a continuous layer over the entire body. It makes it difficult for harmful substances, bacteria and fungi to get into the body. It keeps down the loss of water from the body and it helps to control the body temperature.

Functions of the Skin

Protection

A brown or black pigment, melanin, in the skin absorbs the harmful ultraviolet rays from sunlight. Skin containing only a little melanin may be damaged by these rays. This happens when white-skinned people become sunburned. Many white-skinned people, however, produce extra melanin and so acquire a 'sun-tan'. This helps to protect the skin from the effects of ultraviolet light.

The layer of dead cells at the surface of the skin stops harmful bacteria getting into the living tissues beneath. It also greatly reduces the evaporation of water from the body, so helping to maintain the composition of the body fluids.

Sensitivity

Scattered through the skin are a large number of tiny sense organs which give rise to feelings of touch, pressure, heat, cold and pain. These make us aware of changes in our surroundings. Thus we can act to avoid damage, recognize objects by touch and manipulate objects with our hands (see page 195).

Vitamin D production

The ultraviolet rays in sunlight act on natural fats in the skin to produce a form of vitamin D. This is an important source of vitamin D. If people with deeply pigmented skins live and work in industrial towns where they receive little sunlight, they may develop a shortage of vitamin D unless their diets contain enough of this vitamin.

Immunological function

Some of the cells in the epidermis can recognize antigens (page 134). They then 'programme' lymphocytes (which arrive via the blood) to attack these antigens or the micro-organisms that produce them. In this, the skin has a function similar to that of the thymus gland (page 133).

Temperature regulation

The way in which the skin helps to keep the body temperature constant is described on pages 161-2.

QUESTION

1 To what dangers is the body exposed if (a) a small area of skin is damaged, (b) a large area of skin is damaged?

Structure of the Skin

There are two main layers in the skin, an outer **epidermis** and an inner **dermis**. The thickness of these two layers depends on which part of the body they are covering. The skin on the palms of the hands and soles of the feet has a very thick epidermis and no hairs (Figure 2). Over the rest of the body, the epidermis is thinner and has hairs (Figure 3). The diagram of a section through the skin (Figure 1) is a generalized one. It shows all the structures that are in skin as a whole, even though not all are present in all areas.

Epidermis

Basal layer (Malpighian layer) This is the innermost layer of cells in the epidermis. The cells of the basal layer keep dividing and producing new

cells. The new cells are pushed towards the surface of the skin, forming the **granular layer**.

Some of the cells in the basal layer produce granules of the pigment melanin. This pigment is passed to the other epidermal cells to give the skin its colour. Skin with little melanin looks pink because of the haemoglobin in the blood capillaries. Skin with a lot of melanin, evenly distributed, looks black.

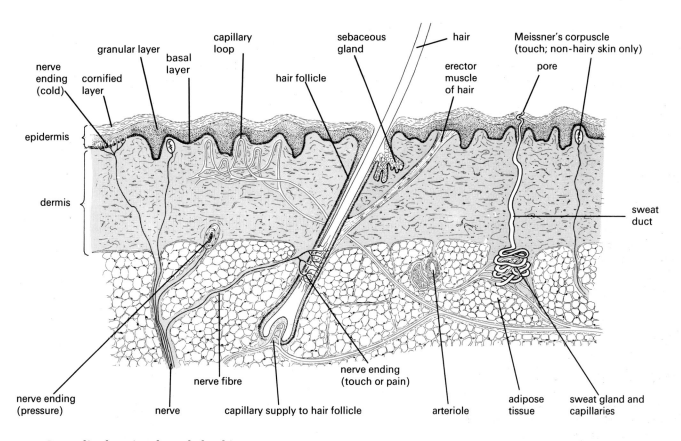

Figure 1   Generalized section through the skin

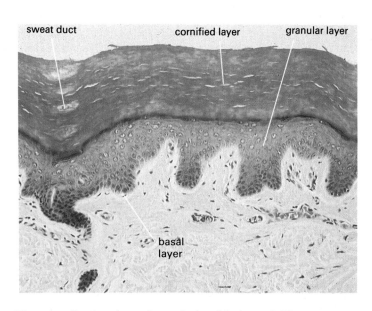

Figure 2   Section through non-hairy skin (×300). The sweat ducts are contorted as they pass through the cornified layer.

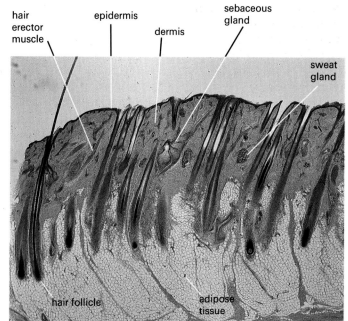

Figure 3   Section through hairy skin (×20)

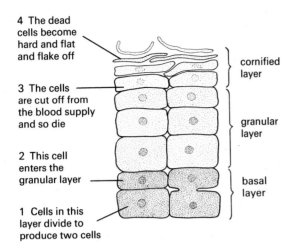

4 The dead cells become hard and flat and flake off

3 The cells are cut off from the blood supply and so die

2 This cell enters the granular layer

1 Cells in this layer divide to produce two cells

cornified layer

granular layer

basal layer

Figure 4 Growth of the epidermis

Granular layer The cells produced by the basal layer move through the granular layer and then die, so forming the cornified layer.

Cornified layer This consists of dead, flattened cells. It is the outermost layer of the epidermis, and helps to cut down evaporation and keep bacteria out. The cells on the surface are constantly worn away, and are replaced from below by the basal and granular layers (Figure 4).

Dermis

The dermis is a layer of connective tissue containing capillaries, sensory nerve endings, lymphatics, sweat glands and hair follicles.

Capillaries These bring oxygen and food to the skin and remove its carbon dioxide and nitrogenous waste. They supply the hair follicles and sweat glands. The capillary loops close to the surface (just beneath the epidermis) play an important part in regulating heat loss from the body (see page 161).

Sweat glands A sweat gland is a coiled tube deep in the dermis. When the body temperature is too high, the sweat gland takes up water from the capillaries around it. The water collects in the gland, travels up the **sweat duct**, and comes out of a **pore** in the epidermis on to the skin surface. When the sweat evaporates, it takes heat from the body and so cools it down. Unless the sweat evaporates, it has no cooling effect.

Sweat is mainly water but there are some dissolved salts and urea in it. Some people regard this as a form of excretion (page 153). But sweating is a response to a rise in temperature, not to excess water or salt in the body.

Hair follicles A hair follicle is a deep pit lined with granular and basal cells. The basal cells keep dividing and adding cells to the base of the hair,

making it grow. A hair is a lot of cornified cells formed into a tube. The hair follicle has nerve endings which respond when the hair is touched, or give a feeling of pain if the hair is pulled.

In furry mammals, the hairs trap a layer of air close to the body. Air is a bad conductor of heat and so this layer of air insulates the body against heat loss. When the **hair erector muscle** contracts, it pulls the hair more upright. This makes the fur stand up more and so provides a thicker layer of insulating air in cold weather. Most of the human body is covered with short hairs, but they trap very little air. And when the hair erector muscles contract, they produce only 'goose pimples'.

Sebaceous glands The sebaceous glands open into the top of the hair follicles. They produce an oily substance that keeps the epidermis waterproof and stops it drying out.

Sensory nerve endings These are described more fully on page 195.

Fat layer The fat stored in the adipose tissue beneath the skin not only provides a store of food, but also forms an insulating layer and reduces the heat lost from the body.

QUESTIONS

2 Is a hair made by the epidermis or the dermis?
3 Why do you think dead cells are better than living cells in reducing water loss from the skin?
4 Describe the path taken by a water molecule that enters the skin in the blood plasma of a capillary and ends up in sweat on the surface of the skin.

Heat Balance

Body temperature

Different parts of the body are at different temperatures. The skin temperature is lower than the liver temperature, and the feet and hands may be colder than the abdomen. However, 'body temperature' usually means the temperature deep inside the body. You cannot put a thermometer far inside the body, so it is usually placed in the mouth, under the tongue, and held there for two minutes with the mouth closed.

The type of thermometer used is called a **clinical thermometer** (Figure 5). It is calibrated from 35 to 42 °C (95–110 °F) and can be read to 0.1 of a degree. The bulb has to be small and so the mercury column needs to be very thin to show the expansion of the mercury. The stem of the thermometer is shaped so that the glass magnifies the mercury column, making it easier to see.

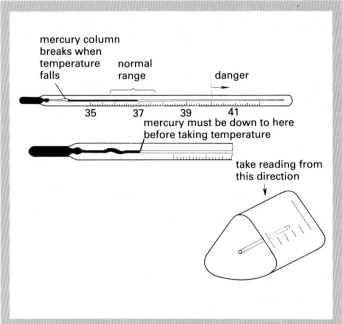

Figure 5   The clinical thermometer

When you remove the thermometer from the mouth to take the reading, the bulb cools and the mercury starts to contract. This does not affect the reading, however. The reason is that there is a constriction (a narrowing of the tube) just above the bulb, at which the retreating thread of mercury breaks. So the thread above the constriction is left unchanged.

Before you can take the next reading, you have to shake the mercury back into the bulb. Then sterilize the thermometer by placing it in an anti-septic solution before you use it again.

The body temperature varies during the day and there is no single 'correct' body temperature. Body temperatures between 35.8 and 37.7 °C (96.4 and 99.8 °F) are normal. A fall below 34 °C (93 °F) or a rise above 40 °C (104 °F) may be dangerous if it lasts for long (see page 162).

The body may gain or lose heat as a result of internal changes or external influences. These are explained below.

Heat gain

Internal   Many of the chemical reactions in the cells produce heat. The chief heat-producers are the abdominal organs, the brain and contracting muscles. Any increase in muscular activity of the body will result in more heat being produced.

External   Direct heat from the Sun will be absorbed by the body. If the air temperature is above 37 °C, the body will absorb heat. Hot food and drink also add heat to the body.

Heat loss

Heat is lost to the air from the exposed surfaces of the body by conduction, convection and radiation. Heat is lost in evaporation from the skin, which takes place all the time. The cold air breathed into the lungs and cold food or drink taken into the stomach all absorb heat from the body.

The heat lost from the body is largely balanced by the heat absorbed or produced. However, changes in the temperature of the surroundings or in the rate of activity may upset this balance. In humans, any change in the temperature balance is regulated mainly by changes in the skin (see below).

We also control our heat loss and gain by taking conscious action. We remove clothing or move into the shade to cool down. We put on more clothes or take exercise to keep warm.

QUESTIONS

5 What conscious actions do we take to reduce the heat lost from the body?
6 What sort of chemical reaction in the liver and in active muscle will produce heat? How does this heat get to other parts of the body? (See pages 28, 121 and 129.)
7 Draw up a balance sheet to show all the possible ways the human body can gain or lose heat. Make two columns, with 'Gains' on the left and 'Losses' on the right.

Temperature Control

Skin structure

The structures in the skin which play a part in temperature control are the small blood vessels and the sweat glands. In furry mammals, the hairs and hair muscles also have a role.

The arterioles and capillaries near the surface of the skin can increase or decrease in width and so increase or reduce the amount of blood flowing through them. An increase in width of the vessel is called **vaso-dilation**. A reduction in width is **vaso-constriction**.

The sweat glands are not active when the loss and gain of heat are balanced. But as soon as the body temperature starts to rise, the sweat glands of the trunk, limbs and face produce sweat as described above. Sweating from the hands, feet and armpits is a response to emotional stress rather than over-heating.

Over-heating

If the body gains or produces heat faster than it is losing it, the following processes occur:

Vaso-dilation   The widening of the blood vessels in the dermis allows more warm blood to flow near the surface of the skin and so lose more heat (Figure 6 (a)).

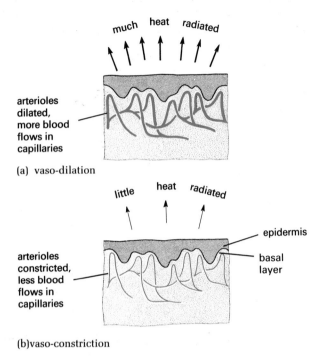

(a) vaso-dilation

(b)vaso-constriction

Figure 6   Vaso-dilation and vaso-constriction

Figure 7   Sweating. During vigorous activity the sweat evaporates from the skin and helps to cool the body. When the activity stops, continued evaporation of sweat may over-cool the body unless it is towelled off.

Sweating   The sweat glands pour sweat on to the skin surface. When this layer of liquid evaporates it takes heat (latent heat) from the body and so cools it down (Figure 7).

Over-cooling

If the body begins to lose heat faster than it can produce it, the following changes occur:

Sweat production stops   Thus the heat lost by evaporation is reduced.

Vaso-constriction   Constriction of the blood vessels in the skin reduces the amount of warm blood flowing near the surface (Figure 6 (b)).

Shivering   Uncontrollable bursts of rapid muscular contraction in the limbs release heat as a result of the chemical changes in the muscles.

These processes keep the body temperature of an adult within a degree or so either side of 37 °C, even when the external temperature changes. The average temperature recorded by a thermometer under the tongue is 36.7 °C, and is called the **core temperature** of the body. The temperature of the skin can vary very widely without affecting the core temperature. It is the sensory nerve endings in your dermis which make you feel hot or cold. You do not feel anything if there are small changes in your core temperature.

Keeping the body temperature steady is part of the homeostasis of the body (see pages 121 and 156).

Hypothermia

If the body loses heat faster than the tissues can produce it, the core temperature may fall. If it drops below 35 °C speech becomes slurred, and sight is affected. The person may behave illogically and unreasonably. If body temperature drops below 32 °C, he or she becomes unconscious. This lowering of core temperature is called **hypothermia**. Unless the body is gently rewarmed, the sufferer will die.

Young people may become hypothermic in conditions such as immersion in cold water or exposure in wet clothing. In elderly people, hypothermia may result simply from inactivity in chilly surroundings, and from insufficient food.

Cold can also kill elderly people by causing a prolonged rise in blood pressure. This can lead to strokes and heart attacks.

Prevention of hypothermia   The chance of becoming hypothermic can be reduced by eating a good meal before taking part in outdoor pursuits such as fell-walking, climbing or sailing. The food provides the source of energy for heat production.

Warm clothing helps to reduce heat losses and, in particular, should include an outer layer which is wind-proof and rain-proof.

You can help elderly people to avoid hypothermia by regularly visiting them to make sure that they are eating well and keeping their rooms warm enough (above 20 °C).

QUESTIONS

8 What changes take place in human skin to reduce heat loss?

9 If your body temperature hardly changes at all, why do you sometimes feel hot and sometimes cold?

10 Sweating only cools you down if the sweat can evaporate.

(a) In what conditions might the sweat be unable to evaporate from your skin?

(b) What conditions might speed up the evaporation of sweat and so make you feel very cold?

PRACTICAL WORK

Cooling by evaporation

Use a dropping pipette to place a drop of alcohol on the skin on the front of your left wrist. Blow gently on the alcohol and also on the same place on the right wrist. Compare the two sensations.

Alcohol evaporates easily and takes up heat (latent heat) from your skin. This makes the skin feel cold. The evaporation of sweat has the same effect, but sweat evaporates more slowly than alcohol does.

CHECK LIST

- Skin consists of an outer layer of epidermis and an inner dermis.
- The epidermis is growing all the time and has an outer layer of dead cells.
- The dermis contains the sweat glands, hair follicles, sense organs and capillaries.
- Skin protects the body from bacteria and drying out. It contains sense organs which give us the sense of touch, warmth, cold and pain. It also controls the body temperature.
- Chemical activity in the body produces heat. So do muscular contractions.
- Heat is lost to the surroundings by conduction, convection, radiation and evaporation.
- If the body temperature rises too much, the skin cools it down by sweating and vaso-dilation.
- If the body loses too much heat, vaso-constriction and shivering help to keep it warm.

17 Human Reproduction and Life-cycle

Reproductive Systems
Male and female organs. Gamete production.

Fertilization and Development
Mating and fertilization. Development of embryo. Placenta. Twins.

Birth and Parental Care
Normal labour and delivery. Surgical intervention. Breast-feeding, antenatal care, growth.

Puberty and the Menstrual Cycle
Hormones and secondary sexual characteristics. Menstruation and menopause.

Family Planning and Fertility
Birth control. In-vitro fertilization.

Ageing

Reproduction is the process of producing new individuals.

Most animals reproduce sexually. The two sexes, male and female, each produce special types of reproductive cells, called **gametes**. The male gametes are the **sperms** (or **spermatozoa**) and the female gametes are the **ova** (singular = ovum) or eggs (Figure 1).

To produce a new individual, a sperm has to reach an ovum and join with it (**fuse** with it). The sperm nucleus then passes into the ovum and the two nuclei also fuse. This is called **fertilization**.

The cell formed after the fertilization of an ovum by a sperm is called a **zygote**. A zygote grows by cell division to produce first an **embryo** and then a fully formed animal (Figure 2).

The male animal always produces a large number (millions) of small sperms, which can move about. The female produces a smaller number of eggs, which are larger than sperms and cannot move.

In mammals, a small number of eggs is fertilized, from one to twenty. In humans, only one egg is usually fertilized at a time. If two eggs are fertilized twins are produced.

An act of mating or **copulation** brings the sperms close enough to the ova for fertilization to take place. In mammals this act results in sperms from the male animal being put into the female. The sperms swim inside the female's reproductive system and fertilize any eggs that are present. The zygote then grows into an embryo inside the body of the female.

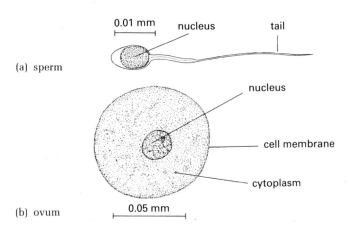

(a) sperm — 0.01 mm, nucleus, tail

(b) ovum — nucleus, cell membrane, cytoplasm, 0.05 mm

Figure 1   Human gametes

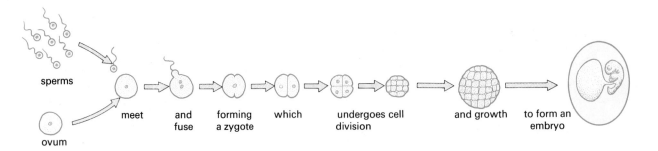

sperms — ovum — meet — and fuse — forming a zygote — which — undergoes cell division — and growth — to form an embryo

Figure 2   Fertilization and development

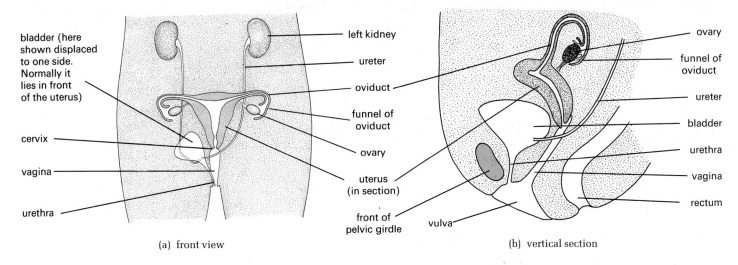

(a) front view

(b) vertical section

Figure 3 The female reproductive organs

The Human Reproductive System

Female

The ova are produced from the female reproductive organs called **ovaries**. These are two whitish oval bodies, 3–4 cm long. They lie in the lower half of the abdomen, one on each side of the **uterus** (Figure 3 (a) and (b)). Close to each ovary is the funnel-shaped opening of the **oviduct**, the narrow tube down which the ova pass when they leave the ovary. The oviduct is sometimes called the **Fallopian tube**.

The oviducts open into a wider tube, the uterus or womb, lower down in the abdomen. When there is no embryo developing in it, the uterus is about 80 mm long. It leads to the outside through a muscular tube, the **vagina**. A ring of muscle, the **cervix**, closes the lower end of the uterus where it joins the vagina. The urethra, from the bladder, opens into the **vulva** just in front of the vagina.

Male

Sperms are produced in the male reproductive organs (Figures 4 and 5), called the **testes** (singular = testis). These lie outside the abdominal cavity in a special sac called the **scrotum**. In this position they are kept slightly cooler than the rest of the body. This is the best temperature for sperm production.

Each testis consists of a mass of sperm-producing tubes (Figure 6). These tubes join to form ducts leading to the **epididymis**, a coiled tube about 6 metres long lying on the outside of each testis. The epididymis, in turn, leads into a muscular **sperm duct**. The two sperm ducts, one from each testis, open into the top of the urethra just after it leaves the bladder. A short, coiled tube called the **seminal vesicle** branches from each sperm duct just before it

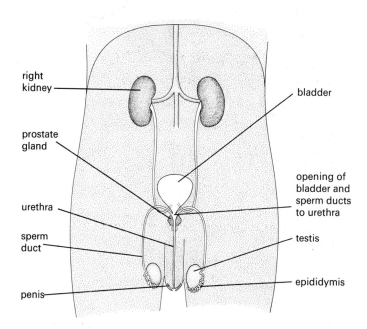

Figure 4 The male reproductive organs (front view)

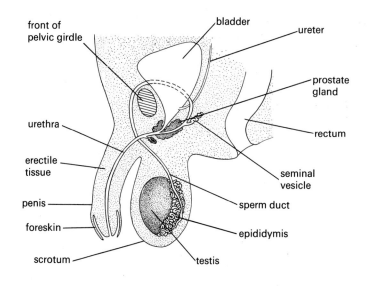

Figure 5 The male reproductive organs (side view)

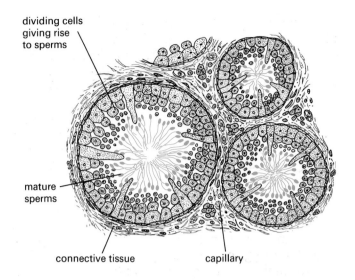

Figure 6   **Section through tubules of testis**

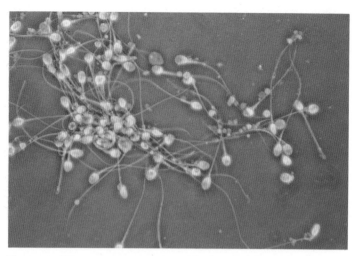

Figure 7   Human sperms (×700). The head of the sperm has a slightly different appearance when seen from the 'side' or from the 'top'.

enters the **prostate gland**, which surrounds the urethra at this point.

The urethra passes through the **penis**. Urine and sperms pass through it at different times. The penis consists of connective tissue with many blood spaces in it. This is called **erectile tissue**.

QUESTIONS

1 How do sperms differ from ova in their structure? (See Figure 1.)
2 List the structures, in the correct order, through which the sperms must pass from the time they are produced in the testis to the time they leave the urethra.
3 What structures are shown in Figure 5 which are not shown in Figure 4?
4 In what ways does a zygote differ from any other cell in the body?

Production of Gametes

Sperm production

The lining of the sperm-producing tubules in the testis consists of rapidly dividing cells (Figure 6). After several divisions, the cells grow long tails and become sperms (Figure 7) which pass into the epididymis.

During copulation, waves of peristaltic contraction pass down the epididymis and sperm ducts and force sperms out through the urethra. The prostate gland and seminal vesicle add fluid to the sperms. This fluid plus the sperms it contains is called **semen**. The ejection of sperms through the penis is called **ejaculation**.

Ovulation

The ova (egg cells) are present in the ovary at the time a baby girl is born. No more are formed during

her lifetime. Between the ages of 10 and 14 the ova start to ripen. About every four weeks an ovum is released, often (but not always) from alternate ovaries. As each ovum ripens, the cells around it divide rapidly and produce a fluid-filled sac. This sac is called a **follicle** (Figures 8 and 9). When mature, the follicle juts out on the surface of the ovary like a small blister. Finally it bursts and releases the ovum with its coating of cells into the funnel of the oviduct. This is called **ovulation**.

From the ovary, the ovum is wafted down the oviduct by the action of cilia (page 15) in the lining of the tube. If the ovum meets sperm cells in the oviduct, one of them may fertilize it.

The freshly released ovum is enclosed in a jelly-like layer called the **zona pellucida** and is still surrounded by a layer of follicle cells. Before fertilization can occur, sperms have to get through this layer of cells. The successful sperm has then to make its way through the zona pellucida, using enzymes secreted by its head.

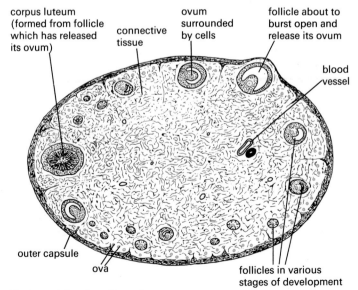

Figure 8   **Section through an ovary**

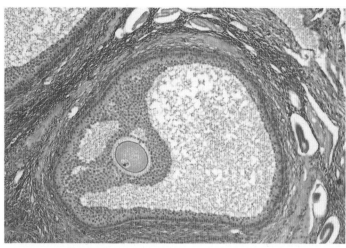

Figure 9 Mature follicle, as seen in a section through part of an ovary (×100). The ovum is surrounded by follicle cells. These produce the fluid which fills most of the follicle.

Mating and Fertilization

Mating

Sexual stimulation causes the male's penis to become erect. This is due to blood flowing into the erectile tissue round the urethra. In the female, the lining of the vagina produces mucus which makes it possible for the penis to enter it. The sensory stimulus (sensation) produced by copulation causes a reflex (page 209) in the male which results in the ejaculation of semen into the top of the vagina.

The last paragraph is a very simple description of a biological event. In humans, however, the sex act has intense psychological and emotional importance. Most people feel a strong sexual drive, which has little to do with the need to reproduce. Sometimes the sex act is simply the meeting of an urgent physical need. Sometimes it is an experience that both man and woman enjoy together. At its 'highest' level it is both of these, and is also an expression of deeply felt affection within a lasting relationship.

Fertilization

The sperms swim through the cervix and into the uterus by wriggling movements of their tails. They pass through the uterus and enter the oviduct, though we do not know by what method they do this. If there is an ovum in the oviduct, one of the sperms may bump into it and stick to its surface. The sperm then enters the cytoplasm of the ovum and the male nucleus of the sperm fuses with the female nucleus. This is the moment of fertilization and is shown in more detail in Figure 10.

Although a single ejaculation may contain five hundred million sperms, only a few hundred reach the oviduct and only one will fertilize the ovum. The function of the others is not understood. Probably very few manage to travel from the vagina to the oviduct.

The released ovum may survive for about 24 hours. The sperms might be able to fertilize an ovum for about two or three days. So fertilization is possible for only a short period of about four days each month.

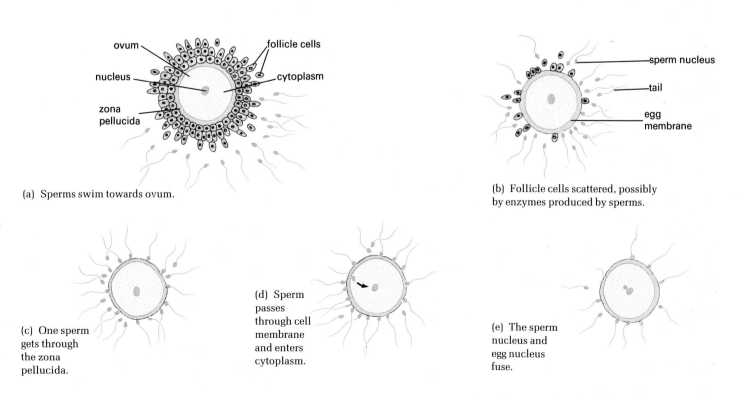

(a) Sperms swim towards ovum.

(b) Follicle cells scattered, possibly by enzymes produced by sperms.

(c) One sperm gets through the zona pellucida.

(d) Sperm passes through cell membrane and enters cytoplasm.

(e) The sperm nucleus and egg nucleus fuse.

Figure 10 Fertilization of an ovum. (The diagrams show what is thought to happen, but the details are not known for certain.)

QUESTIONS

5 Suppose that a woman starts ovulating at 13 and stops at 50.

(a) How many ova are likely to be released from her ovaries?

(b) About how many of these are likely to be fertilized?

6 List, in the correct order, the parts of the female reproductive system through which sperms must pass before reaching and fertilizing an ovum.

7 State exactly what happens at the moment of fertilization.

8 If mating takes place (a) two days before ovulation, (b) two days after ovulation, is fertilization likely to occur? Explain your answers.

Pregnancy and Development

The fertilized ovum first divides into two cells. Each of these divides again, so producing four cells. The cells continue to divide in this way to produce a solid ball of cells (Figure 11), an early stage in the development of the **embryo**. This early embryo travels down the oviduct to the uterus. Here it sinks into the lining of the uterus, a process called **implantation** (Figure 12 (a)). The embryo continues to grow and produces new cells, which form tissues and organs (Figure 13). When all the organs are formed, the embryo is called a **fetus**. One of the first organs to form is the heart, which pumps blood round the body of the embryo.

As the embryo grows, the uterus gets larger to contain it. Inside the uterus the embryo becomes enclosed in a sac called the **amnion**. This sac is filled with **amniotic fluid**, which protects the embryo from damage and prevents unequal pressures from acting on it (Figures 12 (b) and (c)). The embryo gets oxygen and food from the mother's blood through a structure called the placenta.

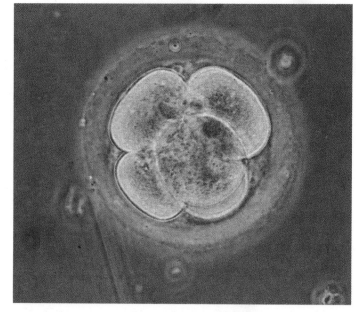

Figure 11   Human embryo at the five-cell stage (×230). The embryo is surrounded by the zona pellucida

Placenta

Soon after the ball of cells reaches the uterus, some of the cells grow into a disc-like structure, the **placenta** (Figure 12 (c)), instead of forming the organs of the embryo. The placenta develops branching outgrowths called **placental villi** (Figure 15). These villi grow into the lining of the uterus and provide a large surface area of close contact. The placenta is connected to the embryo by blood vessels running in the **umbilical cord** (Figure 12 (c)). After a few weeks, the embryo's heart has developed and is circulating blood through the umbilical cord and placenta as well as through its own tissues.

The blood vessels in the placenta are very close to the blood vessels in the uterus. Oxygen, glucose, amino acids and salts can pass from the mother's blood to the embryo's blood (Figure 14 (a)). So the blood flowing in the umbilical vein from the

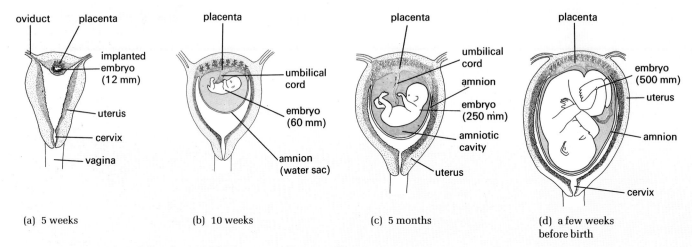

(a) 5 weeks

(b) 10 weeks

(c) 5 months

(d) a few weeks before birth

Figure 12   Growth and development in the uterus (not to scale).

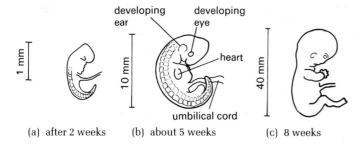

Figure 13   **Human embryo: the first 8 weeks**

(a) after 2 weeks   (b) about 5 weeks   (c) 8 weeks

placenta carries food and oxygen to be used by the living, growing tissues of the embryo.

In a similar way, the carbon dioxide and urea in the embryo's blood escape from the vessels in the placenta and are carried away by the mother's blood in the uterus (Figure 14 (b)). The embryo can thus get rid of its excretory products.

The mother's blood does not mix with the embryo's. The exchange of substances takes place across the thin walls of the blood vessels. In this way, the mother's blood pressure cannot damage the delicate vessels of the embryo. Also the placenta can select the substances allowed to pass into the embryo's blood. The placenta can prevent some harmful substances in the mother's blood from reaching the embryo. It cannot keep all of them away, however. Cigarette smoke and alcohol can both harm the embryo (see below).

> The placenta produces hormones, including oestrogens and progesterone. These hormones are believed to play an important part in maintaining the pregnancy and preparing for birth. Exactly how they act is not known. They may influence the development and activity of the muscle layers in the wall of the uterus. They may also prepare the mammary glands in the breasts for milk production.

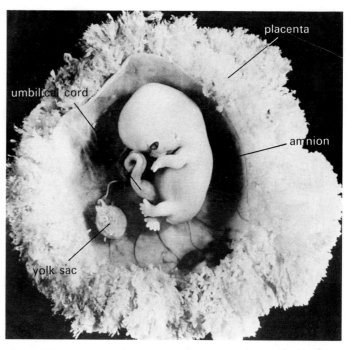

Figure 15   **Human embryo, 7 weeks** (×1.5). The embryo is enclosed in the amnion. Its limbs, eye and ear-hole can be seen clearly. The amnion is surrounded by the placenta. The fluffy-looking structures are the placental villi, which penetrate into the lining of the uterus. The umbilical cord connects the embryo to the placenta.

Twins

Sometimes a woman releases two ova when she ovulates. If both ova are fertilized, they may form twin embryos, each with its own placenta and amnion. Because the twins come from two separate ova, each fertilized by a different sperm, it is possible to have a boy and a girl. Twins formed in this way are called **fraternal twins**. Although they are born within a few minutes of each other, they are no more alike than other brothers or sisters.

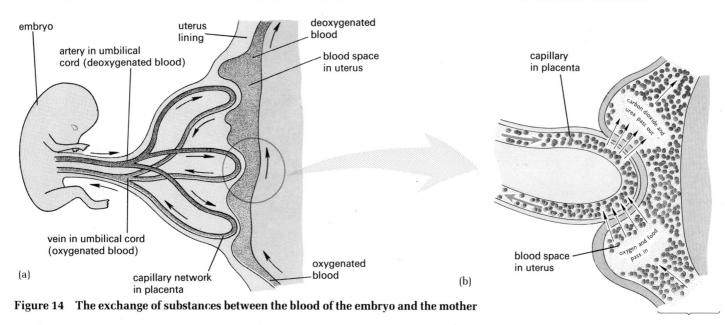

Figure 14   **The exchange of substances between the blood of the embryo and the mother**

Figure 16   Identical twins

Twins will also be produced when a single fertilized egg, during an early stage of cell division, forms two separate embryos. Sometimes these may share a placenta and amnion. Twins formed from a single ovum and sperm must be the same sex, because only one sperm (X or Y, see page 231) fertilized the ovum. These 'one-egg' twins are sometimes called **identical twins** because, unlike fraternal twins, they closely resemble each other in every respect (Figure 16).

QUESTIONS

9 In what ways will the composition of the blood in the umbilical vein differ from that in the umbilical artery?

10 An embryo is surrounded with fluid, its lungs are filled with fluid and it cannot breathe. Why doesn't it suffocate?

11 If a mother gives birth to twin boys, does this mean that they are identical twins? Explain.

Antenatal Care

'Antenatal' or 'prenatal' refers to the period before birth. Antenatal care is the way a woman should look after herself during pregnancy, so that the birth will be safe and her baby healthy.

The mother-to-be should make sure that she eats properly, and perhaps takes more iron and folic acid (page 101) to prevent anaemia. If her job is a light one, she may go on working for the first six months of pregnancy. She should not do heavy work, however, or repeated lifting or stooping.

Pregnant women who drink or smoke are more likely to have babies with low birth weights. These babies are more likely to be ill than babies of normal weight. Smoking may also make a miscarriage more likely. So a woman who smokes should give up smoking during her pregnancy. Heavy drinking is strongly suspected of damaging the developing brain of the foetus, so it is wise to avoid alcoholic drinks too.

During pregnancy, a woman should not take any drugs unless they are strictly necessary and prescribed by a doctor. In the 1950s, a drug called thalidomide was used to treat the bouts of early morning sickness which often occur in the first three months of pregnancy. Although tests had appeared to show the drug to be safe, it had not been tested on pregnant animals. About 20 per cent of pregnant women who took thalidomide had babies with deformed or missing limbs.

If a woman catches **rubella** (German measles) during the first four months of pregnancy, there is a danger that the virus may affect the foetus and cause abortion or stillbirth. Even if the baby is born alive, the virus may have caused defects of the eyes (cataracts), ears (deafness) or nervous system. All girls should be vaccinated against rubella between the ages of 11 and 13, to make sure that their bodies contain antibodies to the disease (see page 266).

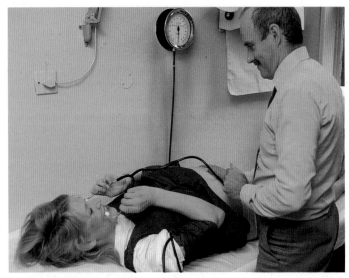

Figure 17   Antenatal examination. The mother is about to listen to the heart beat of her fetus.

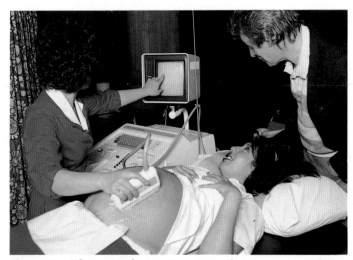

Figure 18   Ultra-sound scan. By moving the scanner over the abdomen, an image of the foetus can be seen on the screen. The size and position of the foetus and the placenta can be observed in this way.

Antenatal clinics

A pregnant woman should attend an antenatal clinic once a month for the first 28 weeks of pregnancy, then fortnightly and, finally, weekly. Regular attendance has the following advantages:

1 The pregnancy can be confirmed, and the expected date of birth worked out.
2 If she has some unsuspected illness, such as diabetes, high blood pressure or anaemia, it can be diagnosed and treated.
3 Anything wrong with the pregnancy will be detected at an early stage. Doctors will then be ready to deal with, for example, a rhesus factor problem or a need for Caesarian section (pages 138 and 172).
4 By weighing the woman and measuring her abdomen, it is possible to check that the pregnancy is proceeding normally.
5 The mother can get advice on diet, clothing, exercise, work, rest, smoking and so on. She can be kept informed about the progress of the foetus and the process of birth. She will also be offered advice about feeding and looking after the baby after it is born.

The tests

Apart from weighing and measuring the mother, samples of her blood and urine will be taken and analysed and her blood pressure will be measured.

The blood sample will show what her ABO blood group is, and whether she is rhesus-positive or rhesus-negative. The haemoglobin content of the blood will show whether she is anaemic and needs extra iron.

The presence of certain hormones in the urine sample will confirm that the woman is pregnant. The presence of sugar would mean that she is diabetic. Later in the pregnancy, the urine is tested for proteins. If proteins are present and her blood pressure is high, she may be advised to rest in bed until her blood pressure falls again. Very high blood pressure usually means that the placenta is not getting enough blood and the growth of the foetus has slowed down or stopped. If this happens late in pregnancy, the birth may be induced (page 172) to prevent harm to the mother and baby.

Amniocentesis

As a woman gets older, she is more likely to have a baby with Down's syndrome (page 227). This can be detected fairly early in the pregnancy (14–15 weeks), by taking a sample of amniotic fluid. Then the chromosomes of the foetal cells floating in it are counted under the microscope. The cells of a Down's syndrome foetus have 47 chromosomes in their nuclei, instead of the normal 46. The mother of a Down's syndrome foetus can then decide whether to end her pregnancy rather than give birth to a mentally handicapped child.

In amniocentesis, a tube is inserted through the wall of the abdomen, through the uterus and into the amnion. A local anaesthetic is used. In 1–2 per cent of cases, amniocentesis leads to a spontaneous abortion. The risk of this has to be balanced against the risk of having an unwanted, defective child. For women over 40, amniocentesis is the lesser risk. Between 35 and 40, the risks are more evenly balanced.

The chromosomes of fetal cells can also be used to find out the sex of the fetus. This is useful where there is a family history of sex-linked genetic disease such as haemophilia (page 233).

Analysis of the sample of amniotic fluid removed by amniocentesis can also detect certain chemicals which, if present, mean that the foetus has other defects.

A newer technique takes a sample of the placental villi, to look for abnormal chromosomes. One advantage is that the sampling tube can be passed through the cervix and does not enter the amnion. Placental sampling can also be carried out earlier in the pregnancy than amniocentesis. So if an abnormality is found and the mother decides the pregnancy should be ended, the experience may be less distressing for her. The risks of this technique are still being studied.

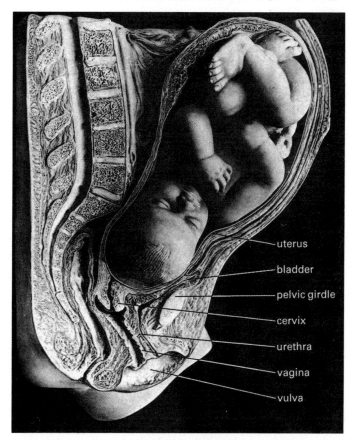

uterus

bladder

pelvic girdle

cervix

urethra

vagina

vulva

Figure 19 Model of human fetus just before birth. The cervix and vagina seem too narrow for the baby to pass through. But they widen quite naturally during labour and delivery.

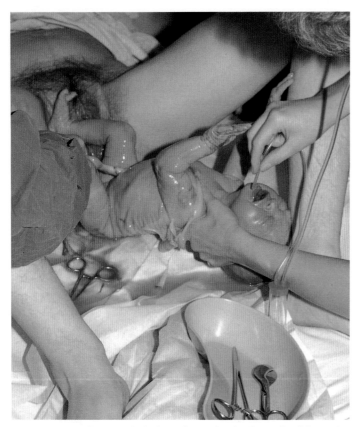

Figure 20   Delivery of a baby. The midwife clears fluid from the baby's mouth. The umbilical cord is still intact.

Birth

From fertilization to birth takes about 38 weeks in humans. This is called the **gestation** period. A few weeks before the birth, the fetus comes to lie head downwards in the uterus, with its head just above the cervix (Figures 12 (d) and 19).

Dilation   When the birth starts, the uterus begins to contract rhythmically. This is the beginning of what is called 'labour'. These regular rhythmic contractions become stronger and more frequent. The opening of the cervix gradually widens (dilates) enough to let the baby's head pass through. Now the contractions of the uterus are helped by muscular contractions of the abdomen. The water sac breaks at some stage in labour and the fluid escapes through the vagina.

Delivery   Finally, the muscular contractions of the uterus and abdomen push the baby head first through the dilated cervix and vagina (Figure 20). The umbilical cord still connects the child to the placenta. A thread is tied tightly round it, and the cord is then cut.

After-birth   Later, the placenta breaks away from the uterus and is pushed out separately as the 'after-birth'.

The sudden fall in temperature felt by the newly born baby stimulates it to take its first breath and it usually cries. In a few days, the remains of the umbilical cord attached to the baby's abdomen shrivel and fall away. The cord leaves a scar in the abdominal wall, called the navel.

Induced birth   Sometimes, when a pregnancy has lasted for more than 38 weeks or when examination shows that the placenta is not coping with the demands of the fetus, birth may be induced. This means that it is started artificially.

This is often done by carefully breaking the membrane of the amniotic sac. Another method is to inject a hormone, **oxytocin**, into the mother's veins. Either of these methods brings on the start of labour. Sometimes both are used together.

Caesarian section   If you study Figure 5 (a) on page 181, you will see the hole in the pelvic girdle through which the baby's head has to pass. During pregnancy, the tissues holding the right and left sides of the girdle together soften. This lets the girdle widen. The bony plates in the baby's skull can overlap during birth and so reduce the diameter of its head.

If, even so, the pelvic girdle is too narrow to allow the baby's head to pass through, the baby can be delivered by Caesarian section. The mother is anaesthetized while a surgeon opens her abdomen and uterus to extract the baby.

A woman may have several children by this method.

Breech delivery   A baby sometimes fails to turn head downwards in the uterus and is delivered feet first or bottom first. If a baby is in the 'feet-first' position and its legs are straight its body can pass through the cervix and vagina easily. But there is a risk that the baby may suffocate if the head does not follow quickly. A 'bottom-first' delivery can be avoided by straightening the legs in the early stages of birth. In either case a Caesarian section may be used instead.

A breech delivery may often be avoided by turning the baby from outside the mother's body, so that it lies head down.

Abortion

The ending of a pregnancy before 24–28 weeks is called an **abortion** because the fetus cannot survive on its own at this early stage. A birth between 28 and 38 weeks might be called **premature** if the baby has not developed enough to keep its body temperature steady or oxygenate its blood without help.

Spontaneous abortion (miscarriage) This occurs usually because the embryo is defective in some way. The embryo dies and is expelled from the uterus. This may happen so early in the pregnancy that it is unnoticed or confused with menstruation.

Perhaps as many as 30 per cent of fertilized ova fail to implant or develop properly, though it is hard to be certain about such figures.

Induced abortion This is a deliberate ending of the pregnancy. It is allowed by law if there are medical reasons. For example, there may be a risk to the mother's health if the pregnancy continues. Or the fetus may be defective, for example, after an attack of rubella in the first three months of pregnancy.

A fetus of less than 12 weeks is sucked out of the uterus through a tube inserted via the cervix. After 12 weeks, abortion is more difficult. Developments are now taking place in the use of chemicals (prostaglandins) which induce early labour to expel the fetus.

Many people feel strongly that abortion should not be used as a means of birth control. It is, after all, the destruction of a fetus which has reached a stage where it might be considered as a real or a potential human being.

Figure 21   Breast-feeding helps to establish an emotional bond between mother and baby

Lactation, Growth and Parental Care

Lactation

About 24 hours after birth, the baby starts to suck at the breast. During pregnancy the mammary glands (breasts) enlarge as a result of an increase in the number of milk-secreting cells. No milk is secreted during pregnancy, but the hormones which start the birth process also act on the milk-secreting cells of the breasts. The breasts are stimulated to release milk by the first sucklings. The continued production of milk (lactation) is under the control of hormones, but the amount of milk produced is related to the quantity taken by the child during suckling.

> The liquid produced in the first week is called **colostrum**. It is sticky and yellow, and contains more protein than the milk produced later. It also contains some of the mother's antibodies.

Milk contains nearly all the food, vitamins and salts that babies need for their energy requirements and tissue-building. It contains no iron, however. All the iron needed to make haemoglobin in the first weeks or months is stored in the body of the foetus during gestation.

The mother's milk supply increases with the demands of the baby, up to 1 litre a day. Solid food replaces it, in part at first and then entirely. The process is known as **weaning**.

Cows' milk is not wholly suitable for babies. It has more protein, sodium and phosphorus than human milk, and less sugar, vitamin A and vitamin C. Manufacturers modify dried cows' milk to make it more like human milk. This makes it more acceptable if the mother cannot breast-feed her baby. (But see page 93.)

Cows' milk and dried milk from the chemist's both lack human antibodies. The mother's milk, however, contains antibodies to any diseases which she has had. It also carries white cells which produce antibodies or ingest bacteria. The antibodies can protect the baby against infection at a time when its own immune responses are not fully developed. Breast milk is free from bacteria, whereas cows' milk or artificial milk feeds may contain the bacteria that cause intestinal diseases. Breast-feeding is usually also a happy and satisfying experience for both mother and baby (Figure 21).

Growth

Growth results from cell division, followed by cell enlargement (Figure 2). In the uterus a single-celled zygote grows into a many-celled foetus weighing about 3.5 kg. Cells become specialized to form bone, skin, muscle, nerve and so on. These cells are then organized into tissues and organs (page 14).

A new-born baby may weigh from 2.5 to 6.5 kg. The average is 3.5 kg (7.5 pounds). In the first week, the baby loses weight and does not get back to its birth weight until the second week. Then the child grows rapidly for a year or two. After that growth is slower and fairly steady until the age of about 18, though there is a growth 'spurt' at adolescence

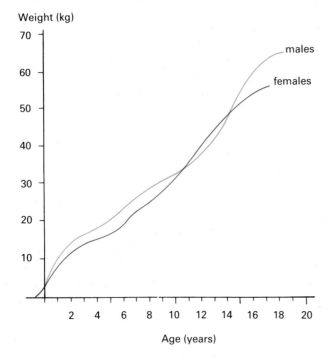

Figure 22   Weight increase in males and females

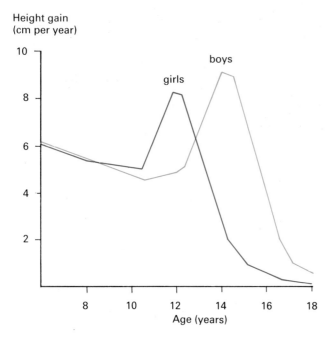

Figure 23   **Rates of growth in boys and girls.** There is a 'growth spurt' at adolescence. Note that the vertical axis represents height gain.
(From J.M. Tanner, *Growth at adolescence*, Blackwell Scientific Publications, 1962)

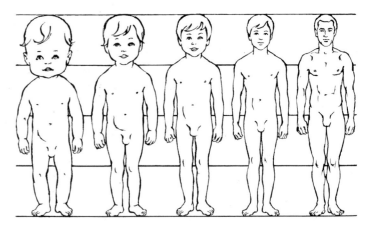

Figure 24   **Human growth.** All the figures are drawn to the same height to show how body proportions change with age.
(After C.M. Jackson)

(12–16). Girls usually start their adolescent growth spurt before boys do. The boys overtake them, however, and on average are taller and heavier by the time they are 18 (Figures 22 and 23).

The different parts of the body do not grow at the same rate. The skull does not grow very much compared with the long bones of the limbs, for example (Figure 24).

Parental care

Most young mammals are independent of their parents after a few weeks or months, though they may stay together as a family group. Young humans, however, depend on their parents for food, clothing and shelter for many years. During this time the young learn to talk, to read and write, and many other skills that help them to survive and be self-sufficient (Figure 25).

Figure 25   **Parental care.** Human parental care includes a long period of education.

QUESTION

12 Apart from learning to talk, what other skills might young humans develop that would help them when they are no longer dependent on their parents in (a) an agricultural society, (b) an industrial society?

Puberty and the Menstrual Cycle

Puberty

Although the ovaries of a young girl contain all the ova she will ever produce, they do not start to be released until she reaches an age of about 10–14 years. This stage in her life is known as **puberty**.

At about the same time as the first ovulation, the ovary also releases female sex hormones into the bloodstream. These hormones are called **oestrogens**. When oestrogens circulate round the body, they bring about the development of **secondary sexual characteristics**. A girl's breasts grow larger, her hips widen and hair grows in the pubic region and in the armpits. The uterus and vagina increase in size. Once all these changes are complete, the girl is capable of having a baby.

Puberty in boys occurs at about the same age as in girls. The testes start to produce sperms for the first time. They also release a hormone, called **testosterone**, into the bloodstream. The male secondary sexual characteristics begin to appear at puberty: the testes and penis enlarge, the voice deepens, and hair grows on the pubic region, armpits, chest and, later, on the face.

Boys and girls both grow rapidly during puberty.

The menstrual cycle

The ovaries release an ovum about every four weeks. As each follicle develops, the amount of oestrogens produced by the ovary increases. The oestrogens act on the uterus and cause its lining to become thicker and develop more blood vessels. These changes help an early embryo to implant, as described on page 168.

Once the ovum has been released, the follicle which produced it develops into a solid body called the **corpus luteum**. This produces a hormone called **progesterone**. It affects the uterus lining in the same way as the oestrogens, making it grow thicker and produce more blood vessels.

If the ovum is fertilized, the corpus luteum goes on releasing progesterone. This keeps the uterus in a state suitable for implantation. The rising level of progesterone also stops further ovulation because it suppresses the production of another hormone from the pituitary gland (see page 216). If the ovum is not

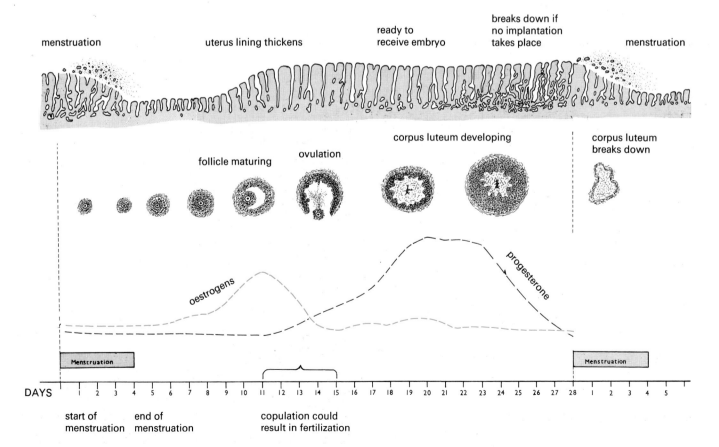

Figure 26 The menstrual cycle
(After G.W. Coner, *The hormones in human reproduction*, Princeton.)

fertilized, the corpus luteum stops producing progesterone. As a result, the thickened lining of the uterus breaks down and loses blood, which escapes through the cervix and vagina. This is known as a **menstrual period**. The appearance of the first menstrual period is one of the signs of puberty in girls. The events in the menstrual cycle are shown in Figure 26.

Menopause Between the ages of 40 and 55, the ovaries stop releasing ova and producing hormones. As a result menstrual periods cease, the woman can no longer have children, and sexual desire is gradually reduced.

QUESTIONS

13 From the list of changes at puberty in girls, select those that are related to child-bearing and say what part you think they play.

14 One of the first signs of pregnancy is that the menstrual periods stop. Explain why you would expect this.

Family Planning and Fertility

As little as four weeks after giving birth, some women are able to conceive again. Frequent breast-feeding may reduce the chances of conception. Even so, many women do have children at about one-year intervals. Most people in Britain do not want, or cannot afford, to have as many children as this. All human communities practise some form of birth control to space out births and limit the size of the family.

Natural methods of family planning

If a woman could know exactly when she ovulated, she could avoid intercourse for three or four days before ovulation and one day after it (see page 167). At the moment, however, there is no simple, reliable way to recognize ovulation. It usually happens 12–16 days before the onset of the next menstrual period. By keeping careful records of the intervals between menstrual periods, a woman can calculate a potentially fertile period of about 10 days in mid-cycle, when she should avoid sexual intercourse if she does not want children.

On its own, this method (the 'rhythm' method) is not very reliable. But some physiological clues help to make it more accurate. During or soon after ovulation, a woman's temperature rises about 0.5 °C. It is reasonable to assume that one day after the temperature returns to normal, a woman will be infertile. Another clue comes from the type of mucus secreted by the cervix and lining of the vagina. As the time for ovulation approaches, this mucus

becomes more fluid. Women can learn to detect these changes and so calculate their fertile period.

By combining the 'rhythm', 'temperature' and 'mucus' methods, it is possible to achieve about 80 per cent 'success', which means only 20 per cent unplanned pregnancies. Conscientious couples may be more successful than this. And, of course, it is a very helpful way of finding the fertile period for couples who do want to have a child.

Contraception

Contraception means the use of artificial methods of preventing conception (fertilization) without having to limit sexual intercourse.

The sheath or condom A thin rubber sheath is placed on the erect penis before sexual intercourse. The sheath traps the sperms and prevents them from reaching the uterus.

The diaphragm A thin rubber disc, placed in the vagina before intercourse, covers the cervix and stops sperms entering the uterus. Condoms and diaphragms, used together with chemicals (spermicidal creams or jellies) that immobilize sperms, are about 95 per cent effective.

Intra-uterine device (IUD) A small metal or plastic strip bent into a loop or coil is inserted and retained in the uterus, where it probably prevents implantation of a fertilized ovum. It is about 98 per cent effective. The woman does have a small risk of developing uterine infections, particularly if she has intercourse with many different men.

The contraceptive pill The pill contains chemicals which have the same effect on the body as the hormones oestrogen and progesterone. When mixed in suitable proportions these hormones suppress ovulation (see 'Feedback', page 217) and so prevent conception. The woman needs to take the pill each day for the 21 days between menstrual periods.

Different kinds of contraceptive pill contain different amounts of oestrogen- and progesterone-like chemicals. They are 99 per cent effective. Long-term use of some types increase the risk of cancer of the breast and cervix, however.

Sterilization

(a) Vasectomy

This is a simple and safe surgical operation in which the man's sperm ducts are cut and the ends sealed. This means that his semen contains the secretions of the prostate gland and seminal vesicle but no sperms. So it cannot fertilize an ovum. Sexual desire, erection, copulation and ejaculation are quite unaffected.

The testis continues to produce sperms and testosterone. The sperms are removed by white cells as fast as they form. The testosterone ensures that there is no loss of masculinity.

The operation is not easy to reverse. The sperm ducts can be rejoined by surgery, but this is not always successful.

(b) Laparotomy

A woman may be sterilized by an operation in which her oviducts are tied, blocked or cut. The ovaries are unaffected. Sexual desire and menstruation continue as before, but sperms can no longer reach the ova. Ova are released, but break down in the upper part of the oviduct.

The operation cannot usually be reversed.

In-vitro fertilization ('test-tube babies')

'In-vitro' means literally 'in glass'. In other words, the fertilization is allowed to take place in laboratory glassware rather than 'in vivo', that is, in the living body.

Some women are infertile because their oviducts are blocked. Sometimes this can be cured by surgery. If not, the woman may be offered the chance of in-vitro fertilization. This process has been given wide publicity since the first 'test-tube baby' was born in 1978.

The woman may be given injections of follicle-stimulating hormone (FSH), and luteinizing hormone (LH) (see page 216). These cause her ovaries to release several mature ova at once. These ova are then collected by sucking them up through a fine tube inserted through the abdominal wall. The ova are mixed with the husband's seminal fluid and watched under the microscope to see if cell division takes place. (Figure 11 on page 168 is a photograph of such an 'in-vitro' fertilized ovum.)

One or more of the dividing zygotes is then introduced to the woman's uterus by means of a tube inserted through the cervix. Usually, only one (or none) of the zygotes develops. Occasionally, however, there are multiple births as with the quadruplets born in the Hammersmith Hospital in 1984.

The success rate for in-vitro fertilization is probably little better than 10–15 per cent. But the main debate seems to be about the fate of the 'spare' zygotes. Some people believe that since these zygotes are potential human beings, they should not be destroyed or used for experiments.

Some zygotes have been frozen at the 2–8 cell stage and stored in liquid nitrogen. They are then used later if the first transplants are not successful.

In Australia, in 1983, an embryo that had been frozen for two months was transferred to the mother's uterus, where it developed successfully. This technique avoided the mother having to undergo a further operation to remove ova from her ovaries.

Ageing (Senescence)

From the age of 30, or perhaps sooner, the body's efficiency steadily declines. The rate of basal metabolism falls (Figure 27). Cells that are not replaced by cell division are lost. The kidney, for example, will in time lose about 50 per cent of its nephrons. The brain loses about 30 cells every minute.

The loss of cells in the skin and blood is less marked but their rate of replacement slows down. For example, the epidermis becomes thinner. Some hair follicles stop producing hairs.

The causes of cell death, the slowing down of cell division and the other degenerative changes of old age are not fully understood. The effects of ageing are well known, however. But it can be hard to separate these from the effects of the diseases which mainly attack elderly people.

The tissues lose elasticity. The skin wrinkles, the capacity of the bladder decreases, and the eye lens loses some of its accommodation (page 200). In the skeleton, bone is constantly re-absorbed and replaced throughout life. In old age re-absorption happens faster than replacement, so the bones become less dense and more easily broken.

Atherosclerosis (thickening of the arteries, page 138) probably starts early in life. By old age it may have reached a stage where strokes or heart attacks are more likely.

Hearing and vision become less acute. Powers of concentration and reaction times lessen. There is a loss of short-term memory. (See also Figure 27.)

This makes a pretty depressing list. But in fact many of the effects of old age (particularly being prone to disease) can be lessened by healthy living – by eating a good diet, taking exercise, not smoking, and keeping the mind active. Moreover, these effects are greatly influenced by a person's mentality and social conditions. Many people with the disabilities of old age, such as arthritis, can lead fulfilling and rewarding lives, especially if they have a positive attitude and some support and encouragement from their friends and families.

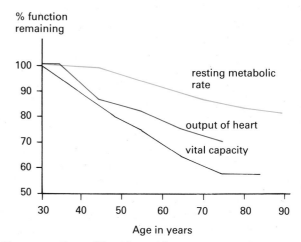

Figure 27   Loss of function with age
(After N.W. Shock, *Geriatrics*, **12**, 40)

CHECK LIST

- The male reproductive cells (gametes) are sperms. They are produced in the testes and expelled through the urethra and penis during mating.
- The female reproductive cells (gametes) are ova (eggs). They are produced in the ovaries. One is released each month. If sperms are present, the ovum may be fertilized as it passes down the oviduct to the uterus.
- Fertilization happens when a sperm enters an ovum and the sperm and egg nuclei join up (fuse).
- The fertilized ovum (zygote) divides into many cells and becomes embedded in the lining of the uterus. Here it grows into an embryo.
- The embryo gets its food and oxygen from its mother.
- The embryo's blood is pumped through blood vessels in the umbilical cord to the placenta, which is attached to the uterus lining. The embryo's blood comes very close to the mother's blood so that food and oxygen can be picked up and carbon dioxide and nitrogenous waste can be got rid of.
- When the embryo is fully grown, it is pushed out of the uterus through the vagina by contractions of the uterus and abdomen.
- Each month, the uterus lining thickens up in readiness to receive the fertilized ovum. If an ovum is not fertilized, the lining and some blood is lost through the vagina. This is menstruation.
- The release of ova and the development of an embryo are under the control of hormones like oestrogen and progesterone.
- Twins may result from two ova being fertilized at the same time or from a zygote forming two embryos.
- At puberty, (1) the testes and ovaries start to produce mature gametes, (2) the secondary sexual characteristics develop.
- Human milk and breast-feeding are best for babies.
- Good antenatal care improves a woman's chances of having a successful pregnancy and a healthy baby.
- Young humans are dependent on their parents for a long time. During this period much essential learning takes place.
- There are effective natural and artificial methods for spacing births and limiting the size of a family.
- Changes in tissues and organs are inevitable during ageing, but these need not be disabling.

18 The Skeleton, Muscles and Movement

Structure of the Skeleton
Vertebral column, skull, limbs and joints.

Functions of the Skeleton
Support, protection and movement.

Bone, Cartilage and Muscle
Skeletal and smooth muscle. Muscle contraction.

Movement and Locomotion
Muscles produce movement. Lever action of limbs. Locomotion.

Lifting, Posture and Back Pain
Backache caused by faulty lifting or posture.

Exercise
Immediate and long-term benefits.

Practical Work
Structure of bone.

Structure of the Skeleton

Figure 1 shows a human skeleton. The **vertebral column** (sometimes called the 'backbone', 'spine' or 'spinal column') supports the skull. Twelve pairs of ribs are attached to the upper part of the vertebral column. The limbs are attached to the vertebral column by means of **girdles**.

The hip girdle (pelvic girdle) is joined rigidly to the lower end of the vertebral column. The shoulder girdle (pectoral girdle) consists of a pair of shoulder-blades and collar-bones. These are not rigidly fixed to the vertebral column but are held in place by muscles.

The upper arm bone (humerus) fits into a socket in the shoulder-blade. The thigh bone (femur) fits into a socket in the hip girdle.

The vertebral column and skull are sometimes called the **axial skeleton** (they form the axis of the body), while the ribs, girdles and limbs are called the **appendicular** skeleton (the appendages).

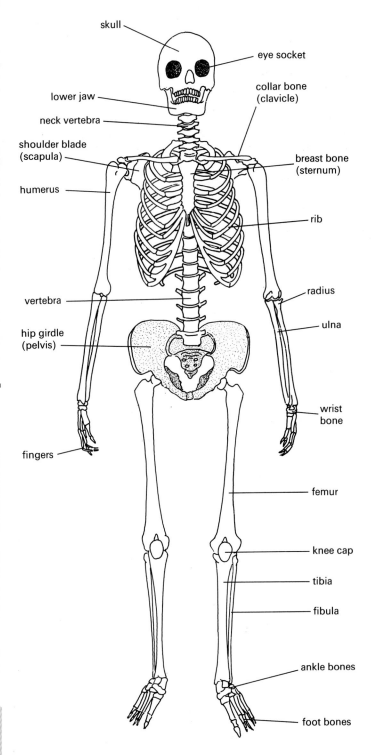

Figure 1 The skeleton

179

Vertebral column

This forms the central supporting structure of the skeleton. It consists of 33 individual bones called **vertebrae** (singular = vertebra), separated by **intervertebral discs** of fibrous cartilage (Figure 2 (b)). These discs allow the vertebrae to move slightly. This means that the vertebral column can bend backwards and forwards or from side to side.

Each intervertebral disc consists of a central core of jelly-like material enclosed in a tough, fibrous capsule, which is slightly flexible. The discs thus act as shock absorbers.

The spinal cord (page 212) runs through a bony tunnel formed by the **neural arches** of the vertebrae. The bone protects the cord from accidental damage (Figure 2 (a)).

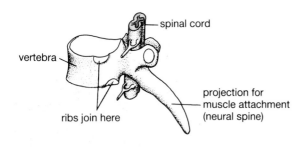

(a) a single thoracic vertebra

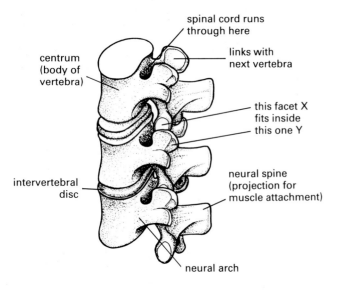

(b) three lumbar vertebrae

Figure 2   The vertebral column

The structures of the vertebrae vary from one region of the vertebral column to the next (Figure 3). The variations are related to the differences in function. For example, the centrum of a lower vertebra is larger than that of an upper vertebra, as the weight carried by the lower part of the vertebral column is greater.

A lumbar vertebra (Figure 2) has a large, sturdy centrum and projections (facet joints X and Y in the drawing) which form joints that restrict twisting movements.

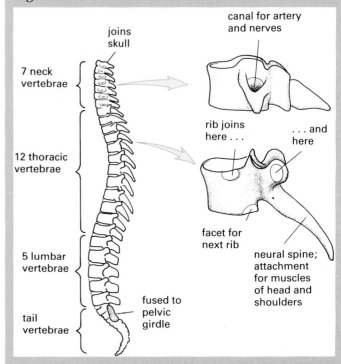

Figure 3   Regions of the vertebral column

A thoracic vertebra (Figure 3 (b)) has projections and shallow 'sockets' to which the ribs are attached. It also has a long neural spine to which the muscles holding up the head are attached.

The neck vertebrae have only a small centrum. The joint between the skull and the first vertebra makes a nodding movement possible. The joint between the first and second vertebrae allows the head to turn. The remaining joints of the neck vertebrae allow rather more flexibility than in the rest of the column.

The skull

This is made up of many bony plates joined together (Figure 4). It encloses and protects the brain and also carries and protects the eyes, ears and nose, which are the main sense organs. The upper jaw is fixed to the skull, but the lower jaw is hinged to it in a way which allows chewing.

The base of the skull makes a joint with the top vertebra of the vertebral column. This joint allows the head to make nodding movements.

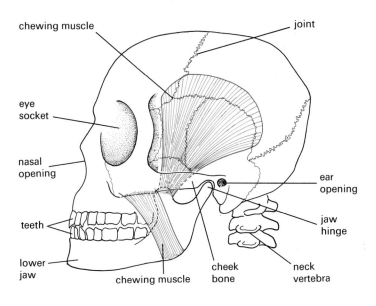

Figure 4   The skull and chewing muscles

Joints

Where two bones meet they form a joint. It may be a **fixed joint** like the joint between the hip girdle and the vertebral column (Figure 5 (a)). Or it may be a **movable joint** like the knee. Two important types of movable joint already mentioned are the **ball and socket joints** of the hip and the shoulder (Figure 5 (b)) and the **hinge joints** of the elbow and knee. The ball and socket joint allows movement forwards, backwards and sideways. The hinge joint allows movement in only one direction.

Where the surfaces of the bones in a joint rub over each other they are covered with smooth cartilage which reduces the friction between them. Friction is also reduced by a thin layer of lubricating fluid called **synovial fluid** (Figures 5 (b) and (d)). (Movable joints are sometimes called **synovial joints**.) The bones forming the joint are held in place by tough bands of fibrous tissue called **ligaments** (Figure 5 (f)). Ligaments keep the bones together but do not stop their various movements.

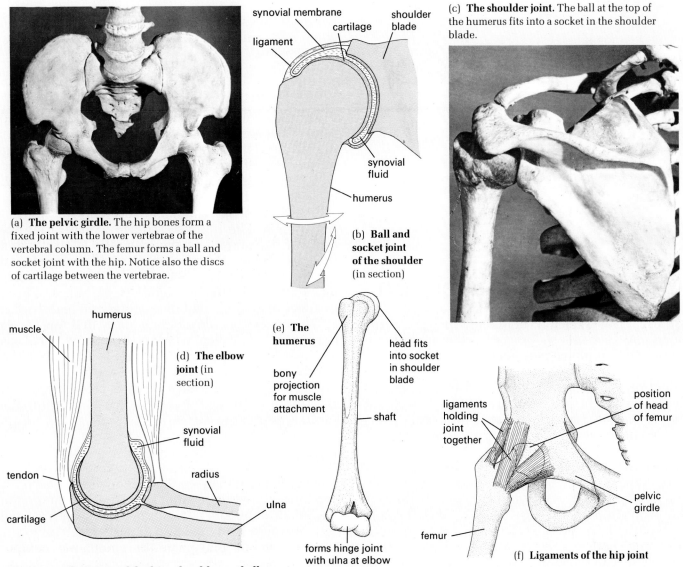

(a) **The pelvic girdle.** The hip bones form a fixed joint with the lower vertebrae of the vertebral column. The femur forms a ball and socket joint with the hip. Notice also the discs of cartilage between the vertebrae.

(b) **Ball and socket joint of the shoulder** (in section)

(c) **The shoulder joint.** The ball at the top of the humerus fits into a socket in the shoulder blade.

(d) **The elbow joint** (in section)

(e) **The humerus**

(f) **Ligaments of the hip joint**

Figure 5   The joints of the hip, shoulder and elbow

The limbs

Arm   The upper arm bone is the **humerus**. It is attached by a hinge joint to the lower arm bones, the **radius** and **ulna** (Figure 6). These two bones make a joint with a group of small wrist bones which in turn join to a series of five hand and finger bones. The ulna and radius can partly rotate round each other, so that the hand can be held palm up or palm down.

Leg   The thigh bone or **femur** is attached at the hip to the pelvic girdle by a ball joint. At the knee it makes a hinge joint with the **tibia**. The **fibula** runs parallel to the tibia but does not form part of the knee joint. The ankle, foot and toe bones are similar to those of the wrist, hand and fingers.

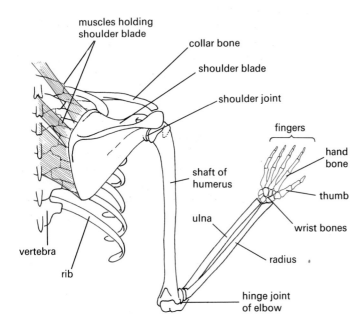

Figure 6   Skeleton of the arm and shoulder

Functions of the Skeleton

Support   The skeleton holds the body off the ground and keeps its shape even when muscles are contracting to produce movement.

Protection   The brain is protected from injury by being enclosed in the skull. The heart, lungs and liver are protected by the rib cage. The spinal cord is enclosed inside the neural arches of the vertebrae.

Movement   Many bones of the skeleton act as levers. When muscles pull on these bones, they produce movements such as the raising of the ribs during breathing (see page 142), or the chewing action of the jaws. For a skeletal muscle to produce movement, both its ends need to have a firm attachment. The skeleton provides suitable points of attachment for the ends of most muscles.

Production of blood cells   Some bones, such as the vertebrae, ribs, breastbone and the heads of the limb bones, contain red marrow. This produces both red and white blood cells (page 126).

QUESTIONS

1 Study Figure 1. Then write down the biological names of the following bones: upper arm bone, upper leg bone, hip bone, breastbone, 'backbone', lower arm bones.
2 Apart from the elbow and knee, what other joints in the body function like hinge joints?
3 What types of joint are visible in Figure 5 (a)? Name the bones which form each type of joint that you mention.
4 Which parts of the skeleton are concerned with both protection and movement?

Cartilage, Bone and Muscle

All these tissues are formed by living cells, though bone and cartilage do contain some non-living components.

Cartilage

This occurs in several forms. One form is firm and semi-transparent. It makes up the rings which keep the trachea and bronchi open (page 141), it covers the surfaces of movable joints (reducing friction and wear) and it supports that part of the nose which projects from the face.

Fibrous cartilage contains many fibres as well as living cells. The fibrous cartilage which forms the external ear pinna and the epiglottis is elastic and flexible. Less flexible but very strong fibres are found in the fibro-cartilage which forms part of some ligaments and attaches tendons to bones. Fibro-cartilage also forms part of the intervertebral discs.

When a foetus is developing in the first few weeks (page 169) its skeleton is first formed in cartilage. The cartilage is then gradually replaced by bone in the course of development, before the baby is born.

Cartilage does not have its own blood supply. It gets its oxygen and food by diffusion from the capillaries of nearby tissues.

Bone

Bone is harder than cartilage, and less flexible. It contains living cells and non-living fibres (the 'organic' component). The fibrous tissue between the cells becomes hardened by a deposit of calcium salts such as calcium phosphate (the 'inorganic' component).

Bone contains a high proportion of non-living

material. The blood vessels that run through it keep the cells alive and allow growth and repair to take place.

Muscle

There are three types of muscle. One kind is called **skeletal muscle** (or striated, or voluntary muscle). Another kind is called **smooth muscle** (or unstriated, or involuntary muscle). A third kind occurs only in the heart.

Skeletal muscle   This is made up of long fibres. Each fibre is formed from many cells, but the cells have fused together. The cell boundaries cannot be seen but the individual nuclei are still present (Figure 7 (c)).

The muscle fibres are arranged in bundles which form distinct muscles (Figure 7 (b)). Most of these are attached to bones, and produce movement as described below. Each muscle has a nerve supply. When a nerve impulse is sent to a muscle, it makes the muscle contract (get shorter and fatter). We can usually control most of our skeletal muscles. For this reason they are called **voluntary muscles**.

Branches from the end of a nerve fibre go to many individual fibres in a muscle (see Figure 3 (a) on page 208). The number of muscle fibres which are stimulated to contract will depend on the number of nerve fibres involved. The more muscle fibres that contract, the stronger will be the contraction of the muscle as a whole. Usually, only a proportion of the fibres take part in a muscle contraction.

Smooth muscle   This is made up of long cells which are not fused together to form fibres (see Figure 13 (c) on page 16). The cells make layers of muscle tissue rather than distinct muscles. Examples are found in the walls of the alimentary canal (page 113), the uterus (page 165) and the arterioles (page 130).

When the cells are arranged at right angles to the organ, they form a layer of circular muscle. When circular muscle contracts it makes the gut or the arteriole narrower. This is the basis for the processes of peristalsis (page 113), vaso-constriction (page 162) and labour (page 172). A band of circular muscle may form a **sphincter**. Examples are the pyloric sphincter at the exit of the stomach (page 115), the sphincter at the base of the bladder (page 153), the anal sphincter at the anus and the sphincter muscle in the iris of the eye (page 201).

We do not have conscious control over most of the smooth muscle in our bodies (though we do for the anal and bladder sphincters). This is why smooth muscle is sometimes called **involuntary muscle**.

Muscle contraction   The fibres of skeletal muscle and the cells of smooth muscle are able to contract (shorten) when stimulated by nerve impulses. However, the fibres and cells cannot make themselves longer (elongate). They can only contract and relax. So they have to be pulled back into their elongated shape by other muscles which work in the opposite direction (see 'Muscles and movement', below).

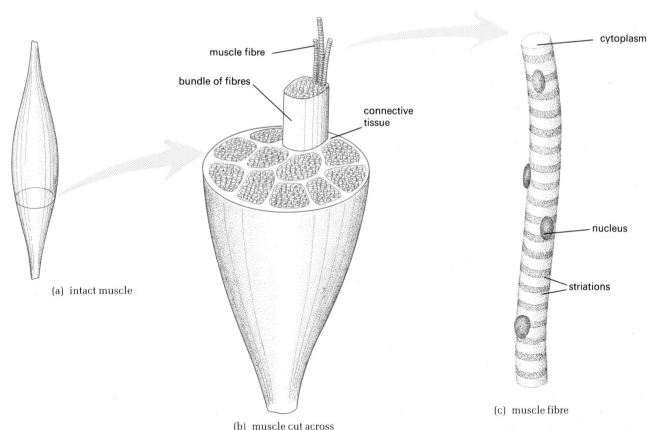

(a) intact muscle

(b) muscle cut across

muscle fibre

bundle of fibres

connective tissue

cytoplasm

nucleus

striations

(c) muscle fibre

Figure 7   Skeletal (striated) muscle

QUESTIONS

5 What are the main differences in structure and function between skeletal and smooth muscle?

6 If a tendon is damaged, it may take a long time to heal. A damaged bone heals more quickly. Suggest a reason for this difference.

Movement and Locomotion

Muscles and movement

The ends of the limb muscles are drawn out into **tendons** which attach each end of the muscle to the skeleton (Figure 5 (e)).

Figure 8 shows how a muscle is attached to a limb to make it bend at the joint. The tendon at one end is attached to a non-moving part of the skeleton, while the tendon at the other end is attached to the movable bone close to the joint.

When a muscle contracts it pulls on the bones and makes one of them move. The position of the attachment means that a small contraction of the muscle will produce a large movement at the end of the limb. Figure 9 is a model which shows how the

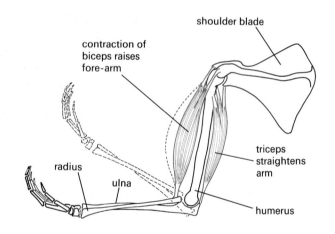

Figure 8   Antagonistic muscles of the fore-arm

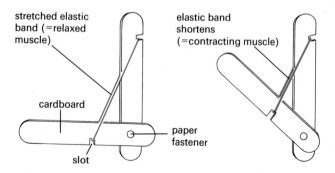

Figure 9   Model to show how muscles pull on bones to produce movement

shortening of muscle can move a limb. Figure 8 shows how a contraction of the **biceps muscle** bends (or **flexes**) the arm at the elbow, while the **triceps** straightens (or **extends**) the arm.

The non-moving end of the biceps is attached to the shoulder-blade while the moving end is attached to the ulna, near the elbow joint.

Limb muscles are usually arranged in pairs having opposite effects. This is because muscles can only shorten or relax, they cannot make themselves longer. This is why the triceps is needed to pull the relaxed biceps back to its elongated shape after it has contracted. Pairs of muscles like this are called **antagonistic** muscles. Antagonistic muscles are also important in holding the limbs steady, both muscles keeping the same state of tension or 'tone'.

The contraction of muscles is controlled by nerve impulses. The brain sends out impulses in the nerves so that the muscles are made to contract or relax in the right order to make a movement. For example, when a muscle contracts to bend the limb, its antagonistic muscle must be kept in a relaxed state.

Many muscular activities bring about movements but do not result in locomotion. Chewing, breathing, throwing, swallowing and blinking are examples of such movements.

Energy for muscle contraction

All muscles need energy to make them contract. This energy comes from respiration (page 28). In the muscle cells, glucose or glycogen is broken down to carbon dioxide and water, releasing energy for the contraction.

The first stage of the respiration is anaerobic (page 28), and breaks glucose down only as far as pyruvic acid ($CH_3COCOOH$). The second stage of respiration is aerobic, and the pyruvic acid is oxidized completely to carbon dioxide and water.

If you are exercising hard, the pyruvic acid is formed faster than it can be broken down. It is converted to lactic acid and carried away in the bloodstream to the liver. Here the lactic acid is built up once again to glycogen, or oxidized to carbon dioxide and water. Oxygen is needed for these reactions for some time after the exercise has finished. The build-up of lactic acid has therefore produced what is called an **oxygen debt**.

Muscle fatigue may also be caused by lactic acid forming in the muscle tissue faster than it can be removed by the blood, though this is not certain. There may be other causes of fatigue.

The energy from breakdown of glucose or glycogen is not used directly for muscle contraction, but for building up stocks of ATP (page 29). It is the breakdown of ATP to ADP that provides the energy for repeated muscle contraction.

The chemical reactions that take place during respiration do not only cause muscle contraction. They also produce heat. A contracting muscle therefore becomes warm. The blood will carry the heat away to other parts of the body. If this raises the general body temperature, vaso-dilation and sweating may follow (see page 162).

Locomotion

Locomotion is brought about by the limb muscles contracting and relaxing in an orderly (co-ordinated) manner. Figure 10 shows a sprinter at the start of a race. Figure 11 shows how some of his leg muscles act on the bones to thrust him forward. When muscle A contracts, it pulls the femur backwards. Contraction of muscle B straightens the leg at the knee. Muscle C contracts and pulls the foot down at the ankle. When these three muscles contract at the same time, the leg is pulled back and straightened and the foot is extended, pushing the foot down-

wards and backwards against the ground. If the ground is firm, the straightening of the leg pushes upwards against the pelvic girdle. This in turn pushes the vertebral column and so lifts the whole body upwards and forwards.

While muscles A, B and C are contracting to extend the leg, their antagonistic muscles are relaxed. At the end of the extension movement, muscles A, B and C relax, and their antagonistic partners contract to flex the leg.

There are at least two different types of muscle fibre in mammalian muscle: slow-contracting and fast-contracting. They are sometimes called type 1 (red muscle) and type 2 (white muscle). White muscle is powerful and contracts rapidly, but it also fatigues quickly. Red muscle contracts more slowly and uses energy more economically.

In general terms, white muscle is important for vigorous bursts of activity, such as sprinting. Red muscle is used to keep the body standing upright, and for activities requiring endurance. Physiologists disagree about whether the ratio of red and white muscle in a person is determined by heredity, or whether the ratio can be changed by training.

Limbs as levers

Most limb bones act as levers, and greatly magnify the movement of the muscles that act on them. Figure 12 (a) shows a very simple lever effect. Figure 12 (b) shows the lever effect of the foot. The **load** is the resistance of the ground against the weight of the body which is being lifted by the foot. In Figure 12 (c) the biceps muscle is providing the **effort** to lift a load held in the hand, using the elbow joint as a **fulcrum**.

Figure 10   Leg muscles used in running. Compare with Figure 11 (a).

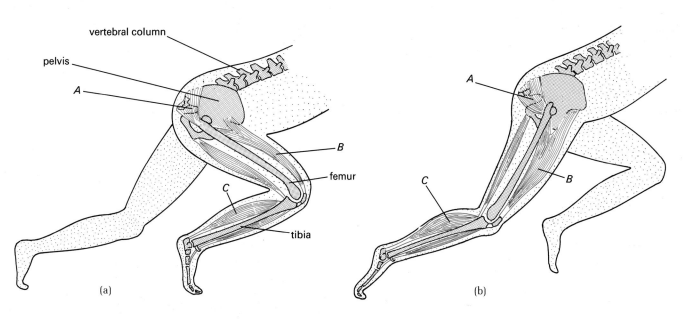

Figure 11   Action of leg muscles. There are many other muscles in the leg which are not shown here. A, B and C are all contracting to straighten the leg and foot.

QUESTIONS

7 What is the difference between the functions of a ligament and a tendon?
8 What is the main action of (a) your calf muscle, (b) the muscles in the front of your thigh and (c) the muscles in your forearm? If you don't already know the answers, try making the muscles contract and feel where the tendons are pulling.
9 Look at Figure 11.
   (a) To what bone is the non-moving end of muscle *B* attached?
   (b) Which muscle is the antagonistic partner to *C*?

Lifting, Posture and Back Pain

Back pain

Most people will have some back pain during their lifetime. Most backache is caused by standing for a long time, or lying or sitting awkwardly. The pain usually wears off quickly.

In about 40 per cent of people, back pain may be so bad, or last so long, that they have to see a doctor or take time off work. The ligaments of the back may have become stretched and inflamed. In more severe cases, the ligaments or muscle attachments may be torn. Sometimes the intervertebral disc is damaged.

The damage to ligaments, muscles and discs is usually the result of lifting, carrying or moving heavy objects.

The joints between the lower (lumbar) vertebrae cannot twist freely because of their interlocking facet joints (see Figure 2 (b) on page 180). However, a sudden twisting movement while the back is bent, particularly if one is lifting something heavy, can force these vertebrae to twist. This can tear the ligaments or the muscle attachments of the vertebrae, or damage the fibrous capsule of an intervertebral disc. If the capsule of the disc is badly damaged, the weight of the body compressing the disc may force part of the jelly-like centre into the weakened part of the damaged capsule. This makes it bulge outwards. If the bulge presses on the spinal cord or on a spinal nerve, it can cause severe pain. If the nerve comes from the leg, the pain may seem to be in the leg.

The ligaments or discs of the lumbar vertebrae can be damaged by lifting an awkward load. Examples are lifting heavy shopping into or out of a car, or lifting a child from a play-pen or cot. Any sudden twisting movement with bent back can cause damage.

The 'cure' is usually to rest on a flat, firm surface, perhaps for a day or two. The damaged tissues heal or the disc goes back more or less to its proper shape

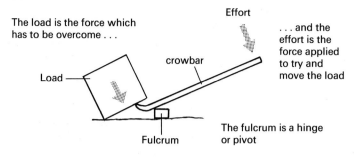

(a) the lever effect

The load is the force which has to be overcome . . .

Effort

. . . and the effort is the force applied to try and move the load

crowbar

Load

Fulcrum

The fulcrum is a hinge or pivot

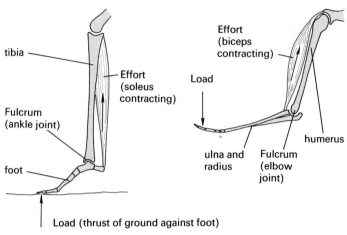

(b) lever effect in the foot

tibia

Effort (soleus contracting)

Fulcrum (ankle joint)

foot

Load (thrust of ground against foot)

(c) lever effect in the arm

Effort (biceps contracting)

Load

humerus

ulna and radius

Fulcrum (elbow joint)

Figure 12   The limb as a lever

(but can quite easily be damaged further). In a very few people, a damaged disc has to be repaired surgically.

Lifting

Most severe back pain is caused by lifting heavy loads. So it is worth taking care to avoid damage.

Firstly, it is best not to try to lift anything which you judge to be too heavy. Divide it into smaller

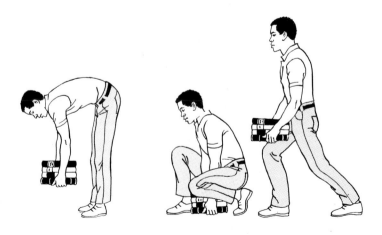

(a) **Incorrect.** The back is curved and the ligaments and discs are over-stressed.

(b) **Correct.** The load is close to the body and the back is nearly upright. The lifting force comes from the legs.

Figure 13   Lifting heavy objects

loads, roll it, use a trolley or a hoist, or get help. If the load is within your powers, use the strength of your leg muscles rather than your back for lifting.

Figure 13 (a) shows the wrong way to lift. The load is too far away and the bent back will put the vertebral joints under a type of strain that they are not adapted to take.

Figure 13 (b) shows a better way to lift. The load is close to the body, the back is almost upright, and one foot is flat on the floor alongside the load. The effort for the lift comes from the leg muscles and not from the back. If you carry a heavy object, hold it as close to your body as you can.

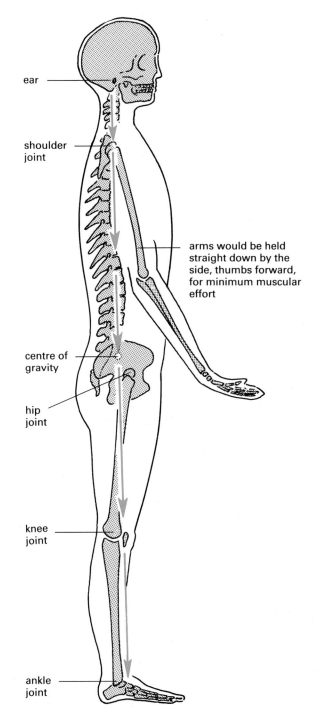

Figure 14 Standing posture. The minimal muscular energy is needed to maintain this posture.

Posture

Poor posture probably does not cause back injuries. But it can certainly cause backache, and may make an already damaged disc worse.

Standing   A jointed skeleton cannot keep standing upright by itself. If you relaxed all your muscles, you would collapse in a heap. You are kept standing upright by the tension of antagonistic muscles keeping the knees straight, holding the back upright, and supporting the head.

To maintain posture, only a small proportion of the fibres of any one muscle have to contract. But even these use up energy and can become fatigued. A good standing posture uses the minimum amount of energy (Figure 14). The skull is balanced on the spinal column. The ear, shoulder, centre of gravity and knee caps are in a straight line vertically above the ankle joint. The knee joints are 'locked' back against their ligaments.

In this 'balanced' position, the minimum amount of muscular energy is needed to stay upright and the ligaments of the back are not stretched. The balanced upright position is difficult to achieve during pregnancy, when the centre of gravity moves forward. This is why pregnant women get backache if they stand for long. High-heeled shoes and obesity also make it hard to hold a relaxed, upright position.

The spinal column cannot be held straight. It has natural curves, as Figures 3 and 14 show. However, it should be held upright. A long time spent bending over a sink or work surface produces backache. One set of antagonistic muscles has to work overtime and the ligaments of the vertebral column may become stretched and painful. Your work surfaces should be of such a height that you do not need to bend (Figure 15).

Long standing, even with a good posture, may lead to backache. It is best to change your position from time to time.

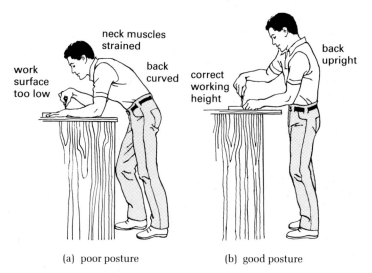

(a) poor posture   (b) good posture

Figure 15   Good and bad standing postures
(After Michael I.V. Jayson, *Back pain: the facts*, Oxford University Press, 1984)

Sitting   The back should be upright and supported, especially in the lumbar region. The seat should support the thighs over most of their length, and the feet should be flat on the floor (Figure 16 (a)).

In this position, the discs are not unevenly stressed and the ligaments are not stretched. Slumping in a soft chair or bending over a desk that is too low can lead to pain in the back or neck (Figure 16 (b)).

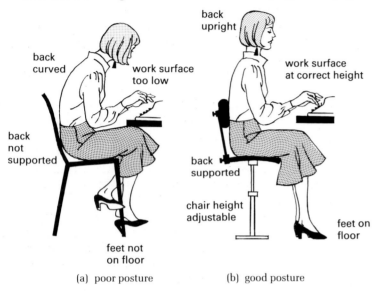

Figure 16   Good and bad sitting postures
(After Michael I.V. Jayson, *Back pain: the facts*, Oxford University Press, 1984)

The feet   The weight of the body is supported by the feet. Each foot is a kind of three-dimensional arch, with the main points of support at the heel, the base of the big toe and the base of the little toe. When the posture is correct, the weight is shared by these three points (Figure 17). Bad posture leads to unequal stresses on the joints and ligaments of the foot. This is uncomfortable, and the arches may become distorted and flattened.

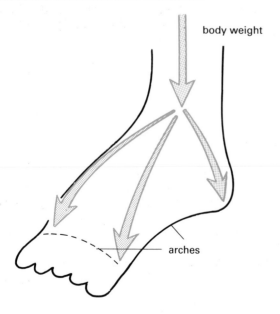

Figure 17   Distribution of weight on the foot

QUESTIONS
10 If you were asked to carry a heavy box of books upstairs, how would you tackle the job in a way that kept the risk of back injury to a minimum?
11 In what circumstances do you think you adopt a poor standing or sitting posture during the day?

Exercise

The immediate effects of exercise

The body responds to strenuous exercise in the following ways:

1 The heart rate increases (to about twice its resting rate) and so does its **stroke volume**. This means that the ventricles contract more and expel more blood at each beat. This increases the output from the heart up to five times.
2 The breathing rate and tidal volume increase (page 144) so that the volume of air exchanged in a given time goes up about ten times.
3 The arterioles and capillaries in the active muscles widen (dilate), so the blood flow increases up to four times.
    At the same time, the blood vessels in the alimentary canal and skin constrict. So more blood can reach the muscles.
4 The rate at which energy is released in the active muscles goes up about twenty times and lactic acid begins to build up in the blood.
5 The insulin level drops and the adrenalin level rises (pages 214–15). This causes the liver to convert glycogen to glucose, and the fat depots to release fatty acids.
6 The body temperature rises. The blood vessels in the skin which at first constricted may now dilate. Sweating may begin.

All these changes increase the rate at which (a) oxygen and food are delivered to the muscles, (b) carbon dioxide and lactic acid are removed, (c) heat is lost.

Recovery   After light exercise, such as walking, or after a short burst of strenuous activity, all these systems return to their resting rates within minutes. After long and strenuous exercise, it may take hours for the resting rates to be restored. This is because an oxygen debt (page 184) has built up, and time is needed for oxidation of the lactic acid.

Long-term benefits of exercise

Some of the evidence for the benefits of exercise comes from experiments on laboratory animals, some from observations and measurements on athletes and some from studies of large samples from the general population.

Whatever benefits exercise may bring, they do not persist unless you exercise regularly. Taking part in sport at school will help to make you fit, but you will not stay fit unless you keep up a regular pattern of exercise.

To be useful, exercise has to be strenuous, last about 20 minutes or more and be repeated at least three times per week. Examples are brisk walking, jogging, cycling, disco dancing, playing football, rugby, hockey, netball, tennis, squash and so on.

Regular strenuous exercise can produce the following physiological changes, which are beneficial:

(a) *The resting heart rate goes down.* The ventricles enlarge and the heart muscle grows stronger, so that the stroke volume is increased. This means that when you take exercise, your heart can deliver more blood to the muscles without its rate of beating rising too far. Coronary blood flow may possibly increase, either because the vessels widen or because more branches develop. But the evidence for this is not very strong.

(There is no evidence that exercise has any beneficial effect on the lungs or breathing mechanism.)

(b) *The muscles used in exercise grow larger.* At first the muscle fibres grow thicker and then their number increases. The capillaries in the muscle develop more branches. Thus the muscles become stronger. But this only happens if the exercise makes them work to about 80 per cent of their maximum capacity.

(c) *More enzymes are made in the muscle tissue.* These are the enzymes needed for breaking down glucose, glycogen or fatty acids. Thus the muscle is able to take up oxygen and food more rapidly from the blood and increase the rate of energy production.

All these changes increase your strength, and also your stamina and endurance. That means that you can take more strenuous exercise, for longer periods, without getting tired or out of breath. Weight training improves strength but not stamina. Walking improves stamina but not strength.

Only the muscles taking part in the exercise will grow stronger. So training for one sport probably won't make you better at another. Improved stamina is useful in all active sports, however.

(d) *Your ligaments and tendons become stronger.* This reduces the chance of injury during sudden vigorous activity. Back injury is less likely if the muscles and ligaments of the vertebral column are strong.

(e) *Your joints become more flexible,* giving a greater range of movement with a lower risk of 'pulling' a muscle or spraining a joint.

The changes (a) to (e) help to postpone the effects of old age, but only if the pattern of exercise is maintained.

Once regular exercise ceases, the muscles get thinner. All the improved physiological functions go back to their original level.

(f) *Losing weight.* It is not clear how far exercise can help you become slimmer if you are over-weight. Immediate weight loss after exercise comes mainly from using up glycogen stores and the evaporation of water. Losses of adipose tissue are quite small. You would have to cycle hard for hours to use energy equivalent to 500 g fat. Two hours jogging will use up only about 1600 kJ, equal to about one chocolate bar. Exercise may also increase your appetite.

But exercise does use up some energy. Since it has other benefits, it is worth combining with a controlled diet if you want to lose weight.

(g) *Protection from heart attacks.* Studies have been carried out on large groups of adults, comparing those who take regular exercise with those who do not. Some of these suggest that people who take regular exercise are less likely to suffer prematurely from heart disease. Other studies show no benefit, or even the reverse. On balance, however, it does seem likely that regular exercise throughout life reduces the chance of an early heart attack.

The mechanism for this might be increased coronary circulation, a change in the ratio of lipids in the blood, a slowing down in the formation of atheroma (page 138) in the arteries, a reduced tendency for the blood to form clots in the blood vessels, and long-term reduction in blood pressure. Increased efficiency of the muscles might reduce the strain on the heart.

The evidence for these changes comes mainly from animal studies rather than from humans, and is not all clear-cut. However, even if exercise does not make you live longer, you will certainly stay fitter.

(h) *Well-being.* Most people agree that exercise, undertaken willingly, makes you 'feel good'. The 'scientific' evidence for this is lacking but it could be explained in physiological terms.

QUESTIONS

12 Say which of the following you would consider to be beneficial forms of exercise: running for a bus, climbing a mountain, playing badminton, cutting the grass, playing cricket, swimming. Give reasons for your answers.

13 Why do you have to exercise regularly in order to benefit?

14 Two people have taken strenuous exercise to the same extent. One looks pale and the other is flushed. Suggest reasons for this difference.

15 Explain what part an oxygen debt might play in the time taken to recover from exercise.

PRACTICAL WORK

The structure of bone

Obtain two small bones, such as limb bones from a chicken. Place one of them in a test-tube or beaker, and cover it with dilute hydrochloric acid. Leave it for 24 hours, during which time the acid will dissolve most of the calcium salts in the bone. After 24 hours pour away the acid, wash the bone thoroughly with water and then try to bend it.

Take the second bone and hold one end of it in a hot bunsen flame, heating it strongly for 2 minutes. At first the bone will char and then glow red as the fibrous organic material burns away, but it will retain its shape. Allow the bone to cool. Then try crushing the heated end against the bench with the end of a pencil.

Result   Both bones retain their shape after treatment, but the bone whose calcium salts had been dissolved in acid is rubbery and flexible because only the organic, fibrous connective tissue is left. The bone that had this fibrous tissue burned away is still hard but very brittle and easily shattered.

Interpretation   The combination in bone of mineral salts and organic fibres produces a hard, strong and resilient structure.

CHECK LIST

- The vertebral column ('backbone') is made up of 33 vertebrae.
- The vertebral column forms the main support for the body and also protects the spinal cord.
- The legs are attached to the vertebral column by the hip girdle.
- The shoulder-blades and collar-bones form the shoulder girdle.
- The arms are attached to the shoulder-blades.
- The skull protects the brain, eyes and ears.
- The ribs protect the lungs, heart and liver, and also play a part in breathing.
- The limb joints are either ball and socket (hip and shoulder) or hinge (knee and elbow).
- The surfaces of the joints are covered with cartilage and lubricated with synovial fluid.
- Skeletal muscles are formed from fibres and can be consciously controlled.
- Smooth muscle is formed from layers of cells and cannot be consciously controlled.

- Limb muscles are attached to the bones by tendons.
- When the muscles contract, they pull on the bones and so bend and straighten the limb or move it forwards and backwards.
- Most limb muscles are arranged in antagonistic pairs. For example, one bends and one straightens the limb.
- By straightening the leg and thrusting it against the ground, an animal can propel itself forwards.
- Severe back pain is often the result of a damaged intervertebral disc.
- The risk of back injury is reduced by learning how to lift properly.
- A poor standing or sitting posture may cause back pain.
- The body's immediate responses to exercise can increase the efficiency of the blood supply to the muscles.
- The long-term benefits of exercise are increases in strength, stamina and flexibility.
- Exercise must be regular to be of lasting benefit.

Functions of Teeth
Incisors, canines, premolars and molars.

Structure of Teeth
Enamel, dentine, pulp and cement.

Milk Teeth and Permanent Teeth

Dental Health
Tooth decay and gum disease. Methods of prevention.

Fluoridation
Fluoride in drinking water.

Functions of Teeth

Before you can swallow food, you have to bite off pieces which are small enough to pass down your gullet into your stomach. Digestion is made easier if you crush these pieces of food into even smaller particles by the action of chewing. Biting and chewing are actions carried out by teeth, jaws and muscles (see Figure 4 on page 181).

The teeth are given different names according to their position in the jaw (Figure 1). In the front of each of the upper and lower jaws there are four **incisors**. Your top incisors pass in front of your bottom incisors and cut pieces off the food, as when you bite into an apple or take a bite out of a sandwich.

On each side of the incisors there is a **canine** tooth.

In carnivorous mammals, like dogs, the canines are long and pointed. But in humans they are something like the incisors but a little more pointed. They function rather like extra incisors.

At the side of each jaw are the **premolars**, two on each side. They are larger than the canines and have one or two blunt points or **cusps**. At the back of each jaw are two or three **molars**. The molars are larger than the premolars and have four or more cusps. The premolars and molars function similarly. Their knobbly surfaces meet when the jaws are closed, and crush the food into small pieces.

As well as breaking the food into a suitable size for swallowing, the crushing action of the molars and premolars reduces food to quite small particles. Small particles of food are easier to digest than large pieces because the digestive enzymes can act over a greater surface area.

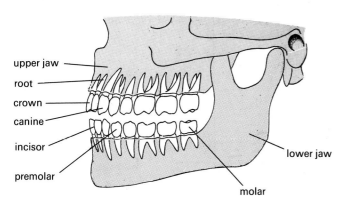

(a) teeth and jaws, side view

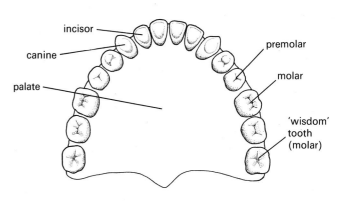

(b) teeth in upper jaw

Figure 1   Human dentition

QUESTIONS

1 How many incisors, canines, premolars and molars are there in a human upper jaw (see Figure 1 (b))? How many teeth are there in a full set?

2 The words 'biting', 'crushing' and 'chewing' have been used several times in this section. Say exactly what you think each word means.

3 Look at the position of the jaw muscles in Figure 4 on page 181. Which teeth do you think exert the greatest force on the food?

Structure of Teeth

Figure 2 (a) shows the structure of an incisor or canine tooth as it would appear in vertical section (cut from top to bottom). Figure 2 (b) shows a section through a molar tooth.

Enamel Enamel covers the exposed part, or **crown**, of the tooth and makes a hard biting surface. It is a non-living substance containing 97 per cent calcium salts and only 3 per cent organic matter. Although the enamel is laid down before the tooth comes through the gum, it can be thickened and strengthened by salts from the saliva or from food and drink. Fluoride ions taken up by the enamel increase its resistance to decay.

Dentine This is rather like bone and softer than enamel. It is a living tissue with threads of cytoplasm running through it. The hardness of both enamel and dentine depends on there being enough calcium in the diet and enough vitamin D to help calcium absorption in the intestine.

Pulp In the centre of the tooth is soft connective tissue. It contains cells which make the dentine and keep the tooth alive. In the pulp are blood vessels which bring food and oxygen, so that the tooth can grow at first and then remain alive when growth has stopped. There are also sensory nerve endings in the pulp, which are sensitive to heat and cold but give only the sensation of pain. If you plunge your teeth into an ice-cream, they do not feel cold but they do hurt.

Cement This is a bone-like substance which covers the root of the tooth. In the cement are embedded tough fibres which pass into the bone of the jaw and hold the tooth in place.

Milk teeth and permanent teeth

Mammals have two sets of teeth in their lifetimes (Figure 3). In humans the first set, or **milk teeth**, grow through the gum during the first year of life. They consist of four incisors, two canines and four molars in each jaw. Between the ages of 6 and 12 years, these milk teeth gradually fall out (Figure 4). They are replaced by the **permanent teeth**, including six molars in each jaw. The last of these molars, the 'wisdom teeth', may not grow until the age of 17 or later. In some people they do not appear at all. If the permanent teeth are lost for any reason, they do not grow again.

QUESTIONS

4 Which of the permanent teeth are not represented in the set of milk teeth?

5 What are the differences between dentine and enamel?

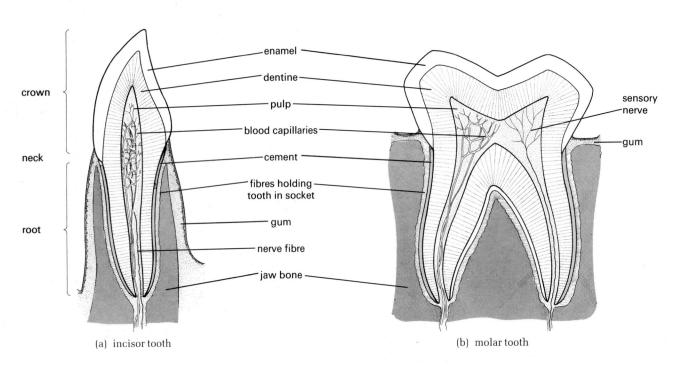

(a) incisor tooth   (b) molar tooth

Figure 2 Longitudinal sections through incisor and molar teeth

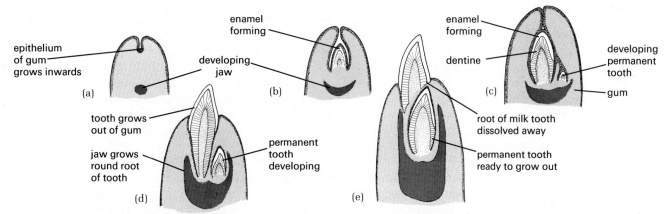

Figure 3   Sections through lower jaw to show development and growth of milk tooth and permanent tooth

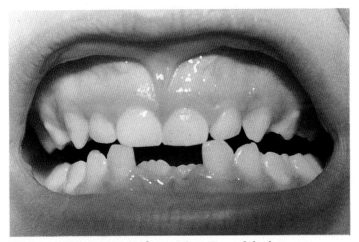

Figure 4   **Permanent teeth erupting.** Two of the bottom incisors are just emerging.

Dental Health

The most likely reasons for the loss of teeth are dental decay and gum disease.

Dental decay (dental caries)

Decay begins when small holes (cavities) appear in the enamel (Figure 5 (b)). The cavities are caused by bacteria on the tooth surface. The bacteria produce acids which dissolve the calcium salts in the tooth enamel. The enamel and dentine are dissolved away in patches, forming cavities. The cavities reduce the distance between the outside of the tooth and the nerve endings. The acids produced by the bacteria irritate the nerve endings and cause toothache. If the cavity is not cleaned and filled by a dentist, the bacteria will get into the pulp cavity and cause a painful abscess at the root. Often, the only way to treat an abscess is to have the tooth pulled out.

Although some people's teeth are more resistant to decay than others, it seems that it is the presence of refined sugar (sucrose) that gives rise to decay.

Western diets contain a good deal of refined sugar, and children suck sweets between meals. The high level of dental decay in western society is thought to be caused mainly by keeping sugar in the mouth for long periods of time.

The best way to prevent tooth decay, therefore, is to avoid the constant eating of sugar, either in the form of sweets or in sweet drinks such as orange squash or cola drinks. It is often said that eating hard fibrous food, such as raw vegetables, removes plaque (see below) and prevents decay. But there is not much evidence to support this.

Brushing the teeth or rinsing the mouth does little to prevent dental decay. However, if a fluoride toothpaste is used it does help to increase the resistance of enamel to bacterial acids. If fluoride is added to drinking water, fewer children's teeth decay. But many people disapprove of this practice (see below). Brushing the teeth is very important in the prevention of gum disease, which causes more tooth loss than caries does.

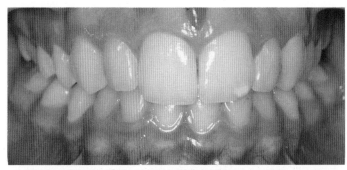

(a) The teeth are free from cavities and the gums are healthy.

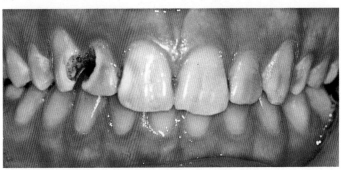

(b) Two of the upper teeth have cavities caused by decay.

Figure 5   **Healthy and decayed teeth**

Gum disease (periodontal disease)

There is usually a layer of saliva and mucus over the teeth. This layer contains bacteria which live on the food residues in the mouth, building up a coating on the teeth, called **plaque**. If the plaque is not removed, mineral salts of calcium and magnesium are deposited in it, forming a hard layer of 'tartar' or **calculus**.

If plaque is not removed regularly, it spreads down the tooth into the narrow gap between the gum and enamel. Here it causes inflammation, called **gingivitis**, which leads to redness and bleeding of the gums and to bad breath. It also causes the gums to recede and expose the cement. If gingivitis is not treated, **periodontitis** develops. The fibres holding the tooth in the jaw are destroyed, so the tooth becomes loose and falls out or has to be pulled out.

Cleaning the teeth does seem to help to prevent gum disease. It is best to clean the teeth about twice a day, using a toothbrush. No one method of cleaning has proved to be any better than any other, but the cleaning should try to remove all the plaque from the narrow crevice between the gums and the teeth.

Drawing a waxed thread ('dental floss') between the teeth helps to remove plaque in these regions.

Disclosing tablets   These contain a harmless dye which colours any plaque present on the teeth. You chew a disclosing tablet before cleaning your teeth and then rinse your mouth with water. Any plaque on your teeth will be stained red. If you now clean your teeth, you will be able to see how efficiently you remove the plaque.

Fluoridation

Fluoride ions occur fairly commonly in drinking water, in concentrations up to about 5 parts per million (ppm). In areas where water naturally contains fluoride ions in concentrations of about 1 ppm, there is up to 60 per cent less decay than in areas where the water contains little or no fluoride. In some American towns fluoride was added to drinking water in concentrations of 1 ppm. The populations of these towns were compared with control areas with little fluoride in the water. Again, tooth decay in children had fallen, with no evidence of unwanted side-effects. Concentrations of 2 ppm or more, however, tend to cause some mottling of the teeth. Experimental fluoridation has been carried out in the USA for over 25 years, and in Britain for over 20 years, with encouraging results.

Fluoride ions are taken up directly from the mouth by the surface layers of enamel. Fluoride which is swallowed gets into the bloodstream. The kidneys excrete 95 per cent of it, and the rest is taken up by the teeth and bones. Fluoride makes enamel resist decay better, especially when the permanent teeth are still developing, but to some extent at all ages.

Some people dislike the fluoridation of drinking water, mainly because the measure is forced upon them, leaving them no choice in the matter. Biologically it may seem a reasonable adjustment of our environment to our needs. Teeth seem to need a supply of fluoride just as they need calcium and phosphate, and the best way, it is claimed, of obtaining this supply in continuous small doses is via the drinking water.

Certainly, any adjustment of our environment which affects the health of millions of people needs very thorough consideration. Though the case for fluoridation seems to have received careful study, people are still arguing both about the interpretations of the evidence, and whether it is right to interfere with the water supplies for medical purposes, rather than just making it safe to drink.

If the fluoride level in your drinking water is less than 0.3 ppm, you can increase your intake by chewing fluoride tablets.

QUESTIONS

6 Does your diet include any refined sugar? If so make a list of the food substances or meals which contain it.
7 What are the most important things to do to avoid dental decay and gum disease?

CHECK LIST

- The roots of our teeth are held in the jawbone.
- The crowns of the teeth are covered with enamel and project into the mouth.
- The pulp and the dentine are kept alive by blood vessels bringing food and oxygen.
- We have incisor, canine, premolar and molar teeth.
- The incisors and canines bite off pieces of food.
- The premolars and molars crush the food ready for swallowing.
- We have two sets of teeth in our lifetime: milk teeth (20) and permanent teeth (32).
- Bacteria in the mouth can cause cavities in teeth if sugar is present.
- Plaque is a layer which forms on the teeth. It consists of saliva, mucus, bacteria and bacterial products.
- If plaque is not removed, it may cause gum disease.
- Cleaning the teeth removes the plaque and helps prevent gum disease.

The Senses

Skin Senses
Touch, pressure, cold.

Taste and Smell
Taste buds. Chemo-receptors.

Proprioceptors
Position of limbs. Tension of muscles.

Sight
Eye structure and function. Image formation. Accommodation. 3-D vision. Colour vision. Long and short sight.

Hearing
Ear structure and function.

Practical Work
Experiments on touch and taste.

Our senses make us aware of changes in our surroundings and in our own bodies. We have sense cells which respond to stimuli (singular = stimulus). A **stimulus** is a change in light, temperature, pressure or any other condition, which produces a reaction in a living organism. Stimuli like touch and heat come from outside the body. Others result from changes within the body, such as blood pressure or temperature.

Structures which respond to stimuli are called **receptors**. Some of these receptors are scattered throughout the skin. Others are concentrated into special sense organs which detect only one kind of stimulus. For example, the eye responds to light, and the tongue detects chemicals.

Sensory cells and sense organs convert one form of energy to another. Structures which can do this are called energy **transducers**. The eyes can convert light energy into the electrical energy of a nerve impulse. The ears convert the energy in sound vibrations into nerve impulses. The forms of energy which make up the stimuli may be very different – mechanical energy, chemical energy, light energy and so on – but they are all transduced into pulses of electrical energy in the nerves.

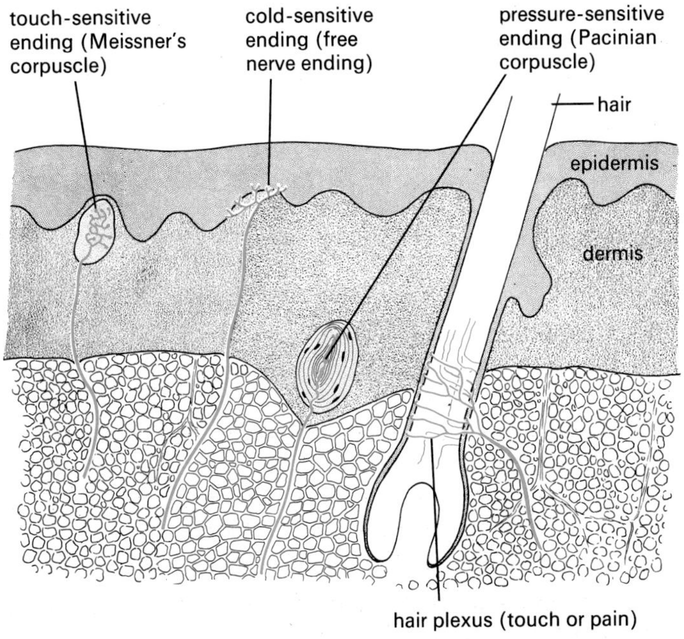

Skin Senses

There are a great many sensory nerve endings in the skin. Some respond to the stimuli of touch, pressure, heat and cold. Some cause a feeling of pain. These sensory nerve endings are very small, and they can be seen only in sections of the skin when studied under the microscope (Figure 1). Some have not yet been identified.

Some of the sensory nerve endings are **encapsulated**, which means they are enclosed in a capsule. Examples are the Meissner's corpuscles (touch) and the Pacinian corpuscles (pressure) (Figure 2). Other sensory nerve endings seem to consist only of fine branches from the nerve fibre. The 'cold' sensors and the hair plexuses are like this. They are called **'free' nerve endings**.

Certain regions of skin have a greater concentra-

touch-sensitive ending (Meissner's corpuscle)

cold-sensitive ending (free nerve ending)

pressure-sensitive ending (Pacinian corpuscle)

hair

epidermis

dermis

hair plexus (touch or pain)

Figure 1 The sense organs of the skin (generalized diagram)

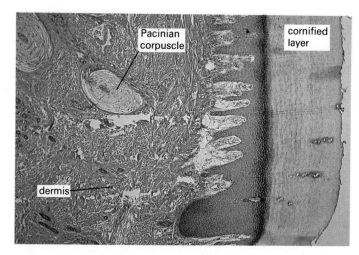

Figure 2   Pacinian corpuscle in human skin (×60)

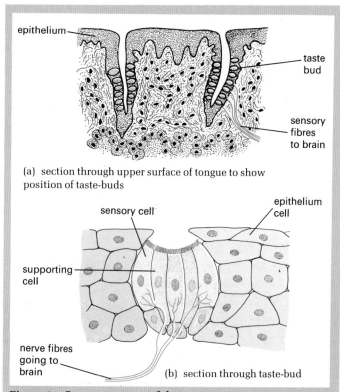

(a) section through upper surface of tongue to show position of taste-buds

(b) section through taste-bud

Figure 3   Sensory system of the tongue

tion of sense organs than others. The finger-tips, for example, have a large number of touch organs, making them particularly sensitive to touch. The front of the upper arm is sensitive to heat and cold. Some areas of the skin have fewer sense organs. You can prick or burn it in certain places without feeling anything.

When the nerve ending receives a stimulus, it sends a nerve impulse to the brain which makes us aware of the sensation. Generally, each type of nerve ending responds to only one kind of stimulus. For example, a heat receptor would send off a nerve impulse if its temperature were raised, but not if it were touched.

Pain is not a stimulus. It is a sensation produced in the brain. The sensation of pain can be produced by various stimuli such as heat, cold and pressure.

It is not clear whether there are specialized sensory nerve endings for 'pain', or whether we have the sensation of pain when a combination of receptors is stimulated in a particular way.

QUESTIONS

1 What sensation would you expect to feel if a warm pin-head was pressed on to a touch receptor in your skin? Explain.
2 If a piece of ice is pressed on to the skin, which receptors are likely to send impulses to the brain?

Taste and Smell

Taste   In the lining of the nasal cavity and on the tongue are groups of sensory cells, called **chemo-receptors**, which respond to chemicals. On the tongue, these groups are called **taste-buds** and they lie mostly in the grooves of the tongue (Figure 3).

The receptor cells in the taste-buds can recognize only four classes of chemicals. These are the chemicals which give the taste sensations of sweet, sour, salt or bitter. Nearly all acids, for example, give the taste sensation we call 'sour'. Many quite different chemicals give the sensation of 'sweet'. Generally, the taste cells are sensitive to only one or two of these classes of chemical. For a substance to produce a sensation of taste, it must be able to dissolve in the film of water covering the tongue.

Smell   The epithelium lining the top of the nasal cavity contains chemo-receptors. Fine processes from these chemo-receptors extend into the film of mucus which lines the nasal epithelium (Figure 4). A wide range of airborne chemicals stimulates the nasal receptors, and they send nerve impulses to the brain.

Our sense of smell can distinguish a great many more chemicals than our sense of taste. But the types of smell we can recognize have never been properly classified. And we cannot explain how we recognize them.

The sensation we call 'flavour' (as distinct from 'taste') is the result of vapours, from the food in the mouth, reaching the chemo-receptors in the nose. Flavour is, therefore, largely 'smell'. We lose some of the sensation of flavour when the nose is blocked by a heavy cold.

The sense of smell is easily fatigued. That is to say, after smelling something for a long time we become unaware of it, though a newcomer may detect it at once.

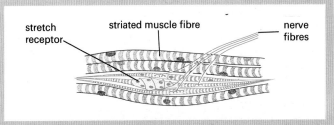

Figure 5 Stretch-receptor in muscle

'know' about the position and movement of our limbs without having to watch them. In this way, the proprioceptors play an important part in co-ordinated movement.

Proprioceptors also represent an important means of **'feedback'** to the central nervous system. They indicate the degree of tension in the muscles and the position of the limbs. In humans, the body is kept upright by keeping opposing sets of muscles in a state of tension (tone) (page 187). However, we cannot stand perfectly still; we sway and tilt very slightly all the time. If we sway slightly forward, the stretch-receptors in the calf muscles will be stimulated and set off a reflex which tightens the calf muscles themselves and other muscles in the back of the legs. This will restore the upright position.

QUESTION

6 Refer back to Figures 8 and 11 on pages 184 and 185. In which muscles will the stretch-receptors be stimulated?

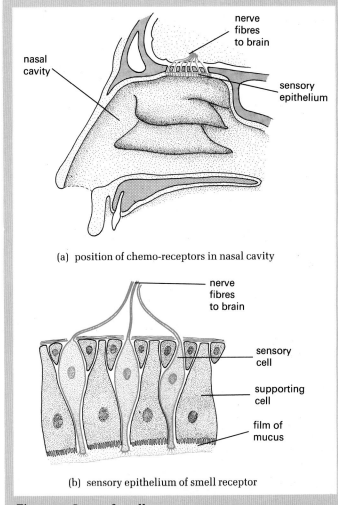

(a) position of chemo-receptors in nasal cavity

(b) sensory epithelium of smell receptor

Figure 4 Sense of smell

QUESTIONS

3 Which types of taste-bud are likely to be stimulated by lemonade?
4 Apart from the cells which detect chemicals, what other types of receptor must be present in the tongue?
5 What is the difference between taste, smell and flavour?

Proprioceptors

Sometimes the term 'proprioceptors' refers to any kind of internal sense organ that responds to changes within the body, such as blood pressure. Usually, it describes muscle receptors which respond to stretching. The **stretch-receptors** are specialized muscle fibres with a sensory nerve supply (Figure 5). They lie parallel to the other muscle fibres and are stretched when the relaxed muscle is extended by the contraction of its antagonistic partner (page 184).

Stretch-receptors trigger off certain reflex actions (see page 209). They control walking patterns in many land vertebrates. They enable us to

Sight

If you do not already know how lenses work, study Figure 6 before reading the next section.

The eye

The structure of the eye is shown in Figures 7 and 8. The **sclera** is the tough, white outer coating. The front part of the sclera is clear and allows light to enter the eye. This part is called the **cornea**. The **conjunctiva** is a thin epithelium which lines the inside of the eyelids and the front of the sclera. It is continuous with the epithelium of the cornea.

The eye contains a clear liquid, whose outward pressure on the sclera keeps the eyeball spherical. The liquid in the back chamber of the eye is jelly-like and called **vitreous humour**. The **aqueous humour** in the front chamber is watery.

The **lens** is a transparent structure, held in place by a ring of fibres called the **suspensory ligament**.

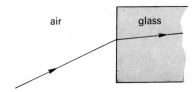

(a) When a ray of light passes at an angle from air to glass or from glass to water, the ray is bent slightly. The bending is called 'refraction'.

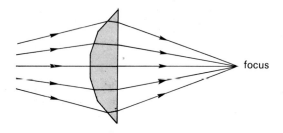

(b) If the rays pass through the curved surface shown here (a lens), they are bent towards each other and come to a focus.

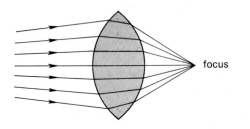

(c) A thick lens bends light more . . .

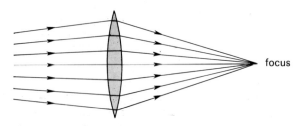

(d) . . . than a thin lens.

Figure 6   How a convex lens works

Unlike the lens of a camera or a telescope, the eye lens is flexible and can change its shape. In front of the lens is a disc of coloured tissue called the **iris**. It is the iris we describe when we say the colour of the eye is brown or blue.

There is a hole in the centre of the iris called the **pupil**. This lets in light to the rest of the eye. The pupil looks black, because all the light entering the eye is absorbed by the black pigment in the **choroid**. The choroid layer, which contains many blood vessels, lies between the retina and the sclera. In the front of the eyeball, it forms the iris and the **ciliary body** (see page 200). The ciliary body produces aqueous humour.

The internal lining at the back of the eye is the **retina**. It consists of many thousands of cells which respond to light. When light falls on these cells, they send off nervous impulses which travel in nerve fibres through the **optic nerve** to the brain, and so give rise to the sensation of sight.

Tear glands under the top eyelid produce tear fluid. This is a dilute solution of sodium chloride

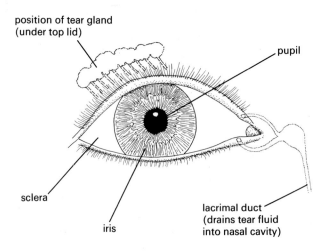

Figure 7   Appearance of right eye from the front

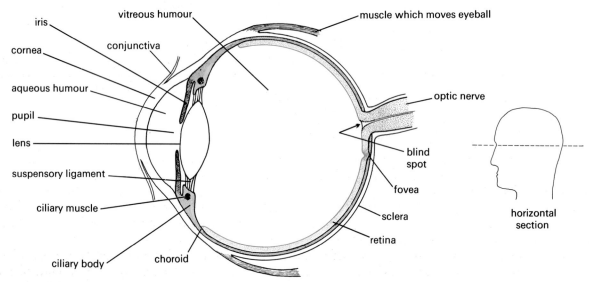

Figure 8   Horizontal section through the left eye

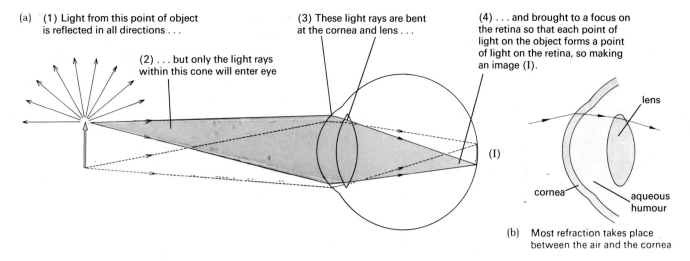

(a) (1) Light from this point of object is reflected in all directions . . .

(2) . . . but only the light rays within this cone will enter eye

(3) These light rays are bent at the cornea and lens . . .

(4) . . . and brought to a focus on the retina so that each point of light on the object forms a point of light on the retina, so making an image (I).

(I)

lens

cornea

aqueous humour

(b) Most refraction takes place between the air and the cornea

Figure 9 Image formation on the retina (eye shown in vertical section)

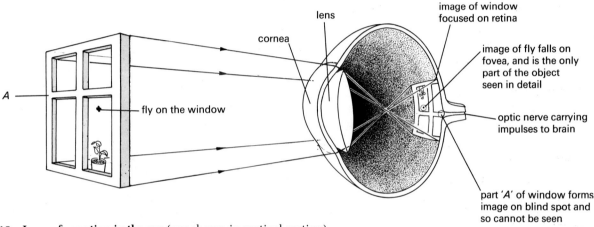

lens

cornea

image of window focused on retina

image of fly falls on fovea, and is the only part of the object seen in detail

optic nerve carrying impulses to brain

A

fly on the window

part '*A*' of window forms image on blind spot and so cannot be seen

Figure 10 Image formation in the eye (eye shown in vertical section)

and sodium hydrogencarbonate. The fluid is spread over the eye surface by the blinking of the eyelids, keeping the surface moist and washing away any dust particles or foreign bodies. Tear fluid also contains an enzyme, **lysozyme**, which attacks bacteria.

Vision

Figures 9 and 10 explain how light from an object produces a focused **image** on the retina (like a 'picture' on a cinema screen). The curved surfaces of the cornea and lens both 'bend' the light rays which enter the eye. They 'bend' in such a way that each 'point of light' from the object forms a 'point of light' on the retina. These points of light will form an image, upside down and smaller than the object.

The cornea and the aqueous and vitreous humours are mainly responsible for the 'bending' (refraction) of light. The lens makes the final adjustments to the focus (Figure 9 (b)).

The pattern of sensory cells stimulated by the image will produce a pattern of nerve impulses sent to the brain. The brain interprets this pattern, using its past experience and learning. We thus gain an impression of the real size, distance and upright nature of the object.

Blind spot At the point where the optic nerve leaves the retina, there are no sensory cells. So no information reaches the brain about that part of the image which falls on this **blind spot** (see Figure 11).

Figure 11 The blind spot. Hold the book about 50 cm away from your eyes. Close your left eye. Concentrate on the cross with your right eye. Slowly bring the book closer to your face. When the image of the dot falls on the blind spot it will seem to disappear.

Retina The millions of light-sensitive cells in the retina are of two kinds, the **rods** and the **cones** (according to shape). The cones enable us to tell colours apart. There seem to be three types of cone cell. One type responds best to red light, one to green and one to blue. If all three types are equally stimulated we get the sensation of white. The cone cells are concentrated in a central part of the retina, called the the **fovea** (Figure 8). When you study an

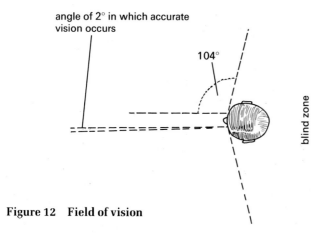

angle of 2° in which accurate
vision occurs

104°

blind zone

Figure 12   Field of vision

object closely, you are making its image fall on the fovea.

The cone cells in the fovea detect colour and give a detailed analysis of the image but they will work only in good light. The rods cannot distinguish colours but will work in poor light. This is why we find it difficult to identify colours in dim light. And we need good light to make out detail, because the fovea (the central, 'accurate' part of the retina) contains only cones, which do not respond to dim light. The peripheral part of the retina (all the rest of the retina surrounding the fovea) will provide a distinct silhouette of an object in dim light, but no detail.

Fovea   Only in the fovea can the eye and brain make a really detailed analysis of the colour and shape of an object. Although we can see objects included in a zone of about 100° from each eye (our **field of vision**), only those objects within a 2° zone can be seen in detail (Figure 12). This is much less than people imagine. For example, only about two letters in any word on this page can be studied in detail at any one moment. Only by constantly moving your eyes can you build up an accurate picture of a scene.

Accommodation (focusing)

The eye can produce a focused image of either a near object or a distant object. To do this the lens changes its shape, becoming thinner for distant objects and fatter for near objects. It does so by contracting or relaxing the circular band of muscle in the ciliary body, the **ciliary muscle** (Figures 13 and 14). When the ciliary muscle is relaxed, the outward pressure of the humours on the sclera pulls on the suspensory ligament and stretches the lens to its thin shape. The eye is now accommodated (focused) for distant objects (Figures 14 (a) and 15 (a)).

To focus a near object, the ciliary muscle contracts to a smaller circle. This takes the tension out of the suspensory ligament (Figures 14 (b) and 15 (b)). The lens is elastic and flexible and so is able to change to its fatter shape. This shape is better at bending the light rays from a close object.

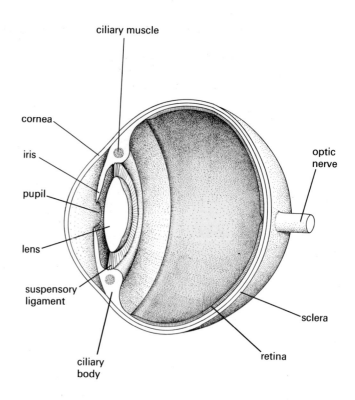

ciliary muscle

cornea

iris

pupil

lens

suspensory
ligament

ciliary
body

optic
nerve

sclera

retina

Figure 13   Vertical section through the left eye

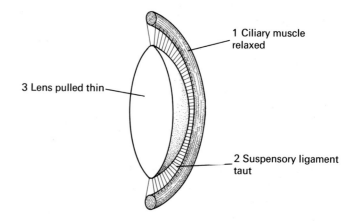

1 Ciliary muscle
relaxed

3 Lens pulled thin

2 Suspensory ligament
taut

(a) accommodated for distant object

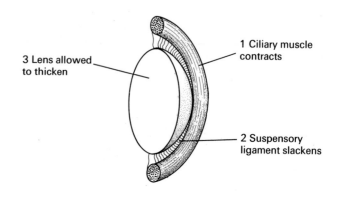

1 Ciliary muscle
contracts

3 Lens allowed
to thicken

2 Suspensory
ligament slackens

(b) accommodated for near object

Figure 14   How accommodation is brought about

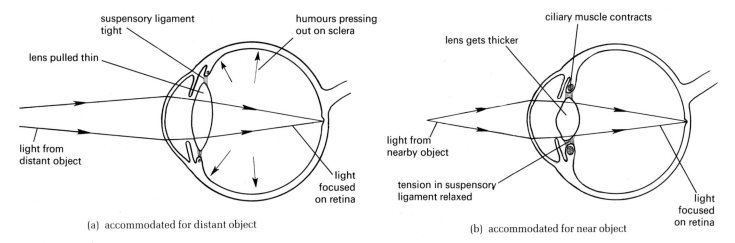

(a) accommodated for distant object

(b) accommodated for near object

Figure 15   Accommodation

Control of light intensity

The amount of light entering the eye is controlled by altering the size of the pupil. Bright light causes a contraction in a ring of muscle fibres (a sphincter) in the iris. This reduces the size of the pupil and cuts down the intensity of light entering the eye. This reaction protects the retina from high-intensity light, which can damage the retina.

In dim light the sphincter muscle of the iris relaxes and muscle fibres running radially (like wheel spokes) contract. This makes the pupil enlarge and admits more light (see Experiment 3 on page 205).

The change in size of the pupil is caused by an automatic reflex action (page 209). You cannot control it consciously.

3-D vision and distance judgment

When we look at an object, each eye forms its own image of the object. So two sets of impulses are sent to the brain. The brain somehow combines these impulses so that we see only one object and not two. However, because the eyes are spaced apart, they do not have the same view of the object. In Figure 16, the left eye sees more of the left side of the box and the right eye sees more of the right side. When the brain combines the information from both eyes, we get the impression that the object is three-dimensional (3-D) rather than flat.

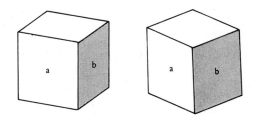

Figure 16   Different views of the same cube seen by left and right eyes. The left eye sees more of side *a*. The right eye sees more of side *b*.

In order to look at a nearby object, the eyes have to turn inwards slightly. (Focusing on a very close object will make you look 'cross-eyed'.) Stretch-receptors in the eye muscles will send impulses to the brain and make it aware of how much the eyes are turning inwards. This is one way by which the brain may be able to judge how close an object is. But it is not likely to be much use for objects beyond 15 metres. We probably judge greater distances by comparing the sizes of familiar objects. The further away an object is, the smaller will be its image on the retina. We use many other clues to help us to judge distances.

We have 3-D vision, and we can judge distances effectively, because our eyes are set in the front of our heads. This gives us what is called **binocular vision**.

Colour vision

The simplest theory of colour vision supposes that there are three different types of cone in the retina. Each type of cone responds best to one particular wavelength of light. (The colour we see depends on the wavelength.) One type of cone responds best to short wavelengths (blue light), one type responds best to long wavelengths (red) and one type responds to intermediate wavelengths (green). The brain checks how many of each type of cone are being stimulated and forms an impression of the colour of the object.

Light from a purely green object would stimulate mainly the green-sensitive cones. Light from a yellow object would stimulate green- and red-sensitive cones. Light from a white object would stimulate all three types equally.

There is plenty of evidence to support the three-colour theory. But there are some experimental results which it cannot explain without more detailed development.

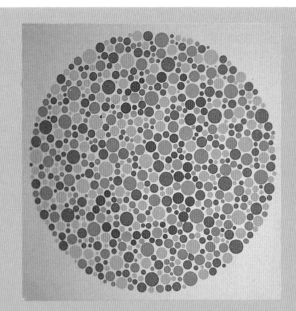

Figure 17   Ishihara colour vision test card. People with normal colour vision see a figure 8. People with red-green colour blindness see a figure 3. Totally colour-blind people cannot see a numeral. Note that for accurate testing the original card must be used.

Colour blindness   Very rarely, a person is totally colour-blind. Such a person sees the world only in black, white and shades of grey. Someone like this probably has no cones in the retina. More commonly, a colour-blind person cannot tell certain groups of colours apart. For example, a red–green colour-blind person is likely to confuse red, brown and green. These colour-blind people probably lack one of the three types of cone.

People may not realize they are colour-blind, because they use other clues to tell colours apart (for example, the green light of a traffic light is always the lowest of the three). Special tests, however, show up this kind of colour blindness (Figure 17).

Red–green colour blindness is more common in men (about 8 per cent) than in women (about 0.4 per cent) because it is inherited on a sex-linked basis (page 234).

Long and short sight

In some people the size of the eyeball does not exactly match the power of the lens. For example, in short-sighted people the eyeball may be too long or the lens too powerful. The image of a distant object then comes into a focus in front of the retina and the image on the retina is blurred. The causes of long and short sight, and how they are corrected, are explained in Figure 18.

Care of the eyes

If dust or other small particles get blown into the eye, they cause reflex blinking (page 209), and the tear glands produce a rapid flow of liquid. These two actions usually wash the particle into the

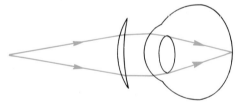

Long sight is caused by short eyeballs or 'weak' lenses. Light from a close object would be focused behind the retina.

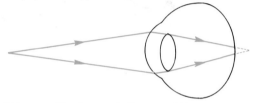

Long sight can be corrected by wearing converging lenses.

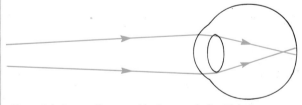

Short sight is usually caused by long eyeballs. Light from a distant object is focused in front of the retina.

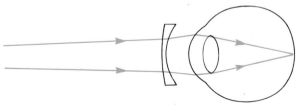

Short sight can be corrected by wearing diverging lenses.

Figure 18   Long and short sight. ('Converging lenses' are thicker in the middle. 'Diverging lenses' are thinner in the middle.)

Figure 19   Protecting the eyes. Always use protective goggles or face shields when doing any experiment which involves vigorous reactions or strong heating.

corner of the eye. It can often then be removed easily with a clean handkerchief. If the particle is not so easily dislodged, the first-aid procedure described on page 279 should be tried before asking for help from a doctor or clinic.

Power tools such as grindstones and sanders, or chisels used with hard objects, can fling particles into the eye with such force that they embed in the cornea. If this happens, a doctor's help is needed.

You can avoid such injuries if you wear protective eye-shields or goggles. You should always wear goggles in the school laboratories when doing experiments which could cause substances to be flung into the eye, such as boiling solutions in test-tubes (Figure 19). Never look into the mouth of a test-tube, in case the liquid spurts out into your eye.

There is no point in bathing the eyes regularly with special solutions. Normal washing with soap and water will keep down the bacterial population round the eyes. Any infections of the eye need to be treated by a doctor.

You should avoid looking straight at very bright lights. In particular, never try to look at the Sun (for example, to watch an eclipse). Light of this intensity can permanently damage the retina.

QUESTIONS

7 In Figure 10, what structures of the eye are not shown in the diagram?
8 In Figure 9, explain what the broken lines are meant to represent.
9 (a) If your ciliary muscles are relaxed, are your eyes focused on a near or a distant object? Explain.
  (b) If you dissected a cow's eye, would you expect the lens to be at its thinnest or its fattest shape? Explain.
10 How do you think animals without binocular vision can judge distances?
11 After the age of about 45, the lens begins to lose its elasticity and does not return to its fatter shape when the ciliary muscle relaxes.
  (a) What effect is this likely to have on vision?
  (b) What sort of spectacles might compensate for this effect?

Hearing

The hearing apparatus is enclosed in bone on each side of the skull, just behind the jaw hinge. Sound vibrations travel through a short, wide tube (the outer ear). They are converted to nerve impulses by the apparatus in the middle ear and inner ear. Figure 20 shows the structure of the ear.

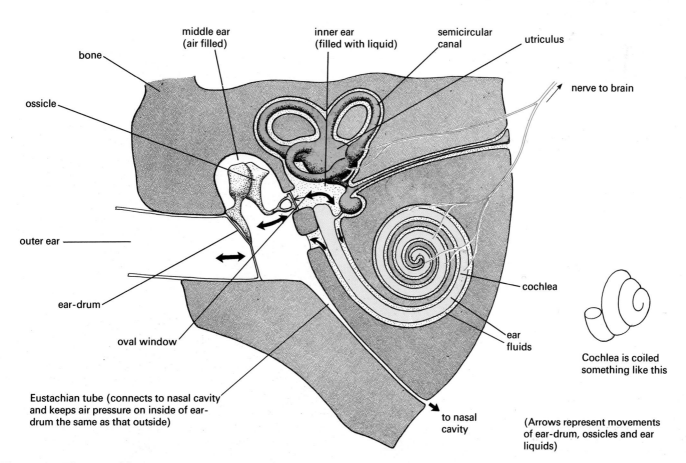

Figure 20 Diagram of the ear

Outer ear

Sound is the name we give to the sensation we get as a result of vibrations in the air. These vibrations are pulses of compressed air. They enter the tube of the outer ear and hit the **ear-drum**, a thin membrane like a drum-skin across the inner end of the tube. The air vibrations cause the ear-drum to vibrate backwards and forwards. If there are 200 pulses of compressed air every second, the ear-drum will move backwards and forwards at the same rate. The vibrations of the ear-drum are converted into nerve impulses by the middle and inner ear.

The ear **pinnae** are the flaps of skin and elastic cartilage which project from the sides of the head and which we usually call our 'ears'. The ear pinnae of mammals, such as dogs and cats, help to direct sound vibrations into the outer ear. The animal can then tell where a sound has come from. Our ear pinnae may have a similar function.

Middle ear

This is a cavity with air in it. It contains a chain of tiny bones or **ossicles**. The first of these ossicles, the **malleus**, is attached to the ear-drum, and the inner ossicle, the **stapes**, fits into a small hole in the skull called the **oval window**. The malleus is connected to the stapes by the **incus** (Figure 21). When the ear-drum vibrates back and forth, it forces the ossicles to vibrate in the same way. So the stapes moves rapidly backwards and forwards like a tiny piston in the oval window. The way the ossicles are attached to each other increases the force of the vibrations and so amplifies the sound.

A narrow tube, called the **Eustachian tube**, connects the nasal cavity (see Figure 6 on page 114) to the middle ear. Although the Eustachian tube is normally closed, it does open to admit or

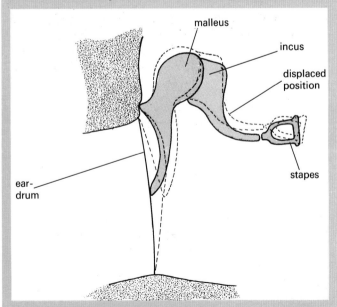

Figure 21 Movement of the ear ossicles in transmitting sound

release air if the air pressure on the outside of the ear-drum changes. Air pressure falls when going up a mountain or in an aircraft. The action of swallowing often causes the Eustachian tube to open. You can then hear a 'popping' sound if there has been a change of pressure.

Inner ear

This is where the vibrations are changed into nerve impulses. The inner ear contains liquid, and the vibrations of the ossicles are passed to this liquid. The sensitive part of the inner ear is the **cochlea**, a coiled tube with sensory nerve endings in it. When the liquid in the cochlea is made to vibrate, the nerve endings send off impulses to the brain. The nerve endings in the first part of the cochlea are sensitive to low-frequency vibration (low notes) and those in the last part are sensitive to high-frequency vibrations (high notes). So if the brain receives nerve impulses coming from the first part of the cochlea, it interprets this as a high-pitched noise or a high musical note. If the impulses come from the top end of the cochlea, the brain recognizes them as being caused by a low note.

In fact, this is a very much simplified account of what happens. The way in which vibrations of different frequencies are converted to nerve impulses by the cochlea has not been fully worked out. It is certainly more complicated than the description above.

Balance The **utriculus** and **semi-circular canals** (Figure 20) are organs of balance. The utriculus detects tilting movements. The semi-circular canals respond to twisting movements in any direction.

The utriculus is important in keeping the body upright. If the body angle changes slightly, it sends nerve impulses to the brain. The brain then sends impulses to the muscles concerned. The muscles increase or reduce their tension to keep the body upright.

The semi-circular canals are important for keeping our balance while moving.

QUESTIONS

12 What is the function of (a) the ear-drum, (b) the ossicles, (c) the liquid of the inner ear, (d) the cochlea?

13 (a) How does the function of a sensory cell in the retina differ from the function of a sensory cell in the cochlea?

(b) If nerve impulses from the cochlea were fed into the optic nerve, what sensations would you expect if somebody clapped their hands?

14 Sometimes, when you have a cold, the middle ear becomes filled with a clear sticky fluid. Why do you think this causes deafness? (The fluid usually drains away through the Eustachian tube when the cold goes.)

PRACTICAL WORK

Experiments 1 and 4 are best done by three people working together: an **experimenter** who applies or offers the stimuli, a **subject** who is given the stimuli, and a **recorder** who watches and makes a note of the responses made by the subject.

1 Sensitivity to touch

The experimenter marks a regular pattern of dots on the back of the subject's hand, using an ink-pad and a rubber stamp like the one in Figure 22, and also stamps the same pattern on to a piece of paper for the recorder to use. The experimenter now tests the sensitivity of the subject's skin by

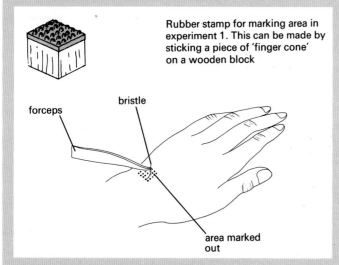

Rubber stamp for marking area in experiment 1. This can be made by sticking a piece of 'finger cone' on a wooden block

forceps

bristle

area marked out

Figure 22   Testing sensitivity to touch

pressing a fine bristle on to each dot in turn. The bristle (a horsehair will do) is glued to a wooden handle or held in forceps and pressed on to each mark until the bristle just starts to bend. The subject must not look, and simply says 'yes' if the stimulus is felt. The recorder marks on his or her pattern how many spots in each row were sensitive to touch.

You can now compare the sensitivity of the back of the hand with the sensitivity of the finger-tips or the back of the neck, by repeating the experiment in these regions.

2   To find which eye is used more

Hold a pencil at arm's length in line with a distant object. Close one eye, and open it again. Then do the same thing with the other eye. With one the pencil will seem to jump sideways. This shows which eye was used to line up the pencil in the first place.

3   The iris diaphragm

For this experiment the room needs to be darkened, but not blacked out.

If you are working in pairs, sit facing each other and take it in turns to hold a bench lamp or torch about 10 cm from the *side* of your partner's face. Switch on the torch or bench lamp and watch the pupil of the eye very carefully. Try switching the light on and off at about 3- or 4-second intervals.

If you are working on your own, you must look closely in a mirror while switching the light on and off.

4   Sensitivity of the tongue to different tastes

(*CAUTION*: It is normally forbidden to taste chemical substances in a laboratory. The substances in this experiment are harmless but should be made up exactly as described on page 285. The test-tubes and other apparatus used must be very clean.)

Sweet, sour, salt and bitter solutions are made up as described on page 285. The subject sticks his tongue out and the experimenter picks up a drop of one of the solutions on the end of a drinking-straw (Figure 23) and touches it on the subject's tongue. The subject must not know in advance which solution is being used, but must leave his tongue out

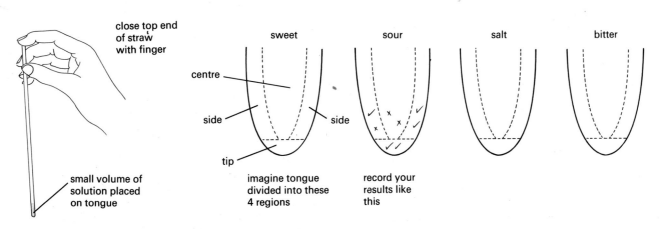

close top end of straw with finger

small volume of solution placed on tongue

sweet

centre

side   side

tip

imagine tongue divided into these 4 regions

sour

record your results like this

salt

bitter

Figure 23   Testing sensitivity to taste

while he decides whether he can recognize the taste or not. If he cannot recognize it, he shakes his head, still leaving his tongue out.

The experimenter now tries a drop of the same solution on a different part of the tongue and keeps doing this until the subject recognizes the taste. At this point, the subject has to pull his tongue in to say what the taste is.

The recorder makes four charts of the tongue, as shown in Figure 23, and puts a tick where each taste was recognized and a cross where it was not. The experimenter now changes to a different solution (and a different drinking-straw) and repeats the experiment. He should try to test all four regions of the tongue equally with all four solutions. He may have to go back several times to any one of the solutions during the course of the experiment if the subject recognizes the taste after only one or two trials.

You can thus build up a picture of the tongue showing which regions are particularly sensitive or insensitive to the four tastes.

There are more experiments on human senses in *Experimental work in biology*, Combined Edition (see page 258).

CHECK LIST

- Our senses detect changes in ourselves and in our surroundings.
- The skin is a sense organ which detects heat, cold, touch and pressure.
- Sensory endings in the nose respond to chemical substances in the air and give us the sense of smell.
- The tongue responds to chemicals in food and drink and gives the sense of taste.

SIGHT

- The lens focuses light from the outside world to form a tiny image on the retina.
- The sensory cells of the retina are stimulated by the light and send nerve impulses to the brain.
- The brain interprets these nerve impulses and so gives us the sense of vision.
- The eye can focus on near or distant objects by changing the thickness of the lens.

- Short sight is corrected by diverging lenses. Long sight is corrected by converging lenses.

HEARING

- The ear-drum is made to vibrate backwards and forwards by sound waves in the air.
- The vibrations are passed on to the inner ear by the three tiny ear bones.
- Sensory nerve endings in the inner ear respond to the vibrations and send impulses to the brain.
- The brain interprets these impulses as sound.

Co-ordination

Co-ordination is the way all the organs and systems of the body are made to work efficiently together (Figure 1). If, for example, the leg muscles are being used for running, they will need extra supplies of glucose and oxygen. To meet this demand, the lungs breathe faster and deeper to obtain the extra oxygen. And the heart pumps more rapidly to get the oxygen and glucose to the muscles more quickly.

The brain detects changes in the oxygen and carbon dioxide content of the blood and sends nervous impulses to the diaphragm, intercostal

muscles and heart. In this example, the systems are co-ordinated by the **nervous system**.

The extra supplies of glucose needed for running come from the liver. Glycogen in the liver is changed to glucose, which is released into the bloodstream (page 120). The conversion of glycogen to glucose is stimulated by, among other things, a chemical called adrenalin (page 214). Co-ordination by chemicals is brought about by the **endocrine system**.

The nervous system works by sending electrical impulses along nerves. The endocrine system depends on the release of chemicals, called **hormones**, from **endocrine glands**. Hormones are carried by the bloodstream. For example, insulin (page 215) is carried from the pancreas to the liver by the circulatory system.

Figure 1 Co-ordination. The badminton player's brain is receiving sensory impulses from her eyes, semi-circular canals, utriculus and muscle stretch-receptors. Using this information, the brain co-ordinates the muscles of her limbs so that even while running or leaping she can control her stroke.

The Nervous System

Figure 2 is a diagram of the human nervous system. The brain and spinal cord together form the **central nervous system**. Nerves carry electrical impulses from the central nervous system to all parts of the body. The nerve impulses make muscles contract, or glands produce enzymes or hormones.

Glands and muscles are called **effectors**, because they go into action when they receive nerve impulses or hormones. The biceps muscle (page 184) is an effector which flexes the arm. The salivary gland is an effector which produces saliva when it receives a nerve impulse from the brain.

The nerves also carry impulses back to the central nervous system from the sense organs of the body, such as the eyes, ears or skin. These impulses make us aware of changes in our surroundings or in

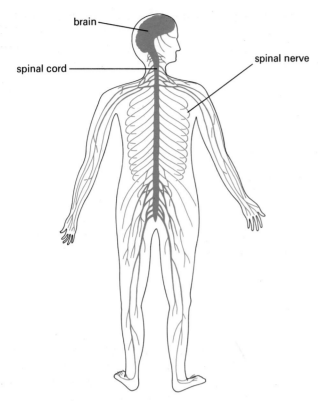

Figure 2   The human nervous system

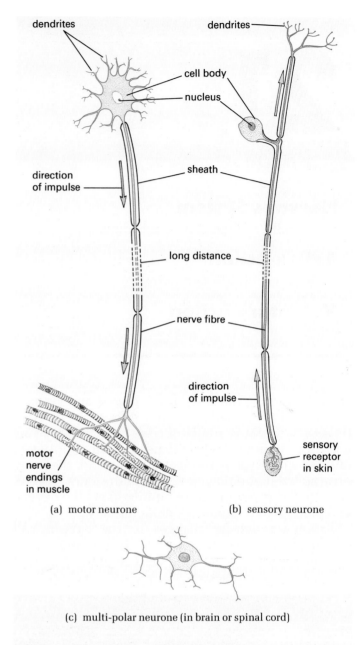

(a) motor neurone   (b) sensory neurone

(c) multi-polar neurone (in brain or spinal cord)

Figure 3   Nerve cells (neurones)

ourselves. Nerve impulses from the sense organs to the central nervous system are called **sensory impulses**. Impulses from the central nervous system to the effectors produce action of some kind. They are called **motor impulses**.

The nerves which connect the body to the central nervous system make up the **peripheral nervous system.**

Nerve cells (neurones)

The central nervous system and the peripheral nerves are made up of nerve cells, called **neurones**. Figure 3 shows three types of neurone. The **motor neurones** carry impulses from the central nervous system to muscles and glands. The **sensory neurones** carry impulses from the sense organs to the central nervous system. The **multi-polar neurones** are neither sensory nor motor. They make connections to other neurones inside the central nervous system.

Each neurone has a **cell body** consisting of a nucleus surrounded by a little cytoplasm. Branching fibres, called **dendrites**, from the cell body make contact with other neurones. A long thread of cytoplasm, surrounded by an insulating sheath, runs from the cell body of the neurone. This thread is called a **nerve fibre** (Figure 3 (a) and (b)). The cell bodies of most neurones are in the brain or in the spinal cord, and the nerve fibres run in the nerves. A **nerve** is easy to see. It is white, tough and stringy and consists of hundreds of microscopic nerve fibres bundled together (Figure 4). Most nerves contain a mixture of sensory and motor fibres. So a nerve can

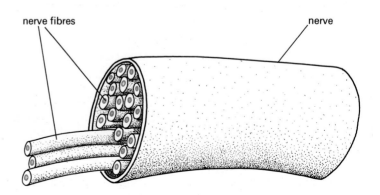

Figure 4   Nerve fibres grouped into a nerve

carry many different impulses. These impulses travel in one direction in sensory fibres and in the opposite direction in motor fibres.

Some of the nerve fibres are very long. For example, the nerve fibres to the foot have their cell bodies in the spinal cord. The fibres run inside the nerves, without a break, down to the skin of the toes or the muscles of the foot. Thus a single nerve cell may have a fibre about 1 metre long.

QUESTIONS

1 What is the difference between a nerve and a nerve fibre?
2 In what ways are sensory neurones and motor neurones similar (a) in structure, (b) in function? How do they differ?
3 Can (a) a nerve fibre, (b) a nerve, carry both sensory and motor impulses? Explain your answers.

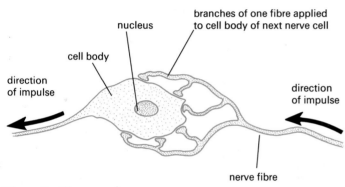

Figure 5 Diagram of synapses

Synapse

Although nerve fibres are insulated, impulses have to pass from one neurone to another. An impulse from the finger-tips must pass through at least three neurones before reaching the brain to produce a sensation of touch. The regions where impulses can cross from one neurone to the next are called **synapses**.

At a synapse, a branch at the end of one fibre is in close contact with the cell body or dendrite of another neurone (Figure 5). When an impulse arrives at the synapse, it releases a tiny amount of a chemical substance (called a chemical transmitter) which sets off an impulse in the next neurone. Sometimes several impulses have to arrive at the synapse before enough chemical is released to fire off an impulse in the next neurone.

The nerve impulse

The nerve fibres do not carry sensations like pain or cold. These sensations are felt only when a nerve impulse reaches the brain. The impulse itself is a series of electrical pulses. Each pulse lasts about 0.001 second and travels down the fibre at speeds of up to 100 metres per second. All nerve impulses are similar. There is no difference between nerve impulses from the eyes, ears or hands.

We can only tell where the sensory impulses have come from and what caused them because the impulses are sent to different parts of the brain. The nerves from the eye, for instance, go to the part of the brain concerned with sight. So when impulses are received in this area, the brain recognizes that they have come from the eyes and we 'see' something.

QUESTIONS

4 Look at Figure 7. (a) How many cell bodies are drawn? (b) How many synapses are shown?
Look at Figure 9 and answer the same questions.
5 If you could intercept and 'listen to' the nerve impulses travelling in the spinal cord, could you tell which ones came from pain receptors and which from cold receptors? Explain your answer.

The reflex arc

A **reflex action** is an automatic response to a stimulus. When a particle of dust touches the cornea of the eye, you will blink – you cannot prevent yourself from blinking. A particle of food touching the lining of your windpipe will set off a coughing reflex which you cannot suppress. When a bright light shines in your eye, the pupil contracts (see page 201). You cannot stop this reflex, and you don't even know that it is happening.

The nervous pathway for such reflexes is called a **reflex arc**. Figure 6 shows the nervous pathway for a well-known reflex called the 'knee-jerk' reflex.

One leg is crossed over the other and the muscles are totally relaxed. If the tendon just below the kneecap of the upper leg is tapped sharply, a reflex arc makes the thigh muscle contract and the lower part of the leg swings forward.

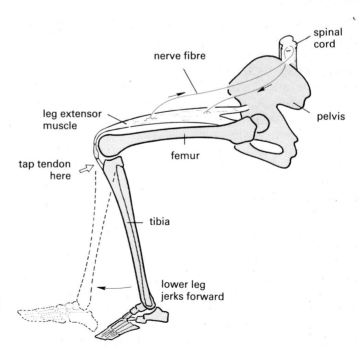

Figure 6 The reflex knee jerk

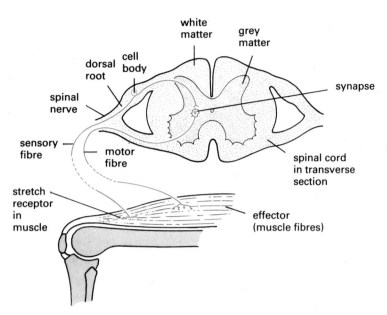

Figure 7 Reflex arc for knee-jerk response. This reflex arc needs only one synapse for making the response. Most reflex actions need many more synapses, both to adjust other muscles in the body, and to send impulses to the brain.

Figure 7 traces the pathway of this reflex arc. Hitting the tendon stretches the muscle and stimulates a stretch-receptor (page 197). The receptor sends off impulses in a sensory fibre. These sensory impulses travel in the nerve to the spinal cord.

In the central region of the spinal cord, the sensory fibre passes the impulse across a synapse to a motor neurone which conducts the impulse down the fibre, back to the thigh muscle. The arrival of the impulses at the muscle makes it contract, and jerk the lower part of the limb forward. You know that this is happening (which means that sensory impulses must be reaching the brain), but there is nothing you can do to stop it.

Spinal cord Figure 10 shows the spinal cord drawn in transverse section. The spinal nerve divides into two 'roots' at the point where it joins the spinal cord. All the sensory fibres enter through the **dorsal root** and the motor fibres all leave through the **ventral root**, but both kinds of fibre are contained in the same spinal nerve. This is like a group of insulated wires in the same electric cable. The cell bodies of all the sensory fibres lie in the dorsal root. They make a bulge called a **ganglion** (Figure 8).

In even the simplest reflex action, many more nerve fibres, synapses and muscles take part than are shown here. Figure 9 shows the reflex arc which would result in the hand being removed from a painful stimulus. On the left side of the spinal cord, an incoming sensory fibre is shown making its first synapse with a **relay neurone** (sometimes called an 'intermediate' neurone). This can pass the impulse on to many other motor neurones, although only one is shown in the diagram. On the right side of the spinal

cord, some of the incoming sensory fibres are shown making synapses with neurones which send nerve fibres to the brain. So the brain is kept informed about what is happening in the body. Also, nerve fibres from the brain make synapses with motor neurones in the spinal cord so that 'commands' from the brain can be sent to the muscles.

Reflexes The reflex just described is a **spinal reflex**. In theory, the brain takes no part in it. Some responses take place in the head, such as blinking, coughing and iris contraction. These have their reflex arcs in the brain, but may still not be consciously controlled.

The reflex closure of the iris protects the retina from bright light (page 201). The withdrawal reflex removes the hand from a dangerously hot object. The coughing reflex dislodges a foreign particle from the windpipe. Thus, these reflexes have a protective function.

There are many other reflexes going on inside our bodies. We are usually unaware of these, but they maintain our blood pressure, breathing rate, heart beat and other body processes.

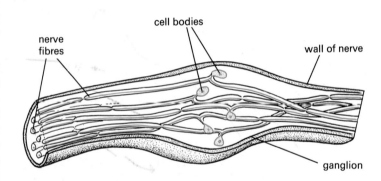

Figure 8 Cell bodies forming a ganglion

Inhibition Motor impulses do not always produce action. Some of them inhibit muscle contraction. That means, they suppress the action of a muscle. Figure 9, for example, shows that a contraction of the biceps muscle will extend the triceps (see Figure 8 on page 184). This makes the stretch-receptors in the triceps fire. These receptors would set off a reflex in the triceps, making it contract and oppose the action of the biceps. However, one of the synapses from the relay neurone in Figure 9 would send a nerve impulse to the triceps, to inhibit it from contracting while the biceps was in action.

This kind of inhibition must be going on all the time during co-ordinated movement. Otherwise every muscle contraction would be immediately opposed by its antagonistic partner.

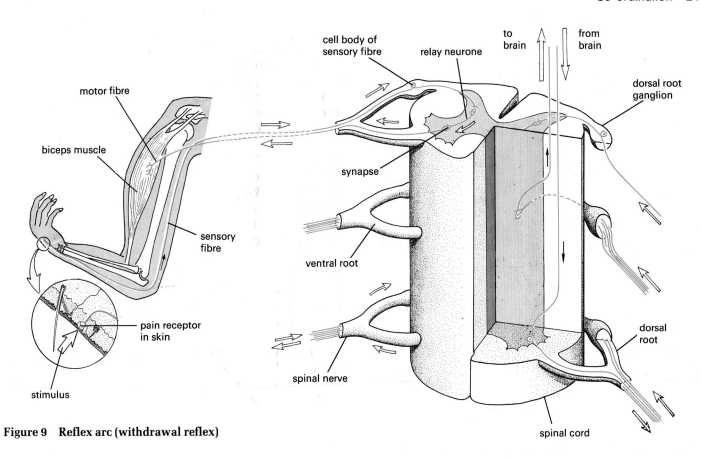

Figure 9   Reflex arc (withdrawal reflex)

Conditioned reflexes

In most simple reflexes, the stimulus and response are related. For example, the chemical stimulus of food in the mouth produces the reflex of salivation. However, an animal can learn, or be trained, to produce a response to an unrelated stimulus. A 'conditioned reflex' has been established, and the animal is said to be **conditioned** to this stimulus. Pavlov, a Russian biologist of the 1890s, carried out a great many experiments on conditioned reflexes with dogs. One of these experiments is now something of a classic.

The taste of food is a stimulus that acts on a dog's salivary glands, making its mouth water. For several days, Pavlov rang a bell at the time the food was given to the dogs. Later, the sound of the bell alone was a sufficient stimulus to make a dog's mouth water, without the taste of food. The original chemical stimulus of the food had been replaced by an unrelated stimulus through the ears. The dog had been conditioned to the sound of the bell.

Humans can be conditioned. When a person's hand is immersed in cold water, the blood vessels of the skin constrict (page 162). In one experiment, a buzzer was sounded each time the hand was immersed. After a few trials, the sound of the buzzer alone caused vaso-constriction in the hand.

Voluntary actions

A voluntary action starts in the brain. It may be the result of external events, such as seeing a book on the floor. However, any resulting action, such as picking up the book, is entirely voluntary. It is not a reflex action: you do not pick it up automatically. You can decide whether or not you pick it up.

The brain sends motor impulses down the spinal cord in the nerve fibres. These make synapses with motor fibres which enter spinal nerves and make connections to the sets of muscles needed to produce effective action. Many sets of muscles in the arms, legs and trunk would be brought into play in order to stoop and pick up the book. Impulses passing between the eyes, brain and arm would direct the hand to the right place and 'tell' the fingers when to close on the book.

One of the main functions of the brain is to co-ordinate these actions so that they happen in the right order and at the right time and place.

QUESTIONS

6 Put the following in the correct order for a simple reflex arc: (a) impulse travels in motor fibre, (b) impulse travels in sensory fibre, (c) effector organ stimulated, (d) receptor organ stimulated, (e) impulse crosses synapse.
7 Which receptors and effectors are involved in the reflex actions of (a) sneezing, (b) blinking, (c) contraction of the iris?
8 Explain why the tongue may be considered to be both a receptor and an effector organ.
9 Discuss whether coughing is a voluntary or reflex action.

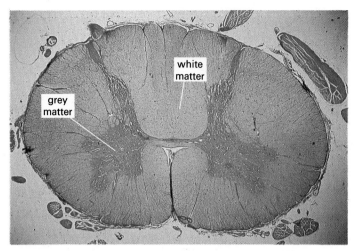

Figure 10 Section through spinal cord (×7). The light area is the white matter. This consists mostly of nerve fibres running to and from the brain. The dark central area is the grey matter. The grey matter consists mostly of cell bodies.

Central Nervous System

Spinal cord

Like all other parts of the nervous system, the spinal cord consists of thousands of nerve cells. Figures 7, 9 and 10 show its structure. Figures 1 (a) and (b) on page 180 show how the vertebrae protect it from harm.

All the cell bodies, apart from those in the dorsal root ganglion, are concentrated in the central region called the **grey matter**. The **white matter** consists of nerve fibres. Some of these pass from the grey matter to the spinal nerves. Others run along the spinal cord connecting the spinal nerve fibres to the brain. The spinal cord is thus concerned with (1) reflex actions involving body structures below the neck, (2) conducting sensory impulses from the skin and muscles to the brain and (3) carrying motor impulses from the brain to the muscles of the trunk and limbs.

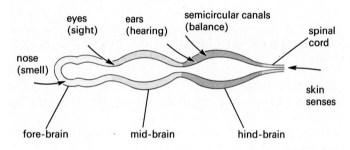

(a) The front end of the spinal cord develops three bulges: the fore-, mid- and hind-brain. Each region receives impulses mainly from sense organs in the head.

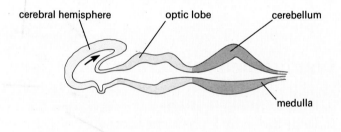

(b) The roofs of the fore-, mid- and hind-brain become thicker and form the cerebral hemispheres, optic lobes and cerebellum. The floor of the hind-brain thickens to form the medulla.

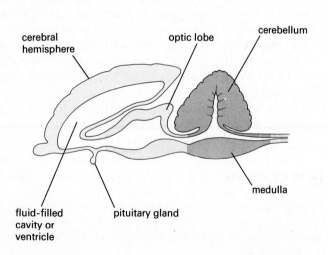

(c) A rabbit's brain would look something like this in vertical section.

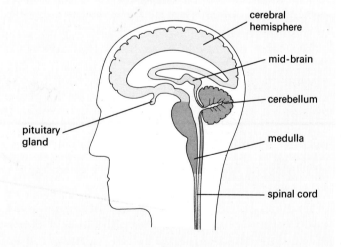

(d) The same regions are present in a human brain. But because of our upright position, the brain is bent through 90°.

Figure 11 Development of the brain of a mammal (vertical sections)

The brain

You can think of the brain as the expanded front end of the spinal cord. Certain areas are greatly enlarged to deal with all the information arriving from the ears, eyes, tongue, nose and semi-circular canals. Figure 11 (d) is a simplified diagram of the main regions of the brain as seen in vertical section. The **medulla** regulates the heart beat, body temperature and breathing rate. The **cerebellum** controls posture, balance and co-ordinated movement. The **mid-brain** deals with reflexes involving the eye. The largest part of the brain, however, consists of the **cerebrum**, made up of two **cerebral hemispheres**. These are very large and highly developed in mammals, especially humans. They are thought to be concerned with intelligence, memory, reasoning ability and acquired skills.

In the cerebral hemispheres and the cerebellum there is an outer layer of grey matter, the **cortex**, containing hundreds of thousands of multi-polar neurones (Figure 3 (c)). These form the outer layers, and make possible an enormous number of synapse connections between the dendrites (Figure 12).

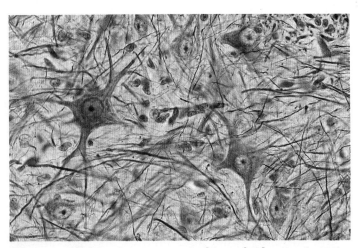

Figure 12   Multi-polar neurones in the cerebral cortex (×800). The cell bodies, nuclei and dendrites of three neurones can be seen.

Localization in the cerebral cortex

Localization in the cerebral cortex   Figure 13 shows the left cerebral hemisphere. The left hemisphere controls the right side of the body; the right hemisphere controls the left side of the body. Scientists have worked out which area of the brain receives impulses from, or sends impulses to, each part of the body.

For example, the region numbered '4' in the motor area on the diagram sends impulses to the hand. If this part of your brain were given a small electrical stimulus your hand would move, whether you wanted it to or not.

The sensory area can be mapped in the same way. If the brain centre concerned with hearing were to be stimulated artificially, you would think you were hearing sounds. Stimulation of the

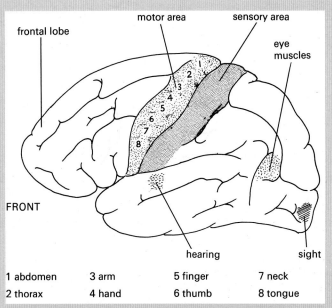

Figure 13   The left cerebral hemisphere

| 1 abdomen | 3 arm | 5 finger | 7 neck |
| 2 thorax | 4 hand | 6 thumb | 8 tongue |

'sight' area would probably cause you to 'see' flashes of light or complete images.

Association centres in the brain are not primarily concerned with any particular sensory or effector system. Association centres receive impulses from many different parts of the brain. They then relay the impulses either to the cortex for further processing or to the motor centres to produce action.

Functions of the brain

Functions of the brain   To sum up:

1 The brain receives impulses from all the sensory organs of the body.
2 As a result of these sensory impulses, it sends motor impulses to the glands and muscles, causing them to function accordingly.
3 In its association centres it correlates the various stimuli from the different sense organs and the memory.
4 The association centres and motor areas co-ordinate bodily activities, so that the mechanisms and chemical reactions of the body work efficiently together.
5 It 'stores' information, so that behaviour can be modified according to past experience.

QUESTIONS

10 Would you expect synapses to occur in grey matter or white matter? Explain your answer.
11 Look at Figure 2. If the spinal cord were damaged at a point about one-third of the way up the vertebral column, what effect would you expect this to have on the bodily functions?
12 (a) With which senses are the fore-, mid- and hind-brain mainly concerned?
   (b) Which part of the brain seems to be mainly concerned with keeping the basic body functions going?
13 Describe the biological events involved when you hear a sound and turn your head towards it.

The Endocrine System

Co-ordination by the nervous system is usually rapid and precise. Nerve impulses travel at up to 100 metres per second to specific parts of the body and produce an almost immediate response. A different kind of co-ordination is brought about by the endocrine system.

This system depends on chemicals, called **hormones**, which are released into the bloodstream from special glands, called **endocrine glands**. The hormones circulate round the body in the blood and in time reach certain organs, called **target organs**. Hormones speed up or slow down or alter the activity of those organs in some way. After being secreted, hormones do not remain in the blood. They are changed by the liver into inactive compounds, which are excreted by the kidneys.

Unlike the digestive glands, the endocrine glands do not deliver their secretions through ducts. This is why they are sometimes called the 'ductless glands'. The hormones are picked up directly from the glands by the blood circulation.

Responses of the body to hormones are much slower than responses to nerve impulses. They depend on the speed of the circulatory system. They also depend on the time it takes for the cells to change their chemical activities. Many hormones affect long-term changes such as growth rate, puberty and pregnancy. Nerve impulses often cause a response in a very limited area of the body, such as an eye-blink or a finger movement. Hormones, however, often affect many organ systems at once.

Serious over- or under-production of hormones gives rise to illnesses. Small differences in hormone activity between individuals may lead to differences of personality and temperament.

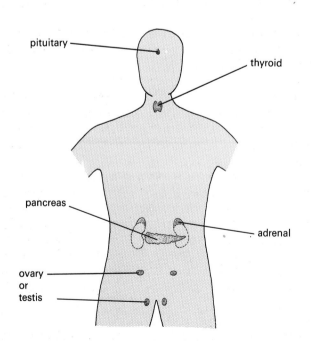

Figure 14   Position of endocrine glands in the body

Figure 14 shows the position of the endocrine glands in the body. Notice that the pancreas and the reproductive organs have dual functions.

Thyroid gland

The thyroid gland lies in the front part of the neck, in front of the windpipe. It produces a hormone called **thyroxine**, which is formed from an amino acid and iodine (page 101). Thyroxine speeds up the metabolic rate of nearly all the body cells. It controls our level of activity, promotes normal skeletal growth and is essential for the normal development of the brain.

Adrenal glands

These glands are attached to the back of the abdominal cavity, one above each kidney. Each adrenal gland is made up of two distinct regions with different functions. There is an outer layer called the **adrenal cortex** and an inner zone called the **adrenal medulla**. The medulla receives nerves from the brain and produces the hormone **adrenalin**. The cortex has no nerve supply and produces several hormones called **corticosteroids**. The corticosteroids help to control the metabolism of carbohydrates, fats, proteins, salts and water.

Adrenalin, from the medulla, has less important but more obvious effects on the body. The brain responds to stress by sending nerve impulses to the adrenal medulla. This releases adrenalin into the blood. As adrenalin circulates round the body it affects a great many organs, as shown in Table 1.

All these effects help us to react quickly and vigorously in dangerous situations where we might need to run away or put up a struggle. However, many stressful situations, such as taking examinations or giving a public performance, do not call for vigorous activity. So the extra adrenalin in our bodies just makes us feel tense and anxious. You may have felt the sensations described in column 4 of Table 1 at times when you were feeling frightened or worried.

Most of the systems affected by adrenalin are also controlled by a section of the nervous system called the **sympathetic nervous system**. This system affects internal organs other than voluntary muscles. It is hard to tell whether adrenalin or the sympathetic nervous system is mainly responsible for the stress reactions. Loss of the adrenal medulla seems to have no ill effects, however.

Adrenalin is quickly converted by the liver to a less active compound, which is excreted by the kidneys. All hormones are similarly altered and excreted, some within minutes, others within days. Thus their effects do not last long. The long-term hormones, such as thyroxine, are secreted all the time, to keep the level in the bloodstream steady.

Table 1   Responses to adrenalin

Organ	Effects of adrenalin	Biological advantage	Effect or sensation
Heart	beats faster	sends more glucose and oxygen to the muscles	thumping heart
Breathing centre of the brain	faster and deeper breathing	increased oxygenation of the blood, rapid removal of carbon dioxide	panting
Arterioles of the skin	constricts them (see page 162)	less blood going to the skin means more is available to the muscles	person goes paler
Arterioles of the digestive system	constricts them	less blood for the digestive system, allows more to reach the muscles	dry mouth
Muscles of alimentary canal	relax	peristalsis and digestion slow down, more energy available for action	'hollow' feeling in stomach
Muscles of body	tenses them	ready for immediate action	tense feeling, shivering
Liver	conversion of glycogen to glucose	glucose available in blood for energy production	no sensation
Fat depots	conversion of fats to fatty acids	fatty acids available in blood, for muscle contraction	

The pancreas

The pancreas is a digestive gland which secretes enzymes into the duodenum through the pancreatic duct (page 116). It is also an endocrine (ductless) gland. Most of the pancreas cells produce digestive enzymes but some of them produce hormones. The hormone-producing cells are arranged in small isolated groups called **islets** (Figure 15) and secrete their hormones directly into the bloodstream. One of the hormones is called **glucagon** and the other is **insulin**.

If the level of sugar in the blood falls, the islets release glucagon into the bloodstream. Glucagon acts on the cells in the liver. It makes them convert some of their stored glycogen into glucose, and so restore the blood sugar level (page 120).

Insulin has the opposite effect to glucagon. If the concentration of blood sugar increases (after a meal, for instance), insulin is released from the islet cells. When the insulin reaches the liver it stimulates the liver cells to remove glucose from the blood and store it as glycogen. Insulin also promotes the conversion of carbohydrates to fat, and slows down the conversion of protein to carbohydrate.

Adrenalin 'antagonizes' insulin. That is, it has the opposite effect to insulin. In moments of stress, adrenalin over-rides the effect of insulin and causes the liver and muscles to convert their glycogen stores to glucose.

All these changes have the effect of keeping the level of glucose in the blood to within narrow limits – a very important example of homeostasis (page 156).

If anything goes wrong with the production or function of insulin, the person will show the symptoms of **diabetes**.

Diabetes   This may develop either because the islet cells fail to produce sufficient insulin, or because the body cells are not able to use it properly. Two forms of diabetes are recognized: juvenile-onset and adult-onset diabetes.

Juvenile-onset diabetes is the less common form. It mainly affects young people and results from the islets producing too little insulin. There is a slight inherited tendency towards the disease, but it may be triggered off by a virus infection which affects the islets. The patient's blood lacks insulin and he or she needs regular injections of the hormone in order to control blood sugar level and so lead to a normal life. This form of the disease is, therefore, sometimes called 'insulin-dependent' diabetes.

Adult-onset diabetes usually affects people after the age of 40. The level of insulin in their blood is

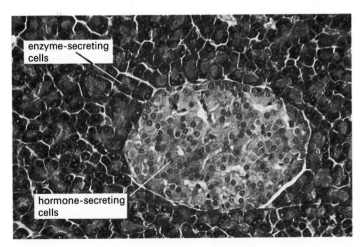

Figure 15   Section of pancreas tissue showing an islet (×250)

often not particularly low but it seems that their bodies are unable to use the insulin properly. This condition can be controlled by careful regulation of the diet and does not usually require insulin injections.

People with either form of diabetes cannot control the level of glucose in the blood. It may rise so high that it is excreted in the urine. Or it may fall so low that the brain cells cannot work properly and the person goes into a coma.

All diabetics need a carefully regulated diet, to reduce their intake of carbohydrates, and to keep the blood sugar within reasonable limits.

Reproductive organs

These produce hormones as well as gametes (sperms and ova). (Their effects have been described on page 175.)

The hormones from the ovary, **oestrogen** and **progesterone**, both prepare the uterus for the implantation of the embryo, by making its lining thicker and increasing its blood supply.

The hormones **testosterone** (from the testes) and oestrogen (from the ovaries) play a part in the development of the secondary sexual characters as described on page 175.

During pregnancy, the placenta produces a hormone which has effects similar to those of progesterone.

Pituitary gland

This gland is attached to the base of the brain (Figure 11 (d)). It produces many hormones. One of these (anti-diuretic hormone, ADH) acts on the kidneys and regulates the amount of water re-absorbed in the kidney tubules (page 155). Another pituitary hormone (growth hormone) affects the growth rate of the body as a whole and the skeleton in particular. Several of the pituitary hormones act on the other endocrine glands and stimulate them to produce their own hormones. For example, the pituitary releases into the blood a **follicle-stimulating hormone** (FSH). When this hormone reaches the ovaries, it makes one of the follicles start to mature and to produce oestrogen. **Luteinizing hormone** (LH) is also produced from the pituitary and, together with FSH, induces ovulation.

A **thyroid-stimulating hormone** (TSH) acts on the thyroid gland and makes it produce thyroxine.

Homeostasis and feedback

Homeostasis   The endocrine system plays an important part in regulating the composition of the body fluids (homeostasis, see page 156).

Blood sugar rises after a meal. This rise stimulates the pancreas to produce insulin. The insulin causes the liver to remove the extra glucose from the blood and store it as glycogen (page 120). This helps to keep the concentration of blood sugar reasonably steady.

The brain checks the concentration of the blood passing through it. If the concentration is too high, the pituitary gland releases ADH (anti-diuretic hormone). When this reaches the kidneys (the target organs) it causes them to re-absorb more water from the blood passing through them (page 155). If the blood is too dilute, production of ADH is suppressed and less water is absorbed in the kidneys. Thus ADH helps to keep the amount of water in the blood at a fairly constant level.

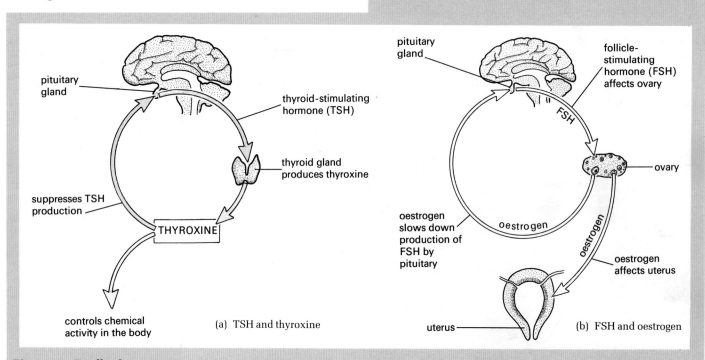

(a) TSH and thyroxine

(b) FSH and oestrogen

Figure 16   Feedback

Feedback Some of the endocrine glands are themselves controlled by hormones. For example, pituitary hormones such as LH (luteinizing hormone) affect the endocrine functions of the ovaries. The output of some hormones is regulated by a process of **negative feedback**.

Figure 16 (a) shows that thyroxine, produced by the thyroid gland, suppresses the production of TSH (thyroid-stimulating hormone) from the pituitary. A drop in the level of TSH reduces the production of thyroxine by the thyroid. Low levels of thyroxine allow the pituitary to produce TSH once again. This feedback causes fluctuations in the production of thyroxine within narrow limits.

The feedback between the pituitary and the ovaries produces wider fluctuations.

When the level of oestrogen in the blood rises, it affects the pituitary gland, suppressing its production of FSH (follicle-stimulating hormone). A low level of FSH in the blood reaching the ovary slows down its production of oestrogen. With less oestrogen in the blood, the pituitary can resume production of FSH. In turn, this makes the ovary start to produce oestrogen again (Figure 16 (b)). This cycle of events takes about one month. It is the basis of the monthly menstrual cycle (page 175).

The oestrogen and progesterone in the female contraceptive pill act on the pituitary and suppress the production of FSH. If there is not enough FSH, none of the follicles in the ovary will grow to maturity. So no ovum will be released.

QUESTIONS

14 Briefly state the differences between co-ordination by hormones and co-ordination by the nervous system, under the headings 'Routes', 'Speed of conduction', 'Target organs', 'Speed of response', 'Duration of effects'.
15 The pancreas has a dual function in producing digestive enzymes as well as hormones. Which other endocrine glands have a dual function, and what are their other functions? (See also page 175.)
16 What are the effects on body functions of (a) too much insulin, (b) too little insulin?
17 Why do you think urine tests are carried out to see if a woman is pregnant?

CHECK LIST

- The body systems are made to work efficiently together by the nervous system and the endocrine system.

NERVOUS SYSTEM

- The nervous system consists of the brain, the spinal cord and the nerves.
- The nerves consist of bundles of nerve fibres.
- Each nerve fibre is a thin thread which grows out of a nerve cell body.
- The nerve cell bodies are mostly in the brain and spinal cord.
- Nerve fibres carry electrical impulses from sense organs to the brain, or from the brain to muscles and glands.
- A reflex is an automatic nervous reaction that cannot be consciously controlled.
- A reflex arc is the nervous pathway which carries the impulses causing a reflex action.
- The simplest reflex involves a sensory nerve cell and a motor nerve cell, connected by synapses in the spinal cord.

- The brain and spinal cord contain millions of nerve cells.
- The millions of possible connections between the nerve cells in the brain allow complicated actions, learning, memory and intelligence.

ENDOCRINE SYSTEM

- The thyroid, adrenal and pituitary glands are all endocrine glands.
- The testes, ovaries and pancreas are also endocrine glands, in addition to their other functions.
- The endocrine glands release hormones into the bloodstream.
- When the hormones reach certain organs they change the rate or kind of activity of the organ.
- Too much or too little of a hormone can cause a metabolic disorder.
- People with diabetes either produce too little insulin, or are unable to use insulin normally.

Examination Questions

Do not write on these pages. Where necessary copy drawings, tables or sentences.

Section 3   Human Physiology

1 A pupil was asked to compare the energy values of sugar and butter. He set up the apparatus shown in the diagram below.

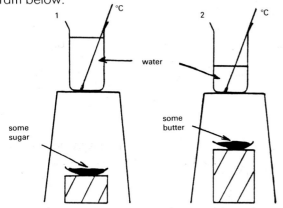

Suggest *three* improvements he could make to his apparatus so that he could compare the energy values accurately. (N1)

2 The graph below shows the amount of glucose in the blood of a person during 25 minutes including a 10 minute period of exercise.

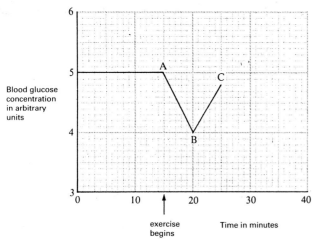

(a) What is the blood glucose level at the end of the exercise period?

(b) Explain the fall in level of blood glucose between A and B.

(c) On the graph show what you would expect to happen during the 10 minutes after C if the subject was resting.

(d) Give a brief explanation of your answer. (L1)

3 Vitamin C turns a blue dye clear. The amount of vitamin C in a solution can be worked out by finding how much must be added to 1 cm^3 of the blue dye to turn it clear.

You are given (a) the blue dye, (b) a solution containing a known amount of vitamin C, (c) a lemon drink.

Design an experiment to find out the concentration of vitamin C in the lemon drink. In your design you should state what apparatus you intend to use. (N1)

4 Describe the different ways we can prevent fresh food from going bad. (N2P)

5 Many experts advise that people in Britain should eat

20% more fibre	10% less fat
30% more fresh fruit	10% less sugar
30% more fresh vegetables	10% less salt

(a) Why is there no advice to increase vitamin intake?

(b) Explain why, if this advice were followed, there would be fewer people suffering from (i) constipation, (ii) heart disease, (iii) dental decay.

(c) Why in (b) is it not correct to state definitely that with the above diet fewer people would suffer from these diseases? (M2)

6 (a) The diagrams below are external views of the human heart. In one the auricles (atria) are shown contracted and in the other the ventricles are shown contracted.

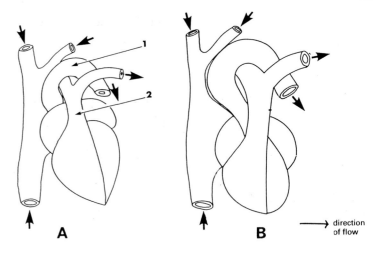

(i) Which diagram shows the contraction of the ventricles?

(ii) Name the vessels numbered 1 and 2 in diagram A.

(iii) Describe *two* important differences in the size of corresponding parts which you can observe in these two diagrams.

(b) Some types of heart disease may be treated by the use of a sound heart transplanted into the patient. Briefly explain *one* problem which may be found in this method of treatment. (W1B)

7 The diagram below shows a section through the human chest.

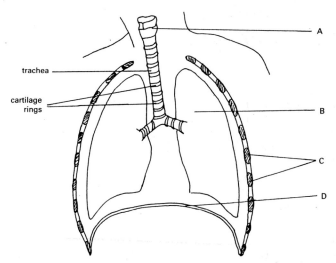

trachea

cartilage rings

A

B

C

D

(a) Label the parts A to D.

(b) What do the cartilage rings do?

(c) Describe the changes which take place in the chest when a person breathes in. It may help you to look at the diagram above.

(d) (i) How does the breathing rate change when a person takes exercise?

(ii) How does regular exercise (training) affect this breathing rate?

(e) What are the dangers of smoking during pregnancy?

(L2)

8 (a) Distinguish between breathing and respiration.

(b) Describe, and explain, the processes occurring during inspiration.

(c) Name *three* chronic diseases or conditions which adversely affect the efficiency of the lungs, explaining for each why and how the efficiency of the lungs is affected.

(M3B)

9 The diagram below shows a vertical section of human skin.

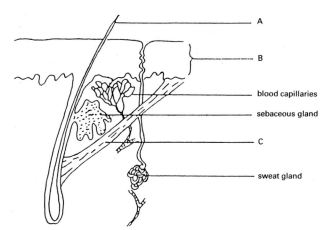

A

B

blood capillaries

sebaceous gland

C

sweat gland

(a) Name the parts A, B and C.

(b) After running a race, your skin is wet and your face is hot.

(i) Why is your skin wet, and how does this help to cool your body?

(ii) Why is your face hot, and how does this help to cool your body?

(c) How do you think the sebaceous glands help to keep hair and skin healthy?

(L2)

10 The diagram below illustrates the principle of an artificial kidney machine. The blood of the patient flows on one side of a partially permeable membrane and dialysing fluid flows on the other side. The dialysing fluid has a composition and concentration equal to that of a normal person.

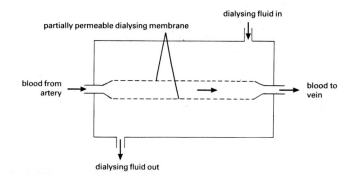

partially permeable dialysing membrane

dialysing fluid in

blood from artery

blood to vein

dialysing fluid out

(a) What process causes excess water from the patient to pass into the dialysing fluid?

(b) (i) Name an excretory product, other than water, which will pass out of the blood into the dialysing fluid.

(ii) Name the process by which this occurs.

(c) Explain why, in the case of permanent kidney failure, it is more satisfactory to a patient to be given a kidney transplant rather than treatment with an artificial kidney.

(N2Q)

11 *Either* Explain how the skin helps to return body temperature to normal after vigorous exercise.

Or Explain how urea passes from the liver where it is made to the bladder.

(L3)

12 Explain the term homeostasis, illustrating your answer by reference to the organs and mechanisms involved in the control of:

(a) body temperature,

(b) blood sugar concentration,

(c) water content of the body.

(M3B)

13 The diagram below shows a section through a ball and socket joint in the human hip.

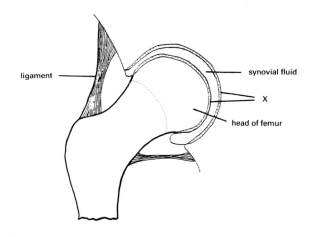

ligament

synovial fluid

X

head of femur

(a) Name the structure X.

(b) The ligament is playing a part in holding the bones together. As well as being strong, suggest another important property of the ligament.

(c) What is the function of the synovial fluid in the joint?

(N2Q)

14 Diagram to show the skull from underneath.

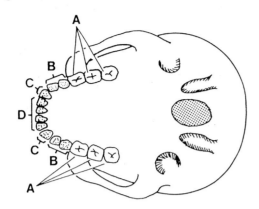

(a) Name the different teeth labelled on the diagram.

(b) Give *one* reason why this skull is *not* that of a young child.

(c) How would you use a red dye which stains bacteria to help you make sure your teeth are properly cleaned?

(W1)

15 The diagram below shows the human female reproductive system.

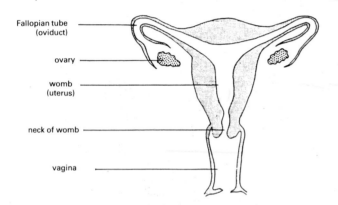

(a) Label the diagram clearly with an X to show where eggs are made.

(b) During mating, sperms pass from the man's penis into the woman's vagina. Describe what happens from the time that the sperms enter the vagina until a baby starts to grow in the womb.

(c) The chart below shows what happens to the thickness of the lining of a woman's womb during the monthly cycle (menstrual cycle).

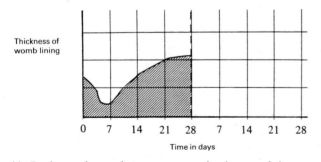

(i) Explain what is happening to the lining of the womb during the first five days.

(ii) On the chart, put a letter E to show the time when an egg is most likely to be released.

(iii) An egg is fertilized during the first month. Draw a line on the chart to show what would happen to the thickness of the lining of the womb during the second month. (N2P)

16 The diagram shows part of the eye.

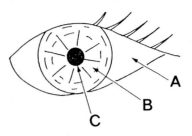

(a) Name the parts labelled A and B and C.

(b) Complete the outline below to show how the eye would look in dim light. (W1)

17 Complete the following description of a simple reflex action by filling in each space with one word. Choose the words from those given below.

motor   relays   spinal   grey   cavities

synapses   white   sensory   neural

If the stretched tendon below the knee is tapped, a receptor is stimulated so that the nerve impulse passes along a _____ nerve fibre into the spinal cord. This nerve fibre ends in the _____ matter of the spinal cord. Before the impulses travel to a muscle they must pass over small spaces called _____ (S1)

18 Match each of the following events in the body with an appropriate hormone chosen from the list below.

A ovulation   B increased heart rate   C control of blood glucose   D implantation   E reduced urine production

Luteinizing hormone (LH)   anti-diuretic hormone (ADH)   progesterone   thyroxine   insulin   testosterone   adrenalin

19

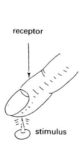

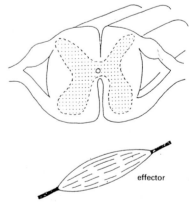

(a) Complete the diagram by drawing the pathway of the reflex arc in the following stages:

(i) Draw single lines to show the following nerve fibres: sensory (afferent); relay (intermediate); motor (efferent).

(ii) Label the nerve fibres clearly.

(iii) Draw arrows on the nerve fibres to show the direction of a nerve impulse.

(b) Describe *two* differences between a reflex action and an action brought about by hormones. (W1)

SECTION 4
Genetics and Evolution

Cell Division and Chromosomes

Heredity and Genetics
Explanation of terms.

Chromosomes and Mitosis
Mitosis: the movement of chromosomes at cell division. Function of chromosomes: genes on the chromosomes control the cell's physiology and structure. Number of chromosomes: a fixed number for each species.

Gamete Production and Chromosomes
Meiosis: the chromosomes are shared between the gametes. Meiosis and mitosis compared.

Mutations
Changes in genes and chromosomes.

Practical work
Observing chromosomes in plant cells.

Heredity and Genetics

We often talk about people inheriting certain characteristics: 'John has inherited his father's curly hair', or 'Mary has inherited her mother's blue eyes'. We expect tall parents to have tall children. The inheritance of such characteristics is called **heredity**. The branch of biology which studies how heredity works is called **genetics**.

Genetics also tries to forecast what sort of offspring are likely to be produced when plants or animals reproduce sexually. What will be the eye colour of children whose mother has blue eyes and whose father has brown eyes? Will a mating between a black mouse and a white mouse produce grey mice, black-and-white mice or some black and some white mice?

To understand the method of inheritance, we need to look again at the process of sexual reproduction and fertilization.

In sexual reproduction, a new organism starts life as a single cell called a **zygote** (page 164). This means that you started from a single cell. Although you were supplied with oxygen and food in the uterus, all your tissues and organs were produced by cell division from this one cell. So, the 'instructions' that dictated which cells were to become liver, or muscle, or bone must all have been present in this first cell. The 'instructions' which decided that you should be tall or short, dark or fair, male or female must also have been present in the zygote.

To understand how these 'instructions' are passed from cell to cell, we need to look in more detail at

what happens when the zygote divides and produces an organism consisting of thousands of cells. This type of cell division is called **mitosis**. It takes place not only in a zygote but in all growing tissues.

QUESTION

1 (a) What are gametes? What are the male and female gametes of humans called, and where are they produced?
   (b) What happens at fertilization?
   (c) What is a zygote and what does it develop into?
(The information needed to answer these questions is given on pages 164 and 167.)

Chromosomes and Mitosis

Mitosis

When a cell is not dividing, there is not much detailed structure to be seen in the nucleus even if it is treated with special dyes called stains. Just before cell division, long, thread-like structures appear in the nucleus and show up very clearly when the nucleus is stained (Figures 1 (a) and 2). These thread-like structures are called **chromosomes**. Although they are present in the nucleus all the time, they show up clearly only at cell division because at this time they get shorter and thicker.

Each chromosome is made up of two parallel strands, called **chromatids**. When the nucleus

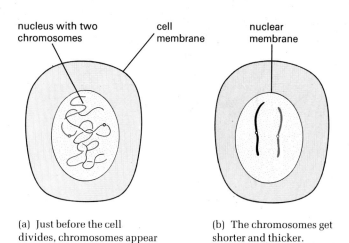

(a) Just before the cell divides, chromosomes appear in the nucleus.

(b) The chromosomes get shorter and thicker.

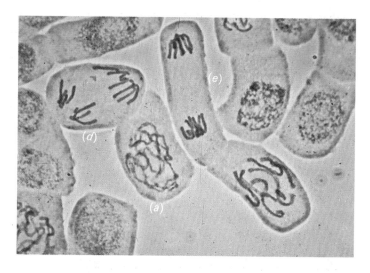

Figure 2   Mitosis in a root tip (×500). The letters refer to the stages described in Figure 1. (The tissue has been squashed to separate the cells.)

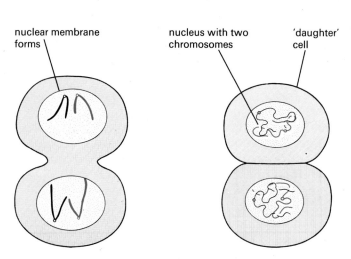

(c) Each chromosome is now seen to consist of two chromatids.

(d) The nuclear membrane disappears and the chromatids are pulled apart to opposite ends of the cell.

(e) A nuclear membrane forms round each set of chromatids, and the cell starts to divide.

(f) Cell division completed, giving two 'daughter' cells, each containing the same number of chromosomes as the parent cell.

Figure 1   Mitosis. Only one pair of chromosomes is shown. Three of the stages here can be seen in Figure 2.

divides into two, one chromatid from each chromosome goes into each daughter nucleus. The chromatids in each nucleus now become chromosomes. Later they will make copies of themselves, ready for the next cell division. The process of copying is called **replication**, because each chromosome makes a replica (an exact copy) of itself. Figure 1 is a diagram of mitosis. It shows only two chromosomes, but there are always more than two. A human cell contains 46 chromosomes.

Mitosis takes place in any part of a plant or animal which is producing new cells for growth or replacement. Bone marrow produces new blood cells by mitosis. The epidermal cells of the skin are replaced by mitotic divisions in the basal layer. New epithelial cells lining the alimentary canal are produced by mitosis. Muscle and bone in animals grow by mitotic cell divisions. So do the roots, leaves, stems and fruits of plants.

An exception to this occurs in the final stages of gamete production in the reproductive organs of plants and animals. The cell divisions which give rise to gametes are not mitotic. They are described on page 225.

Cells which do not take part in the production of gametes are called **somatic cells**. Mitosis takes place only in somatic cells.

QUESTIONS

2 In the nucleus of a human cell just before cell division, how many chromatids will there be?

3 Why can chromosomes not be seen when a cell is not dividing?

4 Look at Figure 4 on page 160. Where would you expect mitosis to be occurring most often?

5 In which tissues would you expect mitosis to be going on in (a) a five-year-old child, (b) an adult human?

The function of chromosomes

When a cell is not dividing, its chromosomes are very long and thin. Along the length of each chromosome is a series of chemical structures called **genes** (Figure 3). The chemical which forms the genes is called DNA (which is short for deoxy-ribose-nucleic acid). Each gene controls some part of the chemistry of the cell. These genes provide the 'instructions' mentioned at the beginning of the chapter. For example, one gene may 'instruct' the cell to make the pigment which is formed in the iris of brown eyes. One chromosome will carry a gene which causes the cells of the stomach to make the enzyme pepsin. When the chromosome replicates, it builds up an exact copy of itself, gene by gene (Figure 4). When the chromatids separate at mitosis, each cell will receive a full set of genes. In this way, the chemical instructions in the zygote are passed on to all the cells of the body. All the chromosomes, all the genes and, therefore, all the 'instructions' are faithfully reproduced by mitosis and passed on complete to all the cells.

Which of the 'instructions' are used depends on

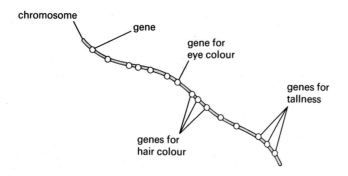

Figure 3 Relationship between chromosomes and genes. The drawing does not represent real genes or a real chromosome. There are probably thousands of genes on a chromosome.

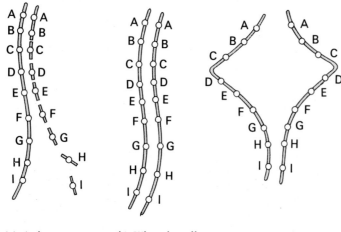

(a) A chromosome builds up a replica of itself.

(b) When the cell divides, the original and the replica are called chromatids.

(c) Mitosis separates the chromatids. Each new cell gets a full set of genes.

Figure 4 Replication. A, B, C, etc. represent genes.

kangaroo (12) man (46)

domestic fowl (36) fruit fly (8)

Figure 5 Chromosomes of different species. The chromosomes are always in pairs.

where a cell finally ends up. The gene which causes brown eyes will have no effect in a stomach cell. The gene for making pepsin will not function in the cells of the eye. So the gene's chemical instructions are carried out only in the right place.

Number of chromosomes

1 There is a fixed number of chromosomes in each species. Human body cells each contain 46 chromosomes, mouse cells contain 40, and garden pea cells 14 (see also Figure 5).

2 The number of chromosomes in a species is the same in all of its body cells. There are 46 chromosomes in each of your liver cells, in every nerve cell, skin cell and so on.

3 The chromosomes have different shapes and sizes. These can be recognized by a trained observer.

4 The chromosomes are always in pairs (Figure 5) – two long ones, two short ones, two medium ones and so on. This is because when the zygote is formed, one of each pair comes from the male gamete and one from the female gamete. Your 46 chromosomes consist of 23 from your mother and 23 from your father.

5 The number of chromosomes in each body cell of a plant or animal is called the **diploid number**. Because the chromosomes are in pairs, it is always an even number.

The chromosomes of each pair are called **homologous** chromosomes. In Figure 7 (b), the two long chromosomes form one homologous pair and the two short chromosomes form another.

Gamete Production and Chromosomes

The genes on the chromosomes carry the 'instructions' which turn a single-cell zygote into a wren or a rabbit or an oak tree. The zygote is formed at fertilization, when a male gamete fuses with a female gamete. Each gamete brings a set of chromosomes to the zygote. The gametes, therefore, must each contain only half the diploid number of chromosomes. Otherwise the chromosome number would double each time an organism reproduced sexually. Each human sperm cell contains 23 chromosomes and each human ovum has 23 chromosomes. When the sperm and ovum fuse at fertilization (page 164), the diploid number of 46 (23+23) chromosomes is produced (Figure 6).

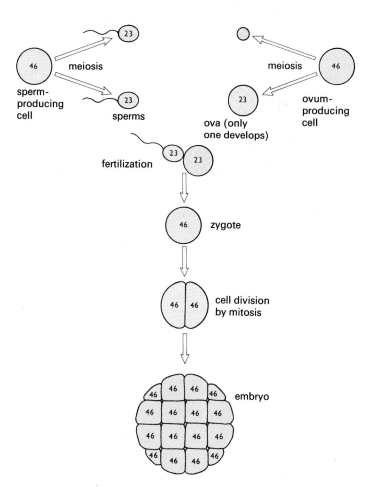

Figure 6   Chromosomes in gamete production and fertilization

So gametes cannot be produced by mitosis. They must be formed by a different kind of cell division which will produce cells containing only half the diploid number of chromosomes. This number is called the **haploid number**. The process of cell division which gives rise to gametes is called **meiosis**.

Meiosis takes place only in reproductive organs.

Meiosis

In a cell which is going to divide and produce gametes, the diploid number of chromosomes shorten and thicken as in mitosis. The pairs of homologous chromosomes – for example, the two long ones and the two short ones in Figure 7 (b) – lie alongside each other. When the nucleus divides for the first time, it is the chromosomes (*not* the chromatids) which separate. So only half the total number of chromosomes goes to each daughter cell. In Figure 7 (c) the diploid number of four chromosomes is being reduced to two before the first cell division.

By now (Figure 7 (d)), each chromosome consists of two chromatids. A second division of the nucleus (Figure 7 (e)) separates the chromatids into four distinct nuclei (Figure 7 (f)). This gives rise to four

(a) The chromosomes appear. Those in colour are from the organism's mother. The black ones are from its father.

(b) Homologous chromosomes lie alongside each other.

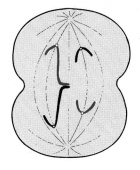

(c) The nuclear membrane disappears and corresponding chromosomes move apart to opposite ends of the cell.

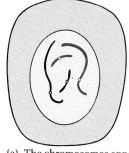

(d) By now each chromosome has become two chromatids.

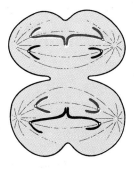

(e) A second division takes place to separate the chromatids.

(f) Four gametes are formed. Each contains only half the original number of chromosomes.

Figure 7   Meiosis

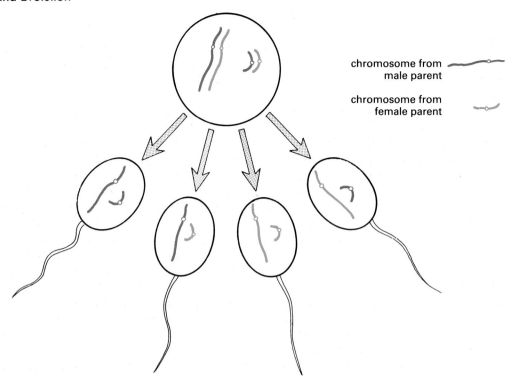

chromosome from male parent

chromosome from female parent

Figure 8 Some possible combinations of maternal and paternal chromosomes in the gametes, as a result of meiosis. Each gamete must receive one chromosome from each pair in the mother cell, but which one is a matter of chance.

gametes, each with the haploid number of chromosomes. In the testis of an animal, meiosis in each sperm-producing cell forms four sperms. The cells of the ovary of a mammal each produce four gametes at first. But only one of them turns into a mature ovum which can be fertilized.

Variability The 46 chromosomes in each of your body cells are in the form of 23 pairs. One of each pair came from your mother and the other from your father. In meiosis the pairs separate, so that a gamete receives either a maternal or a paternal chromosome from each pair.

However, it is a matter of chance which of each pair goes into any one gamete. So there are many possible combinations of maternal and paternal chromosomes in each gamete. Figure 8 shows the possible combinations with only two pairs of chromosomes. With 23 pairs, there are 2^{23} possible combinations.

Mitosis is different, because all the daughter cells have identical sets of chromosomes. The importance of this variability in gametes is explained on page 238.

QUESTIONS

6 How many chromosomes would there be in the nucleus of (a) a human muscle cell, (b) a mouse kidney cell, (c) a human skin cell that has just been produced by mitosis?.
7 What is the diploid number in humans?
8 What is the haploid number for (a) humans, (b) fruit fly?
9 Write down which of the following cells would be haploid and which diploid: white blood cell, basal cell of the skin, bone cell, ovum, sperm.
10 Where in the body of (a) a human male and (b) a human female would you expect meiosis to be taking place?
11 How many chromosomes would be present in (a) a mouse sperm cell, (b) a mouse ovum?

Mitosis and meiosis compared

Mitosis	**Meiosis**
Occurs during cell division of somatic cells.	Occurs in the final stages of cell division leading to production of gametes.
A full set of chromosomes is passed on to each daughter cell. This is the diploid number of chromosomes.	Only half the chromosomes (the haploid number of chromosomes) are passed on to the daughter cells.
The chromosomes and genes in each daughter cell are identical.	The homologous chromosomes and their genes are randomly shared between the gametes. (See page 238 for a fuller explanation of this.)

Mutations

A mutation is a spontaneous change in a gene or a chromosome. A change in a gene or chromosome usually has a harmful effect on the cell in which it occurs. A mutation in a gamete will affect all the cells of the individual which develops from the gamete. Thus the whole organism may be affected. A mutation in a somatic cell (body cell) will affect only those cells produced, by mitosis, from the affected cell.

Thus mutations in gametes may result in genetic disorders in the offspring. Mutations in somatic cells may give rise to cancers of the affected tissues.

Down's syndrome   An inherited form of mental and physical handicap, known as Down's syndrome, results from a chromosome mutation. The ovum which gives rise to the child carries an extra chromosome. The affected child, therefore, has 47 chromosomes in his or her cells instead of the normal 46.

The extra chromosome gives rise to a group of characteristics (a syndrome) which includes short stature, flattened nose, high cheek bones, a fold of skin across the top eyelid, a large tongue and broad hands. People with Down's syndrome pick up infections easily, and have varying degrees of mental handicap.

Sickle-cell anaemia is caused by a gene mutation. The affected gene controls the production of haemoglobin in red blood cells. As a result of the mutation, the red cells produce a defective form of haemoglobin. In low oxygen concentrations, the defective haemoglobin forms rod-like structures which damage the red cells (see page 241).

Drug-resistant bacteria   Mutations in bacteria often produce resistance to drugs. Bacterial cells reproduce very rapidly, perhaps as often as once every 20 minutes. Thus a mutation, even a rare one, is likely to appear in a large population of bacteria. A population of bacteria might contain only one or two mutants that can resist a certain drug. But even if that drug kills all the non-resistant bacteria, the drug-resistant mutants will survive. Mutant genes are inherited in the same way as normal genes. So when the surviving mutant bacteria reproduce, all their offspring will be resistant to the drug (Figure 9).

Mutations are quite rare. Perhaps only one in every 100 000 replications results in a mutation. Nevertheless they do occur all the time. (There are bound to be some mutants in the 200 million sperms produced in a human ejaculate.) And exposure to ultraviolet light, X-rays, ionizing radiation and certain chemicals (**mutagenic** chemicals) all increase the rate of mutation.

QUESTION

12 Why is it particularly important to prevent radiation from reaching the reproductive organs?

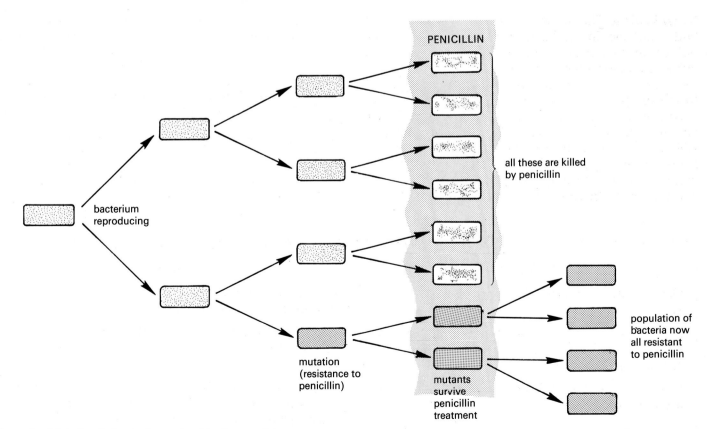

Figure 9   Mutation in bacteria can lead to drug resistance

PRACTICAL WORK

Squash preparation of chromosomes using acetic orcein

Material   1   Prepare *Allium cepa* (onion) root tips. Support onions over beakers or jars of water. Keep the onions in darkness for several days until the roots growing into the water are 2–3 cm long. Cut off about 5 mm of the root tips, and place them in a watch glass.

2   Cover them with 9 drops acetic orcein and 1 drop molar hydrochloric acid.

3   Heat the watch glass gently over a very small bunsen flame till the steam rises from the stain, but do not boil.

4   Leave the watch glass covered for at least 5 minutes.

5   Place one of the root tips on a clean slide, cover with 45 per cent ethanoic (acetic) acid and cut away all but the terminal 1 mm.

6   Cover this root tip with a clean cover slip and make a squash preparation as described below.

Making the squash preparation   Squash the softened, stained root tips by lightly tapping on

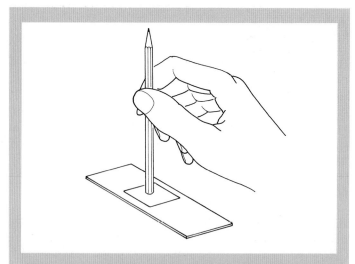

Figure 10   Tap the cover slip gently to squash the tissue

the cover slip with a pencil: hold the pencil vertically and let it slip through the fingers to strike the cover slip (Figure 10). The root tip will spread out as a pink mass on the slide. The cells will separate and the nuclei, many of them with chromosomes in various stages of mitosis (because the root tip is a region of rapid cell division), can be seen under the high power of the microscope (×400).

CHECK LIST

- In the nuclei of all cells there are thread-like structures called 'chromosomes'.
- The chromosomes are in pairs. One of each pair comes from the male and one from the female parent.
- On these chromosomes are carried the genes.
- The genes control the chemical reactions in the cells and, as a result, determine what kind of organism is produced.
- Each species of plant or animal has a fixed number of chromosomes in its cells.
- When cells divide by mitosis, the chromosomes and genes are copied exactly and each new cell gets a full set.
- At meiosis, only one chromosome of each pair goes into the gamete.
- A mutation is a spontaneous change in a gene or chromosome. Most mutations produce harmful effects.

Patterns of Inheritance

If we understand mitosis and meiosis we can explain, at least to some extent, how heredity works. A gene in a mother's body cells causes her to have, say, brown eyes. This gene may be present on one of the chromosomes in each ovum she produces. If the father's sperm cell contains a gene for brown eyes on the corresponding chromosome, the zygote will receive a gene for brown eyes from each parent. These genes will be reproduced by mitosis in all the embryo's body cells. Then, when the embryo's eyes develop, the genes will make the cells of the iris produce brown pigment. So the child will have brown eyes.

In a similar way, the child may receive genes for curly hair. Figure 1 shows this happening. But it does not, of course, show all the other chromosomes with thousands of genes for producing enzymes, making different types of cell and all the other processes which control the development of the organism.

Single-factor inheritance

It is impossible to follow the inheritance of the thousands of characteristics controlled by genes. So we will start with the study of a single gene that controls one characteristic. We will go on using eye colour as an example (although in fact more than one gene pair may decide the colour of a child's eyes).

We have seen how a gene for brown eyes from each parent would result in the child having brown eyes. Suppose, however, that the mother has blue eyes and the father brown eyes. The child might receive a gene for blue eyes from its mother and a gene for brown eyes from its father (Figure 2). If this happens, the child will, in fact, have brown eyes.

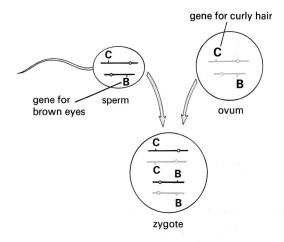

Figure 1   Fertilization. Fertilization restores the diploid number of chromosomes and combines the genes from the mother and father.

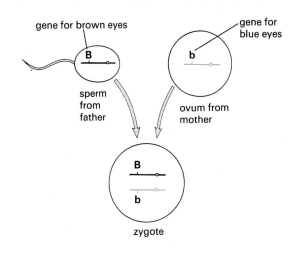

Figure 2   Combination of genes in the zygote (only one chromosome is shown). The zygote has both genes for eye colour. So the child will have brown eyes.

229

The gene for brown eyes is said to be **dominant** to the gene for blue eyes. Although the gene for blue eyes is present in all the child's cells, it does not contribute to the eye colour. It is said to be **recessive** to the gene for brown eyes.

This example illustrates the following important points:

1 There is a pair of genes for each characteristic, one gene from each parent.
2 Although the gene pairs control the same character, such as eye colour, they may have different effects. One tries to produce blue eyes, the other tries to produce brown eyes.
3 One gene is often dominant over the other.
4 The genes of each pair are on corresponding chromosomes and occupy corresponding positions. For example, in Figure 1 the genes for eye colour are shown in corresponding positions on the two short chromosomes, and the genes for hair curliness are in corresponding positions on the two long chromosomes.

In diagrams and explanations of heredity:

(a) genes are represented by letters;
(b) genes controlling the same characteristic are given the same letter; and
(c) the dominant gene is given the capital letter.

For example, in rabbits, the gene for black fur is dominant, and is labelled **B**. The recessive gene for white fur is labelled **b** to show that it corresponds to **B** for black fur. If it were labelled **w**, we would not see any connection between **B** and **w**. **B** and **b** are obvious partners. In the same way **L** could represent the gene for long fur and **l** the gene for short fur.

Alleles

The genes which are in corresponding positions on homologous chromosomes and control the same character are called **allelomorphic genes** or **alleles**. The word 'allelomorph' means 'alternative form'. The genes **B** and **b** are alleles.

There are often more than two alleles of a gene. The human ABO blood groups (page 136) are controlled by three alleles, I^A, I^B and i, though only two of these can be present in one genotype.

QUESTIONS

1 Some plants occur in one of two sizes, tall or dwarf. This characteristic is controlled by one pair of alleles. Tallness is dominant to shortness.
　　Choose suitable letters for the pair of alleles.
2 Why are there two genes controlling one characteristic? Do the two genes affect the characteristic in the same way?
3 The allele for red hair is recessive to the allele for black hair. What colour hair will a person have if he inherits the allele for red hair from his mother and the allele for black hair from his father?

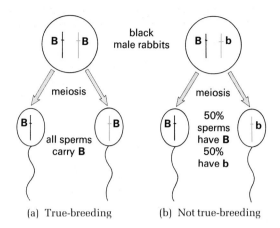

(a) True-breeding   (b) Not true-breeding

Figure 3   Breeding true

Breeding true

A white rabbit must have both the recessive alleles **b** and **b**. If it had **B** and **b**, the dominant allele for black (**B**) would override the allele for white (**b**) and produce a black rabbit. A black rabbit, on the other hand, could be either **BB** or **Bb**. You could not tell the difference by just looking at the rabbit. When the male black rabbit **BB** produces sperms by meiosis, each one of the pair of chromosomes carrying the **B** alleles will end up in different sperm cells. Since the alleles are the same, all the sperms will have the **B** allele for black fur (Figure 3 (a)).

The black rabbit **BB** is called a 'true-breeding' black. It is said to be **homozygous** for black coat colour ('homo-' means 'the same'). If this rabbit mates with another black (**BB**) rabbit, all the babies will be black because each will receive a dominant allele for black fur. When all the offspring have the same characteristic as the parents, we say the parents 'breed true' for this characteristic.

When the **Bb** black rabbit produces gametes by meiosis, the chromosomes with the **B** alleles and the chromosomes with the **b** alleles will end up in different gametes. So 50 per cent of the sperm cells will carry **B** alleles and 50 per cent will carry **b** alleles (Figure 3 (b)). Similarly, in the female, 50 per cent of the ova will have a **B** allele and 50 per cent will have a **b** allele. If a **b** sperm fertilizes a **b** ovum, the offspring will have two **b** alleles (**bb**). So it will be white. The black **Bb** rabbits are not true-breeding, because they may produce some white babies as well as black ones. The **Bb** rabbits are called **heterozygous** ('hetero-' means 'different').

The black **BB** rabbits are homozygous dominant.
The white **bb** rabbits are homozygous recessive.

QUESTIONS

4 (a) Read question 3 again. Choose letters for the alleles for red hair and black hair and write down the allele combination for having red hair.
　　(b) Would you expect a red-haired couple to breed true?
　　(c) Could a black-haired couple have a red-haired baby?

5 Use the words 'homozygous', 'heterozygous', 'dominant' and 'recessive' (where suitable) to describe the following combination of alleles: **Aa, AA, aa**.

6 A plant has two varieties, one with red petals and one with white petals. When these two varieties are cross-pollinated, all the offspring have red petals. Which allele is dominant? Choose suitable letters to represent the two alleles.

Genotype and phenotype

The two kinds of black rabbit **BB** and **Bb** are said to have the same **phenotype**. This is because their coat colours look exactly the same. But they have different alleles for coat colour, and they are said to have different **genotypes** (different combinations of genes). One genotype is **BB** and the other is **Bb**.

You and your brother might both be brown-eyed phenotypes but your genotype could be **BB** and his could be **Bb**. You would be homozygous dominant for brown eyes. He would be heterozygous for eye colour.

If an allele produces a noticeable effect in the phenotype, it is said to be **expressed**. A recessive allele is not expressed in the phenotype if its dominant partner is present.

Co-dominance and incomplete dominance

Co-dominance Sometimes both genes of an allelomorphic pair produce their effects in an individual, so that neither allele is dominant to the other. The alleles are said to be co-dominant.

The inheritance of the human ABO blood groups includes an example of co-dominance. In the ABO system there are four phenotypic blood groups, A, B, AB and O (page 136). The alleles for groups A and B are co-dominant. If a girl inherits alleles for group A and group B, her red cells will carry both antigens.

However, the alleles for groups A and B are both completely dominant to the allele for group O. (Group O people have neither *A* nor *B* antigens on their red cells.)

Table 1 shows the genotypes and phenotypes for the ABO blood groups. (The allele for group O is represented here as **i**. Sometimes it is written as I^O.)

Table 1   The ABO blood groups

Genotype	Blood group (phenotype)
$I^A I^A$ or $I^A i$	A
$I^B I^B$ or $I^B i$	B
$I^A I^B$	AB
ii	O

Since the alleles for groups A and B are dominant to that for group O, a group A person could have the genotype $I^A I^A$ or $I^A i$. Similarly a group B person could be $I^B I^B$ or $I^B i$. There are no alternative genotypes for groups AB and O.

Incomplete dominance This term is sometimes taken to mean the same as 'co-dominance'. Strictly, however, an incompletely dominant allele partly, though not wholly, masks the effect of the recessive allele.

An example occurs with sickle-cell anaemia (page 241). If a person inherits both recessive alleles ($Hv^S Hb^S$) for sickle-cell haemoglobin, then he or she will show obvious signs of the disease, such as mis-shapen red cells and bouts of severe anaemia.

A heterozygote ($Hb^A Hb^S$), however, will have a condition called 'sickle-cell trait'. Although there may be mild symptoms of anaemia, the condition is not serious. In this case, the normal haemoglobin gene (Hb^A) is not completely dominant over the recessive (Hb^S) gene.

QUESTIONS

7 What are the blood groups likely to be inherited by children born to a group A mother and a group B father? Explain your reasoning.

8 A woman of blood group A claims that a man of blood group AB is the father of her child. A blood test reveals that the child's blood group is O. Is it possible that the woman's claim is correct? Could the father have been a group B man? Explain your reasoning.

Determination of sex

Whether you are a male or female depends on one particular pair of chromosomes called the 'sex chromosomes'. In females, the two sex chromosomes are the same size. They are called the X chromosomes. In males, the two sex chromosomes are of different sizes. One looks like the female sex chromosomes and is called the X chromosome. The other is smaller and is called the Y chromosome. So the female genotype is XX and the male genotype is XY.

When meiosis takes place in the female's ovary, each ovum receives one of the X chromosomes. So all the ova are the same in this. Meiosis in the male's testes results in 50 per cent of the sperms getting an X chromosome and 50 per cent getting a Y chromosome (Figure 4). If an X sperm fertilizes the ovum, the zygote will be XX and will grow into a girl. If a Y sperm fertilizes the ovum, the zygote will be XY and will develop into a boy. There is an equal chance of an X or Y chromosome fertilizing an ovum, so the numbers of girl and boy babies are more or less the same.

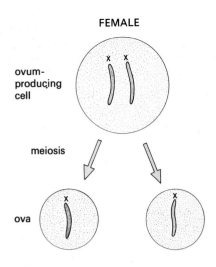

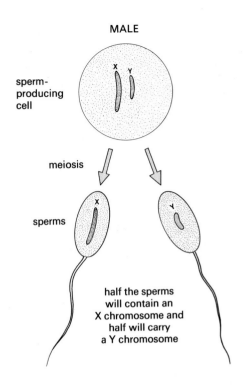

Figure 4   Determination of sex. Note that:
(1) Only the X and Y chromosomes are shown
(2) The Y chromosome is not smaller than the X chromosome in all organisms
(3) Details of meiosis have been omitted
(4) In fact, four gametes are produced in each case, but two are enough to show the sharing of the X and Y chromosomes

The three-to-one ratio

Figure 5 (a) shows the result of a mating between a true-breeding (homozygous) black mouse (**BB**) and a true-breeding (homozygous) brown mouse (**bb**). The diagram leaves out a lot, because it shows only one pair of the 20 pairs of mouse chromosomes and only one pair of alleles on the chromosomes.

Black fur is dominant to brown. So all the offspring from this mating will be black phenotypes, because they all receive a dominant allele for black fur from the father. Their genotypes will be **Bb**, however, because they all receive the recessive **b** allele from the mother. They are heterozygous for coat colour. The offspring resulting from this first mating are called the **F₁ generation**.

Figure 5 (b) shows what happens when these heterozygous, F₁ black mice are mated together. Their offspring are called the **F₂ generation**. Each sperm or ovum produced by meiosis can contain only one of the alleles for coat colour, either **B** or **b**. So there are two kinds of sperm cell, one kind with the **B** allele and one kind with the **b** allele. There are also two kinds of ovum, with either **B** or **b** alleles. When fertilization occurs, there is no way of telling whether a **b** or **B** sperm will fertilize a **B** or a **b** ovum. So we have to look at all the possible combinations as follows:

1 A **b** sperm fertilizes a **B** ovum. Result: **bB** zygote.
2 A **b** sperm fertilizes a **b** ovum. Result: **bb** zygote.
3 A **B** sperm fertilizes a **B** ovum. Result: **BB** zygote.
4 A **B** sperm fertilizes a **b** ovum. Result: **Bb** zygote.

There is no difference between **bB** and **Bb**, so there are three possible genotypes in the offspring – **BB**, **Bb**

and **bb**. There are only two phenotypes – black (**BB** or **Bb**) and brown (**bb**). So, by the laws of chance, we would expect three black baby mice and one brown. Mice usually have more than four offspring and what we really expect is that the **ratio** (proportion) of black babies to brown will be close to 3:1.

If the mouse had 13 babies, you might expect nine black and four brown, or eight black and five brown. But whether a **B** or **b** sperm fertilizes a **B** or **b** ovum is a matter of chance. Even if the mouse had 16 babies you would not expect to find exactly 12 black and four brown. After all, if you spun ten coins, you would not expect to get exactly five heads and five tails. You would not be surprised at six heads and four tails or even seven heads and three tails. In the same way, we would not be surprised at 14 black and two brown mice in a litter of 16.

To decide whether there really is a 3:1 ratio, we need to do a lot of experiments. We could breed the same pair of mice together for a year or so to produce many litters. Or we could mate 20 black and 20 brown mice, and add up the numbers of black and brown babies in the 20 families.

Single-factor inheritance in humans

Humans are not very suitable animals for studying single-factor inheritance. We breed too slowly and have too few offspring. Also, most of the characteristics we think of as important are controlled by more than one pair of alleles, and can be influenced by our environment. Your height, for example, is probably determined

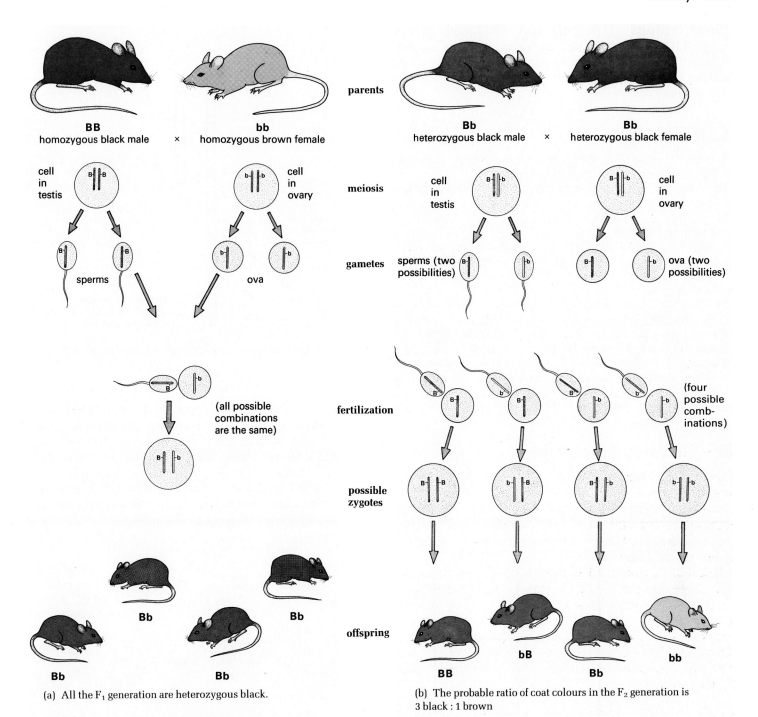

parents

BB
homozygous black male × **bb**
homozygous brown female

meiosis

cell in testis

cell in ovary

gametes

sperms

ova

fertilization

(all possible combinations are the same)

offspring

Bb

Bb

Bb

Bb

(a) All the F₁ generation are heterozygous black.

Bb
heterozygous black male × **Bb**
heterozygous black female

cell in testis

cell in ovary

sperms (two possibilities)

ova (two possibilities)

(four possible comb-inations)

possible zygotes

BB

bB

Bb

bb

(b) The probable ratio of coat colours in the F₂ generation is 3 black : 1 brown

Figure 5   Inheritance of coat colour in mice

by several allelomorphic pairs. It will also depend on whether you get enough food while you are growing.

The most striking single-factor characteristics are those associated with inherited defects such as sickle-cell anaemia, haemophilia, albinism and colour blindness.

Sickle-cell anaemia   (see page 241) is caused by a defective gene (Hb^S) for haemoglobin production. This allele is recessive to the normal haemoglobin allele (Hb^A). A person who inherits two recessive alleles ($Hb^S Hb^S$) will have sickle-cell anaemia.

Haemophilia   is a genetic disease in which blood clots very slowly. The blood of people with the disease lacks one of the plasma proteins, called Factor VIII, which plays a part in clotting. The production of Factor VIII is controlled by a single gene. A person who lacks this gene will be a **haemophiliac**. Quite minor cuts tend to bleed for a long time and internal bleeding may occur.

Although haemophilia is a genetically controlled disease, symptoms vary from mild to severe in different individuals. The condition can be largely controlled by daily or weekly injections of Factor VIII.

Albinism   An albino lacks a gene for producing the pigment melanin (page 158). As a result the iris of the eye is pink, the hair is white or very pale yellow, and the skin is unpigmented and easily damaged by sunlight. The albinism allele is recessive to the pigment-producing allele.

Blood groups The ABO and Rh blood groups (page 136) are determined by single pairs of alleles. Alleles for group A or group B are dominant to alleles for group O. The Rh⁺ allele is dominant to the Rh⁻ allele.

QUESTIONS

9 Look at Figure 5 (a). Why is there no possibility of getting a **BB** or a **bb** combination in the offspring?

10 In Figure 5 (b), what proportion of the F₂ black mice are true-breeding?

11 (a) If two albinos marry, what proportion of their children will be albinos?

(b) If an albino man marries a normally pigmented woman, what proportion of their children might be albino (i) if the woman is homozygous for the melanin allele, (ii) if she is heterozygous for this allele?

12 One way of working out the possible results of an F₂ cross (**Bb**×**Bb**) is to complete a Punnett square. Copy the Punnett square below into your notebook. Enter the possible genotypes of the female gametes (**B** and **b**) in the top two spaces (see Figure 2 on page 238 for guidance). Similarly, enter the possible genotypes for the male gametes in the left-hand spaces. In the four central squares, enter the gene combinations that would result from each possible fertilization.

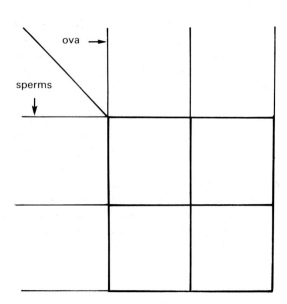

Sex linkage

Some genetic disorders affect males much more often than females. Haemophilia and colour blindness are examples. Such diseases are said to be sex-linked. Sex linkage results from the fact that the X chromosome is longer than the Y chromosome. Thus there are genes on the X chromosome which have no corresponding alleles on the Y chromosome (Figure 6).

The alleles for colour blindness and haemophilia are recessive. But since they lie on the section of the X chromosome which is not matched by the Y, there is no chance of their effects being suppressed by a dominant allele.

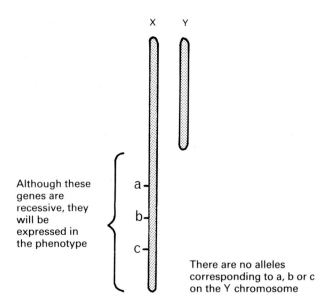

Although these genes are recessive, they will be expressed in the phenotype

a
b
c

There are no alleles corresponding to a, b or c on the Y chromosome

Figure 6   Sex linkage. Genes a, b and c are sex-linked to the X chromosome.

Figure 7 shows the outcome of a cross between a normal man with a normal woman who carries a recessive allele for colour blindness. Although the woman has normal colour vision she is a 'carrier' for the disorder.

There is a 1 in 2 chance that any son will be colour-blind. None of the daughters will be affected, but half of them can be expected to carry the allele.

Parents:	XN Y normal man		XN Xn carrier woman	
Gametes:	XN	Y	XN	Xn
Possible combinations of gametes:	XN XN normal girl	XN Xn girl carrier	XN Y normal boy	Xn Y colour-blind boy

Figure 7   Inheritance of colour blindness

QUESTIONS

13 A married couple has four girl children but no boys. This does not mean that the husband produces only X sperms. Explain why not.

14 A haemophiliac man marries a normal woman. What are the chances of their having an affected son (a) if the woman is a carrier of the recessive allele, (b) if she is homozygous for the normal allele?

15 A man with inherited red–green colour blindness marries a woman with normal colour vision. What are the chances of affected sons and daughters (a) if the woman is homozygous for colour vision, (b) if she is heterozygous for this condition?

Family trees

Family trees (or pedigrees) can give information about human genetics. Two examples are shown in Figures 8 and 9. In these trees, males are always represented by squares and females by circles. Parents are linked by a horizontal marriage line, from which a vertical line is drawn downwards to the children.

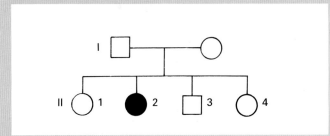

Figure 8   Method of showing a family tree

Figure 8 shows the family tree of a couple who have four children: two girls, a boy and another girl in that order. The parents are generation I. The brothers and sisters in generation II are called siblings or sibs. The girl sibling II/2 is affected by a genetic disorder, shown by the filled-in circle.

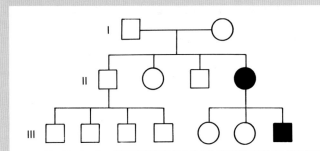

Figure 9   Inheritance of a recessive trait

Figure 9 shows the inheritance of a recessive trait. The birth of an affected daughter (II/4) to unaffected parents shows two things. First, both parents must have been heterozygous for the condition. Secondly, the relevant gene must be recessive. The only other explanation is that the girl's condition is the result of a spontaneous mutation.

Generation III shows that the affected girl must have eventually married a heterozygous man (not shown in the family tree), because one of their children is affected.

Genetic counselling

If normal parents have a child affected by an inherited disorder caused by a single gene, they can be sure that they are both heterozygous (**Nn**) for the gene.

Thus there is a 1 in 4 chance that any one of their later children will be affected too (see page 232). If the condition is serious, the parents may decide that the risk of having another affected child is too high and therefore they will have no more children.

If one member of a couple has a genetic disorder, the chances that they will have an affected child can be worked out. For an albino man (**nn**) marrying a normal woman, this is done as follows:

1 About 1 person in 70 carries the recessive allele for albinism.
2 Thus there is a 1 in 70 chance that the woman is a carrier (heterozygous for albinism, **Nn**).
3 The chance of an affected child being born to an affected man (**nn**) and a heterozygous woman (**Nn**) is 1 in 2.
4 Combining probabilities 2 and 3 gives a chance of $\frac{1}{2} \times \frac{1}{70} = \frac{1}{140}$ that any one child will be an albino.

The parents may decide that this risk is low, and that it is worth starting a family.

Genetic counselling would be more effective if scientists could detect heterozygotes. Unfortunately, this can be done for only a few conditions. For others, they have to wait until an affected child is born.

An inherited disease called **phenylketonuria** (PKU) is caused by a recessive gene. Children who are homozygous for PKU have such a high level of phenylalanine in their blood that their brains are damaged and they became mentally handicapped. However, by using a diet which is free from phenylalanine in the first six years, the damage can be avoided. This is one of the few diseases where heterozygotes can be detected. However, all babies are given a blood test at birth to see if their phenylalanine level is normal.

Anyone with a genetic disorder, or having a family history of one, should seek genetic counselling before starting a family. This can usually be arranged through the family doctor.

QUESTIONS

16 In the family tree of Figure 9, how can you be sure that daughter II/4 did not marry either a homozygous affected or homozygous normal male?

17 The chances of a man being heterozygous for albinism are 1 in 70. The chances of a woman being heterozygous for albinism are also 1 in 70. The chances of two heterozygotes having an affected child are 1 in 4.

What are the chances, therefore, of an apparently normal couple having an albino child?

PRACTICAL WORK

Inherited characteristics

Two fairly trivial human characteristics are known to be genetically controlled. They are (a) the ability to roll the tongue and (b) having free or attached ear lobes (Figure 10).

Make a survey of your class to find (a) the numbers of tongue-rollers and non-rollers, and (b) the numbers of people with free or attached ear lobes.

Do you think that either of these characteristics could be controlled by a single pair of alleles? If so, which gene might be dominant and which recessive?

Some non-rollers can learn how to roll their tongues, with practice. Does this affect your answers?

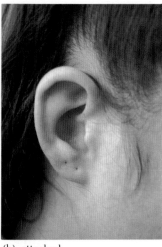

(a) free

(b) attached

Figure 10   Ear lobes

CHECK LIST

- In breeding experiments, the effect of only one or two genes (out of thousands) is studied, such as the colour of fur in rabbits or mice.

- The genes are in pairs, because the chromosomes are in pairs.

- Although each gene pair controls the same character, they do not necessarily have the same effect. For example, of a pair of genes controlling fur colour, one may try to produce black fur and the other may try to produce white fur.

- Alleles, or allelomorphs, are the alternative forms of genes which control the same characteristics.

- Allelomorphic genes occupy corresponding positions on homologous chromosomes.

- Usually, one gene is dominant over the other. For example, the gene (**B**) for black fur is dominant over the allele (**b**) for white fur.

- This means that a rabbit with the allelomorphic pair **Bb** will be black, even though it has an allele for white fur.

- Although **BB** rabbits and **Bb** rabbits are both black, only the **BB** rabbits will breed true.

- **Bb** black rabbits mated together are likely to have some white babies.

- The expectation is that, on average, there will be one white baby rabbit to every three blacks.

- Meiosis is the kind of cell division that leads to production of gametes.

- Only one of each chromosome pair goes into a gamete.

- A **Bb** rabbit would produce two kinds of gametes for coat colour; 50 per cent of the gametes would have the **B** allele and 50 per cent would have the **b** allele.

- Some inherited disorders in humans are the result of single-factor inheritance.

- In some cases, neither one of a pair of alleles is fully dominant over the other. This may be a case either of incomplete dominance or of co-dominance.

- Sex, in mammals, is determined by the X and Y chromosomes. Males are XY. Females are XX.

- Analysis of family trees can often reveal patterns of single-factor inheritance.
- Genetic counselling helps couples to work out the chances of having a child with an inherited disorder.

Variation

The term 'variation' refers to differences that we can observe within a species. All domestic cats belong to the same species – they can all interbreed. But cats show many variations of size, coat colour, eye colour, fur length and so forth.

Those variations which can be inherited are determined by genes. They are genetic or heritable variations.

Some variations are determined by the individual's environment. A kitten which does not get enough food will not grow as big as its litter mates. A cat with a skin disease may have bald patches in its coat. These conditions are not heritable. They are caused by environmental factors.

Figure 1 Acquired characteristics. This over-developed musculature results from long-term weight training.

Similarly, fair-skinned people may be able to change the colour of their skin by exposing it to sunlight, so getting a tan. The tan is an **acquired characteristic**. You cannot inherit a sun tan. The dark skin of a black African, on the other hand, is an **inherited characteristic**.

Many features in plants and animals are a mixture of acquired and inherited characteristics (Figure 1). For example, some fair-skinned people never go brown in the sun, they only become sunburned. They have not inherited the genes for producing the extra melanin in their skin. A fair-skinned girl who does have the genes for producing melanin will only go brown if she goes out into the sun. So her tan is the result of both inherited and acquired characteristics.

Heritable variation may be caused by mutations (page 227) or by new combinations of genes in the zygote.

New combinations of genes If a grey cat with long fur mates with a black cat with short fur, the kittens will all be black with short fur. If these offspring mate together, their litters may include four varieties: black–short, black–long, grey–short and grey–long. Two of these are different from either of the original pair. (See 'Meiosis and new combinations of characteristics', below.)

Mutations Many of the coat variations mentioned above may have arisen, in the first place, as mutations in wild cats. A recent mutation produced the 'rex' variety, in which the coat has curly hairs.

Many of our high-yielding crop plants arose as a result of mutations in which the whole chromosome set doubled.

237

Meiosis and new combinations of characteristics

During meiosis, homologous chromosomes pair up and then at the first nuclear division, separate again (page 225).

One of the homologous chromosomes comes from the male parent and the other from the female parent. The genes for a particular characteristic occupy identical positions on the homologous chromosomes. But they do not necessarily control the characteristic in the same way. The genes for eye colour will be in the same position on the maternal and paternal chromosomes. But one may carry the gene for brown eyes and the other the gene for blue eyes. Separation of homologous chromosomes at meiosis means that the genes for blue and brown eyes will end up in different gametes (Figure 2).

On a second pair of homologous chromosomes there may be allelomorphic genes for hair curliness (**C** = curly; **c** = straight). These chromosomes and their genes will also separate at the first division of meiosis.

Suppose a father has brown eyes and straight hair, and a mother has blue eyes and curly hair. Also suppose that the father is heterozygous for eye colour (**Bb**) and the mother is heterozygous for hair curliness (**Cc**).

In the mother's ovary, the **b** and **b** genes will separate at the first division of meiosis and so will the **C** and **c** genes. The **b** gene could finish up in the same gamete as either the **C** or the **c** gene. So, the genotype of the ovum could be either **bC** or **bc**.

Similarly, meiosis in the father's testes will produce equal numbers of **Bc** and **bc** gametes.

At fertilization, it is a matter of chance which of the two types of sperm fertilizes which of the two types of ovum. (Although usually only one ovum is released, there is a 50:50 chance of its being **bC** or **bc**.)

The Punnett square in Figure 2 (c) shows the possible genotypes of the children in the family.

Offspring (2) and (3) would have the same combination of characteristics as their parents: (2) has brown eyes and straight hair (father's phenotype), and (3) has blue eyes and curly hair (mother's phenotype). Offspring (1) and (4), however, would have different combinations of these two characteristics, and these combinations are not present in either parent. They are (1) brown eyes and curly hair, and (4) blue eyes and straight hair.

The separation of parental chromosomes at meiosis and their recombination at fertilization means that new combinations of characteristics are possible. This is because the homologous chromosomes from one parent do not all go into the same gamete, but move independently of each other (see also page 234).

This recombination of characteristics as a result of meiosis is important for plant and animal breeding programmes (page 243). It is also important as a source of variation for natural selection to act on (page 240).

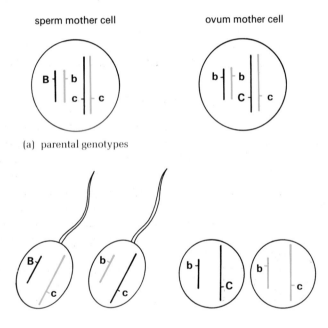

(a) parental genotypes

(b) possible gene combinations in gametes

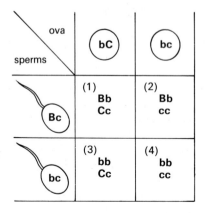

(c) possible combinations of genes in the children

Figure 2   New combinations of characteristics

QUESTIONS

1 (a) Bearing in mind the role of the sex chromosomes, suggest two other new variations which might occur among the children in the example given above.

(b) In the example given above, suppose that the mother had been homozygous for hair curliness and the father had been homozygous for eye colour. Is there a possibility of new combinations of those characters in the offspring?

2 State which of the following you think are (a) mainly inherited characters, (b) mainly acquired characteristics or (c) a more or less equal mixture: manual skills, facial features, body build, language, athleticism, ability to talk.

3 What new combinations of characters are possible as a result of crossing a tall plant with yellow seeds (**TtYy**) with a dwarf plant with green seeds (**ttyy**)?

Discontinuous variations

These are variations under the control of a single gene pair or a small number of genes. The variations take the form of distinct, alternative phenotypes with no intermediates (Figure 3 (a)). The mice in Figure 5 on page 233 are either black or brown. There are no intermediate colours. You are either male or female. Apart from a small number of abnormalities, sex is inherited in a discontinuous way.

Discontinuous variations cannot usually be altered by the environment. You cannot change your blood group or eye colour by altering your diet. A genetic dwarf cannot grow taller by eating more food.

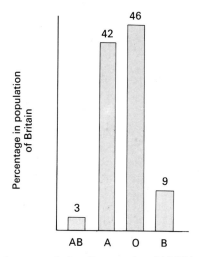

(a) **Discontinuous variation.** Frequencies of ABO blood groups in Britain. The figures could not be adjusted to fit a smooth curve because there are no intermediates.

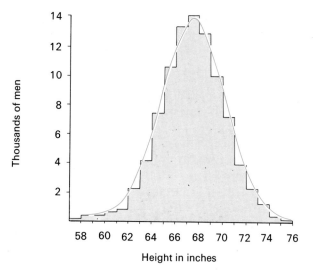

(b) **Continuous variation.** Heights of 90 000 recruits in 1939. The apparent 'steps' in the distribution are the result of arbitrarily chosen categories, differing in height by one inch. But heights do not differ by exactly one inch. If measurements could be made accurately to the nearest millimetre, there would be a smooth curve like the one shown in colour.

Figure 3   Discontinuous and continuous variation

Continuous variation

On the other hand, people are not either tall or short. There are all possible intermediates between very short and very tall. This is a case of continuous variation (Figure 3 (b)).

Continuously variable characteristics are usually controlled by several gene pairs. There might be five pairs of genes for height – **Hh, Tt, Ll, Ee** and **Gg** – each dominant gene adding 4 cm to a person's height. If you inherited all ten dominant genes (**HH, TT,** etc.) you could be 40 cm taller than a person who inherited all ten recessive genes (**hh, tt,** etc.). In fact, we do not know how many genes control height, intelligence or even the colour of hair and skin.

Many characteristics are difficult to classify as either wholly continuous or discontinuous variations. Human eye colour has already been mentioned. People can be classified roughly as having blue eyes or brown eyes. But some people's eyes can be described as grey, hazel or green. Probably there is a small number of genes for eye colour and a dominant gene for brown eyes which overrides all the others when it is present.

Similarly, red hair is a discontinuous variation but it is masked by genes for other colours. So there is a continuous range of hair colour from blond to black.

Environment and genotype

Many continuously variable characteristics are affected by the environment or by what happens during the individual's lifetime. A person may inherit the genes for tallness and yet not get enough food to grow tall. You may carry the genes for melanin production, but if you stay out of the sun you will not get a tan. You might have a genotype which determines a strong physique, but unless you take exercise you will stay weak and flabby.

In humans, continuous variations such as height, physique and intelligence are always the result of an interaction between the genotype and the environment.

Studies of identical twins

One way of studying the effects of heredity and environment is to look at identical twins. Identical twins are formed from the same zygote (page 170). So they must have the same genotype. Any observable difference between twins must therefore be the result of something in the environment. Even while twins are in the uterus they may have different positions or different blood supplies. These may produce differences before the twins are born.

Scientists have measured differences between identical twins and compared them with differences between non-identical (fraternal) twins. This gives us some idea of the parts played by the genotype and the environment. For example, the average difference in height of fifty pairs of identical twins reared together was only 1.7 cm, while the average difference for the same number of non-identical twins was 4.4 cm. These and other comparisons are given in Table 1.

Table 1   Average differences in selected physical characteristics between pairs of twins

Difference in:	50 pairs of identical twins reared together	50 pairs non-identical twins reared together	19 pairs of identical twins reared apart
Height (cm)	1.7	4.4	1.8
Weight (kg)	1.86	4.54	4.50
Head length (mm)	2.9	6.2	2.2
Head width (mm)	2.8	4.2	2.85

(From Freeman, Newman and Holzinger, *Twins: A study of heredity and environment*, Univ. Chicago Press, 1937)

QUESTIONS

4 State which of the following you would expect to be inherited in (a) a continuous way and (b) a discontinuous way: presence of horns in sheep, black colour in cats, number of seeds in an ear of wheat, size of apples, colour of roses, ability to sing, physical strength.

5 In Table 1, why do you think there is so little difference in weight variation between identical twins reared apart and non-identical twins reared together?

Figure 4   Variation. Notice the variations in the colour and curliness of hair in this family.

Natural Selection

Theories of evolution have been put forward in various forms for hundreds of years. In 1858, Charles Darwin and Alfred Russel Wallace published a theory of evolution by natural selection. The theory is still widely accepted today.

The theory of natural selection suggests that

1 Individuals within a species are all slightly different from each other (Figure 4). These differences are called **variations**.
2 If the climate or food supply changes, some of these variations may be better able to survive than others. If one variety of animal can eat the leaves of shrubs as well as grass, it is more likely to survive a drought than one that feeds only on grass.
3 If one variety lives longer than others, it is also likely to leave behind more offspring. A mouse that lives for twelve months may have ten litters of five babies (50 in all). A mouse that lives for six months may have only five litters of five babies (25 in all).
4 If some of the offspring inherit the variation that helped the parent survive better, they too will live longer and have more offspring.
5 In time, this particular variety will outnumber and finally replace the original form.

Thomas Malthus, in 1798, suggested that the human population would grow faster than the rate of food production. He predicted that the number of people would eventually be regulated by famine, disease and war. When Darwin read the Malthus essay, he applied its principles to other populations of living organisms.

He observed that animals and plants produce far more offspring than can possibly survive to maturity. He reasoned that, therefore, there must be 'a struggle for survival'.

For example, a pair of rabbits might have eight offspring. When these grow up they could form four pairs and have eight offspring per pair. In four generations the number of rabbits stemming from the original pair would, in theory, be 512 ($2 \rightarrow 8 \rightarrow 32 \rightarrow 128 \rightarrow 512$). The population of rabbits remains more or less constant, however. Many of the offspring in each generation must, therefore, have died before they could reproduce.

Competition and selection   Members of the rabbit population will **compete** for food, burrows and mates. If food is scarce, space is short and the number of potential mates limited, then only the healthiest, most vigorous, most fertile and otherwise well-adapted rabbits will survive and breed.

Competition does not necessarily mean direct conflict. The best-adapted rabbits may be able to run faster from predators, digest their food more efficiently, have larger litters or grow coats which camouflage them better or more effectively reduce heat losses. These rabbits will survive longer and leave more offspring. If the offspring inherit the advantages of their parents, they may give rise to a new race of faster, different coloured, thicker furred and more fertile rabbits. The new race will gradually replace the original, less well-adapted varieties. The new variations are said to have **survival value**.

This is natural selection. The better adapted varieties are 'selected' by the pressures of the environment (**selection pressures**).

For natural selection to be effective, the variations have to be heritable. Variations which are not heritable are of no value in natural selection. Training may give athletes more efficient muscles, but their children will not inherit this characteristic.

Evolution The theory of evolution tries to explain the origin and diversity of all the living organisms on the Earth. The theory supposes that at one time, perhaps more than three billion years ago, there were no living organisms on the Earth. Conditions on the Earth at that time might have been suitable for the development of very simple organisms from chemicals in the waters of the oceans.

A series of gradual changes took place involving mutation and natural selection over hundreds of millions of years. In this way organisms became more numerous, more complicated and more diverse.

There is a good deal of direct evidence from the fossil record to support this theory. Most biologists accept the theory of evolution as the best scientific explanation of the origin of living organisms. They do argue, however, about the speed of the changes, the role of natural selection and the dates and relationships of the fossil organisms. One day, they may find evidence that makes it necessary to amend the theory.

Some explanations of the origin of living organisms are based on literal interpretation of the Bible's account in *Genesis* or on similar religious beliefs. These views are more acceptable to some people than the evolutionary theory, and must be respected. But they are not scientific, because they are unlikely to be modified or abandoned no matter what scientific evidence is presented.

Selection in human populations

Most biologists accept the theory that humans have evolved from ape-like ancestors by processes of natural selection lasting several million years. Selection probably acted to produce characteristics such as the upright posture which leaves the hands free to manipulate tools, and the unspecialized, five-fingered hands which carry out these manipulations. Another such characteristic is the enlarged cerebral cortex (page 213), which gives humans their intelligence and helps them to adapt to a wide variety of environments and exploit many sources of food.

Selection must still operate to some extent. Today, however, medical science has greatly reduced the selection pressure on human populations. People with inborn defects such as poor vision, diabetes or haemophilia would have been unlikely to survive selective pressures in an early hunting-gathering community (page 89).

In modern society, selection will act only on genetic defects which impair reproduction or cause death before reproductive age. You might think that selection would have wiped out such defects (for example, Down's syndrome) altogether. But they continue to occur as a result of mutations (page 227).

Conditions such as susceptibility to coronary heart disease or cancer are not affected by selection because these diseases mainly take their toll after reproductive age.

Selection and the sickle-cell gene A person with sickle-cell disease (page 233) has inherited two recessive genes ($\mathbf{Hb^SHb^S}$) for defective haemoglobin. In low oxygen concentrations, their red blood cells become mis-shapen and die. This leads to bouts of severe anaemia (Figure 5).

In many African countries, sufferers have less chance of reaching reproductive age and having a family. There is thus a selection pressure which tends to remove the homozygous recessives from the population. You might expect that the harmful $\mathbf{Hb^S}$ gene would be selected out of the population altogether. However, the heterozygotes ($\mathbf{Hb^AHb^S}$)

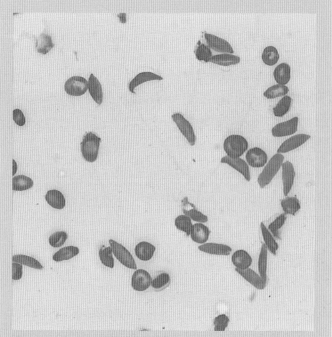

Figure 5 Sickle-cell anaemia. At low oxygen concentration the red cells become mis-shapen.

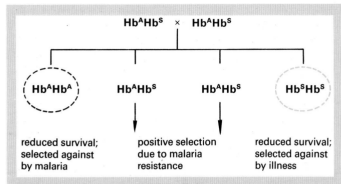

Figure 6   Selection in sickle-cell disease

have virtually no symptoms of anaemia. And they also have the advantage that they are more resistant to malaria than the homozygotes **Hb^A^Hb^A^**.

The selection pressure of malaria, therefore, favours the heterozygotes over the homozygotes. So the potentially harmful **Hb^S^** gene is kept in the population (Figure 6).

When Africans migrate to countries where malaria does not occur the selective advantage of the **Hb^S^** gene is lost. The gene then becomes less common in the population.

Human evolution

There is plenty of evidence that humans evolved from ape-like ancestors. This is *not* the same as saying that 'humans evolved from apes'. The claim is that humans and modern apes evolved from a common ancestral stock some 16 million years ago. During this time, apes and humans have both changed in many ways in the course of

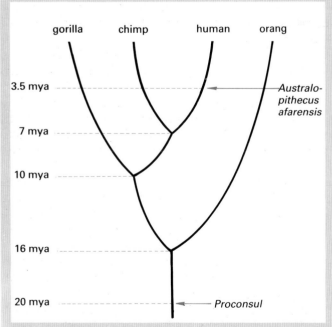

Figure 7   Possible evolutionary lines of apes and humans
mya = million years ago

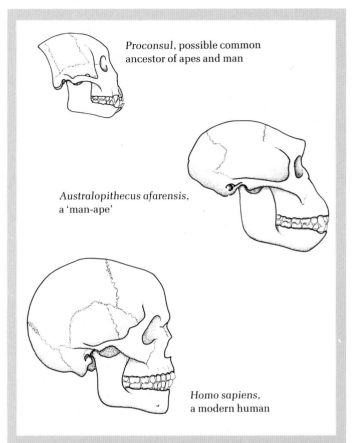

Figure 8   Skulls of possible human ancestors, compared with a modern human

evolution. So the modern apes are now as different from the common ancestor as we are.

Figure 7 shows the possible connections between the common ancestor, modern apes and humans. It is based on evidence from fossil skeletons and from studies of similarities between amino acid sequences in the proteins of the living species (page 19). Bear in mind, however, that as new fossils are found and new analytical and dating techniques are used, the picture is likely to change.

Figure 8 shows three skulls from representatives of the evolutionary sequence. *Proconsul* is a fossil ape thought to be similar to the common ancestor of apes and humans. *Australopithecus afarensis* is a fossil of a human-like ape (or ape-like human).

The drawings show some of the changes which have taken place in the course of evolution. The jaws have become smaller and the forehead higher, so that the face is flatter and more vertical. The canine teeth have become much smaller. Between *Australopithecus* and *Homo*, the prominent brow ridges have disappeared.

These changes probably came about as a result of changes in feeding habits and the increasing size of the cerebral hemispheres. There are also changes in other parts of the skeleton, such as the limbs and pelvic girdle. These changes may be the result of adaptation to an upright, walking posture.

QUESTIONS

6 What sort of evidence or discovery do you think could throw doubt on the theory of evolution?

7 Why do you think that haemophiliacs or very short-sighted people might not have survived to reproductive age in a community of hunter-gatherers?

Artificial Selection and Cross-breeding

Artificial selection

Human communities practise a form of selection when they breed plants and animals for specific characteristics. The many varieties of dog that you see today have been produced by selecting individuals with short legs, curly hair, long ears and so forth. One of the puppies in a litter might vary from the others by having longer ears. This individual, when mature, is allowed to breed. From the offspring, another long-eared variant is selected for the next breeding stock, and so on, until the desired or 'fashionable' ear length is established in a true-breeding population (Figure 9).

More important are the selective programmes to improve farm livestock or crop plants.

Stock-breeders will breed selectively from cows which give a high milk yield. They will select pigs with long backs (more bacon rashers) and sheep which grow quickly but do not lay down too much fat. They will also look for efficient reproduction (sheep which regularly have twin lambs, for example). They will also select for disease resistance.

Characteristics such as milk yield and growth rate are probably under the control of many genes. At each stage of selective breeding the farmer is, in

effect, keeping the most useful genes and discarding the less useful ones from the animals.

The same principles are applied to crop plants. The breeder may pick the largest fruit on a tomato plant and plant its seeds in the following year. In the next generation, again only seeds from the largest tomatoes are planted. In time, a true-breeding large-fruited variety of tomato plant can be produced. Other qualities such as disease resistance, colour and flavour can also be selected.

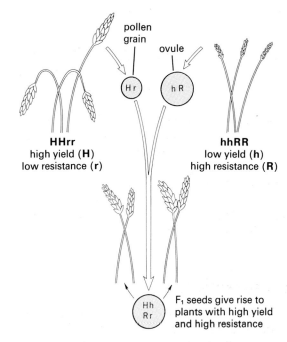

Figure 10   Combining useful characteristics

Cross-breeding and selection

Instead of selecting from varieties which occur naturally, geneticists can produce new varieties and select from these.

For example, suppose one variety of wheat produces a lot of grain but is not resistant to a fungus disease. Another variety is resistant to the disease but has only a poor yield of grain. If these two varieties are cross-pollinated (Figure 10), the F_1 offspring should be disease-resistant *and* give a good yield of grain. (This assumes that the useful characteristics are controlled by dominant genes.)

Suppose **R** represents a dominant gene for resistance to disease, and **r** is the recessive gene for poor resistance. **H** is a dominant gene for high yield and **h** is the recessive gene for low yield. The high-yield/low-resistance variety (**HHrr**) is crossed with the low-yield/high-resistance variety (**hhRR**). Each pollen grain from the **HHrr** plant will contain one **H** and one **r** gene (**Hr**). Each ovule from the **hhRR** plant will contain an **h** and an **R** gene (**hR**). The seeds will, therefore, all be **HhRr**. The F_1 plants which grow from these seeds will have dominant genes for both high yield and good disease resistance.

Figure 9   Selective breeding. Three varieties of dog produced by artificial selection over many years.

The offspring from crossing two varieties are called **hybrids**. If the F_1 hybrids from this cross bred true, they could give a new variety of disease-resisting, high-yielding wheat. But the F_1 generation from a cross does not necessarily breed true (page 230). The F_2 generation of wheat may contain four types of plant:

1 high yield, disease resistant
2 low yield, disease prone
3 low yield, disease resistant ⎫ parental types
4 high yield, disease prone   ⎭

This would not give such a successful crop as the F_1 plants.

With some commercial crops, the increased yield from the F_1 seed makes it worth while for the seedsman to make the cross and sell the seed to the growers. The hybrid corn (maize) grown in America is one example. The F_1 hybrid gives nearly twice the yield of the standard varieties.

Some cross-breeding programmes can produce a hybrid that breeds true (Figure 11). If instead of the **HhRr** in Figure 10 an **HHRR** could be produced, it would breed true.

QUESTIONS

8 Suggest some good characteristics that an animal-breeder might try to combine in sheep by mating different varieties together.

9 A variety of barley has a good ear of seed but has a long stalk and is easily blown over. Another variety has a short, sturdy stalk but a poor ear of seed.

Suggest a breeding programme to obtain and select a new variety which combined both of the useful characteristics.

Choose letters to represent the genes and show the genotypes of the parent plants and their offspring.

(a)   (b)   (c)   (d)   (e)

Figure 11   The genetics of bread wheat. A primitive wheat (a) was crossed with a wild grass (b) to produce a better-yielding hybrid wheat (c). The hybrid wheat (c) was crossed with another wild grass (d) to produce (e), which is one of the varieties of wheat used for making flour and bread.

CHECK LIST

- Variations within a species may be inherited or acquired.
- Inherited variations arise from different combinations of genes or from mutations.
- At meiosis the maternal and paternal chromosomes are randomly distributed between the gametes.
- Because the gametes do not carry identical sets of genes, new combinations of genes may arise at fertilization.
- Discontinuous variation results, usually, from the effects of a single gene pair. It produces distinct and consistent differences between individuals.
- Discontinuous variations cannot be changed by the environment.
- Continuous variations are usually controlled by a number of genes affecting the same characteristic.

- Continuous variation can be influenced by the environment.
- Members of a species compete with each other for food and mates.
- Some members of a species may have variations which enable them to compete better.
- These variants will live longer and leave more offspring.
- If the beneficial variations are inherited, the offspring will also survive longer.
- The new varieties may gradually replace the older varieties.
- Natural selection involves the elimination of the less well-adapted varieties by the pressure of the environment.
- Cross-breeding and artificial selection are used to improve commercially useful plants and animals.

Examination Questions

Do not write on these pages. Where necessary copy drawings, tables or sentences.

Section 4   Genetics and Evolution

1 The diagram below shows a set of chromosomes of a human female.

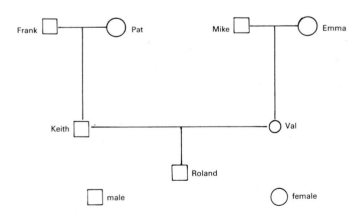

A B

  (a) How many chromosomes are present in this female's genotype?
  (b) What information in the diagram confirms that the person is female?
  (c) In what way will chromosomes A and B differ as regards their origin?
  (d) The diagram shows a family tree. Roland is a haemophiliac, as was one of his grandfathers. Haemophilia is a sex-linked condition, the gene being present on the X chromosome only.

  (i) Which person must have been Roland's haemophiliac grandfather?
  (ii) Explain the reason for your choice.
  (iii) What would be Roland's genotype?   (N2Q)

2 (a) (i) What is a mutation and what are the possible causes of mutation?
  (ii) Name *one* example of a condition brought about by a mutation, describing the symptoms and explaining the cause as fully as possible.
  (b) (i) State what is meant by sex linkage.
  (ii) State how red–green colour blindness is inherited by the offspring from the marriage of a normal-sighted woman with a colour-blind man.   (M3B)

3 (a) The diagrams show some of the stages in the division of a simplified cell which has four chromosomes in the diploid condition.

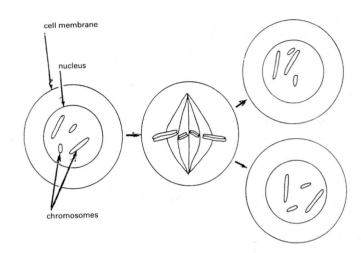

Give *two* reasons, seen from the diagrams, which show that this division was by mitosis.
  (b) (i) Name *one* organ in the human body in which meiosis occurs.
  (ii) Briefly explain the importance of meiosis in the human life cycle.   (W2B)

4 Some people are able to roll their tongues. These people are described as 'rollers'. Those who cannot roll the tongue are described as 'non-rollers'. The letter **R** represents the allele which gives rise to 'rollers' and the letter **r** represents the allele which gives rise to 'non-rollers'. If Mrs Brown's genotype was **Rr** and Mr Brown's was **RR**, explain why
  (a) they were both rollers,
  (b) all their children would also be rollers.   (L1)

5 Mr Brown is able to taste the bitter substance present in the skin of grapefruit but his wife is unable to taste the substance. Of their four children, Jim and Jane can taste the substance but Alan and Linda cannot. The ability to taste this substance is dominant.
  (a) (i) Using the symbols **T** for taster and **t** for non-taster, complete the diagram below to show the genetic make-up of the various members of the family.

Mr Brown		Mrs Brown	
_ _ _ _		_ _ _ _	
Alan	Jane	Jim	Linda
	Tt		
_ _ _ _		_ _ _ _	_ _ _ _

  (ii) Explain why the genetic make-up you have shown for Mr Brown is the only possible correct one.
  (b) Jane marries a man with the same genetic make-up as herself. Draw a diagram to show the possible combination of genes in their children.   (W2B)

6 A woman gives birth to four identical baby boys.
(a) How many eggs were fertilized?
(b) Which of these alternatives describes the chromosomes in the fertilizing sperm?

A   XX and 44 other chromosomes
B   XY and 44 other chromosomes
C   XX and 22 other chromosomes
D   X and 22 other chromosomes
E   Y and 22 other chromosomes

(c) Roman nose is caused by a dominant gene (**R**) and snub nose by a recessive gene (**r**).
If the father of the boys had a roman nose and the mother had a snub nose, complete this diagram to show how the boys inherited snub noses.

gametes ➡		

(W1A)

7 (a) What is the importance of meiosis (reduction division) in the human life cycle?
(b) State two ways in which mitosis differs from meiosis.
(S1)

8 A set of triplets, two of whom were identical, were separated at birth and brought up by different families. When they were 19 years old the following data were recorded.

	Susan	Jane	Amanda
Height	188 cm	188 cm	180 cm
Weight	62 kg	67 kg	77 kg
Blood type	O	AB	O
Measure of intelligence	138	142	125

(a) Name the *two* girls who were identical twins.
(b) Suggest why these *two* girls were different from each other in *one* of the three ways shown in the table.   (N1)

SECTION 5
Health and Disease

25 Micro-organisms and Humans

Bacteria
Structure and physiology. Harmless and pathogenic bacteria.

Viruses
Structure and multiplication. Virus diseases.

Fungi
Structure and nutrition. Parasitic fungi.

Protozoa
Malaria.

Biotechnology
Fermentation. Single-cell protein. Antibiotics. Genetic engineering.

Practical work
Culturing bacteria, effect of antibiotics.

The term 'micro-organism' includes viruses, bacteria, protozoa and some fungi and algae. Most of these organisms are, indeed, microscopic.

Bacteria and protozoa are single-celled organisms. Fungi and algae are multicellular. (That means, their bodies are made up of many cells.) Viruses do not have a cellular structure.

'Micro-organisms' is a convenient term by which to refer to a wide variety of fairly simple organisms. But the word is not used in classifications, in the way we use words like 'mammal' or 'vertebrate'.

DNA stands for **deoxy-ribose-nucleic acid**. DNA is a very large molecule made up of a chain of units called **nucleotides**. Each nucleotide consists of a sugar molecule (deoxy-ribose) combined with a phosphate group and an organic base. Several hundred of these nucleotides make up a gene.

Individual bacteria may be spherical, rod-shaped or spiral. Some have filaments, called **flagella**, projecting from them. The flagella can flick, and so move the bacterial cell about.

Bacteria

Bacterial structure

Bacteria (singular = bacterium) are very small organisms. Each consists of a single cell, rarely more than 0.01 mm in length. They can be seen only with the higher powers of the microscope.

They have cell walls, made of a complex mixture of proteins, sugars and lipids. Some bacteria have a **slime capsule** outside the cell wall. Inside the cell wall is the cytoplasm, which may contain granules of glycogen, lipid and other food reserves (Figures 1 and 2).

Each bacterial cell contains a single chromosome, consisting of a circular strand of DNA. The chromosome is not enclosed in a nuclear membrane but is coiled up to occupy part of the cell.

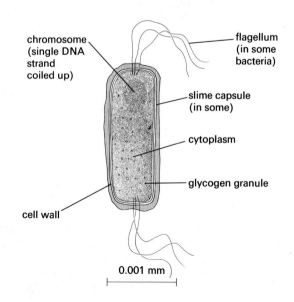

Figure 1   Generalized diagram of a bacterium

248

Bacterial physiology

Nutrition A few species of bacteria contain a photosynthetic pigment like chlorophyll, and can build up their food by photosynthesis. Most bacteria, however, live in or on their food. They produce and release enzymes which digest the food outside the cell. The liquid products of digestion are then absorbed back into the bacterial cell. This is called **saprophytic** nutrition.

Respiration The bacteria which need oxygen for their respiration are called **aerobic bacteria**. Those which do not need oxygen for respiration are called **anaerobic bacteria**. The bacteria used in the first stages of sewage treatment (page 77) are aerobic. Anaerobic bacteria are used to digest sewage sludge and produce methane.

Reproduction Bacteria reproduce by cell division or **fission**. Any bacterial cell can divide into two. Each daughter cell becomes an independent bacterium (Figure 3). Sometimes this cell division takes place every 20 minutes. This produces a large colony of bacteria in a very short time. This is one reason why a small number of bacteria can seriously contaminate our food.

Effect of heat Bacteria, like any other living organisms, are killed by high temperatures. Cooking destroys any bacteria in food, provided high enough temperatures are used. If drinking-water is boiled any bacteria present are killed.

However, some bacteria can produce spores, which can resist heat. When the cooked food or boiled water cools down, the spores germinate to produce new colonies of bacteria, particularly if the

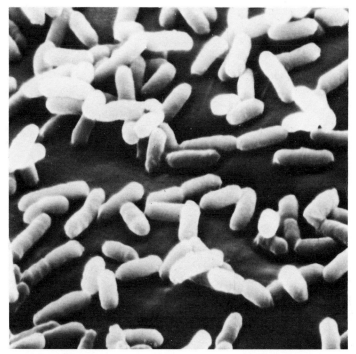

Figure 2 Bacteria as seen by the scanning electron microscope (×11 000)

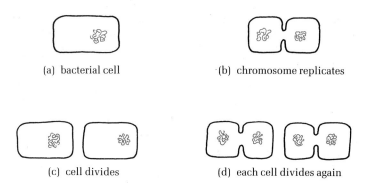

(a) bacterial cell

(b) chromosome replicates

(c) cell divides

(d) each cell divides again

Figure 3 Bacterium reproducing. This is asexual reproduction by cell division.

food is left in a warm place for many hours. For this reason cooked food should be eaten at once or immediately refrigerated. (Refrigeration slows down bacterial growth and reproduction.) After refrigeration food should not merely be warmed up. It should be either eaten cold or heated to 100 °C or more, which will kill any bacteria that have grown in it.

QUESTIONS

1 State which of the following structures are present in both bacterial cells and plant cells: cytoplasm, cellulose, DNA, cell wall, nucleus, chromosome, vacuole, glycogen.
2 If five bacteria landed in some food and reproduced at the maximum possible rate, what would be the population of bacteria after four hours?

Useful or harmless bacteria

When people talk about bacteria, they are usually thinking about those which cause disease or spoil our food. In fact, only a tiny minority of bacteria are harmful. Most of them are harmless. Some are extremely useful.

Bacteria which feed saprophytically bring about decay. They secrete enzymes into dead organic matter and liquefy it. This may be a nuisance if the organic matter is our food. But most bacteria feed on the excreta and dead bodies of organisms. If it were not for the activities of the decay bacteria (and fungi), we should be buried in ever-increasing layers of dead vegetation and animal bodies.

The decay bacteria also release essential elements from the dead remains. For example, they break down proteins to ammonia. The ammonia is turned into nitrates by nitrifying bacteria (page 57). The nitrates are taken up from the soil by plants, which use them to build up their proteins. Sulphur, phosphorus, iron, magnesium and all the elements essential to living organisms are similarly recycled in the course of bacterial decomposition.

Many species of bacteria live and reproduce on our skin or in our breathing passages or intestines. These bacteria are usually harmless. They may in fact keep more harmful competitors away.

Some bacteria in the human large intestine digest vegetable fibre in our food to form fatty acids, and others produce vitamin K. It is possible that we absorb and use these substances.

Humans use bacteria in yoghurt- and cheese-making and also in genetic engineering and the production of single-cell protein (page 257). Bacteria are also used in sewage treatment (page 77).

Pathogenic bacteria

Organisms that live inside or on the skin of other creatures are called **parasites**. The organism that supports these parasites is called the **host**. The parasites get their food from the host and may weaken it. Some may produce poisonous products which harm the host.

Some species of parasitic bacteria cause disease when they invade our bodies. These are called **pathogenic bacteria**.

Species of the bacterium *Streptococcus* cause sore throats, blood poisoning and scarlet fever. Species of *Clostridium* bacteria cause tetanus and botulism. *Staphylococcus* species cause tonsillitis and boils. Tuberculosis, cholera, typhoid, diphtheria, food poisoning, gonorrhoea and syphilis are all bacterial diseases.

The ill effects of a bacterial disease are caused mainly by poisonous products produced either by the bacteria or by the cells which they invade. Bacterial poisons are called **toxins**. Toxins damage the cells in which the bacteria are growing. They also upset some of the systems in the body. This gives rise to a raised temperature, headache, tiredness and weakness, and sometimes to diarrhoea and vomiting.

Some bacteria release **exotoxins** into the body of their host. These exotoxins are extremely poisonous. One milligram of the botulism toxin is enough to kill 300 million mice. (Botulism is a severe and often fatal form of food poisoning.)

Exotoxins also tend to attack specific systems in the body. For example, the tetanus (lock-jaw) toxin damages the nervous system.

Endotoxins are produced inside the bacteria and not released till the bacteria die and break down. They are less harmful than exotoxins but still upset the normal body functions.

Salmonella food poisoning   One of the commonest forms of food poisoning is caused by the bacterium *Salmonella typhimurium*. This bacterium lives in the intestines of cattle, pigs, chickens and ducks. Humans may develop food poisoning if they drink milk or eat meat or eggs which are contaminated with *Salmonella* bacteria from the alimentary canal of an infected animal (Figure 4).

The symptoms are diarrhoea and vomiting, which

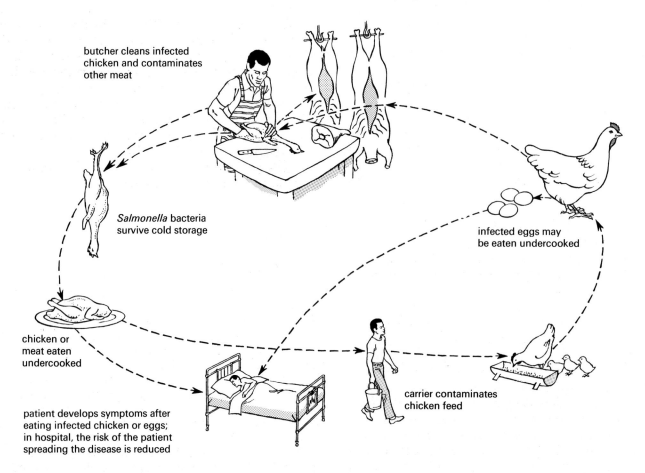

butcher cleans infected chicken and contaminates other meat

Salmonella bacteria survive cold storage

chicken or meat eaten undercooked

patient develops symptoms after eating infected chicken or eggs; in hospital, the risk of the patient spreading the disease is reduced

carrier contaminates chicken feed

infected eggs may be eaten undercooked

Figure 4   Transmission of *Salmonella* food poisoning (after Brian Jones, *Introduction to human and social biology*)

occur from 12 to 24 hours after eating the contaminated food. Although these symptoms are unpleasant, the disease is usually not serious and does not need treatment with drugs. Elderly people and very young children, however, may be made very ill by food poisoning.

The *Salmonella* bacteria are killed when meat is cooked or milk is pasteurized (heated for 30 minutes at 62 °C). Infection is most likely if untreated milk is drunk, meat is not properly cooked, or cooked meat is contaminated with bacteria transferred from raw meat. Frozen poultry must be thoroughly defrosted before cooking. Otherwise, the inside of the bird may not get hot enough during cooking to kill the *Salmonella*.

It follows that to avoid the disease all milk should be pasteurized and meat should be thoroughly cooked. People like shop-assistants and cooks should not handle cooked food at the same time as they handle raw meat. If they must do so, they must wash their hands thoroughly between the two activities. (See also page 264.)

The liquid which escapes when a frozen chicken is defrosted may contain *Salmonella* bacteria. The dishes and utensils used while the bird is defrosting must not be allowed to come into contact with any other food.

In the past few years there has been an increase in the outbreaks of *Salmonella* food poisoning in which the bacteria are resistant to antibiotics. Some scientists suspect that their rise stems from the practice of feeding antibiotics to farm animals to increase their growth rate. This could allow populations of drug-resistant *Salmonellae* to develop (see page 227).

In the 1970s another bacterium, *Campylobacter jejuni* was identified as a cause of food poisoning. This bacterium causes acute abdominal pains and diarrhoea for about 24 hours. The sources of infection are thought to be undercooked poultry and unpasteurized milk. In recent years, *Campylobacter* outbreaks have become more common than those due to *Salmonella*.

Gonorrhoea This is a sexually transmitted disease. That means that it is almost always caught by having sexual intercourse with an infected person. The disease is caused by a bacterium, *Neisseria gonorrhoeae*.

The first symptoms in men are pain and a discharge of pus from the urethra. In women, there may be similar symptoms, or no symptoms at all.

In men, the disease leads to a blockage of the urethra and to sterility. A woman can pass the disease to her child during birth. The bacteria in the vagina invade the baby's eyes and cause blindness.

The disease can be cured with penicillin, but some strains of *Neisseria* have become resistant to this antibiotic. There is no immunity to gonorrhoea. Having had the disease once does not prevent you catching it again.

Syphilis is also a sexually transmitted disease. It is caused by a bacterium called *Treponema pallidum*.

In the first stage of the disease, a lump or ulcer appears on the penis or the vulva, one week to three months after being infected. The ulcer usually heals without any treatment after about six weeks. By this time the bacteria have entered the body and may affect any tissue or organ. There may be a skin rash, a high temperature and swollen lymph nodes. But the symptoms are variable and the infected person may appear to be in good health for many years. But if the disease is not treated in the early stages, the bacteria will in time cause inflammation almost anywhere in the body. They can do permanent damage to the blood vessels, heart or brain, leading to paralysis and insanity.

In a pregnant woman, the bacteria can get across the placenta and infect the foetus.

Penicillin will cure syphilis. But unless it is used in the early stages of the disease, the bacteria may do permanent damage.

Chlamydia trachomatis *Chlamydia* is a bacterium that can live only in other cells and is therefore difficult to culture and study. It is transmitted by sexual intercourse. It is probably responsible for 50 per cent of cases of **non-specific urethritis** (NSU) in men and 40 per cent of instances of **pelvic inflammatory disease** (PID) in women.

The term 'non-specific urethritis' just means that the organism causing the urethritis (inflammation of the urethra) is not easily identified. The symptoms are an itching or burning sensation in the urethra and pain when urinating.

In women, the bacteria may cause no obvious symptoms at first. But if the condition is not treated, they will invade the uterus and oviducts and cause inflammation (PID).

The *Chlamydia* are killed by the antibiotics tetracycline and erythromycin.

QUESTIONS

3 Explain why re-warming cooked meat might lead to food poisoning.

4 In preparing for a reception, a cook defrosted a frozen chicken, placed it in the oven and then sliced some cooked ham which he put into the refrigerator. Then he washed his hands before preparing the salad.

After the reception several guests who ate the cold chicken and ham salad suffered from food poisoning.

(a) How could they have become infected, in spite of the chicken being cooked at a high temperature and the ham being refrigerated?

(b) How could the outbreak have been avoided?

5 Syphilis and gonorrhoea are sexually transmitted diseases. So how is it that babies can be infected?

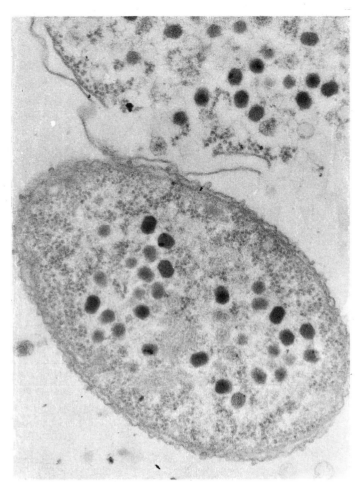

Figure 5   Viruses attacking a bacterium (×60 000). The viruses have invaded the bacterial cell and can be seen as black blobs. The viruses reproduce inside the cell. The cell at the top has burst open and the viruses are escaping.

Viruses

Most viruses are very much smaller than bacteria and can be seen only with the electron microscope at magnifications of about ×30 000. Figure 5 shows virus particles inside a bacterial cell.

Virus structure

There are many different types of virus and they vary in their shape and structure. All viruses, however, have a central core of DNA or RNA, surrounded by a protein coat. Viruses have no nucleus, cytoplasm or cell membrane, and no structures such as mitochondria. Some forms do have a membrane outside their protein coats, however.

RNA (ribose-nucleic acid) is similar to DNA. But the sugar in the nucleotides is ribose, instead of deoxy-ribose.

Virus particles are not cells. They do not feed, respire, excrete or grow. Biologists disagree about whether they can be classed as living organisms.

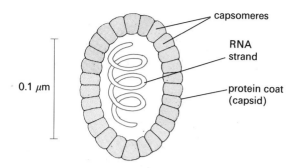

Figure 6   Generalized structure of a simple virus

Viruses do reproduce, but they do so only inside the cells of living organisms, using materials provided by the host cell.

Viruses can be destroyed by high temperatures.

Figure 6 shows a generalized virus particle. The nucleic acid core is a coiled single strand of RNA. The coat is made up of regularly packed protein units.

The protein units are called **capsomeres**. Each contains many protein molecules. The protein coat is called a **capsid**. Outside the capsid, in the influenza and some other viruses, is an envelope which is probably derived from the cell membrane of the host cell (Figure 7).

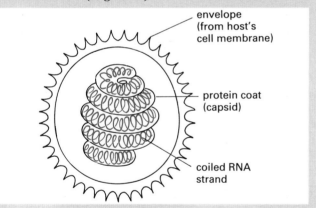

Figure 7   Structure of the influenza virus

Multiplication of viruses

Viruses can survive outside the host cell, but in order to reproduce they must find their way into a living cell. How they do this, in many cases, is not known for certain. Usually the virus particle first sticks to the cell membrane. It may then 'inject' its DNA or RNA into the cell's cytoplasm. Or the whole virus may be taken in by a kind of endocytosis (page 35).

Once inside the host cell, the virus is 'uncoated'. Its capsid is dispersed, exposing its DNA or RNA. The DNA or RNA then takes over the host cell's physiology. It stops the normal syntheses in the cell and makes the cell produce new viral DNA or RNA and new capsomeres. The nucleic

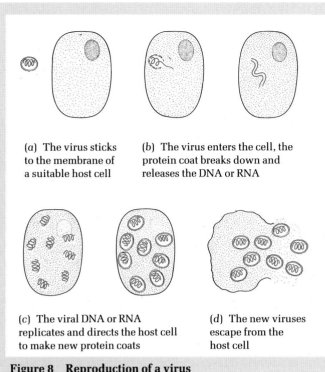

(a) The virus sticks to the membrane of a suitable host cell

(b) The virus enters the cell, the protein coat breaks down and releases the DNA or RNA

(c) The viral DNA or RNA replicates and directs the host cell to make new protein coats

(d) The new viruses escape from the host cell

Figure 8   Reproduction of a virus

acid and the capsomeres are put together in the cell to make new virus particles which escape from the cell (Figure 8).

Sometimes the cell is destroyed in this process. Sometimes the viruses escape, wrapping themselves in pieces of the host's cell membrane as they do so. These activities give rise to the signs and symptoms of disease.

QUESTIONS

6 (a) Why is a virus particle not considered to be a cell?
(b) Why are viruses not easy to classify as living organisms?

7 How does the reproduction of a virus differ from that of a bacterium?

Virus diseases

Viruses can reproduce only inside other cells, and so all viruses are parasitic. In humans they cause diseases such as colds, influenza, herpes, mumps, measles, chicken-pox, rubella, hepatitis and AIDS. Some viruses can remain dormant (inactive) in certain body cells without immediately producing symptoms of disease.

Viruses do not produce toxins. The harm they cause is probably the result of the destruction of the cells they invade. When they destroy cells in, for example, the lining of the windpipe and bronchi, bacteria can invade the damaged tissues.

After entering the body and reproducing in a small group of cells, the viruses may be carried to other organs in the circulation.

Although there are many effective drugs against bacterial infections, drugs against viral infections are only just being developed. However, some viral infections do confer long-term immunity, and many virus diseases can be prevented by immunization (page 265).

The common cold   This is caused by a **rhinovirus**. It is spread by droplet infection and contact. The symptoms of the disease develop within 12–78 hours after infection and are very familiar: dry throat, watering of the eyes, a copious secretion of watery mucus from the nose, swollen (congested) nasal membranes making it difficult to breathe through the nose.

These symptoms last for a few days. But the damage done by the virus to the nose and throat membranes often allows *Streptococcus* bacteria to invade. This secondary bacterial infection may give rise to a sore throat, a cough and catarrh.

Although the body develops immunity to the 'cold' virus, there are at least 80 different strains of rhinovirus. And other species of virus also cause colds. Immunity to one of these strains does not extend to the others. This is why you can have one cold after another.

There is no cure for a cold. Antibiotics are ineffective against rhinoviruses, but they may be prescribed if an acute or persistent secondary bacterial infection appears.

Influenza ('flu) is caused by a virus which exists in three strains, A, B and C. The virus attacks the lining of the throat and respiratory passages, giving rise to inflammation of the trachea, bronchi and bronchioles. The patient will have a raised temperature, headache, dry cough and a mild sore throat and will feel generally 'rotten'. The symptoms subside in 2–4 days, but the damage to the respiratory linings may allow *Streptococci* to invade, causing a secondary bacterial infection.

There are no specific drugs. Aspirin helps to lower the temperature, and antibiotics may be used against any secondary infection.

A bout of infection confers immunity for several years. But the 'A' strain of the virus undergoes mutations (page 227) very readily and immunity to one form is not effective against other mutants.

There are sometimes severe epidemics of influenza. If it is known which mutant is responsible, it is possible to prepare a vaccine which gives protection for a few months to people most at risk and to doctors and nurses dealing with the epidemic.

Herpes   One variety of the herpes virus causes the 'cold sore'. The virus remains in the skin in 'dormant' condition, but may be activated by sunlight or by catching a cold. It produces small blisters which eventually break and form a dry scab under which the skin heals spontaneously, usually in a few days.

One strain of the herpes virus causes **genital herpes**. The blisters and 'sores', in this case, appear on the penis or scrotum in men and on the labial lips of the vulva in women. Genital herpes is spread mainly by sexual contact.

The sores usually heal in a week or two. There are drugs which ease the symptoms. The drugs do not destroy the viruses, however. They remain dormant in the tissues and cause further outbreaks from time to time.

If a woman catches genital herpes in the late stages of pregnancy the infection can harm the foetus, or even kill it.

Another form of herpes virus causes chicken-pox in the young, and shingles in older people.

AIDS The initials stand for Acquired Immune Deficiency Syndrome. (A 'syndrome' is a pattern of symptoms associated with a particular disease.) The virus which causes AIDS has only recently been identified. It attacks certain kinds of lymphocyte (page 134), and thus weakens the body's immune responses.

As a result, the patient has little or no resistance to a range of diseases that normally could not invade the body. Once the symptoms appear, the patient's chances of survival are slim. Death does not result from the virus itself, but from diseases such as pneumonia, blood disorders, skin cancer or damage to the nervous system which the body cannot resist.

After a person has been infected, years may pass before symptoms develop. So people may carry the virus yet not show any symptoms. They can still infect other people, however. It is not known for certain what proportion of carriers will eventually develop AIDS: perhaps 30–50 per cent, or even more, may do so.

AIDS is transmitted by direct infection of the blood. Drug users who share needles contaminated with infected blood run a high risk of the disease. It can also be transmitted sexually, both between men and women and, especially, between homosexual men who practise anal intercourse.

Haemophiliacs (page 233) have also fallen victim to AIDS. Haemophiliacs have to inject themselves with a blood product which contains a clotting factor. Before the risks were recognized infected carriers sometimes donated blood which was used to produce the clotting factor.

Children born to AIDS patients may also contract the disease.

There is no evidence to suggest that the disease can be passed on by droplets (page 261), by saliva or by normal everyday contact.

The disease has appeared only recently in the industrialized countries. There are not yet any effective drugs or vaccines against it, though intensive work is taking place on both fronts.

QUESTIONS

8 Antibiotics are ineffective against virus diseases. Why then are antibiotics sometimes given to people suffering from a virus infection such as influenza?

9 Blood donors now have their blood tested to see if it contains antibodies to AIDS. What do you think is the value of this test?

10 People living in closed, isolated communities, such as Arctic explorers, often get a cold or two at first and then have several months free from colds. However, when the supply ship arrives the colds start again. Try to explain this phenomenon.

Fungi

The kingdom of the fungi includes fairly familiar organisms such as mushrooms, toadstools, puffballs, and the bracket fungi that grow on tree-trunks. There are also the less obvious, but very important, mould-fungi which grow on stale bread, cheese, fruit or other food. Many of the mould-fungi live in the soil or in dead wood. The yeasts are single-celled fungi similar to the moulds in some respects.

Some fungal species are parasites and live in other organisms, particularly plants, where they cause diseases which can affect crops.

Structure and nutrition

Many fungi are not made up of cells but of micro-scopic threads called **hyphae**. The branching hyphae spread through the material on which the fungus is growing, and absorb food from it. The network of hyphae that grows over or through the food material is called the **mycelium** (Figure 9).

Mushrooms and toadstools are the reproductive structures – 'fruiting bodies' – of a mycelium that spreads right through the soil or dead wood on which the fungus is growing.

The hyphae are like microscopic tubes lined with cytoplasm. In the centre of the older hyphae there is a vacuole. The cytoplasm contains mitochondria and there may be lipid droplets or granules of glycogen.

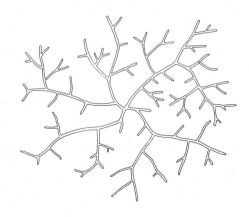

Figure 9 The branching hyphae form a mycelium

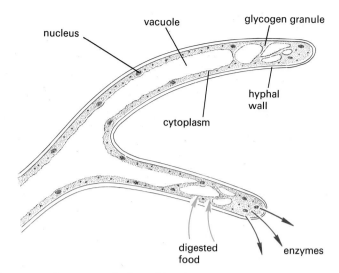

Figure 10   Structure of a fungal hypha

But, unlike plants, there are no chloroplasts or starch grains (Figure 10).

The hyphal wall may contain cellulose or chitin or both, according to the species. Chitin is similar to cellulose but the chitin molecule contains nitrogen atoms.

One family of fungi, the **yeasts**, is rather unusual. Only a few of the several species form true hyphae. Most consist of separate spherical cells which can be seen only under the microscope (Figure 11).

Fungi reproduce by forming microscopic, single-celled spores which are carried about in air currents.

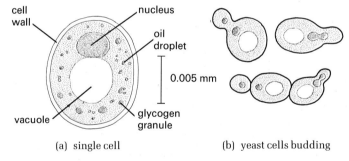

(a) single cell   (b) yeast cells budding

Figure 11   Yeast

Figure 12   Fungi growing on dead wood

When a spore lands on a suitable surface, it germinates to produce a new hypha.

A great many fungi are saprophytic (page 55). They grow in the soil, in rotting wood or other dead vegetation (Figure 12) and on our food. Their hyphae penetrate their surroundings and produce digestive enzymes at their tips. The enzymes dissolve the organic matter and the soluble products are absorbed back into the hypha.

Fungi growing in our food usually make it unfit to eat. In the natural environment, however, fungi are important decomposers (they take part in decay, and help to recycle organic matter – see page 55).

Some fungi are parasitic. The parasitic fungi that most concern us are those that attack crops. Examples are blight of potato, mildew on grapes and rust

Figure 13   **Parasitic fungus growing on crops.** The brown spots on the wheat leaf are caused by a rust fungus.

of wheat (Figure 13). These fungus diseases can cause heavy losses if they are not controlled.

A few fungi are parasitic in humans.

Fungal parasites of humans

Tinea ('ringworm')   Several species of fungus give rise to the various forms of this disease. The fungus attacks the cornified layer of the skin and produces a patch of inflamed tissue. On the skin of the body, face or limbs, the infected patch spreads outwards and heals in the centre, giving a ring-like appearance ('ringworm').

The different species of tinea fungi may live on the skin of humans or domestic animals, or in the soil. The region of the body affected will depend on the species of fungus.

One kind affects the scalp and causes circular bald patches. The hair usually grows again when the patient recovers from the disease.

The species of fungus which affect the feet usually cause cracks in the skin between the toes. This is known as 'athlete's foot'.

Tinea of the crutch is a fungus infection, occurring usually in males, which affects the inner part of the thighs on each side of the scrotum. It causes a spreading, inflamed area of skin with an itching or burning sensation.

All forms of the disease are very contagious. That means, they are spread by contact with an infected person or their personal property. Tinea of the scalp is spread by using infected hair brushes, combs or pillows. Tinea of the crutch can be caught by using towels or bedclothes contaminated by the fungus or its spores, and 'athlete's foot' by wearing infected socks or shoes, or from the floors of showers and swimming pools.

When an infection is diagnosed, the clothing, bed linen, hair brushes, combs or towels must be boiled to destroy the fungus. It is best, anyway, to avoid sharing these items as their owners may be carrying the infection without knowing or admitting it.

In young people, tinea infections often clear up without treatment. Where treatment is needed, a fungicide cream or dusting powder is applied to the affected areas of skin. Infected feet may be dipped in a solution of potassium permanganate (potassium manganate(VII)).

Candidiasis ('thrush')   This fungus may live harmlessly in the mouth or vagina and may cause disease only if a person is unwell from other causes. In the mouth, the fungus causes white patches and general inflammation. In the vagina, infection causes itching and sometimes a discharge.

The fungus is normally kept in check by competition with the harmless bacteria present in the mouth or vagina. If these bacteria are killed by antibiotics, the fungus may grow rapidly and produce disease symptoms.

QUESTIONS

11 When stale food goes mouldy, what is actually happening to it?

12 Suggest why bread, wood and leather may go mouldy, while glass and plastic do not.

Protozoa

The protozoa are microscopic organisms whose bodies consist of a single cell (Figure 14). All protozoa live in water – in the sea, rivers and lakes, in puddles and in the body fluids of animals. Protozoa differ from bacteria: they have a definite nucleus enclosed in a nuclear membrane, and they do not have cell walls.

Some protozoa feed by absorbing liquids through their cell membranes. Others ingest small particles or organisms, such as bacteria, and digest them in their cytoplasm.

The protozoa that are of particular interest to humans are those near the base of the food web in

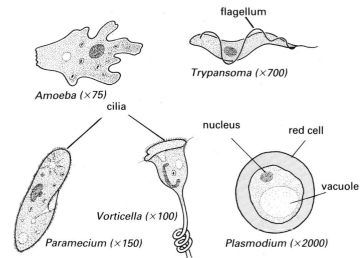

Figure 14   Some protozoa. *Trypanosoma* and *Plasmodium* are parasites in human blood

the sea (page 51), those that play a part in sewage treatment (page 77), and the parasitic protozoa that cause disease in humans and their domestic animals.

A protozoan, *Trypanosoma*, causes sleeping sickness, an amoeba-like protozoan (*Entamoeba*) causes one form of dysentery, and the parasite *Plasmodium* causes malaria. These are very important diseases in tropical countries.

Malaria   Probably about 250 million people suffer from malaria. There are about 150 million new cases each year. In Africa alone, as many as a million children die every year from malaria.

The malarial parasite, *Plasmodium*, enters the human bloodstream when a person is bitten by an infected mosquito. The parasitic protozoa enter the red blood cells and digest the cytoplasm (Figure 15).

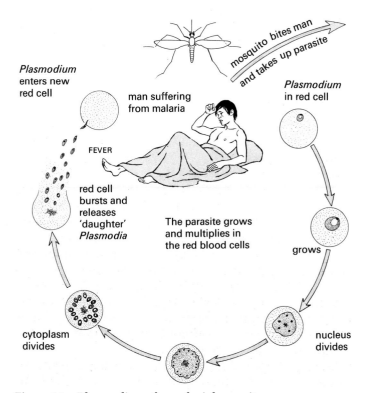

Figure 15   *Plasmodium*, the malarial parasite

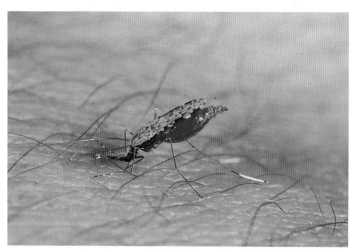

Figure 16   Mosquito biting. The mosquito is sucking blood from a blood vessel in the skin. Its abdomen is swollen with the blood it has taken in.

They also reproduce by cell division inside the red cell. After a few days, the red cells break down releasing the daughter *Plasmodia*. At the same time, the patient suffers a bout of fever. The daughter *Plasmodia* enter new red cells and the cycle starts again. Some of the parasites enter cells of the liver. They remain dormant there for a time, and then re-emerge to cause further bouts of fever.

If a mosquito sucks blood from an infected person (Figure 16), it will take up some of the parasites. These will then be injected into the bloodstream of the next person the mosquito bites.

There are drugs which can kill the parasites in the bloodstream, but these cannot reach those lying dormant in the liver. Mutant forms of the parasites are resistant to these drugs. At one time people thought that malaria could be wiped out by a campaign to kill mosquitoes with DDT. This worked well for a time in some areas. But before long mutant mosquitoes appeared, which were resistant to the insecticide.

Biotechnology

Biotechnology can be defined as the industrial application of biological organisms, systems or processes.

Although biotechnology is 'hot news', we have been making use of it for thousands of years. Wine-making, beer-brewing, the baking of bread and the production of cheese all depend on fermentation processes brought about by yeasts, other fungi and bacteria, or enzymes from these organisms.

Antibiotics, such as penicillin, are produced by mould-fungi or bacteria. The production of some industrial chemicals, such as citric acid and lactic acid, needs bacteria or fungi to bring about essential chemical changes (see below).

Sewage disposal depends on bacteria and protozoa in the sewage treatment plants. They form the basis of the food chain that purifies the effluent.

Biotechnology is not concerned solely with the use of micro-organisms. Cell cultures and enzymes also feature in modern developments. In this chapter, however, there is space to consider only one or two uses of bacteria and fungi.

Fermentation

Traditionally, this refers to the breakdown of carbohydrate to alcohol (ethanol) and carbon dioxide by yeasts (page 255), as in the brewing industry. The term also includes many other reactions, mostly brought about by bacteria and fungi, to produce substances we need.

Brewing   Yeast cells contain many enzymes, some of which can break down sugar into carbon dioxide and ethanol. This chemical change provides energy for the yeast cells to use in their vital processes.

$$C_6H_{12}O_6 \rightarrow 2CO_2 + 2C_2H_5OH + 118 \text{ kJ}$$
$$\text{ethanol}$$

Alcoholic fermentation is a form of anaerobic respiration (page 29). But if the yeast is supplied with carbohydrates other than sugar, it needs oxygen to convert these substances to sugar first.

In brewing, barley is allowed to germinate. During germination, the barley grains convert their starch reserves into maltose (page 21). The germinating barley is then killed by heat and the sugars are dissolved out with water. Yeast is added to this solution and ferments it to carbon dioxide and ethanol.

In making beer, hops are added to give the brew a bitter flavour. The liquid is sealed into casks or bottles so that the carbon dioxide is under pressure. When the pressure is released, the dissolved carbon dioxide escapes from the liquid. This gives it a 'fizz'.

In making spirits such as whisky, the fermentation is allowed to go on longer and the ethanol is distilled off. Wine is made from the juice extracted from fruit, usually grapes. The yeasts that live on the surface of the fruit then ferment the sugar in the juice to ethanol.

Baking   In baking, flour, salt, fat and water are mixed to produce 'dough'. Enzymes in the flour start to convert the flour-starch to sugar. When yeast is added, it ferments the sugar and produces carbon dioxide. The bubbles of carbon dioxide make the dough 'rise'. The bubbles also expand when the dough is baked and so give the bread a 'light' texture.

Other microbiological conversions   Certain bacteria can oxidize ethanol to produce ethanoic acid. Vinegar is produced in this way when bacteria are allowed to act on wine. Some species of *Streptococcus* and *Lactobacillus* convert milk to yoghurt, and others are used in cheese-making.

A mould fungus, *Aspergillus*, is used on an industrial scale to make citric acid from molasses.

Lactic acid is produced by the fermentation of starch or milk products by species of *Streptococcus* or *Lactobacillus*.

A good deal of research is taking place to find ways of using bacteria to convert industrial and farming waste, such as sawdust and straw, to useful products.

An increasingly important conversion process exploits bacteria in extracting metals from low-grade ores and old mining wastes. For example, spoil heaps of residues from copper mines are sprayed with acidified water. This promotes the growth of a species of *Thiobacillus*, which can use the sulphur in the ore and produce sulphuric acid. The acid dissolves out the copper as copper sulphate. The solution drains out at the bottom of the spoil heap and the copper is reclaimed.

Similar bacterial processes may be used to convert toxic wastes to less harmful compounds.

More and more, biotechnologists are using enzymes extracted from micro-organisms instead of the micro-organisms themselves. This often increases the efficiency of the process. Microbial enzymes are used in some washing powders to digest away stains caused by organic materials.

Single-cell protein (SCP)

The principle is that bacteria, yeasts and other fungi, or algae are grown in a 'feedstock'. In the right conditions of temperature, aeration and so on, the micro-organisms grow very rapidly. They are separated from the feedstock, dried and used as food for animals – and possibly, one day, for humans.

The feedstock may be a petroleum product, an agricultural product or waste material from agriculture or the food industry, such as whey from cheese-making.

Before 1985, ICI manufactured a single-cell protein called 'Pruteen' (Figure 17). The feedstock was

Figure 17   ICI's 'Pruteen' factory. The tall building in the centre houses the fermentation tanks. The storage containers are on the left. In between is the drying unit.

methanol produced from the methane in natural gas, and the bacterium used was *Methylophilus methylotrophus.* The bacteria were allowed to grow in a dilute solution of methanol with air, ammonia and essential elements added. In the fermentation tanks, the bacterial cells multiplied and were then separated from the liquid medium by centrifugation and drying. The product is a creamy white powder with no smell and little taste. It could be added in powder form to animal feedstuffs, or made into pellets for cattle.

Since the single cells consist mainly of protoplasm, the product is very rich in protein.

Antibiotics

Many of the fungi which live in the soil compete with bacteria and each other for supplies of organic material to use as food. Some compete by producing chemicals which stop the growth of competitors. We have learned to extract these chemicals, now called antibiotics, and to use them against some of the bacteria that cause human diseases.

Pure cultures of the fungi are grown on nutrient solutions on a large scale and the antibiotics are extracted and purified from the growth medium. A well-known example is the production of penicillin from the mould *Penicillium*.

Some soil bacteria produce similar antibiotics. For example, streptomycin is produced by *Streptomyces*. Some antibiotics are now made synthetically rather than by culturing micro-organisms.

Genetic engineering

The genes (page 224) that control the processes going on within living cells are pieces of the chemical DNA (page 248). If the DNA is altered, as happens in mutations (page 227), the cell's metabolism is altered too. Scientists can now extract a gene from one organism and insert it into the DNA of another species.

For example, the human gene for producing insulin (page 215) can be inserted into bacteria. The genetically engineered bacteria produce insulin when they are cultured and the insulin can be separated and purified from the culture medium. This process produces insulin in a purer form than that extracted from animal pancreas tissue. It may also be a cheaper process in due course.

Although several of these techniques are being successfully developed in the laboratory, some are running into problems when production is stepped up to an industrial scale. But there are many possible applications of genetic engineering in the future. A blood-clotting factor (Factor VIII) has been made by genetic engineering. This factor is needed by people suffering from one form of haemophilia, a genetic disease in which the blood fails to clot adequately.

It may prove possible to insert genes for disease resistance into crop plants, or to improve the nitrogen-fixing process in root nodule bacteria (page 57). Enzymes may be commercially produced by genetic engineering. It may even become possible, one day, to replace defective human genes with genetically engineered normal ones.

QUESTIONS

13 Make a table of examples of industrial processes which use micro-organisms. Where possible name the organism and state the starting substance and the product.
14 In baking, the oven temperature must kill the yeast and yet the bread continues to rise. Explain why this happens.
15 When making substances by biotechnology, it is important that the feedstock (starting substance) and the fermenting vessels do not contain any micro-organisms other than the one that is meant to carry out the conversion. Why is this?

PRACTICAL WORK

Bacteria culture

In order to identify and study bacteria, you have to culture them. This is done by mixing fruit juice, meat extract or other nutrients with agar jelly to form a medium in which the bacteria can grow and reproduce. (Agar jelly, derived from seaweed, is used because bacteria cannot grow on it unless nutrients are added, and because it is not liquefied by bacterial enzymes.)

The bacteria multiply and form visible colonies (Figure 18) whose colour and chemical reactions make them identifiable. By including or excluding

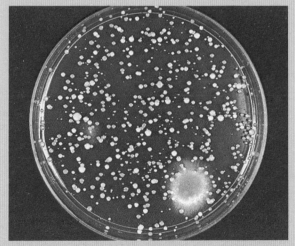

Figure 18 Micro-organisms from the air. The agar was exposed to the air for a few minutes. Each colony has grown from a single micro-organism that fell on the plate.

certain substances from the culture medium, the essential conditions for the growth and reproduction of a particular bacterial species can be found. The effects of drugs, antibiotics and disinfectants can be studied too.

Bacteria are everywhere, in the air, on surfaces, on clothing and the skin. If you want to culture one particular species of bacteria, you must make sure that all other species are excluded. This means using **aseptic techniques**. You must sterilize the glassware and the culture media, and avoid allowing bacteria from the air or from your own body to contaminate the experiments.

You sterilize the glassware and media by heating them to temperatures which destroy all bacteria and their spores. You avoid contamination by handling the apparatus in a way which reduces the chances of unwanted bacteria entering the experiments.

1   Culturing bacteria

Sterilize the glassware by super-heated steam in an autoclave or pressure cooker for 15 minutes at 1 kg/cm², so that the unwanted bacteria on the glassware are destroyed.

Stir 1.5 g agar into 100 cm³ of hot distilled water. Add 1 g beef extract, 0.2 g yeast extract, 1 g peptone and 0.5 g sodium chloride. Sterilize the mixture in an autoclave, and pour it into sterile petri dishes. Cover the dishes at once and allow them to cool.

Precautions   Culture methods can give rise to very dense colonies of potentially harmful bacteria. Treat *all* bacteria as if they were harmful. When the petri dishes have been inoculated with the bacterial samples seal the lids in place with adhesive tape. Do not remove the tape until the plates have been sterilized again at the end of the experiment. Examine any colonies that appear, with the lids still on the dishes.

Inoculating the plates   If a little cooked potato or other vegetable is allowed to rot for a few days in water, bacteria will arrive and grow in the liquid.

Sterilize a wire loop by heating it to redness in a bunsen flame. Pick up a drop of the liquid containing bacteria and streak it lightly across the surface of the agar jelly. Only lift the lid of the dish just far enough to admit the wire loop, but not enough to let bacteria from the air fall on to the agar (Figure 19). Seal the lid on the dish with

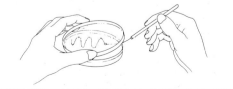

Figure 19   Lift the lid as little as possible

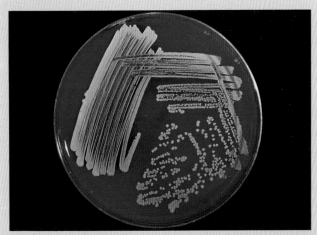

Figure 20   A 'streak plate'. Notice how the bacterial colonies have grown where the plate was streaked.

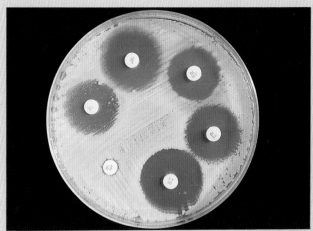

Figure 21   Testing antibiotics. Antibiotics have diffused out from the discs and suppressed the growth of bacteria.

adhesive tape. Keep the dish, upside down, in an incubator or similar warm place for about two days. (If water condenses in the petri dish, it will fall on the lid and not spread over the surface of the agar.)

Prepare a 'control' dish, but do not inoculate it. Incubate it in the same way as the first dish.

Bacterial colonies should grow on the streaked dish, following the path taken by the loop (Figure 20). There should be no growth of bacteria in the control dish, showing that the bacteria in the experiment came from the inoculating liquid and not from the glassware or the medium.

Sterilize all the dishes, still sealed, once more in the autoclave before washing them up.

2   The effect of antibiotics

Make up the culture medium as before. When it is cool but before it sets, add a few drops of pure bacteria culture (use *Escherichia coli* or *Staphylococcus albus* from a reputable dealer). Mix it thoroughly with the medium. Pour the medium into sterile petri dishes and allow it to set.

Using sterile forceps, place some discs containing antibiotics on the surface of the agar. Seal the lids on. Incubate the dishes at about 35 °C for 24 hours.

The bacteria, which are dispersed in the agar, will grow and make the medium look cloudy. But in regions surrounding some of the antibiotic discs, bacterial growth will have been suppressed and the agar will look clear (Figure 21).

If the bacteria are able to grow right up to the edge of a disc, it means that the antibiotic in that disc is unable to suppress the growth of the species of bacteria used in the trial.

QUESTION

16 Suggest the reasons for the variation in extent of the clear areas round the discs in Figure 21.

CHECK LIST

- Bacteria are single cells. They have a cell wall, cytoplasm and a single chromosome.
- Bacteria produce enzymes which digest the surrounding medium.
- Bacteria reproduce by cell division.
- Bacteria are killed by heat but the spores survive.
- Most bacteria are saprophytes and bring about decay.
- Bacterial decay releases essential substances for recycling.
- Viruses are smaller than bacteria and cannot, strictly, be classed as living organisms.
- Each virus particle consists of a DNA or RNA core enclosed in a protein coat.
- Viruses can reproduce only inside a living cell.

- Viruses take over the host cell's physiology and make it produce new virus particles.

- Viruses and bacteria can cause disease.
- Influenza, colds, herpes and AIDS are virus diseases.
- Tuberculosis, *Salmonella* food poisoning, gonorrhoea and syphilis are bacterial diseases.
- Sexually transmitted diseases include syphilis, gonorrhoea, herpes and AIDS.
- Antibiotics are effective against many bacterial diseases but few drugs are effective against virus diseases.
- Fungi are useful as decomposers, but some of them are parasitic on our crops or on ourselves.
- Protozoa are single-celled creatures, some of which cause disease. Malaria is caused by a protozoan.

- Biotechnology exploits bacteria and other microorganisms by making them produce materials useful to us.

26

Transmission and Control of Diseases

Non-Transmissible and Transmissible Diseases
Inherited and acquired disorders.

Disease Transmission
By air, water, food and contact.

Methods of Preventing Spread of Disease
Water treatment, hygiene, immunization, drugs and disinfectants.

Non-Transmissible and Transmissible Diseases

Non-transmissible diseases

These are the diseases which cannot be transmitted (passed) from one person to another (because they are not caused by pathogens, such as viruses or parasitic bacteria). Some are inherited at birth. Others are acquired during the lifetime.

Inherited disorders Examples are haemophilia, sickle-cell anaemia, phenylketonuria and Down's syndrome (pages 233 and 235). Genetic counselling (page 235) can reduce the frequency of these diseases.

Some inherited disorders can be treated effectively. Haemophilia is treated by injections of a blood-clotting factor (Factor VIII). The effects of phenylketonuria can be reduced by excluding phenylalanine from the diet for the first six years (see page 235).

Acquired disorders Some of these are degenerative diseases (diseases that are associated with old age). Most people will sooner or later experience them to some extent. Examples of degenerative diseases are atherosclerosis (page 138) and osteoarthritis. A healthy lifestyle may help to delay the onset of some degenerative diseases.

Other non-transmissible diseases may be unrelated to age. Juvenile diabetes and rickets can affect young people.

Some of the acquired diseases have fairly obvious environmental causes. Many cases of coronary heart disease, bronchitis, emphysema and lung cancer stem from smoking (pages 138 and 148). Poor nutrition can cause vitamin-deficiency diseases (page 101). Working with certain chemicals or radioactive sources may increase the risk of cancer.

Arthritis and diabetes do not have obvious environmental causes, though there is some evidence that they may be triggered by virus infections.

Transmissible diseases

These are the infectious diseases, such as tuberculosis, chicken-pox, measles, whooping cough and syphilis. Most are caused by viruses or bacteria. These organisms can be passed from sick people to healthy people by various means. The rest of this chapter deals with the ways in which these diseases are transmitted and how they can be prevented.

QUESTION

1 State which of the following diseases you think are infectious: influenza, tuberculosis, scurvy, rheumatism, polio, chicken-pox, appendicitis, haemophilia.

Disease Transmission

Air-borne, 'droplet' or aerosol infection

When we sneeze, cough, laugh, speak or just breathe out, we send a fine spray of liquid drops into the air. These droplets are so tiny that they remain floating in the air for a long time. They may be breathed in by other people or fall on to exposed food (Figure 1). If the droplets contain viruses or bacteria, they may cause disease when they are inhaled or eaten with food.

Virus diseases like colds, 'flu, measles and chicken-pox are spread in this way. So are the bacteria

Figure 1 Droplet infection. The visible drops expelled by this sneeze will soon sink to the floor, but smaller droplets will remain suspended in the air.

(streptococci) that cause sore throats. When the water in the droplets evaporates, the bacteria often die as they dry out. The viruses remain infectious, however, floating in the air for a long time.

In buses, trains, cinemas and discos, the air is warm and moist, and full of floating droplets. These are places where you are likely to pick up one of these infections.

Contamination of water

If disease bacteria get into water supplies used for drinking, hundreds of people can become infected. Diseases of the alimentary canal, like typhoid and cholera, are especially dangerous. Millions of bacteria infest the lining of the intestine of a sick person. Some of these bacteria will pass out with the faeces. If the faeces get into streams or rivers, the bacteria may be carried into reservoirs of water used for drinking. Even if faeces are left on the soil or buried, rain water may wash the bacteria into a nearby stream.

To prevent this method of infection, faeces are made harmless, and drinking-water is purified.

Contamination of food

Contamination by people The bacteria most likely to get into food are the ones which cause diseases of the alimentary canal such as typhoid and *Salmonella* food poisoning. The bacteria are present in the faeces of infected people and may reach food from the unwashed hands of the sufferer.

People recovering from one of these diseases may feel quite well. But bacteria may still be present in their faeces. If they don't wash their hands thoroughly after going to the lavatory, they may have small numbers of bacteria on their fingers. If they then handle food, the bacteria may be transferred to the food. When this food is eaten by healthy people, the bacteria will multiply in their bodies and give them the disease (see page 264 and Figure 4 on page 250).

People working in food shops, kitchens and food-processing factories could infect thousands of other people in this way if they were careless about their personal cleanliness.

Some forms of food poisoning result from poisons (toxins) that are produced by bacteria which get into food. Cooking kills the bacteria in the food, but does not destroy the toxins which cause the illness. Only one form of this kind of food poisoning, called **botulism**, is dangerous. It is also very rare.

Contamination by houseflies Flies walk about on food. They place their mouth parts on it and pump saliva on to the food. Then they suck up the digested food as a liquid.

This would not matter much if flies fed only on clean food, but they also visit decaying food or human faeces. Here they may pick up bacteria on their feet or their mouth parts. They then alight on our food and the bacteria on their bodies are transferred to the food. Figure 2 shows the many ways in which this can happen.

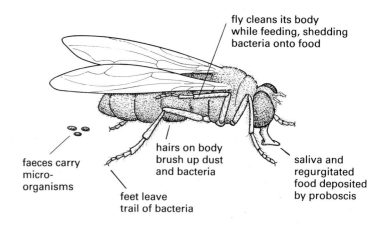

faeces carry micro-organisms

fly cleans its body while feeding, shedding bacteria onto food

hairs on body brush up dust and bacteria

feet leave trail of bacteria

saliva and regurgitated food deposited by proboscis

Figure 2 Transmission of bacteria by houseflies.
(After Brian Jones, *Introduction to human and social biology*)

Vectors

A vector is an animal, often an insect, which carries pathogens from one person to another. Some species of mosquito carry the protozoa which cause malaria (page 256), and other species carry the viruses of yellow fever. Rat fleas carry the bacteria of bubonic plague. Houseflies spread polio, and a variety of intestinal diseases, such as food poisoning.

Contagion

A contagious disease can be spread by contact with an infected person, or with their clothing, bed linen or towels. The fungus disease tinea (described on page 255) is very contagious.

Colds may also be spread by contact. The viruses are transferred from the hands of an infected person to the hands of healthy people, who then infect themselves by touching their eyes or nose.

Sexually transmitted diseases Syphilis, gonorrhoea, *Chlamydia*, genital herpes and non-specific urethritis (page 251) are spread almost exclusively by sexual intercourse with an infected person. AIDS too is spread mainly by sexual contact, though haemophiliacs and drug addicts who share contaminated needles are also at risk.

There is no easy way of recognizing an infected person. People who have many sexual partners, such as prostitutes, are the most likely to be infected.

QUESTIONS

2 Why should people who sell, handle and cook food be particularly careful about their personal hygiene?
3 Coughing or sneezing without covering the mouth and nose with a handkerchief is thought to be inconsiderate behaviour. Why is this?
4 Inhaling cigarette smoke can stop the action of cilia in the trachea and bronchi for about 20 minutes. Why should this increase a smoker's chance of catching a respiratory infection?
5 Although wasps often walk on our food, they are not suspected of spreading disease. Why do you think they are less harmful in this respect than houseflies?

Methods of Preventing Spread of Disease

Natural barriers

Although many bacteria live on the surface of the skin, the outer layer of the epidermis (page 158) seems to act as a barrier which stops them getting into the body. But if the skin is cut or damaged, the bacteria may then get into the deeper tissues and cause infection.

The sweat glands and sebaceous glands produce substances which kill bacteria and keep down their numbers on the skin. Tears contain an enzyme called **lysozyme**. This dissolves the cell walls of some bacteria and so protects the eyes from infection.

The acid conditions in the stomach destroy most of the bacteria which may be taken in with food. The moist lining of the nasal passages traps many bacteria. So does the mucus produced by the lining of the trachea and bronchi. The ciliated cells of these organs carry the trapped bacteria away from the lungs.

When bacteria get through these barriers, the body has two more lines of defence – the white cells and the antibodies. The way these work is described on page 134.

Air-borne infection

There is no single way to prevent the spread of air-borne pathogens, apart from programmes of immunization against individual diseases.

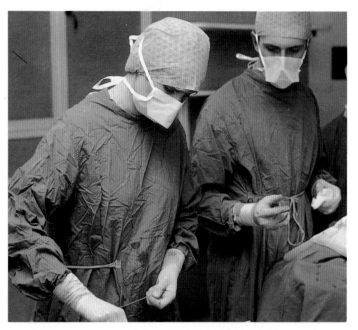

Figure 3   Prevention of infection in an operating theatre. Staff wear sterile masks and clothing in order to protect the patient from bacteria from their own bodies.

Children with infectious diseases such as rubella or chicken-pox are usually kept away from school during their infectious period. However, it is probably better to catch these 'childhood' diseases when young and so develop immunity, because older people are more severely affected.

You might perhaps reduce your chances of catching a cold or 'flu by avoiding crowded, humid, poorly ventilated places. But you might not enjoy living in permanent isolation.

Similarly, you can hardly stay at home every time you have a cold. But you might infect fewer people if you cough and sneeze into a handkerchief, rather than spraying droplets over a wide area.

In an operating theatre, the surgeon and staff wear sterile gauze masks to trap any droplets that might otherwise infect the patient (Figure 3).

Water-borne infection

On a small scale, simply boiling the water used for drinking will destroy any pathogens. On a large scale, water supplies are protected by (a) ensuring that untreated human sewage cannot reach them and (b) treating the water to make it safe.

Sewage treatment This has been described on pages 76–8.

Water treatment Rain water may be acid, but it is unlikely to contain pathogens. Water from fast-flowing rivers which come from deserted hills is not likely to be contaminated. Underground water that has filtered through permeable rock should contain few bacteria. Slow-moving rivers that pass near human settlements are likely to contain some disease bacteria, however.

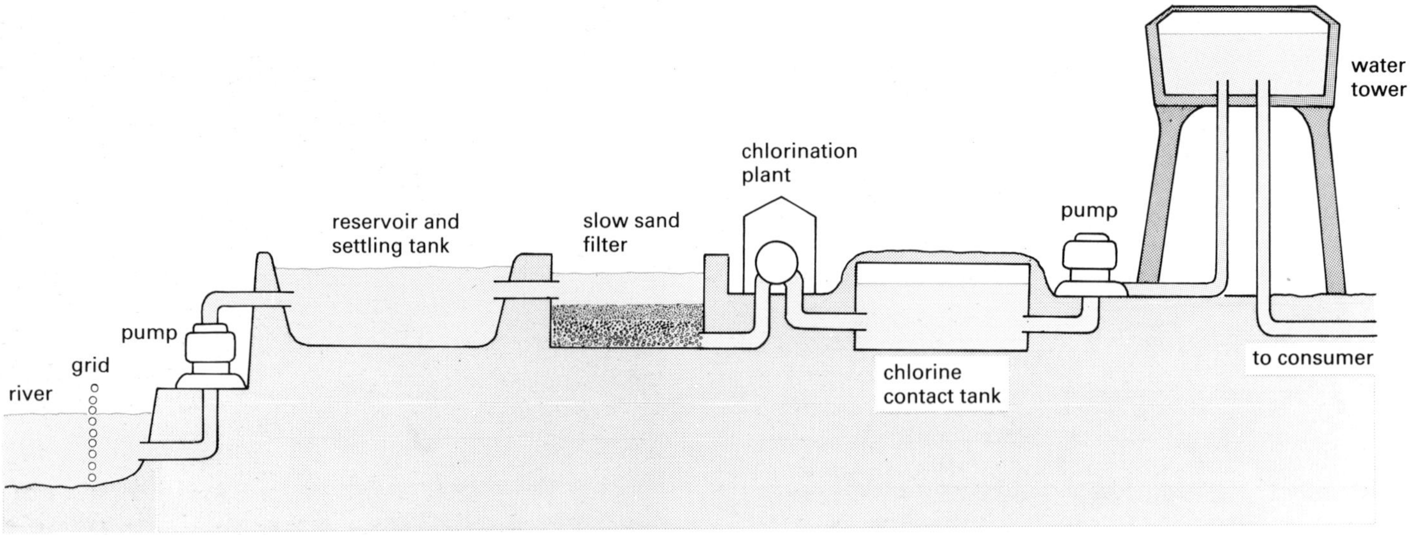

Figure 4   The principles of water purification

Figure 5   **Hampton water purification works.** The main building contains the pumping equipment and the chlorination plant. The 'ponds' in the foreground are slow sand filters, one of which is drained for cleaning. Behind the pumping station are more filters (left) and two reservoirs (right).

The treatment used to purify water depends on how clean the source is. Usually it is similar to the process shown in Figure 4.

Water is pumped from a river or an underground source. River water is passed through a grid to remove floating objects, such as twigs or bottles. The water is allowed to remain for some time in a settling tank where small suspended particles settle out.

The next step is to remove bacteria from the water by passing it through a filter. There are various types of filter. In all of them the water passes through a layer of jelly-like material supported on a bed of sand. In most cases the gelatinous layer is formed by bacteria and protozoa (single-celled animals) growing on the sand. The filters eventually become clogged. So from time to time they are cleaned and the jelly layer is re-formed.

Chlorine gas is added to the filtered water and remains in contact with it for long enough to kill any bacteria which have passed through the filter. How much chlorine is added and the length of the contact time both depend on how contaminated the water source is likely to be. Most of the chlorine disappears before the water reaches the consumers.

The purified water is pumped to a high-level reservoir or water tower. These are enclosed to ensure that no pathogens can get into the water. The height of the reservoir provides the pressure needed to deliver the water to the consumer.

Food-borne infection

People   People who handle and prepare food need to be extremely careful about their personal hygiene. It is essential that they wash their hands before touching food, particularly after they have visited the lavatory (Figure 6). Hand-washing is also important after handling raw meat, particularly poultry (see page 250).

Figure 6   **Prevention of contamination.** Washing your hands after using the toilet reduces the chances of contaminating food or utensils.

Figure 7 Hygienic handling of food. A shop assistant avoids handling meat with her fingers.

Figure 8 Protection of food on display. The glass barrier stops customers from touching the food. It also helps to keep flies and air-borne droplets from coughs and sneezes away from the food.

Some people carry intestinal pathogens without showing any symptoms of disease. These people are called 'carriers'. Once identified, they should not be allowed to work in canteens or food-processing factories.

Houseflies must be prevented from carrying pathogens to food. There are four main ways to do this.

1 Keep all unwrapped food in fly-proof containers such as refrigerators or larders.
2 Enclose all food waste in fly-proof dustbins so that the flies cannot pick up bacteria.
3 Never leave human faeces where flies can reach them (if faeces cannot be flushed into the sewage system, they must be buried).
4 Destroy houseflies, wherever possible, in the places where they breed, such as rubbish tips and manure heaps.

Processing Cooking destroys any bacteria present in food. Refrigeration and freezing slow down or prevent bacterial reproduction. Dehydration, pickling, salting and canning are methods of preserving food. These processes destroy the bacteria which might cause disease. They also stop the food from going bad (see page 107).

Contagion

Prevention of the spread of tinea is described on page 256. The methods listed there apply equally well to any contagious disease other than those transmitted sexually.

Sexual transmission The best way to avoid sexually transmitted diseases is to avoid having sexual intercourse with an infected person. Unfortunately, infected people cannot easily be identified.

Clearly, if sexual intercourse is restricted to one partnership, neither partner will contract a sexually transmitted disease (provided both are free from infection in the first place). This is one good reason, among many others, for being faithful to one partner.

If this restriction is unacceptable, however, the risk of catching a sexually transmitted disease can be greatly reduced if the man uses a condom (page 176). This acts as a barrier to bacteria or viruses.

If a person suspects that he or she has caught a sexually transmitted disease, treatment must be sought at once. Information about treatment can be obtained by phoning one of the numbers listed under 'Venereal disease' in the telephone directory. Treatment is always confidential. The patients must, however, ensure that anyone with whom they have had sexual contact also gets treatment. There is no point in one partner being cured if the other is still infected.

Immunization

In the course of an infectious disease, the patient makes antibodies to the pathogen. The antibodies to some diseases remain in the blood for a long time. Others can be produced again very rapidly. So a pathogen which gets into the body for the second time is quickly destroyed. The person is said to be **immune** to that disease. Immunity may last for a few

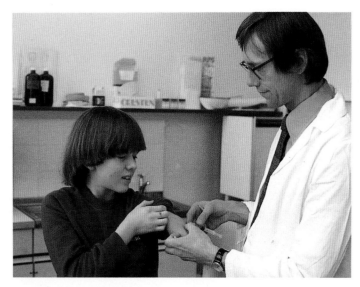

Figure 9   Immunization. The girl is being immunized against rubella (German measles).

months or for many years, depending on the disease (see also page 134).

Not all diseases produce immunity. There seems to be no immunity to syphilis or gonorrhoea.

You can acquire immunity to some diseases without actually catching them. One way is to be injected with a harmless form of the pathogen or its toxin (page 134). This makes your body produce the antibody, without suffering the symptoms of the disease. Then if the real pathogens enter your body, you have the antibodies ready to attack them. You have been immunized against that disease.

The substance with which you are injected is called a **vaccine**. The vaccine against whooping cough consists of the killed bacteria. The dead bacteria cannot cause the disease, but they do stimulate the antibody reaction. The vaccines for diphtheria and tetanus are the toxins extracted from the bacteria and made harmless by heat or chemicals. The BCG vaccine against tuberculosis consists of a harmless form of bacteria closely related to the TB bacteria. The polio vaccine is a harmless form of the virus and can be taken by mouth.

You were probably immunized against diphtheria, polio, tetanus, whooping cough and measles during your first five years, and against tuberculosis between 10 and 13 years. Girls are usually immunized against rubella (Figure 9). In future, babies can receive a combined inoculation against measles, mumps and rubella (MMR) at 18 months. This will replace the measles vaccination at 15 months and the later rubella inoculation.

There is a small risk of serious side-effects from vaccines, just as there is with all medicines. These risks are always far lower than the risk of catching the disease itself. For example, the measles vaccine carries a risk of 1 in 87 000 of causing encephalitis (inflammation of the brain). This is much less than the risk of getting encephalitis as a result of catching measles. Also, the vaccines themselves are becoming much safer, and the risk of side-effects is now almost nil.

Routine immunization not only protects the individual but also prevents the spread of infectious disease. Diseases like diphtheria and whooping cough were once common, and are now quite rare. This is the result of improved social conditions and routine immunization. Smallpox was completely wiped out throughout the world by a World Health Organization programme of immunization between 1959 and 1980.

Disinfectants and antiseptics

These are chemicals which destroy bacteria. They are poisons which can destroy living cells and so must be used with care. An antiseptic differs from a disinfectant in that it can be used on the skin.

Doctors and surgeons put antiseptics on to the skin to kill all the bacteria present before making an incision. However, antiseptics should not be used routinely or for treating minor cuts. One reason is that the antiseptics destroy the harmless bacteria that normally keep pathogens at bay. Another is that the chemicals damage healthy tissues and slow down the healing process.

Figure 10   Disinfectants. A strong disinfectant is used to destroy bacteria that may be present in a lavatory.

Figure 11   Disinfectants. A mild disinfectant is used to sterilize the teat of a baby's feeding bottle.

Soap is a mild, safe antiseptic.

Disinfectants such as sodium chlorate(I) (hypochlorite), which is in 'Domestos' and similar 'bleaches', are used to destroy bacteria in drains and lavatories, and on the walls, floors and working surfaces of canteens and kitchens (Figure 10). Milder disinfectants are used to sterilize utensils or containers such as babies' feeding bottles, or soiled clothing such as babies' nappies (Figure 11).

Drug therapy

Drugs cure diseases rather than prevent them. But if a drug cures a disease before the infectious period is over, it might help to reduce the spread of that disease.

Although drugs play a valuable part in keeping us healthy, many people have come to rely on them for trivial ailments. Many diseases are self-limiting – the patient will get better quite quickly without using drugs. However, when some people consult a doctor, they may feel cheated if medicine of some kind or other is not prescribed. In addition, high-pressure advertising gives the idea that headaches, coughs and colds, indigestion and other minor complaints can be relieved by taking patent medicines. In some cases this may be true. But many of these conditions will get better anyway.

There are fewer effective drugs against viruses than against bacteria. This is because the virus is so closely involved in its host cell's physiology that any chemical that harms the virus will also harm the cell.

Antibiotics The ideal drug for curing disease would be a chemical that destroyed the pathogen without harming the tissues of the host. In practice, modern antibiotics such as penicillin come pretty close to this ideal, for bacterial infections. Antibiotics seem to interfere with chemical processes in the bacterial cell wall and so cause it to break down. Since these processes do not occur in animal cells, the host tissues are unaffected. Nevertheless, many antibiotics cause some side-effects, such as allergic reactions in some people.

Not all bacteria are killed by antibiotics. Some bacteria have a nasty habit of mutating to forms which are resistant to these drugs. For this reason it is important not to use antibiotics in a diluted form, for too short a period or for trivial complaints. These practices lead to a build-up of a resistant population of bacteria. The drug resistance can be passed from harmless bacteria to pathogens.

QUESTIONS

6 How might a harmful bacterium be destroyed or removed by the body if it arrived (a) on the cornea, (b) on the hand, (c) in a bronchus, (d) in the stomach?

7 After a disaster such as an earthquake, the survivors are urged to boil all drinking-water. Why do you think this is so?

8 Revise pages 134-5. Now explain why immunization against diphtheria does not protect you against polio as well.

9 Even if there have been no cases of diphtheria in a country for many years, children may still be immunized against it. What do you think is the point of this?

10 State which of the following measures might be effective in stopping the spread of *Salmonella* food poisoning: (a) using disinfectants, (b) killing mosquitoes, (c) immunization, (d) washing the hands, (e) boiling the drinking-water, (f) genetic counselling, (g) killing houseflies.

CHECK LIST

- Transmissible diseases are infections caused by viruses, bacteria, fungi or protozoa.
- Non-transmissible diseases may be inherited, or acquired during the lifetime.
- Infectious diseases may be transmitted by air, water, food or contact.
- Sexually transmitted diseases are caught during sexual intercourse with an infected person.
- Water-borne diseases are controlled by sewage treatment and water purification.
- Food-borne diseases are controlled by (a) hygienic handling, (b) wrapping or covering, (c) preservation and processing, (d) control of houseflies.
- Sexually transmitted diseases can be prevented by avoiding sexual contact with infected people.
- A vaccine stimulates the blood system to produce antibodies against a disease, without causing the disease itself.
- The presence of antibodies in the blood, or the ability to produce them rapidly, gives immunity to a disease.
- Systematic immunization can protect whole populations.
- Antibiotics are very effective against disease bacteria. But bacteria can become resistant if the antibiotics are used unwisely.

27

Personal Health

Diet; Exercise; Smoking

Mood-influencing Drugs
Tolerance and dependence. Stimulants. Alcohol.
Analgesics. Hallucinogens.

Solvent Misuse
'Gluc-sniffing'.

Mental Health and Mental Illness
Psychosis, neurosis and personality disorders.

Health is not merely the absence of disease but a state of physical and mental well-being. However, you are not usually aware of your state of health until you are unwell. Therefore you may need to make a conscious effort to maintain good health.

The general rules for health are:

Do   eat a balanced diet
       take regular vigorous exercise
       develop a positive attitude to life

Don't   smoke
       drink too much
       misuse drugs.

If you feel this recipe for health is 'boring', ask yourself whether being fat, having bronchitis, craving drugs and alcohol, and looking forward to premature heart failure are likely to make you happy and content.

You may know middle-aged or elderly people who claim to have smoked, got drunk, over-eaten and taken no exercise all their lives, and still remain healthy. You will also have heard of fit people who exercise regularly and do not smoke but die suddenly from a heart attack.

These stories prove nothing. We inherit part of our 'constitution' from our parents. So some people are more able than others to resist disease and to ill-use their bodies. You can do nothing about your genes, but you can do a lot to make the best of the constitution you have inherited.

You can find physiological reasons for some of the 'Do's and Don'ts' listed above in Section 3 of this book ('Human Physiology'). This chapter will refer to them only briefly.

In some cases, such as smoking and drug abuse, there is overwhelming evidence to support the advice. In others, such as diet and exercise, the evidence is less strong, but the advice given represents most expert opinion.

Diet

To remain healthy, you must eat enough food to meet all your energy requirements. It must contain protein and fat to make new cells. You also need vitamins and salts (see pages 100–106).

A healthy diet should contain only a little salt and refined sugar (if any) and a low proportion of fat. The diet also needs to include plenty of vegetable fibre. A low fat intake may help reduce the chances of atherosclerosis and coronary heart disease (page 138). A high fibre intake probably helps to prevent diseases of the large intestine.

In some people, over-eating can led to obesity with its attendant problems (such as high blood pressure and diabetes).

A healthy digestive system also depends on regular meals eaten in a relaxed atmosphere. Hasty snacks and irregular heavy meals can lead to digestive disorders.

The health aspects of diet are discussed more fully on pages 100–106.

Figure 1   Some components of a healthy diet

Mood-influencing Drugs

Any substance used in medicine to help our bodies fight illness or disease is called a **drug**. One group of drugs helps to control pain and ease feelings of distress. These are the mood-influencing drugs.

Things that happen to you make you feel excited, depressed, anxious or angry. All these feelings must arise from changes taking place in your nervous and endocrine systems (page 214). When the chemical substance adrenalin (page 214) is released into your blood, it makes you feel tense and anxious or excited. In a similar way, chemicals produced by nerve endings in your brain are thought to give rise to most of your emotional feelings.

It is not always easy to be sure which is cause and which is effect. Feelings of anxiety may cause the production of adrenalin. Or adrenalin may cause feelings of anxiety. But we do know that swallowing or injecting certain substances can give rise to distinct changes of mood. It is often not known how these substances produce their effect. Even the method of action of alcohol, one of the oldest known mood-influencing drugs, is not understood.

If these drugs are used wisely and under medical supervision, they can be very helpful. A person who feels depressed to the point of wanting to commit suicide may be able to lead a normal life with the aid of an anti-depressant drug which removes the feeling of depression. However, if drugs are used for trivial reasons, to produce feelings of excitement or calm, they may be extremely dangerous. This is because they can cause **tolerance** and **dependence**.

Tolerance

This means that if the substance is taken over a long period, the dosage has to keep increasing in order to have the same effect. People who take sleeping pills containing barbiturates may need to increase the dose from one to two or three tablets in order to get to sleep. People who drink alcohol in order to relieve anxiety may find that they have to keep drinking more and more before they feel relaxed. If the dosage continues to increase it will become so large that it causes death.

Dependence

This is the term used to describe the condition in which the user cannot do without the substance.

Sometimes a distinction is made between emotional and physical dependence, though the distinction is not always clear. A person with emotional dependence may feel a craving for the substance, may be bad-tempered, anxious or depressed without it, and may commit crimes in order to obtain it. Cigarette-smoking is one example of emotional dependence.

Figure 2   Exercise. Regular exercise contributes to good health.

Exercise

Exercise increases stamina, improves flexibility, makes muscles stronger and more efficient, and helps to keep your weight down. Exercise may also reduce your chance of a premature coronary heart attack, though the evidence is not clear-cut.

Most people agree that exercise makes you 'feel good'. But to enjoy the benefits, you need to take exercise throughout your life.

Exercise is discussed in more detail on pages 188–9.

Smoking

There is a long list of diseases associated with smoking. It includes lung cancer, bronchitis, emphysema, arterial disease, stomach ulcers and bladder cancer.

This does not mean that all smokers will develop these diseases. But the chances of their doing so are far higher than they are for non-smokers.

See pages 138–9 and 148–9 for more detail.

QUESTIONS

1 List the features of your diet over the last two days which might be considered to make it (a) healthy, (b) unhealthy.
2 List the forms of exercise which you normally take during a school week. Which of these would you class as 'vigorous'?

Physical dependence involves the same experiences. But there are also physical symptoms, called **withdrawal symptoms**, when the substance is withheld. These may be nausea, vomiting, diarrhoea, muscular pain, uncontrollable shaking and hallucinations. Physical dependence is sometimes called **addiction**.

Not everyone who takes a mood-influencing drug develops tolerance or becomes dependent on it. Millions of people can take alcoholic drinks in moderation with no obvious physical or mental damage. Those who become dependent cannot drink in moderation. Their bodies seem to develop a need for permanently high levels of alcohol and dependent people (**alcoholics**) get withdrawal symptoms if they do not drink.

Physical and emotional dependence are very distressing states. Getting hold of the substance becomes the centre of the addicts' lives, and they lose interest in their personal appearance, their jobs and their families. Because the substances they need cannot be obtained legally or because they need the money to buy them, they turn to crime. Cures are slow, difficult and usually unpleasant.

There is no way of telling in advance which person will become dependent and which will not. Dependence is much more likely with some drugs than with others, however. These are, therefore, prescribed with great caution. Experimenting with drugs for the sake of emotional excitement is extremely unwise. Some people may become dependent on almost any substance which gives them a conscious sensation.

Some of the mood-influencing drugs will now be considered.

Stimulants

Caffeine   This is the active substance present in tea, coffee and cocoa. It acts on the nervous system: it makes you wakeful and reduces feelings of tiredness. In moderation, it does not seem to have harmful effects or to build up tolerance. Too much caffeine, however, may cause tension and anxiety, hand-tremor, over-excitability and sleeplessness. Some people are probably emotionally dependent on tea- and coffee-drinking.

Amphetamines   Drugs in this class make people feel alert and they reduce fatigue. Often they increase confidence, but they also cause a reduction of accuracy. They increase the heart rate and give a sensation of excitement but this is followed by feelings of depression. Unlike caffeine, the users can become both tolerant of and dependent on amphetamines. At one time they were used to relieve depression. But their value for this is now doubtful and there are better drugs for this condition.

Amphetamines can cause dangerously high blood pressure if taken by athletes who are trying to improve performance. Also they are quite useless for

helping examination candidates because although they increase confidence, they also reduce accuracy.

Cocaine   This is extracted from the leaves of the coca plant, which grows in South America. Natives of this region chew the leaves which are said to give them relief from fatigue and hunger. The drug also produces dependence. Pure cocaine, taken as snuff or eaten, gives a temporary feeling of excitement, followed by depression and listlessness. Prolonged use constricts the arteries and causes mental disorders.

Cocaine was once used as a local anaesthetic but it has now been replaced by less poisonous compounds.

Alcohol

The alcohol (ethanol) in wines, beer and spirits is a **depressant** of the central nervous system. Small amounts give a sense of well-being, with a release from anxiety. However, this is accompanied by a fall-off in performance in any activity requiring skill. It also gives a misleading sense of confidence, even though in fact one's judgment is clouded. The drunken driver usually thinks he or she is driving very well.

Even a small amount of alcohol in the blood increases our reaction time (the interval between receiving a stimulus and making a response). In some people, the reaction time is doubled even when the alcohol in the blood is well below the legal limit laid down for car drivers (Figure 3). This can make a big difference in the time needed for a driver to apply the brakes after seeing a hazard such as a child running into the road.

Alcohol causes vaso-dilation in the skin, giving a sense of warmth but in fact leading to a greater loss of body heat (see page 162). A concentration of 500 mg of alcohol in 100 cm^3 of blood results in unconsciousness. More than this will kill, by stopping the action of the breathing centre in the brain.

Some people build up a tolerance to alcohol. This may lead to both emotional and physical dependence (alcoholism).

High doses of alcohol can cause the liver cells to form too many fat droplets, leading to the disease called **cirrhosis**. A cirrhotic liver is less able to stop poisonous substances in the intestinal blood from reaching the general circulation (see page 120).

Pregnancy   Alcohol can cross the placenta and damage the foetus. Pregnant women who take as little as one alcoholic drink a day are at risk of having babies with lower than average birth weights. These under-weight babies are more likely to become ill.

Heavy drinking during pregnancy can lead to deformed babies. All levels of drinking are thought to increase the risk of miscarriage.

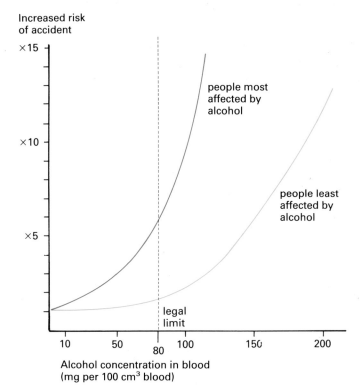

Figure 3   Increased risk of accidents after drinking alcohol. People vary in their reactions to alcohol. Body weight, for example, makes a difference.

Figure 4   Alcohol content of drinks. All these drinks contain the same amount of alcohol. Although the alcohol is more dilute in the beer than in the whisky, it has the same effect on the body.

Behaviour   Alcohol reduces inhibitions, because it depresses that part of the brain which causes shyness. This may be considered an advantage in 'breaking the ice' at parties. But it can also lead to irresponsible behaviour such as vandalism and aggression.

There has been a great increase in drinking by young people, including those under the legal age. In 1984, the under-21 age group contributed to 25 per cent of drink-related offences, compared with 8 per cent in the 1950s. Between 1982 and 1985, drink-related offences in 16-year-olds increased by 47 per cent, offences by 15-year-olds went up by 63 per cent and those by 14-year-olds by 138 per cent.

Moderate drinking   A moderate intake of alcoholic drink seems to do little physiological harm (except in pregnant women). But what is a 'moderate' intake?

Figure 4 shows a variety of drinks which all contain the same amount of alcohol. Beer is a fairly dilute form of alcohol. Whisky, however, is about 40 per cent alcohol. Even so, half a pint of beer contains the same amount of alcohol as a single whisky. This amount of alcohol can be called a 'unit'. It is the number of units of alcohol, not the type of drink, which has a physiological effect on the body. The liver can metabolize one unit of alcohol per hour. Taking more than this, over a long period, can cause liver damage.

Table 1 shows the possible effect of a weekly intake of different amounts of alcohol.

Analgesics

Analgesics are drugs which relieve pain. Although the cause of pain may start in the body, the feeling of pain occurs in the brain. Depressants such as alcohol and barbiturates have analgesic effects because they alter the brain's reaction to pain.

Table 1   Effects of weekly intake of alcohol

Units per week		Possible effects
Men	Women	
20	13	Probably no long-term harm (except for pregnant women) if drinking spread out over the week.
21–36	14–24	Probably no long-term effect if drinking spread evenly, but bouts of drunkenness increase the risk of accidents and unsociable behaviour.
37–50	25–35	For some people, this may be the level at which physiological and behavioural damage begins.
51–95	36–63	An unsafe level of drinking. Disorders of the liver and stomach may occur, and mental processes can be affected.
96+	64+	Probably permanent damage to liver, brain and nervous system. Probably dependent (alcoholic).

Aspirin This is a mild analgesic, particularly useful for relief of pain resulting from inflammation of tissues. It is also used to lower the body temperature during a fever. The side-effects with small irregular doses are mild but about 1 in 15 of aspirin users suffer from indigestion, irritation and possibly bleeding of the stomach lining if they take aspirin frequently.

Tolerance and dependence do not seem to be serious problems for most users. World consumption of aspirin is thousands of tonnes per year.

Young children should not be given aspirin. It can cause serious side-effects, including liver damage, in some cases.

Paracetamol and phenacetin are mild analgesics which do not cause indigestion or gastric bleeding. Phenacetin has been suspected of causing serious kidney disorders, however.

Narcotic analgesics Morphine, codeine and heroin are narcotics made from opium. Morphine and heroin relieve severe pain and produce short-lived feelings of well-being and freedom from anxiety. They can both lead to tolerance and physical dependence within weeks, and so they are prescribed with caution.

The illegal use of heroin has terrible effects on the unfortunate addict. The overwhelming dependence on the drug leads many addicts into prostitution and crime in order to obtain the money to buy it. There are severe withdrawal symptoms and a 'cure' is a long and often unsuccessful process.

An additional hazard is the blood poisoning, hepatitis and AIDS that may result from the use of unsterilized needles when injecting the drug.

Codeine is a less effective analgesic than morphine, but does not lead to dependence so easily. It is still addictive if used in large enough doses.

Tranquillizers These substances are used to relieve tension and anxiety, or in some cases as sleeping pills. They do not usually lead to tolerance and dependence, as long as they are used for short periods only.

Some tranquillizers have been extremely valuable in treating severe mental illnesses such as schizophrenia and mania. Many thousands of mental patients have been enabled to leave hospital and live normal lives as a result of using the tranquillizing drug **chlorpromazine**.

Nowadays, tranquillizers are being prescribed in their millions for the relief of anxiety and tension. Some people think that these drugs are being used merely to escape everyday stresses that could be overcome by a little more will-power and determination. Others think that there is no reason why people should suffer the distress of acute anxiety when drugs are available for its relief. On the other hand, some degree of anxiety is probably needed for mental and physical activity. These activities are unlikely to be very effective in people who tranquillize themselves into apathy every time a problem crops up.

Hallucinogens

Cannabis and other extracts of Indian hemp are chewed or smoked to produce a sense of well-being, detachment and sometimes hallucinations. There does not seem to be much evidence of tolerance or emotional and physical dependence. But unstable individuals looking for more 'exciting' experiences are thought to be likely to move on from cannabis to the 'hard drugs' such as morphine and heroin. Cannabis has little medical value.

Very little is known about the possible harmful effects of smoking cannabis. This is because there have been few long-term studies of regular cannabis-smokers. Experiments on animals suggest the possibility of brain damage, changes in hormone levels and in the structure of the ovaries and sperms (including human sperms), failed pregnancies and lung irritation. In humans there is evidence that products from cannabis-smoking remain in the body for a long time. It is generally accepted that smoking cannabis has a harmful effect on short-term memory and reaction time.

It has taken a great many years of careful study and scientific research to collect the evidence which now shows tobacco smoke to be so harmful. It would be irresponsible to legalize the smoking of another substance which might, after the same intensive study, turn out to be just as harmful.

LSD This substance (lysergic acid) has little medical use. It has been studied because it can cause symptoms similar to the mental disorder called schizophrenia.

The sensations after taking LSD vary from one person to another. Some people report feelings of happiness and heightened awareness, visual distortions and hallucinations. Others experience fearfulness, depression and terrifying illusions. Some individuals commit violent and pointless acts when the drug is active. Some experience the terrifying symptoms at intervals long after the initial dose has worn off. The possible benefits of new sensations are greatly outweighed by the chance of short- or long-term mental damage.

Solvent Misuse

Solvent misuse or 'glue-sniffing' is the inhaling of vapours from various organic solvents (not only glue) in order to become intoxicated. The vapours produce effects similar to drunkenness, but they are more intense and last for only a few minutes. They include dizziness and stupor, followed by a loss of co-ordination and control and eventually by unconsciousness.

The short-term after-effects are headache, nausea, vomiting and, in some cases, convulsions. After-effects which last for several weeks include runny nose, bloodshot eyes, an acne-like rash round the mouth, irritability, lethargy and depression. In the long term, the liver and kidneys may be damaged.

The number of deaths resulting from solvent misuse has been increasing steadily in the last few years. It is estimated that 39 people died in the United Kingdom in 1981, 62 in 1982 and 117 in 1985. Death may result from (1) accidents while the person is intoxicated and out of control, (2) suffocation by the plastic bag used for inhaling, (3) choking on vomit while unconscious and (4) toxic effects of the solvent.

Solvent misusers are mostly adolescents of 14 or 15 years old. They may experiment with 'glue-sniffing' as a form of rebellion against authority, to 'keep in' with their friends, to relieve boredom or for 'kicks' (risk-taking for the sake of a thrill). These reasons can, of course, be motives for other forms of drug misuse and destructive behaviour.

It is not clear whether solvent misuse leads to tolerance and dependence. Most 'glue-sniffers' do not continue once they are old enough to buy alcoholic drinks. But they are likely to drink too much, and to be tempted to move on to other drugs.

QUESTIONS

3 What is the difference between (a) becoming tolerant of a drug and (b) becoming dependent on a drug? Which of these do you think is meant by being 'hooked' on a drug?
4 Why are amphetamine stimulants unsuitable for improving performance in (a) athletics, (b) examinations?
5 Why should drinking alcohol make you 'feel' warm, but cause you to lose heat?
6 Why is it dangerous to take alcoholic drinks before driving?
7 If morphine and heroin make addicts 'feel good', why can't they keep taking steady low doses to stay in this 'happy' state?
8 What is the long-term danger of taking LSD? (Ignore its immediate effects.)

Mental Health and Mental Illness

When you are physically well, you don't usually spend much time thinking about it. Similarly, you are unlikely to give much thought to your mental health as a rule. Physical and mental health are closely inter-related. Physical illness may cause mental symptoms, and mental illness often gives rise to physical symptoms.

Mental illness is quite different from mental handicap. Mental handicap may arise from defective brain development which is either inherited or caused by damage to the foetus. It may be the result of Down's syndrome, untreated PKU or rubella. Mental handicap can also result from brain damage due to an injury or to complications of meningitis, measles or whooping cough.

Mental illness is usually recognized by a person's abnormal behaviour. It is almost impossible to say what is meant by 'normal' behaviour, so it is even more difficult to define abnormal behaviour. It may lie anywhere between mere oddity to obvious insanity. People should not be classed as 'abnormal' simply because they do not conform to the particular social, moral or political customs of the society in which they live.

Mental illnesses are usually classified into psychoses, neuroses and personality disorders. There are no hard and fast boundaries between these categories, however.

Psychosis

Psychotic people are out of touch with reality. They may have a view of the world and themselves which is quite unreasonable (irrational). For example, they may have delusions about their own importance or believe that everyone is plotting against them. There is no obvious external cause of a psychosis. It seems to arise from some fault in the chemical processes in the brain.

Schizophrenia is a psychosis. It is, in fact, a group of related symptoms which probably have a variety of causes, rather than a single illness. Schizophrenics may feel separated from their own bodies. Some have delusions about who they are, or believe themselves to be persecuted by imaginary people. Many hear 'voices' of people who are not there, a symptom known as 'auditory hallucinations'.

Because schizophrenia is caused by faulty chemistry in the brain, some forms of it can be treated with drugs. The drug chlorpromazine and similar compounds have enabled many schizophrenics to live in society rather than in a mental hospital. Schizophrenics can be difficult to live with but do not usually harm other people.

Neurosis

Neuroses are usually brought on by external events such as stress. Almost anyone may develop a neurosis, though some people are much more liable to do so than others. Neurotic people are not irrational like psychotics. But their emotional responses to stress may be out of proportion. For example, they may weep frequently, or refuse to get out of bed and 'face the world'. A neurosis often gives rise to physical symptoms.

Anxiety   Some degree of anxiety probably helps to keep us 'on our toes' and make us give of our best. Persistent anxiety, however, is a neurosis. It is usually accompanied by physical symptoms such as digestive disturbance, sleeplessness, loss of sexual drive, asthmatic attacks or even paralysis. Since these symptoms are often not recognized as having a mental cause, they make the anxiety state worse.

A neurotic person's reasoning powers are unaffected. So once the patient understands the causes of the symptoms, the condition may be relieved. However, some people with anxiety neurosis need to be treated with tranquillizers or by psychotherapy.

Phobias are examples of anxiety neuroses. A phobia is an abnormal fear of something. For example, claustrophobia is an irrational fear of enclosed spaces.

Depression   Most of us get 'fed up' from time to time, but a depressive person remains unhappy for long periods without any obvious reason. Even if the depression is caused at first by some external event, depressives seem unable to do anything about it. They may lose their appetite and lose weight, and often sleep badly.

Although there may be external events which bring on an attack of depression, the patient probably stays depressed because of a disturbance in the brain's activity. So it is pointless to tell a depressive to 'snap out of it', without offering some form of treatment.

Anti-depressant drugs can help some people with depression.

Post-natal depression   Many mothers feel depressed for a few days after giving birth. This may be due to an imbalance of hormones after the birth or to interrupted sleep. Only if the depression persists is it regarded as post-natal depression and as needing treatment.

Personality disorder

People with personality disorders cannot adjust to the needs of society or form lasting personal relationships. Of course, not everyone who fails to conform to the social customs of the day has a personality disorder. This description is kept for people who are persistently disruptive or aggressive for no obvious reason. A person with a personality disorder usually has no concern at all for other people.

In its extreme form the behaviour may become psychopathic. A **psychopath** is often a criminal who feels compelled to destroy things or hurt people, and who takes pleasure in doing so.

Mental health

We are all so different in our personalities and temperaments that it is not easy to suggest a formula for maintaining mental health. A situation that might cause neurosis in one person will leave another person quite unaffected. However, there are one or two guidelines, though they might strike you as obvious.

Physical health   If you are physically fit, you may have less chance of developing a mental illness.

Stable family life   A person's experiences in the first years of a life have a profound effect on his or her mental health. A child from a stable home, looked after by affectionate, caring parents (or other adults), is likely to be mentally stable and able to resist everyday stresses.

A child from a home where there is emotional strife, constant bickering or violence is at more risk of developing a personality disorder in later life.

Adequate sleep and relaxation   Prolonged lack of sleep may cause neurosis. The occasional late night seems to do little harm. A series of late nights might impair performance during the day but, on its own, is unlikely to lead to neurosis. It is more likely that anxiety will lead to insomnia (inability to sleep), and insomnia may contribute to anxiety neurosis.

Overwork can contribute to neurosis. No matter how conscientious you are, it is a good idea to have a break from work and a change of environment from time to time, and to relax both mentally and physically.

QUESTIONS

9 What is the difference between (a) mental illness and mental handicap, (b) a psychosis and a neurosis?

10 Apart from the guidelines given above, what other aspects of life do you think might contribute to good mental health?

CHECK LIST

- A good diet and regular exercise contribute to good health.
- Smoking and excessive drinking contribute to ill-health.
- Mood-influencing drugs may be useful for treating certain illnesses but are dangerous if used for other purposes.
- Tolerance means that the body needs more and more of a particular drug to produce the same effect.
- Dependence means that a person cannot do without a particular drug.
- Withdrawal symptoms are unpleasant physical effects experienced by an addict when the drug is not taken.

- Alcohol is a depressant drug which slows down reaction time and reduces inhibitions.
- Alcohol in a mother's blood can damage her foetus.
- Heroin and morphine are strongly addictive drugs.
- Solvent sniffing produces intoxication and has caused a number of deaths.

- A psychosis is a mental illness in which the sufferer is out of touch with reality.
- A neurosis is a mental illness which may be brought about (in susceptible people) by stress and over-anxiety.

Do not write on this page. Where necessary copy drawings, tables or sentences.

Section 5 Health and Disease

1 In an experiment small pieces of cooked meat were placed in two test-tubes. A small amount of water was added to each tube. Test-tube A was boiled vigorously for a few minutes and then sealed. Test-tube B was not heated and it was left open to the atmosphere. Both tubes were placed in a warm place.

Describe the appearance you would expect the contents of each tube to have several days later. (S1)

2 (a) (i) Why is it important that water supplied for drinking does not contain metals such as lead?

(ii) Suggest why water from a deep well is cheaper to purify for drinking than water from a lake or river.

(iii) Chlorine is added to drinking water. Explain why this is done.

(b) (i) Give one reason why the treatment of sewage is essential for the health of a community.

(ii) In the treatment of sewage solid organic matter (sludge) remains after settlement. This sludge is then treated with anaerobic organisms. Briefly give two reasons why sludge is treated in this way. (S1)

3 (a) Explain what is meant by active immunity to disease.

(b) How can active immunity to tuberculosis be acquired?

(c) In what way does a vaccine differ from an antiserum?

(d) Give an account of the ways by which the body is protected against disease-causing organisms, other than by immunity. (M3)

4 (a) Why should pipes carrying drinking water be made of copper or plastic rather than of lead?

(b) Describe briefly why it is important to have a piped supply of water.

(c) Name *three* stages in the purification of water and state what happens at each stage. (M2)

5 Distinguish between the items in each of the following pairs.

(a) The use of penicillin and aspirin in medicine.

(b) Mental illness and mental handicap.

(c) Insect vectors and insect pests. (L1)

6 The graph shows the amount of alcohol in the blood of a person over a period of several hours after taking a drink of alcohol.

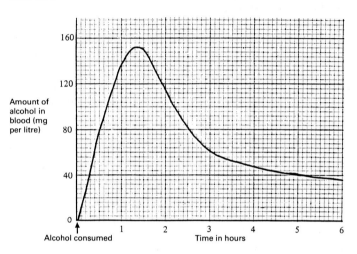

(a) The maximum legal limit for the amount of alcohol in the blood is 80 mg per litre.

(i) Between what times would it be illegal to drive?

(ii) How does alcohol affect a person's ability to drive?

(b) (i) Which organ in the body removes alcohol from the blood?

(ii) What effects may excessive intake of alcohol have on this organ?

Describe *two* other undesirable effects of alcoholism. (N2Q)

7 (a) Explain how each of the following helps to defend the body.

(i) Hydrochloric acid in the stomach.

(ii) The epidermis of the skin.

(iii) The lining of the air passages.

(b) Explain what is meant by each of the terms *antigen* and *antibody*. (S1)

8 *Either*

(a) Describe the harm that may be caused by smoking.

(b) Suggest ways of discouraging smoking.

Or

(a) Describe the harm that may be caused by the misuse of drugs.

(b) What can society do to reduce the problem of drug misuse? (L3)

9 Some people attempt to deal with problems such as stress by regularly taking drugs such as aspirin. Suggest *two* possible dangers of doing this. (S1)

Appendix 1

First Aid and
Emergency Treatment

Objectives

The objects of first aid are to save life, and to prevent an injured person's condition getting any worse while waiting for expert medical help.

Attempts by an unskilled person to treat an injury may do more harm than good. For example, trying to move an injured person or clumsy attempts to put a splint on a broken limb may cause additional damage. On the other hand a very simple, common-sense act may save a person's life. Simply turning an unconscious person on his side may save his life by keeping his mouth and windpipe clear.

Priorities

Non-medical priorities

If you are the first or only person at the scene of an accident you will need to make decisions about what to do first.

Your first action may have nothing to do with 'first aid'. In a road accident, the most important action may be to try and stop oncoming traffic, in order to prevent other vehicles from being involved. If other people are present, your first act might be to send someone to get help while you attend to the injured people. If you are the only able-bodied person present, you should not go for help until you have at least opened the airways (see Figure 2b) of unconscious casualties.

Medical priorities

If there are several injured people, you must decide who to treat first. People who are standing or sitting up, crying out with pain or fright, are certainly conscious and breathing and unlikely to be in immediate danger unless they are bleeding profusely. A person who is lying still and silent is probably unconscious and may not be breathing. If you speak to him or her and there is no response or movement, the person is probably unconscious. This person must be examined first. There are four priorities.

1 Restore breathing.
2 Stop any bleeding.
3 Reduce the effects of shock.
4 Do not leave an unconscious person lying on his or her back.

1 Restore breathing If a person is not breathing, the heart may still be beating but the blood it is pumping to the brain will be deoxygenated (page 126). If the brain cells are deprived of oxygen for more than four minutes they die. Since brain cells cannot be replaced, this will result in permanent brain damage even if the person survives. It is important to restore breathing at once by the method of mouth-to-mouth resuscitation, as described on page 278.

2 Stop any bleeding If the injured person is breathing, your next task is to look for any signs of bleeding. Small cuts and scratches are not likely to need urgent treatment. But if an artery or vein is cut, the casualty may lose blood rapidly and be in serious danger after only a few minutes. You may have to try and stop serious bleeding while still trying to restore the casualty's breathing. Resuscitation may take an hour or more, during which time the casualty could bleed to death if serious bleeding is not stopped.

3 Reduce the effects of shock 'Shock', in the medical sense, does not mean a fright but the drastic fall in blood pressure which often follows injury. This fall in blood pressure may cause death even if the injuries themselves are not fatal. As a first-aider, you cannot treat an injured person for shock but you can do much to prevent it getting worse.

4 Do not leave an unconscious person lying on his or her back In this position, the relaxed tongue, saliva, vomit or blood may block the windpipe and suffocate them. Turn the person very carefully on his side, as shown in Figure 1, pulling the jaw forward and tilting the head back so that the airway is clear and fluids can escape from the mouth. Apart from this, you should not move injured persons more than you can help.

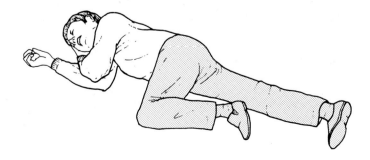

Figure 1   Recovery position

277

First Aid Techniques

Resuscitation

Your exhaled breath contains about 16 per cent oxygen. This is quite enough to oxygenate the casualty's blood. Turn the person carefully on to his back, tilt the head back as far as possible and pull the jaw forward, opening the mouth (Figure 2). This will open the windpipe. Open your mouth wide and place it over that of the casualty. Close his nostrils by pinching his nose with your fingers. Breathe air gently into the casualty's lungs till you see his chest rise.

If there is no chest movement, examine the mouth and pharynx and remove anything that may be blocking the air passage. Then tilt the casualty's head back again as far as possible, pull his jaw well forward and try again. Inflate his lungs about ten times per minute until he starts to breathe or until a doctor tells you to stop. When breathing is restored, turn the patient on his side as described in paragraph 4 above.

Stopping bleeding

Severe bleeding, with the blood flowing out rapidly, must be stopped at once by pressing with the fingers directly on the wound or pressing the edges of the wound together for at least ten minutes. There will be no time to search for sterile dressings or bandages. Make the person lie down. If the wound is in a limb, raise it (provided it is not broken). When the bleeding has slowed down press a pad of material over the wound and tie it firmly in place. If blood oozes through, apply more material on top of the original pad.

You may not be able to get the edges of the wound together if the tissues have been badly torn. In this case, if bleeding is severe, you must plug the wound with a dressing. The 'dressing' may have to be something like a vest or a shirt if you are not carrying a first aid kit. It is more important to stop the bleeding than to worry about infection. Rapid loss of blood may lead to death in as little time as 20 minutes or so and the casualty may not reach hospital alive. If the blood loss is stopped and the casualty gets to hospital, the medical staff will be able to treat any infection introduced by the dressing.

Reducing the effects of shock

Shock is a drop in blood pressure which may result from heart failure, loss of blood or poisoning. Blood may be lost from an external wound, or bleeding may be taking place internally and so not be noticed. At the site of a severe burn, there is a rapid seepage of blood plasma which can cause a fall in blood volume.

If the blood pressure falls, the brain does not work properly and does not send out the right impulses to the heart and circulatory system. As a result, the blood pressure falls even more. Unless the first-aider acts promptly, the victim may die.

The symptoms of shock are a rapid, weak pulse, cold, clammy skin and shallow, rapid breathing. In all cases of electric shock, drowning, burns and serious injury, treat the patient for shock.

Keep the casualty lying down. Raise the legs, if possible, to maintain the blood pressure in the brain. Do not give anything to drink and do not try to warm the casualty. Loosen any tight clothing round the

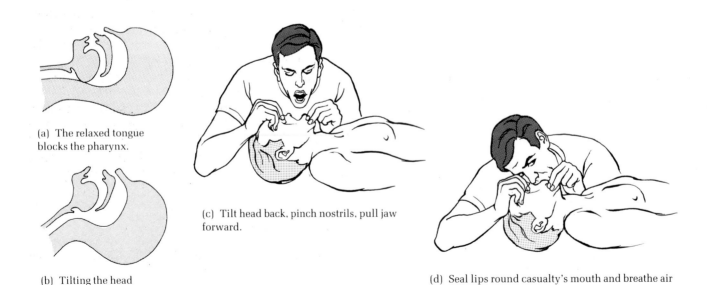

(a) The relaxed tongue blocks the pharynx.

(b) Tilting the head back creates an airway.

(c) Tilt head back, pinch nostrils, pull jaw forward.

(d) Seal lips round casualty's mouth and breathe air into his lungs.

Figure 2 Mouth-to-mouth resuscitation

neck, chest and waist. Do not move the casualty more than absolutely necessary for his or her safety.

The treatment for shock is to restore the blood volume by transfusing blood (page 136) or plasma, so the casualty must be sent to hospital as soon as possible.

Electric shock

A severe electric shock will cause loss of consciousness. On no account should you touch or even go close to an unconscious person who is likely to be still in contact with an electrical supply, because the electricity passing through his body may reach you too. The current must first be switched off by you or somebody who has the necessary skill before touching the unconscious person.

It is likely that the casualty will not be breathing. If so, resuscitation must be started at once, together with precautions against shock and possiby treatment for burns.

Burns and scalds

A *burn* is caused by dry heat, such as a flame or hot object. A *scald* is caused by steam or boiling water. The treatment is the same for both except that, in the case of scalds, any wet clothing should be carefully removed, while burned clothing should be left in place. The treatment is to flood the burned or scalded area with clean, cold water for at least 10 minutes. A burned or scalded hand or arm should be immersed in running cold water.

Do not apply any ointments or lotions. Cover the injured area lightly with a clean, dry cloth to keep bacteria from falling on to the damaged tissue. Remember that shock is likely to result from burns which affect a large area of skin.

Fainting

This is caused by a temporary fall in the blood supply to the brain, sometimes brought on by emotional shock or long standing. Treat the casualty as if he or she were suffering from shock. Unless the unconsciousness was the result of injury or poisoning, there is no need for the person to go to hospital.

Drowning

A person pulled unconscious from the water may not be breathing. In this case, mouth-to-mouth resuscitation must be started at once, followed by efforts to reduce shock. Do not worry about water in the lungs. It is very difficult for water to get into the lungs and even if it does, the first-aider can do

nothing about it. Remember that the casualty is likely to be suffering from hypothermia (see page 162).

Accidental poisoning

If you have reason to suspect that a person, especially a child, has swallowed a harmful substance, ask at once what it was or get hold of a sample so that a suitable antidote can be prepared at the hospital. If the casualty is conscious, he can be given water or milk to drink, to dilute the poison. Do not give solutions of salt or any other mixture intended to induce vomiting. If the casualty is conscious and the poison is not corrosive (has not caused burns to the mouth and throat) get him to make himself vomit, by putting his finger to the back of his throat.

Fractures or dislocations

If a limb or joint is distorted, badly bruised or swollen and the casualty cannot move it, it is probably fractured or dislocated and needs expert attention. The limb should not be moved unless the casualty has to be moved to safety. In that case, support the limb by tying it to the casualty's body. For example, one leg may be tied to the other, or the arm to the chest.

Particles in the eye

'In the eye' really means 'on the cornea or sclera'. The eyes will water and the person will blink. These two actions may wash the particle into one corner of the eye or on to the lower lid. If the object is on the lower lid, in the corner of the eye or free to move on the sclera (white of the eye) it can usually be brushed gently away with the corner of a clean handkerchief or piece of cotton wool soaked in water. If this does not work, the casualty should put his or her face in a bowl of clean water and open and close the eyelids. The object will usually float away.

If the particle is on the cornea or if it appears to be embedded in the surface of the eye and does not move, or cannot be seen clearly, no attempt should be made to dislodge it. Persuade the casualty not to rub the eye. The eyelid should be kept closed and covered with a soft pad held lightly in place with a bandage, while the casualty is taken to a hospital or surgery.

Hypothermia

The causes of, and treatment for, this condition have been described on page 162.

Appendix 2   Keys for Identification

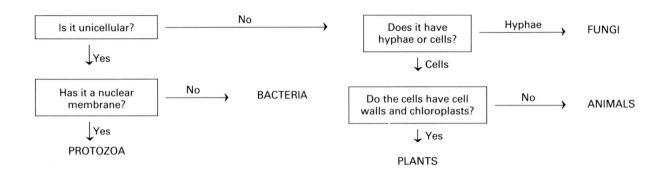

Figure 1   A simple key

Once you know the main characteristics of a group, you can draw up a systematic plan for identifying an unfamiliar organism. One such plan is shown in Figure 1.

An alternative form of key is the **dichotomous key**. 'Dichotomous' means 'two branches', so you meet with two possibilities at each stage.

Figure 2 is an example of a dichotomous key that could be used to place an unknown vertebrate in the correct class. Item 1 gives you a choice between two alternatives. If the animal is 'cold-blooded' you move to item 2 and make a further choice. If it is a 'warm-blooded' animal you move to item 4 for your next choice.

Figure 2   Dichotomous key for vertebrate classes

1 { 'Cold-blooded' → **2**
   { 'Warm-blooded' → **4**

2 { Has fins but no limbs → **fish**
   { Has 4 limbs → **3**

3 { Has no scales on body → **amphibian**
   { Has scales → **reptile**

4 { Has feathers → **bird**
   { Has fur → **mammal**

The same technique may be used for assigning an organism to its order, genus or species. However, the important features may not always be easy to see. You may have to make use of less fundamental characteristics.

In studies of polluted rivers, samples of aquatic invertebrates are taken. The types and abundance of these animals are often a guide to the degree of pollution. The key in Figure 3 is a means of sorting some of these creatures into their major groups (see Figure 4).

Figure 3   Key for some fresh-water invertebrates

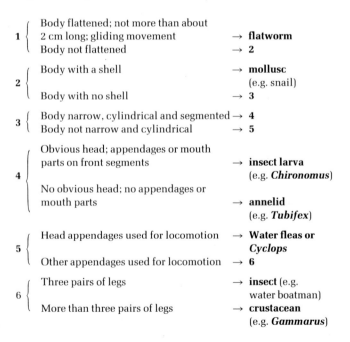

1 { Body flattened; not more than about 2 cm long; gliding movement → **flatworm**
   { Body not flattened → **2**

2 { Body with a shell → **mollusc** (e.g. snail)
   { Body with no shell → **3**

3 { Body narrow, cylindrical and segmented → **4**
   { Body not narrow and cylindrical → **5**

4 { Obvious head; appendages or mouth parts on front segments → **insect larva** (e.g. *Chironomus*)
   { No obvious head; no appendages or mouth parts → **annelid** (e.g. *Tubifex*)

5 { Head appendages used for locomotion → **Water fleas or Cyclops**
   { Other appendages used for locomotion → **6**

6 { Three pairs of legs → **insect** (e.g. water boatman)
   { More than three pairs of legs → **crustacean** (e.g. *Gammarus*)

The key is not based on the fundamental characteristics of the group. For example 'not more than 2 cm long' is not a feature of flatworms, but it is a useful guide to those flatworms that live in ponds. A key such as this is sometimes called an artificial key.

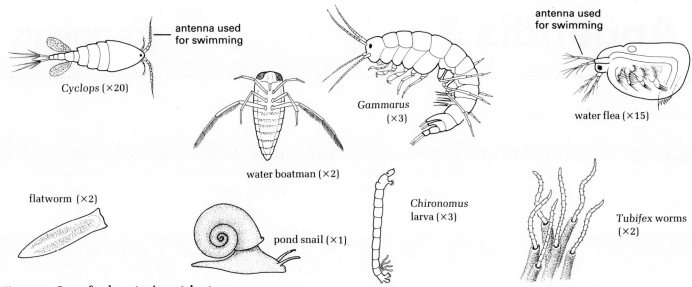

Figure 4   Some fresh-water invertebrates

QUESTION

Figure 14 on page 256 shows some protista. Using only the features shown in the drawings, construct a dichotomous key that could be used to identify these organisms.

Appendix 3

Reagents

Only teachers or technicians should prepare these.

Acetic orcein It is simplest to buy the concentrated solution (3.3% orcein in glacial acetic acid). Dilute 10 cm^3 with 12 cm^3 water just before use. The diluted stain does not keep.

Adenosine triphosphate Purchase 2 cm^3 ampoules from a supplier. (Expensive; over £20 for 5 ampoules. Store in a refrigerator.)

Albumen (1%) Use commercial albumen. It dissolves slowly in cold water. Do not stir or shake vigorously during preparation. Store in a refrigerator or make up fresh when needed.

Ammonia solution (2M) Dilute 11 cm^3 0.880 ammonia with 89 cm^3 water.

Benedict's solution Dissolve 170 g sodium citrate and 100 g sodium carbonate in 800 cm^3 distilled water. Add a solution of copper sulphate made from 17 g copper sulphate in 200 cm^3 distilled water.

Biuret test 10% sodium hydroxide; 1% copper sulphate.

Cobalt chloride paper Dissilve 1 g cobalt chloride in 20 cm^3 distilled water. Soak filter paper in the solution and allow to dry.

Egg-white suspension See **Albumen**.

Ethanoic (acetic) acid (0.1M) Place 6 cm^3 glacial ethanoic (acetic) acid in a graduated flask and make up the volume to 1 litre with distilled water.

Gelatin Make a 10% solution by dissolving the crystals in tap water and heating to boiling point. Keep the solution moving about or it will burn on the bottom. Stopper the solution while hot to reduce the chance of bacterial contamination.

Hydrochloric acid (0.1M) Dilute 10 cm^3 concentrated acid with 990 cm^3 distilled water.

Hydrogen peroxide Use a 20-volume solution, from suppliers or pharmacists.

Iodine solution Grind 1 g iodine and 1 g potassium iodide in a mortar with distilled water. Make up to 100 cm^3 and dilute 5 cm^3 of this solution with 100 cm^3 water for experiments.

Lime water Shake distilled water with an excess of calcium hydroxide and allow the lime to settle. Decant off the clear liquid. Before use, test the liquid by bubbling exhaled air through it.

Methylene blue Dissolve 0.5 g methylene blue in 30 cm^3 ethanol and dilute with 100 cm^3 distilled water.

PIDCP (Phenol-indo-2,6-dichlorophenol). Make a 0.1% solution in distilled water.

Ringer's solution Dissolve 0.85 g sodium chloride, 0.025 g anhydrous calcium chloride, 0.025 g potassium chloride in 100 cm^3 distilled water.

Soda-lime Use the self-indicating form which changes colour when it loses its activity.

Sodium carbonate (0.05M) Dissolve 5.3 g anhydrous sodium carbonate in 1 litre distilled water.

Sodium hydrogencarbonate Use a 10% solution.

Sugar solution (osmosis experiments). Dissolve sucrose in its own weight of tap water.

Starch solution (1%) Shake 1 g starch powder with 100 g water and heat the mixture gently, with stirring, until the liquid just starts to boil.

Taste, solutions for Sweet: 5% sucrose. Sour: 0.5% citric acid. Salt: 2% sodium chloride. Bitter: 1 cm^3 tincture of quinine in 100 cm^3 water, or boil 3 g dried hops in 200 cm^3 water for 30 min. Strain the mixture and make up to 200 cm^3 with water.

Water Unless distilled water is specified in this list of reagents, tap water is adequate.

Appendix 4 Resources

AUDIO-VISUAL MATERIALS

AVP, School Hill Centre, Chepstow, Gwent, NP6 5PH
Wide range of slides, OHP foils, Videos and software.

BBC Education, White City, 201 Wood Lane, London, W12 7TS
Radio and TV programmes, videos, software etc.

Camera Talks Ltd, 197 Botley Road, Oxford, OX2 0HE
Films, videos and tape-slide programmes on anatomy, microbiology, etc.

Concord Films Council Ltd, 201 Felixstowe Road, Ipswich, Suffolk, IP3 9BJ
Films on social and ecological aspects of human biology.

Educational and Scientific Products Ltd, A2 Dominion Way, Rustington, West Sussex BN16 3HQ
Wall charts, models etc.

Focal Point Audio Visual, 251 Copnor Road, Portsmouth, Hants, PO3 5EE
Slides and videos. Health and ecological topics.

Garland Computing, 35 Dean Hill, Plymouth, PL9 9AF
List includes software suitable for human biology.

Guild Sound and Vision, 6 Royce Road, Peterborough, PE1 5YB
Films and videos for hire or sale. Titles include medical, health and social biology topics.

IBA (Independent Broadcasting Authority), 70 Brompton Road, London, SW3 1EY
Educational TV programmes on ITV and Channel 4.

International Centre for Conservation Education, Greenfield House, Guiting Power, Cheltenham, Glos, GL54 5TZ
Slides and filmstrips on conservation.

Longman Micro Software Ltd, Longman House, Burnt Mill Road, Harlow, Essex, CM20 2JE
List includes some titles appropriate to human biology

National Audio Visual Aids Library, The George Building, Normal College, Bangor, Gwynedd, LL57 2PZ
Extensive list of films and videos for hire.

Philip Harris Education, Lynn Lane, Shenstone Lichfield, Staffordshire WS14 0EE
Slides, filmstrips, videos, OHP foils, software, charts, anatomical models, experiment kits.

Slide Centre (Rickitt Educational Media), Ilton, Ilminster, Somerset, TA19 9HS
Slide folios dealing with ecology and wildlife.

Viewtech Films and Video, 161 Winchester Road, Brislington, Bristol BS4 3NJ

CHARTS, BOOKLETS, TEACHING PACKS

English Nature, Northminster House, Peterborough PE1 1UA
Posters and booklets on habitats and wildlife.

Health Education Authority, Hamilton House, Mabledon Place, London WC1H 9TX
Leaflets, booklets, charts and resource lists on health education topics.

Nature Conservancy Council, Interpretive Branch, Attingham Park, Shrewsbury, SY4 4TW
Posters and booklets on habitats and wildlife.

Pictorial Charts Educational Trust, 27 Kirchen Road, London, W13 0UD
Charts on anatomy and physiology.

SATIS (Science and Technology in Society), ASE, College Lane, Hatfield, Herts, AL10 9AA
Teaching units and tape-slide programmes include topics on social aspects of biology.

Thames Water, Marketing Services Department, Room 1503, Nugent House, Vastern Road, Reading, RG1 8DB
Charts and pamphlets on water and sewage treatment.

World Wide Fund for Nature (WWF), Wayside Park, Godalming, Surrey, GU7 1XR
Wall charts, posters, games and books on wildlife and habitat conservation.

OTHER SOURCES OF INFORMATION
ASH (Action on Smoking and Health), 109 Gloucester Place, London W1H 3PH
Information packs, fact sheets and posters.

The Conservation Trust, George Palmer Site, Northumberland Avenue, Reading, RG2 7PW
Study notes, cards, kits and packs on conservation of resources, etc.

Council for Environmental Education, School of Education, University of Reading, London Road, Reading, RG1 5AQ
Lists of resources on environmental topics.

Friends of the Earth, 26-28 Underwood Street, London, N1 7JQ
Newsletters, books and pamphlets on environmental issues.

General Dental Council, 37 Wimpole Street, London, W1M 8DQ
A range of material concerned with dental health.

Greenpeace Environmental Trust, 30-31 Islington Green, London, N1 8XE
Campaigning posters, etc., for conservation and against pollution.

Health Education Centres. Your local centre will have leaflets, booklets and other resources.

National Centre for Biotechnology Education, Department of Microbiology, University of Reading, Whiteknights, Reading RG6 2AJ
Newsletters with up-dating information, ideas for practical work.

PRACTICAL WORK
Experimental Work in Biology, D. G. Mackean, (Murray 1983).
About 140 tested experiments, with detailed instructions to the students. Expected results are not given, but students are asked questions to test their understanding of the experimental design and their ability to make critical interpretations of the results.
A Teacher's Book gives details of the apparatus and materials for each experiment, and suggests answers to the questions.
About 60 of these experiments are relevant to Human Biology and, of these 20 are included in 'GCSE Practical Assessment'. The latter provides photocopiable schedules for assessing the practicals.

Further Examination Questions

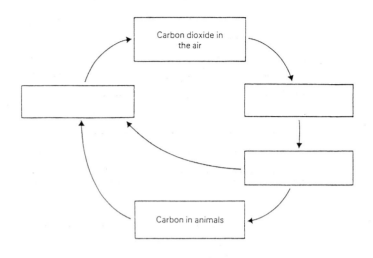

1 (a) Choose, from the list below, the correct words and write them in the boxes provided to complete the diagram of the carbon cycle.

respiration   photosynthesis   carbohydrates

(b) State one other method, other than respiration, by which Man causes huge quantities of carbon dioxide to be returned to the air.   (W1A)

2 The graph below shows the estimated world human population since AD 1000.

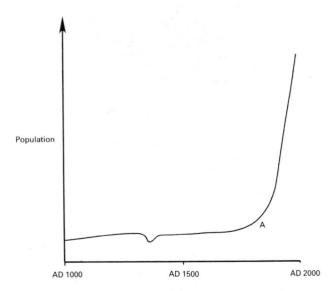

(a) Suggest *one* possible reason for the change in world population beginning at A.

(b) Suggest *two* problems which have been caused by the change in world population beginning at A.   (S1)

3 (a) The list below gives some of Man's effects on the environment. The table contains methods by which these effects may be controlled or prevented. Match each effect to its method of control/prevention by writing the appropriate letter in the table. One example has been done for you.

List – Man's effects on the environment

A increased lead in the air
B sea birds poisoned by mercury
C piles of waste paper
D large animals becoming extinct
E death of fish in rivers due to lack of oxygen
F mineral content of soil reduced

Method of control or prevention	Letter of effect
Reduction of lead content of petrol	**A**
Use of fertilizers	
Sewage treatment	
Recycling	
National parks created	
Treatment of effluent before discharging	

(b) In many areas farmers have moved hedges in order to create larger fields. How does this affect wildlife?   (M2)

4 (a) The simplified graph shows some of the features of a normal menstrual cycle.

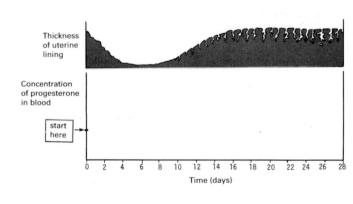

Complete this graph by drawing a line to represent the concentration of progesterone between day 0 and day 28. Start your line at the place shown.

(b) The uterine lining helps to form the placenta.

(i) Briefly explain the importance of the placenta in providing the developing baby with food.

(ii) In a placenta the blood of the mother and embryo do not mix. Briefly give two reasons why this is important for the survival of the embryo.   (S1)

5 Explain how Man is trying to prevent some kinds of animals and plants from dying out.   (N2P)

6 This diagram represents a system in the body.

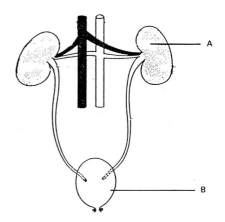

Label the parts A and B.
   (a) Water is lost from the body in other ways, Complete the table below to show how these change on hot and cold days. Use the words *more*, *less* or *no change*.

Ways in which water is lost	Hot day	Cold day
Sweating		
Breathing		
Urine		

   (b) Explain why a person, in between treatments on a kidney machine, can gain up to three kilos in weight. (W1A)

7 (a) Briefly describe *two* ways in which an unborn baby is protected against physical damage.
   (b) The graph shows the growth of the brain and reproductive organs.

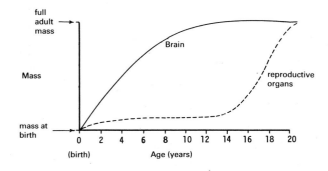

   (i) What does the graph tell you about the growth of the brain?
   (ii) What does the graph tell you about the growth of the reproductive organs?   (S1A)

8 The graph below shows the incidence of five-year-old British children who were free from dental decay between 1900 and 1970.

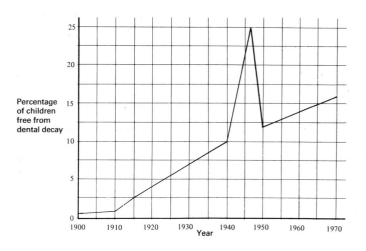

   (a) (i) Describe the general trend shown by the incidence of tooth decay between 1910 and 1970.
   (ii) Suggest why the incidence changed in this way.
   (b) Britain was at war between 1939 and 1945. Suggest why the incidence of tooth decay during this period was different from the incidence between 1947 and 1950.
   (c) (i) State *one* effect of high dietary fat on the circulatory system.
   (ii) State *one* effect of high dietary salt on the circulatory system.
   (d) State *two* possible consequences of low-fibre diets.
   (N2Q)

9 (a) The diagram shows the eye as it is seen from the front.

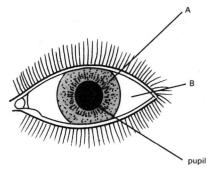

   (i) Name the parts labelled A and B.
   (ii) If a bright light were to be shone into the eye, what would happen to the pupil of the eye?
   (b) From a list of terms A to E choose the one which fits best each description in the table.

   A ciliary muscles   D lens
   B retina   E cornea
   C optic nerve

contains cells which are sensitive to light	
clear bulging region at the front of the eye	

(S1)

10 The diagram below shows the apparatus used in an experiment.

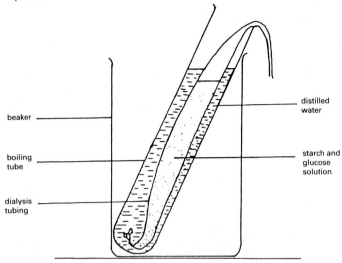

The experiment was set up as follows:

(1) Dialysis tubing, knotted at one end, was filled with a mixture of starch and glucose solution.

(2) The outside of the tubing was washed under a running tap.

(3) The tubing and contents were put into the distilled water in the boiling tube which was supported in a beaker.

(4) Immediately, a small sample of the distilled water was taken and tested for starch and glucose.

(5) The dialysis tubing and contents were left in the distilled water.

(6) After 15 minutes, another sample of the water surrounding the dialysis tubing was taken and tested again for starch and glucose.

(a) What was the purpose of step 2?

(b) How would you take a sample of the distilled water from the boiling tube in step 4?

(c) If, in step 4, both starch and glucose were found to be present, what *two* possible deductions could be made?

(d) (i) In step 6, what results would you expect?

(ii) How would you account for this?

(e) The apparatus is sometimes described as a 'model gut'. What do the following parts of the apparatus represent: dialysis tubing; distilled water? (L1)

11 The diagram below shows three types of structure (X, Y and Z) collected from healthy human blood.

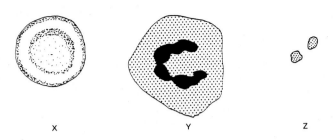

(a) Give the letter of the structure which

(i) increases in number at a site of bacterial infection, such as a pimple or boil,

(ii) will be reduced in number when there is a lack of iron in the diet.

(b) During a blood transfusion, a person with blood group A can safely receive blood from a group O donor, but not from a group B donor, since the red cells will clump together. Explain this.

(c) Explain why, although they know that immunization against a disease such as whooping cough will protect their child, some parents decide not to have their child immunized.

(d) The diagram represents a group of body cells and some parts of the circulatory system. The arrows show the direction of movement of fluids.

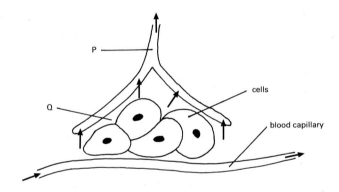

(i) Name the fluids contained in spaces P and Q.

(ii) Describe how the fluid in P is returned to the general blood circulation. (N2Q)

Glossary

(A) SCIENTIFIC TERMS

Acid A sharp-tasting chemical, often a liquid. Some acids can dissolve metals and turn them into soluble salts. Nitric acid acts on copper and turns it into copper nitrate, which dissolves to form a blue-coloured solution. Acids of plants and animals (amino acids, fatty acids) are weaker and do not dissolve metals. Amino acids and fatty acids are organic acids. Hydrochloric, sulphuric and nitric acids are called mineral acids or inorganic acids.

Agar A clear jelly extracted from one kind of seaweed. On its own it will not support the growth of bacteria or fungi, but will do so if food substances (e.g. potato juice or Bovril) are dissolved in it. Agar with different kinds of food dissolved in it is used to grow different kinds of micro-organism.

Alcohol Usually a liquid. There are many kinds of alcohol but the commonest is ethanol (or ethyl alcohol) which occurs in wines, spirits, beer, etc. It is produced by fermentation of sugar. Ethanol vaporizes quickly and easily catches fire.

Alkali The opposite of an acid. An alkali can neutralize an acid and so remove its acid properties. Sodium hydroxide, NaOH, is an alkali. It neutralizes hydrochloric acid to form a salt, sodium chloride.

$$Na\ OH + H\ Cl \rightarrow NaCl + H_2O$$
$$\text{salt} \quad \text{water}$$

Atom The smallest possible particle of an element. Even a microscopic piece of iron would be made up of millions of iron atoms. When we write formulae, the letters represent atoms. So H_2O for water means an atom of oxygen joined to two atoms of hydrogen.

Carbon A black, solid non-metal which occurs as charcoal or soot, for example. Its atoms are able to combine together to make ring or chain molecules. These molecules make up most of the chemicals of living organisms (see 'Organic'). One of the simplest compounds of carbon is carbon dioxide (CO_2).

Carbon dioxide A gas which forms 0.03 per cent (by volume) of the air. It is produced when carbon-containing substances burn ($C + O_2 \rightarrow CO_2$). It is also produced by the respiration of plants and animals. It is taken up by green plants to make food during photosynthesis.

Catalyst A substance which makes a chemical reaction go faster but does not get used up in the reaction. Platinum is a catalyst which speeds up the rate at which nitrogen and hydrogen combine to form ammonia, but does not get used up. Enzymes are catalysts for chemical reactions inside living cells.

Caustic A caustic substance can damage the skin and clothing and therefore should be handled with great care.

Compound Two or more elements joined together form a compound. Carbon dioxide, CO_2, is a compound of carbon and oxygen. Potassium nitrate, KNO_3, is a compound of potassium, nitrogen and oxygen.

Cubic centimetre (cm^3) This is a unit of volume. A tea-cup holds about $200cm^3$ liquid. One thousand cubic centimetres are called a cubic decimetre (dm^3) but this volume is also called a litre. Some measuring instruments are marked in millilitres (ml). A millilitre is a thousandth of a litre and therefore the same volume as a cubic centimetre. So $1\ cm^3 = 1$ ml.

Density This is the weight (mass) of a given volume of a substance. Usually it is the weight in grams of one cubic centimetre of the substance, e.g. $1\ cm^3$ lead weighs 11 grams, so its density is 11 grams per cm^3.
The density of water at 4°C is 1 g per cm^3.

Diffusion The random movement of molecules by which gases or dissolved substances move from a region of high concentration to a region of low concentration.

Dissolve A substance which mixes with a liquid and seems to 'disappear' in the liquid is said to dissolve. Sugar dissolves in water to make a solution.

Element An element is a substance which cannot be broken down into anything else. Sulphur is a non-metallic element. Iron is a metallic element. Oxygen and nitrogen are gaseous elements. Water (H_2O) is not an element because it can be broken down into hydrogen and oxygen.

Energy This can be heat, movement, light, electricity, etc. Anything which can be harnessed to do some kind of work is energy. Food consists of substances containing chemical energy. When food is turned into carbon dioxide and water by respiration, energy is released to do work such as making muscles contract.

Filtrate The clear solution which passes through a filter; e.g. if a mixture of copper sulphate solution and sand is filtered, the blue copper sulphate solution which passes through the filter paper is called the filtrate.

Formula A way of showing the chemical composition of a substance. Letters are chosen to represent elements, and numbers show how many atoms of each element are present. The letter for carbon is C and for oxygen is O. A molecule of carbon dioxide is one atom of carbon joined to two atoms of oxygen and the formula is CO_2. There are more elements than letters in the alphabet, so some of the elements have two letters, e.g. Mg for magnesium. Other elements have letters standing for the latin name, e.g. sodium is Na (= natrium).

Gram (g) A unit of weight in the metric system.
A penny weighs 3½ grams.
A pack of butter is 225 grams.
1000 grams is a kilogram (kg).
One thousandth of a gram is a milligram (mg).

Hydrogen Hydrogen is a gas which burns very readily. It is present in only tiny amounts in the air but forms part of many compounds such as water (H_2O), and organic compounds like carbohydrates (e.g. $C_6H_{12}O_6$ glucose) and fats.

Inorganic Substances like iron, salt, oxygen and carbon dioxide are inorganic. They do not have to come from a living organism. Salt is in the sea, iron is part of a mineral in the ground, oxygen is in the air. Inorganic substances can be made by industrial processes or extracted from minerals.

Insoluble An insoluble substance is one which will not dissolve. Sugar is soluble in water but insoluble in petrol.

Joule Just as a centimetre is a unit of length, a joule is a unit of energy, e.g. heat energy. 4.2 joules of heat energy would be needed to raise the temperature of 1 gram of water by one degree Celsius. The energy available in food is calculated in kilojoules (kJ). 1 kilojoule = 1000 joules. In some cases, the energy value of food is measured in kilocalories (often called just 'Calories'). 1 kilocalorie = 4.2 kilojoules.

Lime water A weak solution of lime (calcium hydroxide) in water. When carbon dioxide bubbles through this solution, it reacts with the calcium hydroxide to form calcium carbonate (chalk) which is insoluble and forms a cloudy suspension. This makes lime water a good test for carbon dioxide.

$$Ca(OH)_2 + CO_2 \rightarrow CaCO_3 + H_2O$$

Mass   This is the amount of matter in an object. The more mass an object has, the more it weighs, so mass can be measured by weighing something. However, if the force of gravity becomes less, as on the Moon, the same object will weigh less even though the amount of matter in it (its mass) has not changed. So mass and weight are related, but are not the same.

Molecule   The smallest amount of a substance which you can have. For example, the water molecule is H_2O, that is, two atoms of hydrogen joined to one atom of oxygen. A drop of water consists of countless millions of molecules of H_2O moving about in all directions and with a lot of space between them.

Organic   This usually refers to a substance produced by a living organism. Organic chemicals are things like carbohydrates, protein and fat. They have very large molecules and are often insoluble in water. Inorganic chemicals are usually simple substances like sodium chloride (salt) or carbon dioxide (CO_2).

$$H-\overset{\displaystyle H}{\underset{\displaystyle H}{C}}-\overset{\displaystyle H}{\underset{\displaystyle H}{C}}-\overset{\displaystyle H}{\underset{\displaystyle H}{C}}-\overset{\displaystyle H}{\underset{\displaystyle H}{C}}-C\overset{\displaystyle O}{\underset{\displaystyle OH}{}}$$

molecule of a fatty acid
C_4H_9COOH (organic)

$$O = C = O$$

molecule of carbon dioxide
CO_2 (inorganic)

Oxygen   Oxygen is a gas which makes up about 20 per cent (by volume) of the air. It combines with other substances and oxidizes them, sometimes producing heat and light energy. In plants and animals it combines with food to release energy.

Permeable   Allows liquids or gases to pass through. A cotton shirt is permeable to rain but a PVC mackintosh is impermeable.

pH   This is a measure of how acid or how alkaline a substance is. A pH of 7 is neutral. A pH in the range 8–11 is alkaline; pH's in the 6–2 range are acid; pH 6 is slightly acid; pH 2 is very acid.

PIDCP   The initials of an organic chemical called phospho-indo-dichlorophenol. It changes from blue to colourless in the presence of certain chemicals including Vitamin C.

Pigment   A chemical which has a colour. Haemoglobin in blood is a red pigment; chlorophyll in leaves is a green pigment. A black pigment called melanin may give a dark colour to human skin, hair and eyes.

Pipette   A glass tube designed to deliver controlled amounts of liquid. A bulb pipette has a plastic squeezer on one end so that it can deliver a drop at a time. A graduated pipette has marks on the side to show how much liquid has run out.

Reaction (chemical)   A change which takes place when certain chemicals meet or are acted on by heat or light. The change results in the production of new substances. When paper burns, a reaction is taking place between the paper and oxygen in the air.

Salt   A salt is a compound formed from an acid and a metal. Salts have double-barrelled names like sodium chloride (NaCl) and potassium nitrate (KNO_3). The first name is usually a metal and the second name is the acid. Potassium (K) is a metal, and the nitrate (NO_3) comes from nitric acid (HNO_3).

Sodium hydrogencarbonate   At one time this was called sodium bicarbonate. It is a salt and its formula is $NaHCO_3$. It is present in blood plasma and in most other body fluids.

Sodium hydroxide (NaOH)   An alkali with caustic properties, i.e. its solution will dissolve flesh, wood and fabrics.

Soluble   A soluble substance is one which will dissolve in a liquid. Sugar is soluble in water.

Solution   When something like sugar or salt dissolves in water it forms a solution. The molecules of the solid become evenly spread through the liquid.

Volume   The amount of space something takes up, or the amount of space inside it. A milk bottle has an internal volume of one pint. Your lungs have a volume of about 5 litres; they can hold up to 5 litres of air. This cube has a volume of 8 cubic centimetres (8 cm^3).

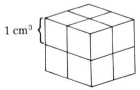

1 cm^3

(B) BIOLOGICAL TERMS
(*References in brackets are to pages.*)

Abdomen (6)   The part of the body below the diaphragm which contains stomach, kidneys, liver, etc.; in insects it refers to the third region of the body.

Accommodation (200)   Changing the shape (and focal length) of the eye lens to focus on near or distant objects.

Active transport (35)   The transport of a substance across a cell membrane with expenditure of energy, often against a concentration gradient.

Alleles (231)   Alternative forms of a gene, occupying the same place on a chromosome and affecting the same characteristics but in different ways.

Anabolism (30)   The building up of complex substances from simpler ones.

Aseptic technique (259)   Method of handling materials or apparatus so that unwanted micro-organisms are excluded.

Assimilation (118)   Absorption of substances which are built into other compounds in the organism.

Basal metabolism (30)   The minimum rate of chemical activity needed to keep an organism alive.

Biodegradable (78)   Able to be broken down to simple inorganic substances by the action of bacteria and fungi.

Biomass (51)   The weight of all the organisms in a population, community or habitat.

Biotechnology (257)   The use of living organisms or biological processes for industrial, agricultural or medical processes.

Cardiac   To do with the heart.

Catabolism (30)   The breakdown of complex substances to simpler substances in the cell, with a release of energy.

Control (25)   An experiment which is set up to ensure that only the condition being investigated has affected the results.

Co-ordination (207)   The process which makes the different systems in an organism work effectively together.

Cortex (150)   An outer layer.

Denature (20)   Destroy the structure of a protein by means of heat or chemicals.

Detoxication (121)   The process by which the liver makes poisonous chemicals harmless.

Dialysis (39)   The separation of small molecules from large molecules in solution by a selectively permeable membrane.

Ecosystem (53)   A community of interdependent organisms and the environment in which they live.

Emulsify (116)   Break-up of oil or fat into tiny droplets which remain suspended in water as an emulsion.

Eutrophic (64) An aquatic environment well supplied with nutrients for plant growth.

Fermentation (29) A form of anaerobic respiration in which carbohydrate is broken down to carbon dioxide and, in some cases, alcohol.

Gastric (115) To do with the stomach.

Gene (224) A sequence of chemicals in a chromosome which controls the development of a particular characteristic in an organism.

Genetic engineering (258) Altering the genetic constitution of an organism by introducing new DNA into its chromosomes.

Genotype (231) The combination of genes present in an organism.

Gestation (172) The period of growth and development of a foetus in the uterus of a mammal.

Hepatic (129) To do with the liver.

Heterozygous (230) Carrying a pair of contrasted genes for any one heritable characteristic; will not breed true for this characteristic.

Homeostasis (156) Keeping the composition of the body fluids the same.

Homologous chromosomes (224) A pair of corresponding chromosomes of the same shape and size; one from each parent.

Homozygous (230) Possessing a pair of identical genes controlling the same characteristic; will breed true for this characteristic.

Hypothesis (44) A provisional explanation for an observation; it can be tested by experiments.

Immunity (134) Ability of an organism to resist infection, usually because it carries antibodies in its blood.

Implantation (168) The process in which an embryo becomes attached to the lining of the uterus.

Incubate (343) Maintain at a raised temperature, e.g. birds' eggs or bacteria cultures.

Inhibit Slow down a process, or prevent its happening.

Inoculation (135) Deliberate infection with a mild form of disease to stimulate the formation of antibodies. (In the case of culture methods for bacteria or fungi, 'inoculation' means introducing the organism to the culture medium.)

Laparoscopy A method of examining the inside of the abdomen by inserting an optical instrument (an endoscope) through the abdominal wall.

Laparotomy (177) making an incision in the abdomen to examine or manipulate the internal organs.

Metabolism (30) All the chemical changes going on in the cells of an organism which keep it alive.

Monoculture (59) Growing a single species of crop plant, usually in the same ground for successive years.

Mutation (227) A spontaneous change in a gene or chromosome, which may affect the appearance or physiology of an organism.

Parasite (250) An organism living in or on another organism (the host). The parasite derives its food from the host.

Pathogen (250) A parasite which causes disease or harms its host in other ways.

Phenotype (231) The observable characteristics of an organism which are genetically controlled.

Plankton (51) The community of small plants and animals floating in the surface waters of an aquatic environment.

Predator (50) An animal which kills and eats other animals.

Proprioceptor (197) A sense organ which detects changes within the body.

Protista (3) Single-celled organisms which have a proper nucleus.

Protozoa (256) Those protista which take in solid food and digest it.

Puberty (175) The period of growth during which humans become sexually mature.

Receptor (195) A sense organ which detects a stimulus.

Recessive (230) A gene which, in the presence of its contrasting allele, is not expressed in the phenotype.

Recycling (55, 81) As a biological term this means the return of matter to the soil, air or water, and its re-use by other organisms. In daily life, it means the re-use of manufactured materials such as paper, glass and metals.

Renal (129) To do with the kidneys.

Replication (223) Production of a duplicate set of chromosomes prior to cell division.

Sensitivity (3) The ability to detect and respond to a stimulus.

Sphincter (153) A band of circular muscle which can contract to constrict or close a tubular organ.

Spore (249) A cell or small group of cells which can grow into a new organism.

Stimulus (195) An event in the surroundings or in the internal anatomy of an organism, which provokes a response.

Toxin (107) A poisonous protein produced by pathogenic bacteria.

Toxoid (135) A toxin which has been treated to make it harmless, but can still cause the body to make antibodies.

Trophic level (51) An organism's position in a food chain, e.g. primary or secondary consumer.

Index